The Communicator's Commentary

Jeremiah, Lamentations

The Communicator's Commentary Series
Old Testament

Lloyd J. Ogilvie

General Editor

The Communicator's Commentary

Jeremiah, Lamentations

John Guest

WORD BOOKS, PUBLISHER • WACO, TEXAS

Library of Congress Cataloging in Publication Data
Main entry under title:

The Communicator's commentary.
  Bibliography: p.
  Contents: OT17. Jeremiah, Lamentations/by John Guest
  1. Bible. O.T.—Commentaries. I. Ogilvie, Lloyd
John. II. Guest, John, 1936–
BS1151.2.C66 1986 221.7'7 86–11138
ISBN 0–8499–0423–4 (v. OT17)

Printed in the United States of America

89801239 AGF 987654321

To the Reverend J. Alec Motyer
my Old Testament professor at Trinity
Theological College, Bristol, England.

He first opened the Prophet Jeremiah to my heart and my
understanding. Of all my seminary professors, his is the most
profound influence on my life and ministry.

Contents

EXPERIENCES AND RELATIONSHIPS OF THE PROPHET:
JEREMIAH 26:1–45:5; 52:1–34

PROPHECIES TO FOREIGN NATIONS:
JEREMIAH 46:1–51:64

LAMENTATIONS OF THE PROPHET:
LAMENTATIONS 1:1–5:22

Editor's Preface

God has called all of His people to be communicators. Everyone who is in Christ is called into ministry. As ministers of "the manifold grace of God," all of us—clergy and laity—are commissioned with the challenge to communicate our faith to individuals and groups, classes and congregations.

The Bible, God's Word, is the objective basis of the truth of His love and power that we seek to communicate. In response to the urgent, expressed needs of pastors, teachers, Bible study leaders, church school teachers, small group enablers, and individual Christians, the Communicator's Commentary is offered as a penetrating search of the Scriptures of the Old and New Testament to enable vital personal and practical communication of the abundant life.

Many current commentaries and Bible study guides provide only some aspects of a communicator's needs. Some offer in-depth scholarship but no application to daily life. Others are so popular in approach that biblical roots are left unexplained. Few offer impelling illustrations that open windows for the reader to see the exciting application for today's struggles. And most of all, seldom have the expositors given the valuable outlines of passages so needed to help the preacher or teacher in his or her busy life to prepare for communicating the Word to congregations or classes.

This Communicator's Commentary series brings all of these elements together. The authors are scholar-preachers and teachers outstanding in their ability to make the Scriptures come alive for individuals and groups. They are noted for bringing together excellence in biblical scholarship, knowledge of the original Hebrew and Greek, sensitivity to people's needs, vivid illustrative material from biblical, classical, and contemporary sources, and lucid communication by the use of clear outlines of thought. Each has been selected to contribute to this series because of his Spirit-empowered ability to help people live in the skins of biblical characters and provide a "you-are-there" intensity to the drama of events of the Bible which have so much to say about our relationships and responsibilities today.

The design for the Communicator's Commentary gives the reader an overall outline of each book of the Bible. Following the introduction, which reveals the author's approach and salient background on the book, each chapter of the commentary provides the Scripture to be exposited. The New King James Bible has been chosen for the Communicator's Commentary because it combines with integrity the beauty of language, underlying Hebrew and Greek textual basis, and thought-flow of the 1611 King James Version, while replacing obsolete verb forms and other archaisms with their everyday contemporary counterparts for greater readability. Reverence for God is preserved in the capitalization of all pronouns referring to the Father, Son, or Holy Spirit. Readers who are more comfortable with another translation can readily find the parallel passage by means of the chapter and verse reference at the end of each passage being exposited. The paragraphs of exposition combine fresh insights to the Scripture, application, rich illustrative material, and innovative ways of utilizing the vibrant truth for his or her own life and for the challenge of communicating it with vigor and vitality.

It has been gratifying to me as editor of this series to receive enthusiastic progress reports from each contributor. As they worked, all were gripped with new truths from the Scripture—God-given insights into passages, previously not written in the literature of biblical explanation. A prime objective of this series is for each user to find the same awareness: that God speaks with newness through the Scriptures when we approach them with a ready mind and a willingness to communicate what He has given; that God delights to give communicators of His Word "I-never-saw-that-in-that-verse-before" intellectual insights so that our listeners and readers can have "I-never-realized-all-that-was-in-that-verse" spiritual experiences.

The thrust of the commentary series unequivocally affirms that God speaks through the Scriptures today to engender faith, enable adventuresome living of the abundant life, and establish the basis of obedient discipleship. The Bible, the unique Word of God, is unlimited as a resource for Christians in communicating our hope to others. It is our weapon in the battle for truth, the guide for ministry, and the irresistible force for introducing others to God.

A biblically rooted communication of the Gospel holds in unity and oneness what divergent movements have wrought asunder. This commentary series courageously presents personal faith, caring for individuals, and social responsibility as essential, inseparable dimensions of biblical Christianity. It seeks to present the quadrilateral Gospel in its fullness which calls us to unreserved commitment to Christ, unrestricted self-esteem in His grace, unqualified love for others in personal evangelism, and undying efforts to work for justice and righteousness in a sick and suffering world.

A growing renaissance in the church today is being led by clergy and laity who are biblically rooted, Christ-centered, and Holy Spirit-empowered. They have dared to listen to people's most urgent questions and deepest needs and then to God as He speaks through the Bible. Biblical preaching is the secret of growing churches. Bible study classes and small groups are equipping the laity for ministry in the world. Dynamic Christians are finding that daily study of God's Word allows the Spirit to do in them what He wishes to communicate through them to others. These days are the most exciting time since Pentecost. The Communicator's Commentary is offered to be a primary resource of new life for this renaissance.

It has been very encouraging to receive the enthusiastic responses of pastors and teachers to the twelve New Testament volumes of the Communicator's Commentary series. The letters from communicators on the firing line in pulpits, classes, study groups, and Bible fellowship clusters across the nation, as well as the reviews of scholars and publication analysts, have indicated that we have been on target in meeting a need for a distinctly different kind of commentary on the Scriptures, a commentary that is primarily aimed at helping interpreters of the Bible to equip the laity for ministry.

This positive response has led the publisher to press on with an additional twenty-one volumes covering the books of the Old Testament. These new volumes rest upon the same goals and guidelines that undergird the New Testament volumes. Scholar-preachers with facility in Hebrew as well as vivid contemporary exposition have been selected as authors. The purpose throughout is to aid the preacher and teacher in the challenge and adventure of Old

Testament exposition in communication. In each volume you will meet Yahweh, the "I AM" Lord who is Creator, Sustainer, and Redeemer in the unfolding drama of His call and care of Israel. He is the Lord who acts, intervenes, judges, and presses His people into the immense challenges and privileges of being a chosen people, a holy nation. And in the descriptive exposition of each passage, the implications of the ultimate revelation of Yahweh in Jesus Christ, His Son, our Lord, are carefully spelled out to maintain unity and oneness in the preaching and teaching of the Gospel.

It is my pleasure to introduce you to the author of this volume, Dr. John Guest. He now adds "commentary author" to his amazingly diverse list of ministry roles: pastor, crusade evangelist, seminary founder, radio teacher, Christian rock musician, and popular writer. Dr. Guest is best known as Senior Rector of St. Stephen's Episcopal Church in Sewickley, Pennsylvania, one of the largest and fastest growing among Episcopal churches.

John Guest affirms his commitment to the goal of the Communicator's Commentary series when he explains: "I have worked as a communicator speaking to other communicators who are primarily concerned with the daily application of these prophetic messages." Upon the bedrock of careful historical scholarship, Dr. Guest allows the prophet Jeremiah to speak to us, to call us to obey God even as he called the children of Israel centuries ago.

A personal reminiscence may help you to understand my enthusiasm for John Guest as a communicator. Recently he spoke at our church's annual family conference. Those in attendance immediately came to appreciate his penetrating insight into the Word of God. His illustrations were moving and compelling. Though many present had not known Dr. Guest before, they were quickly drawn to him through his winsome humor and personal warmth. More significantly, they were drawn again to our Lord as Dr. Guest communicated His call to full discipleship. Many members of our church family mark that weekend as a crucial turning point in their Christian lives.

John Guest is a man with a passion for the gospel of Jesus Christ. He communicates contagiously, inspiring a similar evangelical passion in others. You will encounter and experience this passion as you read Dr. Guest's commentary on Jeremiah and Lamentations. It will guide you into a deeper understanding of God and His call upon our lives. It will equip you to be a fervent, cogent communicator of this call. I am delighted to recommend this commentary to you and to thank John Guest for his excellent contribution to the Communicator's Commentary.

LLOYD OGILVIE

Acknowledgment

I am deeply grateful to Holly Campbell, without whom this work would not have been written. In and of herself, she is a great Bible teacher. The Lord has greatly used her among the people of St. Stephen's Episcopal Church in Sewickley, Pennsylvania, where I am pastor, and in working with me on the preparation of this commentary.

Introduction to Jeremiah

Historical Background

Jeremiah lived between the fall of the Assyrian Empire and the rise of that of Babylon. The restlessness of the seventh century B.C. gave him one of the most difficult enterprises ever to rest on human shoulders. He was sent to pursue a nation that was running away from God. He became the very legs of the "hound of heaven," flinging himself and all the powers of his being into the task of reclaiming the nation of Israel for the purposes of God.

The crescent of land that stretches from the Persian Gulf northwest through the Tigris-Euphrates river valley was the main traffic route between the great powers of Assyria, Babylon, and Egypt. By her very geography, Judah was destined to feel the clash. By the call of God, Jeremiah was destined to warn her that the resultant conflagration was divine judgment upon her sin.

Jeremiah's was a colossal mission, but he was a colossal man, not so much by natural endowment but by obedience to the prophetic call. His mission, however, ended in failure. Nevertheless this man became the outstanding personality of his age, although not recognized as such at the time.[1] The world would have nominated in his place Nebuchadnezzar II, the most famous of the Babylonian monarchs. He ruled for forty-three years. He was a man of troublesome dreams, fits of madness, and strokes of genius, but he built Babylon into one of the most magnificent cities in the ancient world.

Yet Jeremiah built a far more enduring city in his portraits of the kingdom to come and in his steady attention to the prophetic ministry. This ministry went easily during the years of Josiah, the last righteous king of Judah. The reigns of Jehoiakim and Zedekiah that followed, however, brought miseries to Jeremiah as they sank their nation deeper into the mire of sin and idolatry. The political

17

and moral life of Judah took on the dark colors of its spiritual treachery.

In 605 B.C. the battle of Carchemish forever settled the fate of Assyria and Egypt and established Babylon as the monster capable of swallowing Judah, which she did most systematically. In 597 B.C. the first wave of deportees was carried away to serve this monster, and by 587 B.C. the walls of Jerusalem were breached. Several months later the temple was burned and the remaining temple vessels were carried away by brutal soldiers who violated the temple's sanctity in an unbridled effort to erase every trace of God from the face of this earth.

The Man Jeremiah

More is known about Jeremiah than most of the other prophets because of the self-disclosing nature of much of his writing. With poetic candor, he confides in his reader and in his God about the affairs of his heart, his doubts and discouragements, and even his temptations to give up. "Jeremiah has always been a fascination to Christian hearts, because of the close similarity that exists between his life and that of Jesus Christ. Each of them was 'a man of sorrows, and acquainted with grief'; each came to his own and his own received him not; each passed through hours of rejection, desolation, and forsakenness. And in Jeremiah we may see beaten out into detail, experiences that in our Lord, are but lightly touched on by the evangelists."[2]

He was born into a family of exiled priests who lived out their lives in the quiet village of Anathoth. The haunting presence of loneliness and estrangement was ever a reality. From his origins to his death, Jeremiah had very little solace from human approval. He therefore has a special ministry to those of us who are compelled to stand alone at some time in our lives. To every Christian who is called to live contra mundum, Jeremiah stands as a great beacon.

William Petersen titles his book about this man The Prophet Who Wouldn't Quit. Anyone who works for almost half a century at a most unpalatable enterprise and under increasingly adverse circumstances has much to teach today's culture about resilience and resolve. We who are too easily discouraged by failure might plant our feet more firmly after reading this book.

The Book Jeremiah

The arrangement of this material continues to baffle scholars. It is not chronological, neither is it entirely topical. Nonetheless there is a unified message that continues to speak. Obedience to God is the only way ultimately to prosper in a land given to us by Him. It is also the only way to escape judgment.

I have not concerned myself with the textual problems of compilation and transmission. Such technicalities have been avoided along with concern over variations between the Hebrew Masoretic text and the Greek translation of the Old Testament, the Septuagint. Instead I have worked as a communicator speaking to other communicators who are primarily concerned with the daily application of these prophetic messages. They have been called "an anthology of utterances"[3] because they contain so many literary types: for example, sermons, poems, lyric war stanzas, lamentations, narratives, and visions.

Roughly divided, chapters 1–25 contain sermons and poems while chapters 26–45 are rich with narrative accounts of the prophet's relationships and experiences. Chapters 46–51 are largely filled with prophecies to foreign nations. Chapter 52 is a page of history.

Since the Old Testament was the Bible of all New Testament writers and even of the Lord Himself, it is important to note the impact of the Book of Jeremiah upon the New Testament documents. Jeremiah himself is twice mentioned, both times by Matthew (2:17; 16:14). Beyond these two direct references, there are forty-one allusions to his prophecy in the New Testament. Seven of these are direct quotations.

When Herod ordered the slaughter of young babies, Matthew likened the grief it caused to that which Jeremiah had described centuries earlier (Matt. 2:17; cf. Jer. 31:15). At the beginning of His ministry, Jesus entered the temple of Herod and called it a "den of thieves" (Matt. 21:13; cf. Jer. 7:11). What Jeremiah had written became part of the Bible of the Lord Himself. It had indeed given expression to the very heart and life of the Messiah Himself.

When the Apostle James faced a very difficult period in his ministry, he fed on the words of Jeremiah. He gave his judgment concerning the Gentiles to the council in Jerusalem (Acts 15:16) but used the expression of Jeremiah to express his own conviction that the Gentiles were included in the ultimate purposes of God (Jer. 12:15).

Paul, in writing to the Romans concerning the sovereignty of God, borrows imagery from Jeremiah to articulate God's right to choose whom He will and when (Rom. 9:20; cf. Jer. 18:6). In calling the Corinthians away from confidence in things merely human, Paul twice uses a reference from Jer. 9:24.

When Jeremiah wrote the Book of Comfort from the dark hopelessness of his prison cell, he had no way of knowing that centuries later the writer to the Hebrews would feed the hearts of his readers with the self-same introductory words of hope—"Behold the days are coming" (Heb. 8:12; cf. Jer. 31:31). He goes on later to describe the new covenant, again in the language of the great prophet: "I will put my law into their hearts and in their minds I will write them" (Heb. 10:16; cf. Jer. 31:34).

Babylon has always represented the opposing force to Israel and all the things of God. When John expresses the ultimate victory of God over this apostasy in the Apocalypse, he puts the very words of Jeremiah in the mouth of an angel; "Fallen, fallen, is Babylon the great" (Rev. 18:2; cf. Jer. 51:8).[4]

Dare we ignore the work of this great prophet? The very mind of Jesus Himself was satisfied with the expression Jeremiah gave to the image of the kingdom. The original communicators of the gospel— Matthew, James, John, and Paul—saw fit to use his words in their own call to the communication of truth. Dare we do anything but reverently move into a study of this great book?

NOTES

1. James P. Hyatt, "The Book of Jeremiah: Introduction and Exegesis," in *The Interpreter's Bible*, vol. 5, ed. George A. Buttrick et al. (Nashville: Abingdon Press, 1956), 777.

2. F. B. Meyer, *Jeremiah* (Fort Washington, Pa.: Christian Literature Crusade, 1980), 6.

3. R. K. Harrison, *Jeremiah and Lamentations,* The Tyndale Old Testament Commentaries (Downers Grove, Ill.: Inter-Varsity Press, 1973), 27.

4. G. Campbell Morgan, *Studies in the Prophecy of Jeremiah* (Old Tappan, N.J.: Fleming H. Revell, 1969), 279–88.

An Outline of Jeremiah

Sermons and Poems of the Prophet

Jeremiah 1:1–25:38

CHAPTER ONE

The Call and Commission of Jeremiah

Jeremiah 1:1–19

THE VISITED PLACE

1:1 The words of Jeremiah the son of Hilkiah, of the priests who *were* in Anathoth in the land of Benjamin,

2 to whom the word of the LORD came in the days of Josiah the son of Amon, king of Judah, in the thirteenth year of his reign.

3 It came also in the days of Jehoiakim the son of Josiah, king of Judah, until the end of the eleventh year of Zedekiah the son of Josiah, king of Judah, until the carrying away of Jerusalem captive in the fifth month.

Jer. 1:1–3

In the last forty years of Judah, the Southern Kingdom, Jeremiah was called to the prophetic office. Empires were shifting. Nations of the ancient Near East were posturing for war in those turbulent times of the seventh century B.C. The land of the Hebrews, occupying the Fertile Crescent, was under the gaze of Egypt to the south, Assyria to the immediate north, and Babylon due east. It was destined to fall under the crossfire of a convulsive world struggle and under the judgment of God.

That God would intervene on such a turbulent world scene is not what shocks the natural mind. What confounds purely human reason is where God visited and who. Under Pharaoh Psammetichus, Egypt was enjoying a temporary surge of power, but the word of God passed on by. Assyria had just lost its great king, Ashurbanipal, and was clutching to maintain control of an unwieldy and restless empire, but the word of God passed on by.

We watch. What noble place on this earth will receive the heavenly visit? Past the pagan monarchs, their thrones and dominions, the word of God goes in search of a voice. In place of Bethlehem, we might instead sing, "O little town of Anathoth, how still we see thee lie." Seated on a broad range of hills three miles northeast of Jerusalem lay this little, walled village of priests. A speck in the universe becomes the visited place. Its name means "answer to prayer." "Has not God made foolish the wisdom of this world?" (1 Cor. 1:20).

The year was 627 B.C. Josiah had been ruling righteously over the Southern Kingdom for thirteen years, instituting a series of dramatic reforms recorded in 2 Kings 22 and 23. He was trying to overcome the fifty years of wickedness incarnated in the reigns of his grandfather Manasseh and his father Amon. They had systematically plunged the country into a downward spiral of idolatry and corruption.

God honored Josiah by visiting Jeremiah during his reign, which had begun when he was but eight years old—an early age at which to succeed the wicked reigns of godless men. This young king came to power through a coup of righteousness. Under its godly counsel he set about to do right in the sight of the Lord.

Righteous leadership will evoke a calling. We are a people designed to operate under leadership. When it is strong and good it will produce goodness in society. Conversely, when it is wicked or compromising it will ultimately produce calamity, as we will see in the reigns of Jehoiakim and Zedekiah that follow Josiah's.

While providing a climate for the coming of the prophetic voice, Josiah's reforms did not seem to produce any significant change in the apostate hearts of his people. The question we must ask ourselves is how much more in peril might they have been were it not for this good king? The solid answer is in their history, for when they lost him they lost the protection of his righteousness.

Approximately 60 percent of today's population claims a "born-again" experience. Skeptics raise the question, "Why then is our culture fraught with so many social evils." The real issue to ponder is how much worse might we be if it were not for the presence of this renewal, ill-expressed as it often is?

Josiah's leadership received reinforcement from a most unlikely place. Would he have ever dreamed that the answer to his prayers was a young country boy, the son of a priest, from the village of Anathoth?

THE VISITED PROPHET

1:4 Then the word of the LORD came to me, saying:
5 "Before I formed you in the womb I knew you;
Before you were born I sanctified you;
I ordained you a prophet to the nations."
6 Then said I:
"Ah, Lord GOD!
Behold, I cannot speak, for I *am* a youth."
Jer. 1:4–6

In His supreme sovereignty, God visited Anathoth to commission Jeremiah to a role of national and, ultimately, international importance. He says four things to the prophet that completely change our view of what it means to be human.

1. *"I formed you"* (v. 5). Our earthbound little minds imagine conception as only a biological event. Yet here we are forced to think again concerning the origins of human life. The psalmist cries out, "I am fearfully *and* wonderfully made; Marvelous are Your works. . . . My frame was not hidden from You, When I was made in secret, *And* skillfully wrought in the lowest parts of the earth" (Ps. 139:14, 15).

This ought to shock today's culture whose abortion clinics have taken the lives of more than 15 million unborn children since the 1973 *Roe* v. *Wade* Supreme Court decision. If God is present in the process of conception, then the value of human life takes on the implications of eternity. The weight of our glory as humans comes through these words to Jeremiah. Just as they must have shocked him, so must they shock us. We are infinitely more than children of humankind. Our birth is not our real beginning nor will our death be the end. Yet how we live the span between the two will count forever.

2. *"I knew you"* (v. 5). This second mind-boggling claim stretches the prophet's origins beyond the walls of Anathoth, beyond the day of his birth, even beyond the day of his conception. In all of those

"beyonds" God had a plan for his life. His mother first cradled him proudly, innocently in her arms, never knowing that larger arms than hers were wrapped around her child and holding him fast in a relentless purpose that was destined to touch all the power structures of the world. God had a plan for his life.

3. *"I sanctified you"* (v. 5). Because Jeremiah was first known and then, at a point in time, formed in his mother's womb, this third condition becomes possible. He was then set apart for something sacred. When we argue against the sanctity of human life we must come up against this passage.

Jeremiah was about to be sent headlong into a culture that had lost all reverence for human life. They were debauching themselves in the most flagrant disregard for the dignity to which they had been called as the people of God. They had lost every trace of their ordination.

Are we not a society very much like that one? All manner of obscenities have penetrated our culture—our airwaves, our telephones, our music, even our communities and families. The four realities of humanity as God sees it and as He uttered to the prophet should arouse us to action. It has been said that "all that is required for the triumph of evil is that good men and women do nothing."

4. *"I ordained you a prophet to the nations"* (v. 5). The particular form our life is to take on earth is wrapped up in the purposes and foreknowledge of God. We cannot "find" ourselves until we first find Him. I cannot ultimately know who I am until I know whose I am.

The name his father, Hilkiah, had pronounced upon Jeremiah carried in it the nature of his service. It was marked by overtures of gravity and of grandeur. By some "Jeremiah" is said to mean "God hurls." This captures the force and vehemence with which he was sent into a life of perpetual hardship in an attempt to call an apostate people back to their origins. This imagery forever dispels any notion of a "wimpy" God or of a "wimpy" prophet. The grandeur of his name was captured by the meaning "God exults." Jeremiah never gave up. He stood tall to the very end through a life of mostly failure.

Our culture needs more Jeremiahs who sense their ordination in life and who pursue it. We have become an instant society, interested in short-term gains, immediate gratifications, and quick fixes. We have very little loyalty to the long term, perhaps because we have lost the sense of how far back our origins really do go.

Jeremiah decided that if God formed him, if God knew him, and if God sanctified him, then he could persevere. The decision, however, came with a struggle. The awesome presence of God, called in theological terms the *mysterium tremendum*, reduced him to ashes. All that he could utter at first was *"Ah, Lord GOD!"* (v. 6). In that sigh was a painful and humble awareness of his creatureliness, of the fragileness of humanity up against the power of God.

He began to make excuses. *"Behold, I cannot speak, for I am a youth"* (v. 6). Like so many other biblical figures trembling under the weight of their commission, he sighed over his inabilities and inadequacies. God does not want us dwelling on our own incompetence. It belittles His design for us. It might sound humble in the sight of men, but it can be an impertinence to the Creator.

NAIL YOUR COLORS TO THE MAST

1:7 But the LORD said to me:
       "Do not say, 'I *am* a youth,'
       For you shall go to all to whom I send you,
       And whatever I command you, you shall speak.
  8 Do not be afraid of their faces,
       For I *am* with you to deliver you," says the
       LORD.
  9 Then the LORD put forth His hand and touched
my mouth, and the LORD said to me:
       "Behold, I have put My words in your mouth.
10 See, I have this day set you over the nations and
       over the kingdoms,
       To root out and to pull down,
       To destroy and to throw down,
       To build and to plant."

17 "Therefore prepare yourself and arise,
       And speak to them all that I command you.
       Do not be dismayed before their faces,
       Lest I dismay you before them.
18 For behold, I have made you this day
       A fortified city and an iron pillar,
       And bronze walls against the whole land—
       Against the kings of Judah,

31

Against its princes,
Against its priests,
And against the people of the land.
19 They will fight against you,
But they shall not prevail against you.
For I *am* with you," says the LORD, "to deliver
you."

Jer. 1:7–10, 17–19

We never find God pampering cowardice. His response to Jeremiah's self-doubt in the vernacular might sound something like this. "Don't give Me that stuff! *For you shall go to all to whom I send you, And whatever I command you, you shall speak*" (v. 7).

The colossal figure of a redeeming God moves up by the side of Jeremiah and plants Himself between the prophet and the people who will come to hate him for his words. *"I am with you to deliver you"* (v. 8). The large hands that hold the world reach down and touch the mouth of the trembling country boy. *"I have put My words in your mouth"* (v. 9). This touch forever set Jeremiah on an enterprise of courage, *"to root out and to pull down . . . to build and to plant"* (v. 10).

I was converted as a young man. My basic struggle was against cowardice. I did not want to give my life to Jesus Christ because I was afraid of what people would think. The struggle went on for three years. One evening in 1954, I went to hear Billy Graham at Harringay Arena. He spoke about nailing our colors to the mast. It was a phrase from sailing ship days. Your color was the flag flying from your mast. When the man in the crow's nest saw an enemy ship, he would often call to have the color lowered so the enemy could not spot them and blow the ship out of the water.

When Jeremiah nailed his colors to the mast he was in effect saying, "Come what may, this is who I am, and this is my commitment. If an enemy ship wants to try to blow me out of the water, that is up to him. My colors are nailed to the mast." He would face many such enemy ships over the next forty years of his prophetic ministry.

That evening in 1954, Billy Graham said, "I am asking you, those of you who for cowardly reasons have not accepted Christ, to do so this evening." I rose from my seat and took the most important walk of my life. As God takes mourning and gives us joy and dancing, He

32

took my cowardice and gave me courage, just as He had done before for Jeremiah and countless others.

Jeremiah's mission and future lifestyle were certainly not for the fainthearted. Neither is the imagery God uses to confirm what He is building into the person who nails his colors to the mast. Notice the architectural terms "a fortified city," "an iron pillar," and "bronze walls" in verse 18. They are solid and unshakeable like the God who conceived them and the prophet whom they would come to characterize. Jerusalem was soon to be a city no longer fortified. Its pillars were already crumbling. Its walls would be burned by the Babylonians. This was the news Jeremiah would have to deliver to ears that would not hear.

TWO VISIONS

1:11 Moreover the word of the LORD came to me, saying, "Jeremiah, what do you see?" And I said, "I see a branch of an almond tree."

12 Then the LORD said to me, "You have seen well, for I am ready to perform My word."

13 And the word of the LORD came to me the second time, saying, "What do you see?" And I said, "I see a boiling pot, and it is facing away from the north."

14 Then the LORD said to me:
"Out of the north calamity shall break forth
On all the inhabitants of the land.

15 For behold, I am calling
All the families of the kingdoms of the north,"
    says the LORD;
"They shall come and each one set his throne
At the entrance of the gates of Jerusalem,
Against all its walls all around,
And against all the cities of Judah.

16 I will utter My judgments
Against them concerning all their wickedness,
Because they have forsaken Me,
Burned incense to other gods,
And worshiped the works of their own hands."
                                        Jer. 1:11–16

The visions referred to in these verses came to Jeremiah in anything but spectacular terms. Throughout the course of his prophetic ministry, God used the common to speak of the uncommon. Here He spoke about the inevitability of judgment and about the geographic location from which it would come upon the Southern Kingdom. The question-and-answer pattern preserves a conversational intimacy between God and the prophet.

By now, Jeremiah's physical senses were alert with expectancy so that God did not need to thunder or overwhelm but instead could use something as small as the first almond blossom trembling in the January air. The coming of spring was irrevocably working in the forces of nature, as the coming of judgment was working in the forces of Judah's political life.

The tremor of a small flower seems so gentle, but the *"branch of an almond tree"* (v. 11) brings judgment to bear upon the imagery. God has designed into His creation a dynamic that will ultimately punish sin. There is no room here for the thought that God does not care, that He is aloof from our world, indifferent at best. *"I am ready to perform My word"* (v. 12). A picture is formed of God staring fixedly at His people, studying them intently, watching their every move with a heavenly fascination.

The second vision came also from the prophet's everyday experience. A boiling cauldron was a commonplace sight. Now it was infused with new meaning. The direction of the cauldron's steam indicated that the winds of adversity were blowing in from the north. Jeremiah became the confidant of God by being told not to look to Egypt in the south, even though it was presently strong, and not to look to Assyria in the north and its past dominance. Instead he was told to keep his eyes trained on Babylon and on its subtle orchestration for power. This was the nation God would use to judge His people. Jeremiah emerged from the "oval office" knowing exactly what he must preach in his first sermon.

CHAPTER TWO

Afflicting the Comfortable

Jeremiah 2:1–37

It has been said that the word of God must do two things. It must "afflict the comfortable" and it must "comfort the afflicted." Having been called and commissioned in such stirring terms, and having been given the visions of coming political events, the prophet Jeremiah was instructed to make his first foray into Jerusalem. His sermon was designed to "root out and to pull down" before he could ever "build and plant" (1:10).

This unit contains a series of sermons, delivered at different times, that have the same historical frame of reference; namely, the righteous reign of Josiah. The next five chapters of Jeremiah fall into this time period.

These words, uncomfortable as they are to deliver, are only the beginning. Here they have the force of a judicial argument; Judah is on trial. God, the prosecuting attorney, systematically builds a brilliant case against sin. He exposes its irrationality with the mind of an advocate and with the heart of a lover. The case is ironclad.

JUDAH'S HUSBAND PLEADS HIS CASE

2:1 Moreover the word of the LORD came to me, saying,
2 "Go and cry in the hearing of Jerusalem, saying, 'Thus says the LORD:
"I remember you,
The kindness of your youth,
The love of your betrothal,
When you went after Me in the wilderness,
In a land not sown.

35

> 3 Israel *was* holiness to the LORD,
> The firstfruits of His increase.
> All that devour him will offend;
> Disaster will come upon them," says the LORD.'"
> 4 Hear the word of the LORD, O house of Jacob
> and all the families of the house of Israel.
> 5 Thus says the LORD:
> "What injustice have your fathers found in Me,
> That they have gone far from Me,
> Have followed idols,
> And have become idolaters?
> 6 Neither did they say, 'Where *is* the LORD,
> Who brought us up out of the land of Egypt,
> Who led us through the wilderness,
> Through a land of deserts and pits,
> Through a land of drought and the shadow of
>   death,
> Through a land that no one crossed
> And where no one dwelt?'
> 7 I brought you into a bountiful country,
> To eat its fruit and its goodness.
> But when you entered, you defiled My land
> And made My heritage an abomination.
> 8 The priests did not say, 'Where *is* the LORD?'
> And those who handle the law did not know
>   Me;
> The rulers also transgressed against Me;
> The prophets prophesied by Baal,
> And walked after *things that* do not profit."
>
> *Jer. 2:1–8*

God takes the part of the rejected lover and reasons around the central question found in verse 5: *"What injustice have your fathers found in Me, That they have gone far from Me, Have followed idols, And have become idolaters?"* He reaches back to times when they were in love. There is a haunting nostalgia to Jeremiah's poetry like the strains of a sad love song. The voice begins to reminisce over the past recalling four ways in which He had loved them.

1. He married Judah. *"I remember you, . . . The love of your betrothal"* (v. 2). He took on covenant vows and bound Himself to

cherish her. In the wilderness with Moses there had indeed been sweet moments of trust. God chose now to remember those moments rather than the stiff-necked grumbling. The pillar of cloud by day and the fire by night had been enough to set them trustingly on pilgrim feet *"in a land not sown"* (v. 2)

When they had nothing, they loved Him more than when they were led into the lap of luxury. "Things" do not automatically make us happier or our relationships better. He meant such goodness for Judah. The Jews were the *"firstfruits of His increase"* (v. 3). No other nation on earth had ever been married to God. He pleasured in her, as a bridegroom does his bride.

2. He protected her. God chose to "comfort her, honor and keep her in sickness and in health." His guarding of her was, in fact, so zealous that any nation that attempted to harm her was punished (v. 3). The promise He had given her in the wilderness was "I will be an enemy to your enemies and an adversary to your adversaries" (Exod. 23:22).

3. He brought her out of bondage. By bringing her out of Egypt, God signified that here was a people destined for so much more. They walked on dry ground through the Red Sea between high walls of roaring water standing back in obedience to the Hand of the Husband. Yet now they walked after idols (v. 5).

4. He brought them into a bountiful country. God brought them into Canaan, not for some Spartan-like existence but *"To eat its fruit and goodness"* (v. 7). Surely this is a revelation of God's intention for human life. We have a tendency in this culture to think of God as some kind of cosmic kill-joy, out to spoil our fun at every turn. So many have the false notion that becoming a Christian means giving up every opportunity for fun and pleasure—when in fact it is the gaining of that opportunity for the very first time.

Instead of this bounty, Judah chose emptiness, vanity, and futility. In surveying His kindness in marrying, protecting, delivering, and blessing her, what accusation could Jerusalem possibly bring against God? What could possibly be her grounds for divorce? He had every reason to divorce her, yet He remained steadfast and loyal.

Jeremiah describes the senselessness of Judah's ingratitude in three phrases: *"they have gone far from Me, Have followed idols, And have* become idolaters" (v. 5); "You defiled My land And made My heritage an abomination" (v. 7); "And [you] walked after things that do not profit" (v. 8). These accusations were not describing some passive mentality but rather a deliberate going in the wrong direction.

What a dreadful price they had paid for their waywardness! They had become what they worshiped. Here is a principle for all Christians to watch. What we give our imaginations to, our personalities to—that is what we become. The investment of our time, our energy, and our money will result in something, either emptiness or glory. Which it will be depends on what it is we have been worshiping.

Would that this apostasy had been found in only one segment of his culture. Perhaps it could be cured were it localized. This condition, however, was described as all pervasive. The priests, who should have instructed the people in the knowledge of God, had lost sight of Him themselves and had quit seeking. The scribes who handled the Law had no knowledge of His will. The pastors, who should have kept the people from transgressing, were too busy transgressing themselves. The prophets were uttering the words of Baal and not the word of the Lord (v. 8).

She Stands Accused

2:9 "Therefore I will yet bring charges against you,"
     says the LORD,
     "And against your children's children I will
     bring charges.
10 For pass beyond the coasts of Cyprus and see,
     Send to Kedar and consider diligently,
     And see if there has been such *a thing*.
11 Has a nation changed *its* gods,
     Which *are* not gods?
     But My people have changed their Glory
     For *what* does not profit.
12 Be astonished, O heavens, at this,
     And be horribly afraid;
     Be very desolate," says the LORD,
13 "For My people have committed two evils:
     They have forsaken Me, the fountain of living
     waters,

And hewn themselves cisterns—broken cisterns
that can hold no water."

Jer. 2:9–13

After the logic of the lover has been heard in all its penetrating truth, Jeremiah goes on to point out two glaring inconsistencies whereby Judah stands accused.

1. She acted against common practice. It was unprecedented in the history of the nations for a people ever to forsake the gods of their inheritance. Picture Jeremiah in his anguish to communicate, thrusting out a strong arm westward toward the island of Cyprus. *"Pass beyond the coasts of Cyprus and see,"* he exclaims (v. 10). They are being invited to examine other cultures to discover that there is no sociological precedent for their massive defection. Then with his other arm Jeremiah points eastward toward an Arab tribe in the desert beyond Palestine. *"Send to Kedar and consider diligently"* (v. 10). Even the people whose gods are impotent, who are no gods at all, still remain loyal to them. Yet here is Jerusalem, in possession of the one, true God, forsaking Him and going after emptiness.

2. They acted against common sense. Why would anyone take something of great value and deliberately exchange it for something worthless? It defies every law of common sense, so much so that the astonishment can only be felt in heaven because the earth has lost its mind (v. 12). Jerusalem's capacity to comprehend the loss was gone. A shudder ran through the heavens and through the prophet as he contemplated the two evils of verse 13. First, they had forsaken God, the fountain of living waters. Spoken to a people in a semi-arid land, these words would have had a particular intensity. A water source was a matter of survival. An underground fountain was a rare treasure, gurgling bountifully from secret springs that refreshed the weary. It makes no sense to forsake such satisfaction, such a link to life itself. No one parched by the desert sun would have given a moment's consideration to such insanity. Yet this was exactly what Jerusalem had done. Furthermore she had compounded that insanity with another.

Second, they have hewn cisterns of their own making. Tanks out of hard rock, without feeding springs, were unable even to retain what little water might flow into them because they were broken. Judah had given up everything and had gone after nothing. She cheated herself. The loss was poignant and all pervasive. There was nothing now to quench her thirst but mire and filthy sediment. How totally without logic has been her course of action, how purgative the prophet's imagery.

ISRAEL TAKES THE WITNESS STAND

2:14 *"Is* Israel a servant?
      Is he a homeborn *slave?*
      Why is he plundered?
   15 The young lions roared at him, *and* growled;
      They made his land waste;
      His cities are burned, without inhabitant.
   16 Also the people of Noph and Tahpanhes
      Have broken the crown of your head.
   17 Have you not brought this on yourself,
      In that you have forsaken the LORD your God
      When He led you in the way?
   18 And now why take the road to Egypt,
      To drink the waters of Sihor?
      Or why take the road to Assyria,
      To drink the waters of the River?
   19 Your own wickedness will correct you,
      And your backslidings will rebuke you.
      Know therefore and see that *it is* an evil and
         bitter *thing*
      That you have forsaken the LORD your God,
      And the fear of Me *is* not in you,"
      Says the Lord GOD of hosts.
   20 "For of old I have broken your yoke *and* burst
         your bonds;
      And you said, 'I will not transgress,'
      When on every high hill and under every green
         tree
      You lay down, playing the harlot.
   21 Yet I had planted you a noble vine, a seed of
         highest quality.
      How then have you turned before Me
      Into the degenerate plant of an alien vine?
   22 For though you wash yourself with lye, and use
         much soap,

Yet your iniquity is marked before
     Me," says the Lord GOD.
23 "How can you say, 'I am not polluted,
     I have not gone after the Baals'?
     See your way in the valley;
     Know what you have done:
     You are a swift dromedary breaking loose in her
          ways,
24 A wild donkey used to the wilderness,
     That sniffs at the wind in her desire;
     In her time of mating, who can turn her away?
     All those who seek her will not weary themselves;
     In her month they will find her.
25 Withhold your foot from being unshod, and
          your throat from thirst.
     But you said, 'There is no hope.
     No! For I have loved aliens, and after them I
          will go.'
26 "As the thief is ashamed when he is found out,
     So is the house of Israel ashamed;
     They and their kings and their princes, and
          their priests and their prophets,
27 Saying to a tree, 'You *are* my father,'
     And to a stone, 'You gave birth to me.'
     For they have turned *their* back to Me, and not
          their face.
     But in the time of their trouble
     They will say, 'Arise and save us.'
28 But where *are* your gods that you have made
          for yourselves?
     Let them arise,
     If they can save you in the time of your
          trouble;
     For *according to* the number of your cities
     Are your gods, O Judah.
29 "Why will you plead with Me?
     You all have transgressed against Me," says
          the LORD.
30 "In vain I have chastened your children;
     They received no correction.
     Your sword has devoured your prophets
     Like a destroying lion.

41

31 "O generation, see the word of the LORD!
   Have I been a wilderness to Israel,
   Or a land of darkness?
   Why do My people say, 'We are lords;
   We will come no more to You'?
32 Can a virgin forget her ornaments,
   Or a bride her attire?
   Yet My people have forgotten Me days without
       number.
33 "Why do you beautify your way to seek love?
   Therefore you have also taught
   The wicked women your ways.
34 Also on your skirts is found
   The blood of the lives of the poor innocents.
   I have not found it by secret search,
   But plainly on all these things.
35 Yet you say, 'Because I am innocent,
   Surely His anger shall turn from me.'
   Behold, I will plead My case against you,
   Because you say, 'I have not sinned.'
36 Why do you gad about so much to change
       your way?
   Also you shall be ashamed of Egypt as you
       were ashamed of Assyria.
37 Indeed you will go forth from him
   With your hands on your head;
   For the LORD has rejected your trusted allies,
   And you will not prosper by them."

                                           Jer. 2:14–37

Jeremiah has been appealing to the Southern Kingdom because
the Northern Kingdom has already met her demise. He speaks of
her now by way of her bad example. She who was royal born, an
heir of Abraham, has become a slave, has fallen prey to the lions of
Assyria who had roared, attacked, and left her in ruins. The noth-
ingness she had worshiped was what she had become. Let that be
an example to Judah!

Wickedness carries its own chastening. *"Your own wickedness will
correct you, And your backslidings will rebuke you"* (v. 19). Look at
Israel if you don't believe that! God doesn't have to do a thing. There
are circumstances that come into our lives because of choices we

have made. Evil has its own impact upon us. Our natural instinct is to blame someone else. "I am like this because of my mother . . . or my father . . . or the pesky sister whom everybody loved and spoiled and took no notice of me." Our list of excuses is a mile long. Nevertheless there comes a moment of accountability. We must stop blaming someone else for the misfortune that has come to us. We can come back under the covering of God.

Judah was being offered this opportunity. She could profit from the mistakes of her sister to the north, but it does not look as if she was going to. *"And now why take the road to Egypt?"* (v. 18). Jeremiah was advising them not to take the route of political expediency by making the wrong alliance. They were about to drink from the waters of the Nile and of the Euphrates, waters that were from broken cisterns.

Neither Egypt nor Assyria would be faithful allies. Jeremiah stretched continually to create imagery with which to make this uncomfortable news impact on the city of Jerusalem. Like many Hebrew writers, he used a cluster of similes. There were six images to afflict the comfortable.

1. They were like the harlot who prostitutes herself and sells her virtue. She eventually becomes a pitiful figure in any society, merely an object for its lower uses. There was probably reference here to the fertility/sexual cults and their many sanctuaries that sprinkled the hills of Canaan.

2. They were like the choice vine gone wild, an enigma to the husbandman who so carefully planted and so carefully tended it. They had progressively degenerated into something unruly (v. 21).

3. They were soiled and stained in a way that no soap could clean (v. 22). It was more than a cosmetic problem. This was a profound uncleanness that would be explored further in chapter 13 in the public demonstration concerning the linen sash. It is also reminiscent of Jesus' indictment against the Pharisees when he referred to them as "whitewashed tombs" (Matt. 23:27).

4. They were like a swift young camel running through the desert without a driver (v. 24). Her tracks could be seen in the sand, crossing and recrossing each other, betraying their lack of purpose. She was a bundle of contradictions and inconsistencies. They were self-deceived, wild, and on-the-run, getting nowhere fast.

43

5. They were like a wild donkey in heat, racing with sexual desire (v. 24). They had developed a posture that invited trouble. The animal imagery has intensified from the arrogance of the oxen to the errancy of the camel to the deliberate passion of the donkey. Apostasy has a dynamic. It intensifies. It is not neutral or static.

6. They were like the thief who has nothing to show for his life of crime (v. 26). All that was left was the shame of being caught. How shocking when this imagery is applied to dignitaries, kings, princes, priests, and prophets. Both the secular and the religious culture had robbed the people of the truth.

"In vain I have chastened your children; They received no correction" (v. 30). They killed all the prophets sent by God. Here was the highest sense of the lover's frustration. What was it going to take for them to "wise up"? In the section of verses 30–38 we find five things that characterized their forsaking of Him.

1. It defied all logic. Again Jeremiah used bridal imagery. How unnatural for a bride to forget the sash that proclaimed her status as a married woman (v. 32).

2. It was destructive of the morality of others. They seduced neighboring nations by mixing God's ways with those of idolatry. They succeeded in making the wicked more wicked than they would otherwise have been (v. 33).

3. It was destructive of human lives. Innocent blood had been spilled in the practice of child sacrifice (v. 34).

4. It held to a doctrine of "cheap grace." It claimed an innocence in the face of guilt and took forgiveness for granted. *"Surely His anger shall turn from me"* (v. 35). This failure to confess actually compounded the felony.

5. It was fickle. It gadded about from one pagan alliance to the next (v. 36). Yet God would use these nations to punish them as He had already used Assyria to punish Israel.

Afflicting the comfortable is not easy business. Yet it was the business to which Jeremiah was called. This theme characterizes his prophetic ministry. Look at the energy he invested in the task. First, he presented the pleading logic of the lover and his tender reminiscences. Then he listed a courageous outpouring of similes, from the harlot to the wild ass. Then he cited the example of Israel to strike at the heart of Judah. We can never accuse Jeremiah of a lack of passion.

CHAPTER THREE

Comforting the Afflicted

Jeremiah 3:1–4:31

The first sermons delivered by Jeremiah were designed to afflict the comfortable, to strike at the heart of Judah's unfaithfulness to God. With God's word, condemnation was never for its own sake. His only reason for wounding them was to be able to heal them. The second messages begin in this chapter and extend through the sixth chapter. It was not very comfortable news, but it had occasional threads of hope that shone against the fabric of judgment.

FOUR WORDS THAT COULD CHANGE YOUR LIFE

3:1 "They say, 'If a man divorces his wife,
 And she goes from him
 And becomes another man's,
 May he return to her again?'
 Would not that land be greatly polluted?
 But you have played the harlot with many lovers;
 Yet return to Me," says the LORD.
2 "Lift up your eyes to the desolate heights and
  see:
 Where have you not lain *with men?*
 By the road you have sat for them
 Like an Arabian in the wilderness;
 And you have polluted the land
 With your harlotries and your wickedness.
3 Therefore the showers have been withheld,
 And there has been no latter rain.
 You have had a harlot's forehead;
 You refuse to be ashamed.

4 Will you not from this time cry to Me,
'My Father, You *are* the guide of my youth?
5 Will He remain angry forever?
Will He keep it to the end?'
Behold, you have spoken and done evil things,
As you were able."

6 The LORD said also to me in the days of Josiah
the king: "Have you seen what backsliding Israel has
done? She has gone up on every high mountain and
under every green tree, and there played the harlot.

7 "And I said, after she had done all these *things*,
'Return to Me.' But she did not return. And her
treacherous sister Judah saw it.

8 "Then I saw that for all the causes for which
backsliding Israel had committed adultery, I had put
her away and given her a certificate of divorce; yet her
treacherous sister Judah did not fear, but went and
played the harlot also.

9 "So it came to pass, through her casual harlotry,
that she defiled the land and committed adultery with
stones and trees.

10 "And yet for all this her treacherous sister Judah has not turned to Me with her whole heart, but
in pretense," says the LORD.

11 Then the LORD said to me, "Backsliding Israel
has shown herself more righteous than treacherous
Judah.

12 "Go and proclaim these words toward the north,
and say:
'Return, backsliding Israel,' says the LORD;
'I will not cause My anger to fall on you.
For I *am* merciful,' says the LORD;
'I will not remain angry forever.
13 Only acknowledge your iniquity,
That you have transgressed against the LORD
your God,
And have scattered your charms
To alien deities under every green tree,
And you have not obeyed My voice,' says the
LORD.
14 "Return, O backsliding children," says the LORD;
"for I am married to you. I will take you, one from a

city and two from a family, and I will bring you to Zion.

15 "And I will give you shepherds according to My heart, who will feed you with knowledge and understanding.

16 "Then it shall come to pass, when you are multiplied and increased in the land in those days," says the LORD, "that they will say no more, 'The ark of the covenant of the LORD.' It shall not come to mind, nor shall they remember it, nor shall they visit *it*, nor shall it be made anymore.

17 "At that time Jerusalem shall be called The Throne of the LORD, and all the nations shall be gathered to it, to the name of the LORD, to Jerusalem. No more shall they follow the dictates of their evil hearts.

18 "In those days the house of Judah shall walk with the house of Israel, and they shall come together out of the land of the north to the land that I have given as an inheritance to your fathers.

19 "But I said:
'How can I put you among the children
And give you a pleasant land,
A beautiful heritage of the hosts of nations?'
"And I said:
'You shall call Me, "My Father,"
And not turn away from Me.'

20 Surely, *as* a wife treacherously departs from her
husband,
So have you dealt treacherously with Me,
O house of Israel," says the LORD.

21 A voice was heard on the desolate heights,
Weeping *and* supplications of the children of
Israel.
For they have perverted their way;
They have forgotten the LORD their God.

22 "Return, you backsliding children,
And I will heal your backslidings."
"Indeed we do come to You,
For You are the LORD our God.

23 Truly, in vain *is salvation hoped for* from the hills,
And *from* the multitude of mountains;

> Truly, in the LORD our God
> *Is* the salvation of Israel.
> 24 For shame has devoured
> The labor of our fathers from our youth—
> Their flocks and their herds,
> Their sons and their daughters.
> 25 We lie down in our shame,
> And our reproach covers us.
> For we have sinned against the LORD our God,
> We and our fathers,
> From our youth even to this day,
> And have not obeyed the voice of the LORD our
> God."
>
> *Jer. 3:1–25*

The shamelessness of Israel was still under discussion. God began by referring to one of their divorce laws (Deut. 24:1–4). These laws were there to accommodate their human frailties, not because God really approved of divorce.

If a man found an indecency in his wife, he wrote her a certificate of divorce, put it in her hand, and sent her out of the house. If she should go through this process with yet another husband and find herself out of his house, the first husband was not allowed to take her in again. She had been defiled. They all understood these terms.

The Northern Kingdom had been guilty of an infidelity against God. She had not played the harlot on just one occasion but numerous times. *"I had put her away and given her a certificate of divorce,"* says God (v. 8). According to their own legislation that was that. *"Therefore the showers have been withheld, And there has been no latter rain"* (v. 3). Her very environment began to reflect the divorce, to say nothing of her political and economic circumstances. She lay in ruins by the hand of the Assyrians.

Like a bright thread, Jeremiah recorded four words that could change her life. God was unlike any earthly husband; He completely transcended that pattern. No earthly husband in his right mind would take back such a shameless wife. They said put her away, but God said, *"Yet return to Me"* (v. 1). People who talk about the Old Testament being filled with nothing but wrath and anger should look at this most tender piece of long-suffering. God looked past the pollution, the shamelessness, and the whoredom. He looked right into the eyes of Israel and said, *"after she had done all these things, 'Return to Me.' But she did not return"* (v. 7). His first offer was refused. The example of this refusal was held up to the Southern Kingdom. Judah saw this refusal and did not profit from it. Judah saw the certificate of divorce given to her sister Israel, but she did not repent (v. 8). She was therefore more guilty. God put it this way: *"Backsliding Israel has shown herself more righteous than treacherous Judah"* (v. 11).

Divorces are ugly and full of guilt and faultfinding. If any culture could understand this, it ought to be ours. Because of our divorce rate, we are fast becoming a nation of single parents and lonely hearts. This is also a vivid picture of our divorce from God. Therefore, the four words issued here ought to refresh us as they did the prophet who delivered them to the ancient and distant culture of the Hebrews.

"Return," God said a second time to Israel (v. 12). What longsuffering! What exuberance! I can just see Jeremiah now, in full command of his powers, his eyes running with tears so characteristic of him, repeating the invitation to that broken and lonely country of Israel. *"'For I am merciful,' says the LORD; 'I will not remain angry forever'"* (v. 12). The divorce laws said that there was no second chance. Yet God's love transcends our frailties and offers us a new marriage with Him. Here come four more words that would have changed her life. *"Only acknowledge your iniquity"* (v. 13). Eight little words stood between Israel and a new life. As it is true for a nation, so it is also true for an individual. How have we responded?

This second utterance of the four-word invitation was issued with the gusto of a royal proclamation: *"Go and proclaim these words"* (v. 12). Jeremiah must have held his head high, knowing he was in the service of the King. Another factor becomes significant. It was spoken in the days of Josiah the king; his was the last righteous reign that Judah was to know. There was an urgency to the call to repentance. It would not always be offered, a fact that would become painfully evident to the young prophet.

A third time the invitation rang out: *"Return, O backsliding children . . . for I am married to you"* (v. 14). This time there was a new cluster of images, not like those strident images of the harlot, the wild donkey, and the thief from the previous set of sermons.

These images were meant to look beyond all the brokenness to heal and to restore.

1. A personal escort back home was offered the wayward people by the Husband Himself. *"I will take you, one from a city and two from a family, and I will bring you to Zion"* (v. 14). God promised a glorious return of the exiles (v. 18).

2. Good shepherds, with God's heart in them, would feed them with real truth (v. 15). This would become a popular image with Jeremiah, one to which he would return with great triumph in chapter 23.

3. The throne of the Lord, which symbolized God's sovereignty over the earth, would be established in Jerusalem. They would no longer need the ark of the covenant, for the real thing would be established (v. 17).

4. *"You shall call Me, 'My Father,' And not turn away from Me"* (v. 19). This, like the others, was a shocking look into the gospel age to come.

The call to return was repeated a fourth time: *"Return, you backsliding children, And I will heal your backslidings"* (v. 22). After the four refreshing images, they began weeping in repentance. *"A voice was heard on the desolate heights, Weeping and supplications of the children of Israel"* (v. 21). Jeremiah had been waiting for this moment, the time when repentance would come.

Each year I choose one month in which I will lay particular emphasis on repentance. For four Sundays I call my congregation to a public confession. Those who have never before done so are urged to walk down the aisle, to stand at the foot of the cross, and to surrender their lives to the sovereign Lord Jesus. On that last Sunday, there are always those who have struggled with the invitation for three weeks, but their feet have been glued to the floor. Like the house of Israel in this text, they finally respond to those four words that can change their lives. "'If you will return, O Israel,' says the LORD, 're-turn to Me; And if you will put away your abominations out of My sight, Then you shall not be moved'" (4:1).

What comfort for the afflicted heart, for those who act as if they have been divorced from God! Jeremiah's attention now turned to the Southern Kingdom, hoping that Israel's exile could be used to achieve Judah's salvation.

Four Tests for Courageous Preaching

4:1 "If you will return, O Israel," says the Lord,
    "Return to Me;
    And if you will put away your abominations
        out of My sight,
    Then you shall not be moved.
  2 And you shall swear, 'The Lord lives,'
    In truth, in judgment, and in righteousness;
    The nations shall bless themselves in Him,
    And in Him they shall glory."
  3 For thus says the Lord to the men of Judah and
Jerusalem:
    "Break up your fallow ground,
    And do not sow among thorns.
  4 Circumcise yourselves to the Lord,
    And take away the foreskins of your hearts,
    You men of Judah and inhabitants of Jerusalem,
    Lest My fury come forth like fire,
    And burn so that no one can quench it,
    Because of the evil of your doings."
  5 Declare in Judah and proclaim in Jerusalem, and
say:
    "Blow the trumpet in the land;
    Cry, 'Gather together,'
    And say, 'Assemble yourselves,
    And let us go into the fortified cities,'
  6 Set up the standard toward Zion.
    Take refuge! Do not delay!
    For I will bring disaster from the north,
    And great destruction."
  7 The lion has come up from his thicket,
    And the destroyer of nations is on his way.
    He has gone forth from his place
    To make your land desolate.
    Your cities will be laid waste,
    Without inhabitant.
  8 For this, clothe yourself with sackcloth,
    Lament and wail.
    For the fierce anger of the Lord
    Has not turned back from us.

9 "And it shall come to pass in that day," says the
LORD,
"*That* the heart of the king shall perish,
And the heart of the princes;
The priests shall be astonished,
And the prophets shall wonder."

10 Then I said, "Ah, Lord GOD!
Surely You have greatly deceived this people
and Jerusalem,
Saying, 'You shall have peace,'
Whereas the sword reaches to the heart."

11 At that time it will be said
To this people and to Jerusalem,
"A dry wind of the desolate heights *blows* in the
wilderness
Toward the daughter of My people—
Not to fan or to cleanse—

12 A wind too strong for these will come for Me;
Now I will also speak judgment against them."

13 "Behold, he shall come up like clouds,
And his chariots like a whirlwind.
His horses are swifter than eagles.
Woe to us, for we are plundered!"

14 O Jerusalem, wash your heart from wickedness,
That you may be saved.
How long shall your evil thoughts lodge within
you?

15 For a voice declares from Dan
And proclaims affliction from Mount Ephraim:

16 "Make mention to the nations,
Yes, proclaim against Jerusalem,
That watchers come from a far country
And raise their voice against the cities of Judah.

17 Like keepers of a field they are against her all
around,
Because she has been rebellious against Me,"
says the LORD,

18 "Your ways and your doings
Have procured these *things* for you.
This *is* your wickedness,
Because it is bitter,
Because it reaches to your heart."

19 O my soul, my soul!
   I am pained in my very heart!
   My heart makes a noise in me;
   I cannot hold my peace,
   Because you have heard, O my soul,
   The sound of the trumpet,
   The alarm of war.
20 Destruction upon destruction is cried,
   For the whole land is plundered.
   Suddenly my tents are plundered,
   And my curtains in a moment.
21 How long will I see the standard,
   And hear the sound of the trumpet?
22 "For My people *are* foolish,
   They have not known Me.
   They *are* silly children,
   And they have no understanding.
   They *are* wise to do evil,
   But to do good they have no knowledge."
23 I beheld the earth, and indeed *it was* without
       form, and void;
   And the heavens, they *had* no light.
24 I beheld the mountains, and indeed they
       trembled,
   And all the hills moved back and forth.
25 I beheld, and indeed *there was* no man,
   And all the birds of the heavens had fled.
26 I beheld, and indeed the fruitful land *was* a
       wilderness,
   And all its cities were broken down
   At the presence of the LORD,
   By His fierce anger.
27 For thus says the LORD:
   "The whole land shall be desolate;
   Yet I will not make a full end.
28 For this shall the earth mourn,
   And the heavens above be black,
   Because I have spoken.
   I have purposed and will not relent,
   Nor will I turn back from it.
29 The whole city shall flee from the noise of the
       horsemen and bowmen.

> They shall go into thickets and climb up on the
>   rocks.
> Every city *shall be* forsaken,
> And not a man shall dwell in it.
> 30 "And *when* you *are* plundered,
>   What will you do?
> Though you clothe yourself with crimson,
> Though you adorn *yourself* with ornaments of
>   gold,
> Though you enlarge your eyes with paint,
> In vain you will make yourself fair;
> *Your* lovers will despise you;
> They will seek your life.
> 31 "For I have heard a voice as of a woman in
>   labor,
> The anguish as of her who brings forth her
>   first child,
> The voice of the daughter of Zion bewailing
>   herself;
> She spreads her hands, *saying,*
> 'Woe *is* me now, for my soul is weary
> Because of murders!'"
>
> *Jer. 4:1–31*

This section is a series of poems, the pithiest to be found anywhere. They were preached as sermons. Like any good communicator, Jeremiah scorned the vague, the colorless, and the irresolute and
struck right at the heart. After all, the Southern Kingdom, to whom
Jeremiah's words were directed, was in serious trouble, and he must
reach beyond their complacency and stir them to redemption.

Do many ministers look out upon their congregations with that in
mind? Too many are dishing out pabulum as though they were feeding baby sinners. Or worse still, coining euphemisms that are just,
oh, so sweet, but nothing gets said. Jeremiah was not like that. Four
marks of courageous preaching can be found in this section. Those
of us communicating God's truth must ask ourselves these questions.

1. Do we preach for a radical change of heart? (vv. 3, 4, 14).
"Break up your fallow ground, And do not sow among thorns" (v. 3). The
landscape of the heart can lie dormant and become hard. Do our
congregations feel the cut of the plow against that hard soil when we
are preaching or teaching?

"Circumcise yourselves to the LORD, And take away the foreskins of your hearts" (v. 4). Like Judah, we all allow our affections to be mingled with those of the world, ministers included. Do we call for the kind of self-inflicted surgery that this courageous preacher did?

"Wash your heart from wickedness" (v. 14). The same idea appears later, but in slightly different language. For more such language, see 17:1–11.

Jeremiah used imagery common to the society to which he spoke. He took pains to find fresh ways of saying a thing that needed to be said over and over and over again. He has a particular preoccupation with the heart. Do we? Or are we more worried about saying something new and trendy instead of something old and crucial? We must not be ashamed of what is old. The repetition in the Book of Jeremiah is not one of its faults but rather one of its virtues.

2. Do we warn about the dangers that face our culture? (vv. 5–9, 12–18). *"Set up the standard toward Zion. Take refuge! Do not delay! . . . The lion has come up from his thicket, And the destroyer of nations is on his way"* (vv. 6–7). Was there anything compromising about this language? It was spoken in the peaceful times that Josiah provided Judah. It was meant to shake her complacency and cause her to see that a military invasion was imminent. When the other pulpits were preaching peace, Jeremiah was "telling it like it was."

What about the divorce rate, the rise in drug abuse, the disregard for moral absolutes in our education system, and the threats of pornography and child abuse? The list appears endless. The destroyers of nations are on their way. Are we rallying our congregations to respond to these invasions? *"Gather together, . . . Assemble yourselves, And let us go into the fortified cities"* (v. 5). Our churches ought to be fortified cities! They ought to produce a biblically literate citizenry that wishes to change the spirit of the age. Are we?

Jeremiah looked into the eyes of kings, princes, priests, and prophets and warned them of a day coming when the peace about which they had preached would turn to war, when their hearts would sink with embarrassment and emptiness (v. 9). The courageous preacher will find himself standing alone, often against prevailing power structures that resist him at every turn.

3. Do we have private time with God over the issues of our doubts? (vv. 10, 19–22). *"Ah, Lord GOD! Surely You have greatly deceived this people . . . Saying, 'You shall have peace,' Whereas the*

sword reaches to the heart" (v. 10). Here Jeremiah boldly confronted God with what looks like an impropriety. Notice that the preacher does not air this in his pulpit but in his quiet time with God, where the doubts and frustrations are best reviewed and dealt with.

4. Do we have a passion for what we believe? (vv. 19–31). *"O my soul, my soul! I am pained in my very heart! My heart makes a noise in me; I cannot hold my peace"* (v. 19). Do communicators today feel that kind of compulsion about what they have to say to their congregations? Or have we grown so much like the world around us that we have lost such feelings and are merely plying our trade?

This may sound like so much archaic melodrama. It is either that or it is the mark of a great man and a great preacher. Boris Pasternak said to this century, "It is not revolutions and upheavals that clear the road to new and better days, but revelations, lavishness and torments of someone's soul, inspired and ablaze."

"How long will I see the standard, And hear the sound of the trumpet?" (v. 21). The business of seeing ahead into disastrous and frightening times is not for the fainthearted. Jeremiah had to live constantly with the knowledge that Jerusalem would be attacked and that he himself would suffer the consequences along with everyone else. Indeed it was a torment of soul. It caused his own humanity to tremble. Yet it was this very passion that made him brilliant. *"Though you clothe yourself with crimson, Though you adorn yourself with ornaments of gold, Though you enlarge your eyes with paint, In vain you will make yourself fair; Your lovers will despise you; They will seek your life"* (v. 30). We too have the task of communicating to a culture that is "looking for love in all the wrong places." We may not all be poets like Jeremiah, nor possessing of such tender spirits, but we are called to care, to feel that caring in the pit of our stomachs, and to preach that caring with our whole hearts.

We must not let any dullness settle over us. We must find cures for burnout and discouragement. Ours is the business of afflicting the comfortable and comforting the afflicted. We need to line our own hearts up against these four characteristics of Jeremiah the man and Jeremiah the preacher.

CHAPTER FOUR

When God Was Appalled and the People Were Pleased

Jeremiah 5:1–6:30

When something happens that appalls God and at the same time pleases us, we know that we have indeed become a godless society. There can be no gulf wider than this. Chapters 5 and 6, like the sermons of chapter 4, were delivered to the Southern Kingdom that had reached this condition. It can be examined in five dimensions.

THE PROPHET

6:27 "I have set you *as* an assayer *and* a fortress
    among My people,
  That you may know and test their way.
28 They *are* all stubborn rebels, walking as
    slanderers.
  They are bronze and iron,
  They *are* all corrupters;
29 The bellows blow fiercely,
  The lead is consumed by the fire;
  The smelter refines in vain,
  For the wicked are not drawn off.
30 *People* will call them rejected silver,
  Because the LORD has rejected them."

5:14 Therefore thus says the LORD God of hosts:
  "Because you speak this word,
  Behold, I will make My words in your mouth
    fire,

> And this people wood,
> And it shall devour them."
>
> *Jer. 6:27–30; 5:14*

Jeremiah recognized more and more how profound his role to the nations really was. The disparity between God and Judah yawned before him like a dark chasm. He had to stare over its edge and continue "to root out and pull down . . . to build and to plant."

Now the plot thickened. God added to the job description. *"I have set you as an assayer and a fortress among My people, That you may know and test their way"* (v. 27). The very words that Jeremiah was called upon to utter to Judah were the words of testing. When he was called as a country boy, God touched his mouth and put His words in it (1:9). Now God said, *"Behold, I will make My words in your mouth fire, And this people wood, And it shall devour them"* (5:14). Many people do not believe Scripture to be the word of God. They pass such casual judgment upon it, never realizing that in actuality they have been judged by it. When you read your Bible, it also reads you. It is an assayer of the people. Whether they choose to believe that or not makes no difference.

I spoke earlier of the great quality of passion in Jeremiah. Later he would exclaim, *"His word* was in my heart like a burning fire Shut up in my bones; I was weary of holding *it* back, And I could not" (20:9).

THE PROBLEM

> 5:1 "Run to and fro through the streets of Jerusalem;
>   See now and know;
>   And seek in her open places
>   If you can find a man,
>   If there is *anyone* who executes judgment,
>   Who seeks the truth,
>   And I will pardon her.
> 2 Though they say, '*As the* LORD *lives,*'
>   Surely they swear falsely."
> 3 O LORD, *are* not Your eyes on the truth?
>   You have stricken them,
>   But they have not grieved;
>   You have consumed them,

But they have refused to receive correction.
They have made their faces harder than rock;
They have refused to return.

4 Therefore I said, "Surely these *are* poor.
They are foolish;
For they do not know the way of the LORD,
The judgment of their God.

5 I will go to the great men and speak to them,
For they have known the way of the LORD,
The judgment of their God."
But these have altogether broken the yoke
And burst the bonds.

6 Therefore a lion from the forest shall slay
them,
A wolf of the deserts shall destroy them;
A leopard will watch over their cities.
Everyone who goes out from there shall be
torn in pieces,
Because their transgressions are many;
Their backslidings have increased.

7 "How shall I pardon you for this?
Your children have forsaken Me
And sworn by *those that are* not gods.
When I had fed them to the full,
Then they committed adultery
And assembled themselves by troops in the
harlots' houses.

8 They were *like* well-fed lusty stallions;
Every one neighed after his neighbor's wife.

9 Shall I not punish *them* for these *things?*" says
the LORD.
"And shall I not avenge Myself on such a
nation as this?

10 "Go up on her walls and destroy,
But do not make a complete end.
Take away her branches,
For they *are* not the LORD's.

11 For the house of Israel and the house of Judah
Have dealt very treacherously with Me," says
the LORD.

12 They have lied about the LORD,
And said, "*It is* not He.

> Neither will evil come upon us,
> Nor shall we see sword or famine.
> 13 And the prophets become wind,
> For the word *is* not in them.
> Thus shall it be done to them.'
>
> 6:9 Thus says the LORD of hosts:
> "They shall thoroughly glean as a vine the
>   remnant of Israel;
> As a grape-gatherer, put your hand back into
>   the branches."
>
> 15 "Were they ashamed when they had committed
>   abomination?
> No! They were not at all ashamed;
> Nor did they know how to blush.
> Therefore they shall fall among those who fall;
> At the time I punish them,
> They shall be cast down," says the LORD.
>   *Jer. 5:1–13; 6:9, 15*

"Run to and fro through the streets of Jerusalem; See now and know; . . . If you can find a man, If there is anyone who executes judgment, Who seeks the truth" (v. 1). God sent the prophet out into the screaming streets of the city in order to teach him just how horrible the problem really was and just how complacent the people were. No, Jeremiah, you did not exaggerate, you are not guilty of sensationalism. Everything you said was true. As a matter of fact it was worse than you had imagined, for these reasons:

1. *The depravity was total.* In his desperate search through the streets, Jeremiah would not find so much as one person who held to moral standards or who sought the truth. Although they swore by the Lord, it was merely lip service (v. 2).

Imagine the prophet weaving his way through the congested streets, staring into the *"faces harder than rock"* (v. 3), trying to find proof that God was exaggerating. Surely it can't be this bad. The Apostle Paul wrote to the Romans with the same sense of anguish; *"There is none righteous, no, not one; There is none who understands; There is none who seeks after God. They have all turned aside"* (Rom. 3:10–12).

Abraham reeled from the shock concerning the total corruption of Sodom and Gomorrah. God allowed him the bartering prayers and agreed to save the city for the presence of ten righteous men. When Lot and his family were removed, however, there were none left in the city who were not in abject rebellion against God.

Jeremiah moved his search to the high-rent district; *"I will go to the great men and speak to them, For they have known the way of the LORD"* (v. 5). He was thinking that the landed and the educated would not be as diseased with sin. Secular thinking embraces the notion that humankind is about the business of improving itself. With enough education, enough charity, enough economic programs, we will perfect the human race. The revelation of Scripture and of this passage in particular is that the problem is sin. It infects the poor and the rich, the young and the old, male and female, educated and uneducated, nice people and nasty people. All that prevents our catastrophic demise is the presence in a nation of those who, in confession and repentance, have turned their hearts toward God.

2. *The people were shameless.* Not only was the wickedness total, it was also without shame. The people "love to have it so" (v. 31). *"Then they committed adultery And assembled themselves by troops in the harlots' houses"* (v. 7). Theirs were not occasional, clandestine visits to the house of whoredom, under the cover of night. They were actually trooping, in vast numbers, unabashedly. *"They are like well-fed lusty stallions; Every one neighed after his neighbor's wife"* (v. 8). Wife swapping had ceased to be scandalous and had become downright commonplace.

"Were they ashamed when they committed abomination? No! They were not at all ashamed; Nor did they know how to blush" (6:15). I sometimes wonder if in this culture we remember how to blush. There was a time when our professional athletes were content to buy sports cars with their enormous salaries. Now they buy cocaine. Master runners in prestigious marathons are caught cheating. On Wall Street, stockbrokers, whose hefty incomes do not seem to be enough, engage in insider trading. "They *are* wise to do evil" (4:22). One such personage recently struck a deal that allowed him to keep a chunk of his "profits" and avoid jail in return for setting traps to catch associate traders.

People who should be hanging their heads are instead selling their shamelessness for book and movie contracts. Recently an attractive socialite, a descendant of the *Mayflower* Puritans was convicted of running a million-dollar call girl ring. Since then, she has capitalized on the release of a book, the sale of television and movie rights, and an extensive lecture circuit. All because the people love it so.

A team of brothers, former officers in the U.S. Navy, were convicted of leading a spy ring that sold secrets to the Soviet Union. "From the least of them even to the greatest of them, Everyone is given to covetousness" (6:13). The operation remained covert for ten years while its pollution undermined the national security of the country. Even now they are negotiating a book deal from their jail cells. We too are a people who have forgotten how to blush.

THE PENALTY

5:15 "Behold, I will bring a nation against you from afar,
O house of Israel," says the LORD.
"It *is* a mighty nation,
It *is* an ancient nation,
A nation whose language you do not know,
Nor can you understand what they say.
16 Their quiver *is* like an open tomb;
They *are* all mighty men.
17 And they shall eat up your harvest and your
bread,
Which your sons and daughters should eat.
They shall eat up your flocks and your herds;
They shall eat up your vines and your fig trees;
They shall destroy your fortified cities,
In which you trust, with the sword.
18 "Nevertheless in those days," says the LORD, "I will not make a complete end of you.
19 "And it will be when you say, 'Why does the LORD our God do all these *things* to us?' then you shall answer them, 'Just as you have forsaken Me and served foreign gods in your land, so you shall serve aliens in a land *that is* not yours.'"

6:1 "O you children of Benjamin,
Gather yourselves to flee from the midst of
Jerusalem!

Blow the trumpet in Tekoa,
And set up a signal-fire in Beth Haccerem;
For disaster appears out of the north,
And great destruction.

2 I have likened the daughter of Zion
To a lovely and delicate woman.

3 The shepherds with their flocks shall come to
her.
They shall pitch *their* tents against her all
around.
Each one shall pasture in his own place."

4 "Prepare war against her;
Arise, and let us go up at noon.
Woe to us, for the day goes away,
For the shadows of the evening are
lengthening.

5 Arise, and let us go by night,
And let us destroy her palaces."

6 For thus has the LORD of hosts said:
"Cut down trees,
And build a mound against Jerusalem.
This *is* the city to be punished.
She *is* full of oppression in her midst.

7 As a fountain wells up with water,
So she wells up with her wickedness.
Violence and plundering are heard in her.
Before Me continually *are* grief and wounds.

8 Be instructed, O Jerusalem,
Lest My soul depart from you;
Lest I make you desolate,
A land not inhabited."

11 Therefore I am full of the fury of the LORD.
I am weary of holding *it* in.
"I will pour it out on the children outside,
And on the assembly of young men together;
For even the husband shall be taken with the
wife,
The aged with *him who is* full of days.

12 And their houses shall be turned over to others,
Fields and wives together;
For I will stretch out My hand

> Against the inhabitants of the land," says the
> LORD.
>
> 22 Thus says the LORD:
> "Behold, a people comes from the north
>   country,
> And a great nation will be raised from the
>   farthest parts of the earth.
> 23 They will lay hold on bow and spear;
> They *are* cruel and have no mercy;
> Their voice roars like the sea;
> And they ride on horses,
> As men of war set in array against you, O
>   daughter of Zion."
> 24 We have heard the report of it;
> Our hands grow feeble.
> Anguish has taken hold of us,
> Pain as of a woman in labor.
> 25 Do not go out into the field,
> Nor walk by the way.
> Because of the sword of the enemy,
> Fear *is* on every side.
> 26 O daughter of my people,
> Dress in sackcloth
> And roll about in ashes!
> Make mourning *as for* an only son, most bitter
>   lamentation;
> For the plunderer will suddenly come upon us.
>
> *Jer. 5:15–19; 6:1–8, 11–12, 22–26*

Given that Judah's problem was total and shameless, God must ultimately punish her or else apologize to Sodom and Gomorrah. He
questioned repeatedly, "How shall I pardon you for this" (5:7)? "Shall
I not avenge Myself on such a nation as this" (5:9; cf. 5:29)? Just as
Jeremiah could not come up with one just man in Jerusalem, so also
Judah could not come up with one good reason why God should not
punish her.

The very word of God that Judah's priests and prophets scorned
was now like fire and they like wood. The assayer had tested them
and found them guilty. The heat was on. *"Behold, I will bring a nation
against you from afar"* (v. 15). *"For disaster appears out of the north, And*

great destruction" (6:1). *"A great nation will be raised from the farthest parts of the earth"* (6:22). These warnings are obvious references to the Babylonian invasion. It is not some fly-by-night country that would attack, but a large nation of ancient origins, *"A nation whose language you do not know"* (5:15). *"They are cruel and have no mercy"* (6:23). They will destroy sons, daughters, flocks, herds, vineyards, and all aspects of the economy.

Nobody ever wants to hear how bad things are. When we speak like this from our pulpits we get accused of being too emotional, of indulging in sensationalism. Not long ago I addressed a group of sophisticated teenagers, confronting them with the results of sexual promiscuity by explaining the character of AIDS and herpes. Their response was outrage. They accused me of exaggeration. I know how Jeremiah felt.

The problem sounds like total depravity. The penalty sounds like total destruction. Is there not one little strand of hope? God says to the enemy, "Go up on her walls and destroy, But do not make a complete end" (5:10). Again He says, *"Nevertheless in those days, . . . I will not make a complete end of you"* (5:18).

This is reminiscent of chapter 3, of the call to Israel to return to the Lord in the midst of the dark circumstances of her divorce from Him. The prophetic consciousness looks ahead into the gospel age.

THE PEOPLE

5:20 "Declare this in the house of Jacob
      And proclaim it in Judah, saying,
   21 'Hear this now, O foolish people,
      Without understanding,
      Who have eyes and see not,
      And who have ears and hear not:
   22 Do you not fear Me?' says the LORD.
      'Will you not tremble at My presence,
      Who have placed the sand as the bound of the
         sea,
      By a perpetual decree, that it cannot pass
         beyond it?
      And though its waves toss to and fro,

Yet they cannot prevail;
Though they roar, yet they cannot pass over it.
23 But this people has a defiant and rebellious
heart;
They have revolted and departed.
24 They do not say in their heart,
"Let us now fear the LORD our God,
Who gives rain, both the former and the latter,
in its season.
He reserves for us the appointed weeks of the
harvest."
25 Your iniquities have turned these *things* away,
And your sins have withheld good from you.

6:10 To whom shall I speak and give warning,
That they may hear?
Indeed their ear *is* uncircumcised,
And they cannot give heed.
Behold, the word of the LORD is a reproach to
them;
They have no delight in it.

16 Thus says the LORD:
"Stand in the ways and see,
And ask for the old paths, where the good way
is,
And walk in it;
Then you will find rest for your souls.
But they said, 'We will not walk *in it.*'
17 Also, I set watchmen over you, *saying,*
'Listen to the sound of the trumpet!'
But they said, 'We will not listen.'
18 Therefore hear, you nations,
And know, O congregation, what *is* among
them.
19 Hear, O earth!
Behold, I will certainly bring calamity on this
people—
The fruit of their thoughts,
Because they have not heeded My words
Nor My law, but rejected it.
20 For what purpose to Me

Comes frankincense from Sheba,
And sweet cane from a far country?
Your burnt offerings *are* not acceptable,
Nor your sacrifices sweet to Me."
21 Therefore thus says the LORD:
"Behold, I will lay stumbling blocks before this
    people,
And the fathers and the sons together shall
    fall on them.
The neighbor and his friend shall perish."
Jer. 5:20–25; 6:10, 16–21

In the usage of today, the word "fool" suggests someone who is silly and lacking in judgment. The term has a playfulness to it. We might even picture a clown or a jester. In the usage of Scripture, however, the word "fool" is a solemn indictment. "Fools despise wisdom and instruction" (Prov. 1:7). He represents that person who has chosen to turn from God and who, as a result, grows farther and farther away from the light. Nabal, the abusive husband of Abigail, whose stubborn refusal to express gratitude cost him his life, was a personification of the fool. As a matter of fact it was the meaning of his name; "Nabal is his name and folly is his game" (1 Sam. 25:25, my own translation).

The central characteristic of the people of Judah was foolishness. They had become a nation of Nabals. What God thought was horrible, they thought was wonderful. What He hated, they loved. What they loved, He hated. With an anguish the prophet cried, *"O foolish people"* (5:21), and revealed four things about the nature of all folly.

1. Foolishness is without understanding (5:21). Because of their deep-rooted aversion to what was good, their senses had become dull. They had *"eyes and [saw] not, And . . . ears and hear[d] not"* (5:21). They were totally incapable of processing spiritual reality.

Looking at the story of Nabal in 1 Samuel 25, we find an illustration. He totally misunderstood the human dynamic he had created between his enterprise and David's. He was deaf and blind to the explosive and righteous anger that was coming his way—anger that he had in fact created out of his own obtuseness.

2. Foolishness is without reverence. *"Will you not tremble at My presence"* (5:22)? When the Lord revealed His omnipotence to Job by

a series of staggering questions, Job's response was, "I abhor *myself,* And repent in dust and ashes" (Job 42:6). Yet when God addressed this people with questions much the same, He received no response whatsoever. He who "assigned to the sea its limit" (Prov. 8:29) was speaking to them. They heard Him not.

So also Nabal lacked reverence for the protective presence of David in the land, the very presence that encircled his shepherding business with safety. In a surly way, Nabal raised the question, "Who *is* David?" (1 Sam. 25:10). He betrayed his own blind irreverence. Like him, Judah has scorned the protective presence of God.

3. Foolishness is without gratitude. *"Let us now fear the* LORD *our God, Who gives rain, both the former and latter, in its season. He reserves for us the appointed weeks of the harvest"* (5:24). The poetic appeal to their hearts fell on deaf ears. Their self-centeredness was all pervasive.

Listen to the language of Nabal when he refused to compensate David's men for the many sleepless nights given over to his protection. "Shall I then take my bread and my water and my meat that I have killed for my shearers, and give *it* to men when I do not know where they *are* from?" (1 Sam. 25:11). Fools are so self-oriented, they lose their capacity for gratitude.

4. Foolishness is without rest. The Lord says, *"Ask for the old paths, where the good way is, And walk in it; Then you will find rest for your souls"* (6:16); however, they said, *"We will not walk in it."* Foolishness is a condition that results from an act of the will. It is a choice. That is why it is a moral issue and not just an intellectual one.

In refusing the good way, they forfeited the promised rest. We are a nation in desperate search of relaxation. Witness the profusion of stress management courses and the rising problem of drug and alcohol abuse. In our humanity we were designed for rest. We were meant to be a sabbath people. We are going to get that rest one way or the other. "And Nabal's heart *was* merry within him, for he *was* very drunk" (1 Sam. 25:36). In his wine-induced euphoria, Nabal lost touch with reality. At the moment he thought he was most at rest, he was in fact in the most peril. David and his warriors were charging toward Nabal with nothing but revenge in mind.

5. Foolishness is without a sacrifice. *"For what purpose to Me Comes frankincense from Sheba, And sweet cane from a far country? Your burnt offerings are not acceptable, Nor your sacrifices sweet to Me"* (6:20).

Ritual performances, perfumed with imported incense, will never hide the stench of moral disobedience. If we do not come to God on the basis of the sacrifice He has provided, there is none of our own that will ever do.

The foolish people are without understanding, without reverence, without gratitude, without rest, and without an acceptable sacrifice. Indeed, they are the losers.

THE PREDATORS

5:26 'For among My people are found wicked *men;*
They lie in wait as one who sets snares;
They set a trap;
They catch men.

27 'As a cage is full of birds,
So their houses *are* full of deceit.
Therefore they have become great and grown rich.

28 They have grown fat, they are sleek;
Yes, they surpass the deeds of the wicked;
They do not plead the cause,
The cause of the fatherless;
Yet they prosper,
And the right of the needy they do not defend.

29 Shall I not punish *them* for these *things?'* says the LORD.
'Shall I not avenge Myself on such a nation as this?'

30 "An astonishing and horrible thing
Has been committed in the land:

31 The prophets prophesy falsely,
And the priests rule by their *own* power;
And My people love *to have it* so.
But what will you do in the end?"

6:13 "Because from the least of them even to the
greatest of them,
Everyone *is* given to covetousness;
And from the prophet even to the priest,
Everyone deals falsely.

14 They have also healed the hurt of My people
slightly,

Saying, 'Peace, peace!'
When *there is* no peace."

Jer. 5:26–31; 6:13–14

Because of Judah's heart-level blindness and her willful deafness, she provided a culture in which predators can thrive. Blind birds are easy prey for the fowlers and their snares (5:26). Created to fly free, the inhabitants of Judah had become like caged birds. They were trapped and helpless. In examining these passages we learn four things about the dynamic of evil.

1. Evil is an organized system. The confederacies of wicked men were referred to as "houses" (5:27). Judah had fallen victim not simply to random poachers but to a system of organized defiance.

2. Evil is dedicated to bondage. Birds were created to fly, not to sit in cages. The system is out to catch us in its network.

3. Evil is highly sophisticated. *"They have become great and grown rich. They have grown fat, they are sleek"* (5:27–28). The imagery suggests gluttony, eating up everything in sight, and obesity, being larger than they should be.

4. Evil breeds social injustice and inhumanity. *"They do not plead the cause, The cause of the fatherless; . . . And the right of the needy they do not defend"* (5:28). *"Everyone deals falsely. They have also healed the hurt of My people slightly"* (6:13–14). Jeremiah peered over the edge of the gulf created between his people and God. It was a giant wound that they thought to cover with a Band-Aid.

This is not at all unlike the 1980s that some psychiatrists and sociologists have dubbed "The Lite Decade." We are going after lightness in everything from our beer to our personal relationships. We can now get our great literary classics edited into ten minutes on audio cassette. Who cares about the weightiness of these masterpieces? It's lightness we're after, the great virtue of the decade. It's lightness that the false prophets were after. They said, *"Peace, peace,"* when there was no peace (6:14). It was an appealing but dangerous message. In 1940, Neville Chamberlain was forced to resign as prime minister of Great Britain. His message had been that "we have achieved peace in our time." Yet even as he spoke, Adolph Hitler's sinister plans were pushing the world over the brink of war. There are times when we heal the wound of our people lightly.

CHAPTER FIVE

Jeremiah Becomes a Marked Man

Jeremiah 7:1–8:3

THE TEMPLE OF THE LORD

7:1 The word that came to Jeremiah from the LORD, saying,

2 "Stand in the gate of the LORD'S house, and proclaim there this word, and say, 'Hear the word of the LORD, all *you of* Judah who enter in at these gates to worship the LORD!'"

3 Thus says the LORD of hosts, the God of Israel: "Amend your ways and your doings, and I will cause you to dwell in this place.

4 "Do not trust in these lying words, saying, 'The temple of the LORD, the temple of the LORD, the temple of the LORD *are* these.'

5 "For if you thoroughly amend your ways and your doings, if you thoroughly execute judgment between a man and his neighbor,

6 "*if* you do not oppress the stranger, the fatherless, and the widow, and do not shed innocent blood in this place, or walk after other gods to your hurt,

7 "then I will cause you to dwell in this place, in the land that I gave to your fathers forever and ever.

8 "Behold, you trust in lying words that cannot profit.

9 "Will you steal, murder, commit adultery, swear falsely, burn incense to Baal, and walk after other gods whom you do not know,

10 "and *then* come and stand before Me in this house which is called by My name, and say, 'We are delivered to do all these abominations'?

11 "Has this house, which is called by My name, become a den of thieves in your eyes? Behold, I, even I, have seen *it*," says the LORD.

12 "But go now to My place which *was* in Shiloh, where I set My name at the first, and see what I did to it because of the wickedness of My people Israel.

13 "And now, because you have done all these works," says the LORD, "and I spoke to you, rising up early and speaking, but you did not hear, and I called you, but you did not answer,

14 "therefore I will do to the house which is called by My name, in which you trust, and to this place which I gave to you and your fathers, as I have done to Shiloh.

15 "And I will cast you out of My sight, as I have cast out all your brethren—the whole posterity of Ephraim."

Jer. 7:1–15

Anyone who has ever stood against the evil trends of society knows what a costly thing it is to take on the issues of the day or to try to change society for the good. So it was with Jeremiah when he delivered his third and most challenging public address. It was a massive congregation, one that did not want to hear his sermon. The priests of Anathoth, many of whom shared childhood memories with Jeremiah, were ready to serve this swelling crowd in its empty traditions. They did not want to hear Jeremiah speak against their systems; these systems provided their livelihood, even if they were corrupt. Courage calls for lonely moments such as these, for looking out over a sea of familiar faces and seeing them tighten in anger, knowing that they represented a system which would mark him forever and target him for extinction one way or another. Nevertheless Jeremiah stood tall for the God who commissioned him.

Since his messages in chapters 4–6, dramatic events had intervened on the prophet and on his people. In the eighteenth year of his reign, Josiah instituted a restoration of the temple. Nothing had been done to it for more than 250 years. The project was funded by a public collection. Doorkeepers at the temple collected from the people as they passed through. Hilkiah, the high priest, supervised and coordinated the collection and restoration with Shaphan, the king's chancellor and scribe. Carpenters, builders, and masons stirred about the temple precincts. The air was filled with the encouraging sounds of progress and reconstruction. Hilkiah had rolled up his sleeves and was digging through musty relics when he made an amazing discovery. Imagine his smudged but excited face when he shouted to Shaphan over the noise and hurried toward him with the treasure in his arms: "I have found the Book of the Law" (2 Kings 22:8).

Possibly it had been hidden under a heap of stones away from the destructive rampage of wicked King Ahab a century earlier. Or Hilkiah could have found it in the ark which had been concealed under dust and lumber. Whether it was the Book of Deuteronomy alone or the whole Pentateuch, scholars are not in agreement.[1] What we do know is that the two men gasped at the treasure that lay before them. The rediscovery of the written word of God was an answer to the prayers of their prophet and their king.

Shaphan rushed to Josiah and read breathlessly from the long-lost word. Instead of a musty document from antiquity, it was as fresh as the air they breathed and as commanding in its power as the day it was delivered to Moses before the people entered into the Promised Land. "Now it happened, when the king heard the words of the Book of the Law, that he tore his clothes" (2 Kings 22:11). Driven by a sense of impending judgment, Josiah sought the council of the prophetess Huldah, for Jeremiah was yet too young in his ministry. She confirmed that indeed God intended to judge his city, that His anger burned and would not be quenched.

Nevertheless, Josiah pressed forward and called a great convocation of people, priests, and prophets. Jeremiah must have stood in that crowd, feasting his tired eyes on the picture of his king, standing by a pillar of the temple, praying to the Lord and making a personal covenant to serve Him (2 Kings 23:3). It had been years since Jerusalem had experienced this kind of leadership. What a moment in the history of any people to see their leader making a public commitment to the Lord. Moved by this sight, the people entered into this new covenant themselves. A surge of hope must have entered the heart of Jeremiah. Perhaps all was not lost. This to Jeremiah was his king's most heroic moment. There were more such moments.

In the days that followed, Josiah determined that the temple would not only be repaired, but it would be purged of the filth and false gods that had taken residence in its precincts. Daily, strange-looking cultic vessels were carried out of the temple. They were the stuff of Baal and his female consort, Asherah. One day her wooden image was burned in public, its ashes cast on the graveyard. No longer would this rigid, nude figure preside over the worship of sex and fertility. The colleague gods of war and sensuality had lost their stronghold. A ring of male prostitutes was exposed and led out of the temple. The scandal of Israel's idolatry and perversion was out in the open. Its shrines of vice would no longer be legalized.

Watching this, the people of Jerusalem were smitten with a great admiration for Josiah but never with his repentant spirit. He went ahead with his righteous reforms even though Huldah had said they would not be successful, that it was already too late; the people were not going to change their hearts. She told the king to expect judgment but that he himself would be spared the sight of that judgment; "You shall be gathered to your grave in peace" (2 Kings 22:20).

Even still, Josiah lived his life wholeheartedly. He kept on doing what was right. So did Jeremiah. These are not the laid-back, easy-come-easy-go characters that are so admired in today's society. One day, the king himself climbed up on the flat roof of the palace of Ahaz. He could be seen smashing the domestic altars of vice that had been erected there. He took on the evils of his society with the whole force of his personality, investing all of his physical energies and angers in the purging of his beloved Jerusalem.

With this same kind of zeal, Josiah reinstituted the celebration of the Passover. This grand festival was probably the occasion for Jeremiah's temple address. What would he say to this people who were nothing like their king? They came not in sincerity but in pretense, disguised as worshipers but were actually "wolves in sheep's clothing." What would he say to the priests who encouraged their pretense, who made their living upon it? Josiah had gotten the idols out of the temple, but he had not gotten idolatry out of the people. No one knew that better than Jeremiah.

Jeremiah was instructed by God to stand at the gate of the temple, a one-man resistance movement against the culture, as "bronze walls against the whole land" (Jer. 1:18). It was this moment of courage that would forever make him a marked man in the eyes of the world. John Wesley once said, "Give me one hundred men who fear nothing but God, and who hate nothing but sin and we will take over the world for Christ." One such man was Jeremiah. He had two things to say on that fateful day in the temple.

1. Your ways must be amended! If they wished to remain in the land, their cheating, lying lifestyle would have to change. They could not come in, chanting their vain repetitions, and expect the temple to confer safety upon them. The smell of their incense from Sheba could not cover the stench of their crimes. Not for a God who desired obedience rather than oblation! Not for a God who saw innocent blood upon their robes, stolen money in their pockets, and lies upon their lips. Thus began the list of things that had to change.

First, they must cease to oppress the stranger. God's kingdom is meant to be a haven to the orphan, the widow, and the alien; a place where His bounty could be discovered. Instead they were being plundered and exploited (v. 6).

Second, they must stop the stealing, murdering, and adultering. The self-same things that were listed in the Ten Commandments. These were the sins they were sinning against their own humanity. The commandments have a vertical and a horizontal application—those that relate to God and those that relate to man (v. 9).

Third, they must stop walking after other gods. They had gotten Baal and Asherah out of the temple but not out of their hearts. This calls to mind the vertical portions of the commandments; "You shall have no other gods before Me" (Exod. 20:3).

Fourth, they must stop trusting in lies. After participating in all of these scandals, they were then coming to God, standing before Him in His house and saying, *"We are delivered to do all these abominations"* (v. 10). God's salvation is designed to deliver us from sin, not to deliver us for sin. We cannot deliberately continue to sin and then expect God to endorse us because of a little chanting.

2. God has been offended. Incorporated in this temple sermon is an exposure of their scandal and God's sanctity. What a revelation it brings us of God's ways and how God can be offended.

First, God desires good for us. He is not some cosmic kill-joy out to spoil our fun. He desired for them to live in the land, but not just any land; theirs was a land of promise, a land of blessing, a land of prosperity to which all the nations of the earth would be drawn. They were to dwell there, however, on His terms (v. 3).

Second, God is generous. This was not a land they could have found for themselves, not a blessing they could ever have earned. He had given it to their forefathers (v. 7).

Third, God is not deceived. He sees beyond their pretense. He looks down upon the temple and sees it for what it is, a den of thieves. The once sacred precincts have been made into a cover-up for their own scandal, a little coven where thieves gather to hide.

Fourth, God is not going to be patient forever. Not only are goodness and generosity part of His ways but judgment is also. Shiloh's ruins stand as a dreadful testimony to that fact. Once it had been the scene of the tabernacle, the home of the ark of the covenant; now it was a heap of rubble, pleading with them to remember their history and change their ways before it was too late.

QUIT PRAYING, JEREMIAH

7:16 "Therefore do not pray for this people, nor lift up a cry or prayer for them, nor make intercession to Me; for I will not hear you.

17 "Do you not see what they do in the cities of Judah and in the streets of Jerusalem?

18 "The children gather wood, the fathers kindle the fire, and the women knead dough, to make cakes for the queen of heaven; and *they* pour out drink offerings to other gods, that they may provoke Me to anger.

19 "Do they provoke Me to anger?" says the LORD. "*Do they* not *provoke* themselves, to the shame of their own faces?"

20 Therefore thus says the Lord GOD: "Behold, My anger and My fury will be poured out on this place—on man and on beast, on the trees of the field and on the fruit of the ground. And it will burn and not be quenched."

21 Thus says the LORD of hosts, the God of Israel: "Add your burnt offerings to your sacrifices and eat meat.

22 "For I did not speak to your fathers, or command them in the day that I brought them out of the land of Egypt, concerning burnt offerings or sacrifices.

23 "But this is what I commanded them, saying, 'Obey My voice, and I will be your God, and you shall

be My people. And walk in all the ways that I have
commanded you, that it may be well with you.'

24 "Yet they did not obey or incline their ear, but
followed the counsels *and* the dictates of their evil
hearts, and went backward and not forward.

25 "Since the day that your fathers came out of the
land of Egypt until this day, I have even sent to you
all My servants the prophets, daily rising up early
and sending *them.*

26 "Yet they did not obey Me or incline their ear,
but stiffened their neck. They did worse than their
fathers.

27 "Therefore you shall speak all these words to
them, but they will not obey you. You shall also call
to them, but they will not answer you."

Jer. 7:16–27

What shocking words to be coming from God. Imagine having to
be told to quit praying. Does that say something about the constancy
of Jeremiah? Most of us would have given up on these people long
ago for we know so little about endurance, about persistence in anything, particularly in matters of prayer. Jeremiah is so determined
that God Himself has to authorize him to quit.

God was disgusted with His people. They had provoked Him to
anger (v. 19). Now they would get a little taste of what it felt like
to be provoked. Enemies would come upon them. They were no
longer to be the object of Jeremiah's cries or of his prayers. The protective covering that they offered had been removed (v. 16) because
even the ordinary things of life had been contaminated by idolatry.
Children gathered wood, fathers kindled fires, mothers baked for
the queen of heaven (v. 18). "Enough is enough," God said.

They did not want to hear that there was a payday. Neither do we
today. One of the good things about the sports world is that it
teaches that there is a finish to the game. Over the last decade, we
have become attracted to ties and draws. Yet in some sports, "sudden
death" brings a sense of reality. There are winners and there are
losers. We even have replays in order to determine if a rule has been
breached. There really are judgments.

In the more important arenas of life we do not want God to have
any deadlines. We never want there to be a payday. Like those people

in the temple we want to go on saying "we are delivered," even when our ways stand as horrible mockeries of God's ways. This was a dreadful day for Judah, the day the praying ceased. Any reader resistant to God might consider this: Don't ever wish for the day that someone stops praying for you.

I remember the story of a friend of mine in seminary. At the time of his conversion he was a student at Cambridge University and had attended a Billy Graham crusade in London. Thinking he would postpone his decision, this young man got up and was leaving the arena. While still within earshot, he heard Billy quote the text, "He who is often rebuked, *and* hardens *his* neck, Will suddenly be destroyed, and that without remedy" (Prov. 29:1). My friend stopped dead in his tracks, turned around, and went back in. He listened to the rest of the message and finally went forward in glad surrender to the Lord Jesus. Never has he forgotten how close he came. A few more steps and he would have been out of earshot, out into his own reprobate mind and lost condition.

CUT OFF YOUR HAIR, JEREMIAH

7:28 "So you shall say to them, 'This *is* a nation that does not obey the voice of the LORD their God nor receive correction. Truth has perished and has been cut off from their mouth.

29 'Cut off your hair and cast *it* away, and take up a lamentation on the desolate heights; for the LORD has rejected and forsaken the generation of His wrath.'

30 "For the children of Judah have done evil in My sight," says the LORD. "They have set their abominations in the house which is called by My name, to pollute it.

31 "And they have built the high places of Tophet, which *is* in the Valley of the Son of Hinnom, to burn their sons and their daughters in the fire, which I did not command, nor did it come into My heart.

32 "Therefore behold, the days are coming," says the LORD, "when it will no more be called Tophet, or the Valley of the Son of Hinnom, but the Valley of Slaughter; for they will bury in Tophet until there is no room.

33 "The corpses of this people will be food for the birds of the heaven and for the beasts of the earth. And no one will frighten *them away.*

34 "Then I will cause to cease from the cities of Judah and from the streets of Jerusalem the voice of mirth and the voice of gladness, the voice of the bridegroom and the voice of the bride. For the land shall be desolate.

8:1 "At that time," says the LORD, "they shall bring out the bones of the kings of Judah, and the bones of its princes, and the bones of the priests, and the bones of the prophets, and the bones of the inhabitants of Jerusalem, out of their graves.

2 "They shall spread them before the sun and the moon and all the host of heaven, which they have loved and which they have served and after which they have walked, which they have sought and which they have worshiped. They shall not be gathered nor buried; they shall be like refuse on the face of the earth.

3 "Then death shall be chosen rather than life by all the residue of those who remain of this evil family, who remain in all the places where I have driven them," says the LORD of hosts.

Jer. 7:28–8:3

When God told Jeremiah to quit praying, His voice was heard only in the confines of the prophet's heart. How was that to be revealed to the people of Judah? What a colorful God we have. How marvelous are His dramas. The prophetic ministry involves nonverbal as well as verbal communication. Jeremiah was to say nothing except, "Truth has been cut off from your mouth" (7:28). Then he was to ascend one of the surrounding hills, one characterized by barrenness and desolation. Silhouetted against an evening sky, where all could see him, Jeremiah cut off the long dark curls that had been characteristic of him for so long. The wind carried them away once and for all, leaving him shorn of his glory, bent and sorrowful. He had literally become to Judah a mournful portrait of herself and of her lost glory.

The high place that she had occupied in the heart of God was nothing but a desolation. She had built her own high place called

Topheth, where babies screamed in terror, using their little voices for the last time as they were burned on the sacrificial fires kindled there. In the supposed place of worship was the highest apostasy. For slaughtering their children, they themselves would be slaughtered there (7:32). What a cause for weeping was this moment to Jeremiah who could hear in the distance the words of the Savior, "Let the little children come to Me" (Matt. 19:14). Yet the people of Judah were killing them. The chasm between Judah and God could grow no wider.

The voice of gladness, the sounds of mirth and celebration that God had intended their life to be, would be cut off, like pulling the plug on a shining symphony. There sat the silent prophet, shorn of his hair, bent and desolate on the high place that should have been filled with wonder. A time would come when the bones of kings, princes, priests, and prophets would be spread out under the sun and the moon that they had worshiped. They had chosen to serve creation rather than the Creator. They had chosen the cultic fertility practices of the heathen. What had those false gods done for them? The answer was in the parched bones, lying like refuse, unburied, exposed on the face of the earth. They had chosen death rather than life. The awesome testimony throughout Scripture is that we will get what we choose (8:2).

NOTE

1. F. B. Meyer, *Jeremiah* (Fort Washington, Pa.: Christian Literature Crusade, 1980), 35.

CHAPTER SIX

Blessed Is He Who Mourns

Jeremiah 8:4–9:26

Jeremiah, silhouetted against the sky, caught between earth and heaven alone on the barren heights, was like Jesus, "a Man of sorrows and acquainted with grief" (Isa. 53:3). It affords a striking picture of mourning. It means to be in agreement with heaven yet in compassion for earth at one and the same time. We can examine this twofold dynamic at work in the prophet's life in these next two chapters.

HATING THE SIN

8:4 "Moreover you shall say to them, 'Thus says the
LORD:
    "Will they fall and not rise?
    Will one turn away and not return?
5 Why has this people slidden back,
    Jerusalem, in a perpetual backsliding?
    They hold fast to deceit,
    They refuse to return.
6 I listened and heard,
    But they do not speak aright.
    No man repented of his wickedness,
    Saying, 'What have I done?'
    Everyone turned to his own course,
    As the horse rushes into the battle.
7 "Even the stork in the heavens
    Knows her appointed times;
    And the turtledove, the swift, and the swallow
    Observe the time of their coming.

But My people do not know the judgment of the
LORD.

8 "How can you say, 'We *are* wise,
And the law of the LORD *is* with us'?
Look, the false pen of the scribe certainly
works falsehood.

9 The wise men are ashamed,
They are dismayed and taken.
Behold, they have rejected the word of the LORD;
So what wisdom do they have?

10 Therefore I will give their wives to others,
And their fields to those who will inherit *them;*
Because from the least even to the greatest
Everyone is given to covetousness;
From the prophet even to the priest
Everyone deals falsely.

11 For they have healed the hurt of the daughter of
My people slightly,
Saying, 'Peace, peace!'
When *there is* no peace.

12 Were they ashamed when they had committed
abomination?
No! They were not at all ashamed,
Nor did they know how to blush.
Therefore they shall fall among those who fall;
In the time of their punishment
They shall be cast down," says the LORD.

13 "I will surely consume them," says the LORD.
"No grapes *shall be* on the vine,
Nor figs on the fig tree,
And the leaf shall fade;
And *the things* I have given them shall pass
away from them."'"

14 "Why do we sit still?
Assemble yourselves,
And let us enter the fortified cities,
And let us be silent there.
For the LORD our God has put us to silence
And given us water of gall to drink,
Because we have sinned against the LORD.

15 "*We* looked for peace, but no good *came;*
And for a time of health, and there was trouble!

16 The snorting of His horses was heard from
    Dan.
  The whole land trembled at the sound of the
    neighing of His strong ones;
  For they have come and devoured the land and
    all that is in it,
  The city and those who dwell in it."
17 "For behold, I will send serpents among you,
  Vipers which cannot be charmed,
  And they shall bite you," says the LORD.

9:3 "And *like* their bow they have bent their
    tongues *for* lies.
  They are not valiant for the truth on the earth.
  For they proceed from evil to evil,
  And they do not know Me," says the LORD.
 4 "Everyone take heed to his neighbor,
  And do not trust any brother;
  For every brother will utterly supplant,
  And every neighbor will walk with slanderers.
 5 Everyone will deceive his neighbor,
  And will not speak the truth;
  They have taught their tongue to speak lies;
  Weary themselves to commit iniquity.
 6 Your dwelling place *is* in the midst of deceit;
  Through deceit they refuse to know Me," says
    the LORD.
 7 Therefore thus says the LORD of hosts:
  "Behold, I will refine them and try them;
  For how shall I deal with the daughter of My
    people?
 8 Their tongue *is* an arrow shot out;
  It speaks deceit;
  One speaks peaceably to his neighbor with his
    mouth,
  But in his heart he lies in wait.
 9 Shall I not punish them for these *things?*" says
    the LORD.
  "Shall I not avenge Myself on such a nation as
    this?"
10 I will take up a weeping and wailing for the
    mountains,

And for the dwelling places of the wilderness a
   lamentation,
Because they are burned up,
So that no one can pass through;
Nor can *men* hear the voice of the cattle.
Both the birds of the heavens and the beasts
   have fled;
They are gone.

11 "I will make Jerusalem a heap of ruins, a den of
   jackals.
I will make the cities of Judah desolate, without
   an inhabitant."

12 Who *is* the wise man who may understand this?
And *who is he* to whom the mouth of the LORD has
spoken, that he may declare it? Why does the land
perish *and* burn up like a wilderness, so that no one
can pass through?

13 And the LORD said, "Because they have forsaken My law which I set before them, and have not
obeyed My voice, nor walked according to it,

14 "but they have walked according to the dictates
of their own hearts and after the Baals, which their
fathers taught them,"

15 therefore thus says the LORD of hosts, the God
of Israel: "Behold, I will feed them, this people, with
wormwood, and give them water of gall to drink.

16 "I will scatter them also among the Gentiles,
whom neither they nor their fathers have known. And
I will send a sword after them until I have consumed
them."

Jer. 8:4–17; 9:3–16

He hates the sin. The mourner is approaching the vision of sin that
God Himself holds. Jeremiah had long condemned the shallow jovial-
ity and the false comforts of his society. He had sighed over its
claims, "We are delivered" (7:10) and "Peace, peace!" (6:14; 8:11). In
these verses he pointed to the ugly thing that had broken his people.
He exposed the character of sin. First, it was all pervasive. *"No man
repented, . . . Everyone turned to his own course"* (8:6); *"Everyone will
deceive his neighbor"* (9:5). Second, it was unnatural. Even storks and
turtledoves respond to a grand design. Yet humanity, the crown of

creation, chose to defy it (8:7). Third, it was based on lies. Scribes, the supposedly credible communicators of the day, wrote with lying pens when the real truth was available to them (8:9). *"And like their bow they have bent their tongues for lies"* (9:3).

Fourth, it was shameless. *"Nor did they know how to blush"* (8:12). This was a common theme of Jeremiah's and one that has been treated more thoroughly in the preceding chapter. Fifth, it was destined for punishment. The tender-hearted prophet was forced to speak in metaphors of pain, to speak of luscious grapevines that have no grapes, fig trees without figs, and a people unproductive and wasted without ever fulfilling their destiny (8:13). Baking there under a dangerous desert sun, they had found water, but it was mixed with gall (8:14). Serpents and vipers about to strike slide across the desert floor (8:17). This was most likely a reference to military attack. There were no more birds in the sky, their songs were gone, no more cattle in the field, their voices too have been silenced. "The whole creation groans and labors" (Rom. 8:22). Nothing was left but the haunting silence of the wilderness, a heap of ruins with beady-eyed jackals rummaging through it (9:10–16). They, the circumcised, would fall with the uncircumcised (9:25–26).

LOVING THE SINNER

8:18 I would comfort myself in sorrow;
      My heart *is* faint in me.
19 Listen! The voice,
      The cry of the daughter of my people
      From a far country:
      "*Is* not the LORD in Zion?
      Is not her King in her?"
      "Why have they provoked Me to anger
      With their carved images—
      With foreign idols?"
20 "The harvest is past,
      The summer is ended,
      And we are not saved!"
21 For the hurt of the daughter of my people I am hurt.
      I am mourning;
      Astonishment has taken hold of me.

22 *Is there* no balm in Gilead,
   Is there no physician there?
   Why then is there no recovery
   For the health of the daughter of my people?
9:1 Oh, that my head were waters,
   And my eyes a fountain of tears,
   That I might weep day and night
   For the slain of the daughter of my people!
 2 Oh, that I had in the wilderness
   A lodging place for travelers;
   That I might leave my people,
   And go from them!
   For they *are* all adulterers,
   An assembly of treacherous men.

Jer. 8:18–9:2

He loves the sinner. How can it be that Jeremiah would continue in such compassion for his people? These passages reveal intimate glimpses of the private Jeremiah. Rarely was a prophet so self-disclosing, so long-suffering. Shortly after his conversion, Charles Wesley penned a song, "Amazing love, how can it be that thou my Lord shouldst die for me." Jeremiah's patience in mourning the sin while loving the sinner prefigured the final work of Christ on the cross. Two images that the prophet used have become proverbial to today's Western culture.

"The harvest is past, The summer is. ended, And we are not saved!" (8:20). For this he has been called the master of elegy, so brilliant is its literary quality. With tragic eloquence, he lamented the passing of two seasons in Palestine. Our agricultural system only thinks in terms of one harvest. For the Jew, however, April to June was a season of harvest. If for some tragic reason it failed, then they could still look forward to the ingathering of summer fruit.[1] The prophet cried, "We have just exhausted all of our options."

It was not said with any sense of clinical detachment. Jeremiah felt the wound of his people in his own body and being. *"For the hurt of the daughter of my people I am hurt"* (8:21). The prophet spoke of violent emotions in further describing his feelings. *"Astonishment has taken hold of me"* (8:21). The Latin derivation of the word "astonishment" means "to thunder out of." He described a wrenching fit, literally being convulsed with agony. It is all so reminiscent of the pain our Lord took upon Himself in Gethsemane. When the shock and the burden of the sins of the whole world took hold of Him, His sweat turned to blood. We get our word "excruciating" from the events of Calvary, for the word means "out from the cross."

"Is there no balm in Gilead, Is there no physician there?" (8:22). The painful search for comfort and for escape rings out in the second of these famous metaphors, as it does in the cry of Jesus, "Father if it be possible let this cup pass from me." Jeremiah was looking to the east, toward the restful town of Gilead. It had become a symbol of hope for it was the source of healing balsams for the Eastern world. If there was no balm there, then there was no balm anywhere on earth. That is the shocking realization of this passage.

MOURNING IS A LOST ART

9:17 Thus says the LORD of hosts:
"Consider and call for the mourning women,
That they may come;
And send for skillful wailing women,
That they may come.

18 Let them make haste
And take up a wailing for us,
That our eyes may run with tears,
And our eyelids gush with water.

19 For a voice of wailing is heard from Zion:
'How we are plundered!
We are greatly ashamed,
Because we have forsaken the land,
Because we have been cast out of our
dwellings.'"

20 Yet hear the word of the LORD, O women,
And let your ear receive the word of His
mouth;
Teach your daughters wailing,
And everyone her neighbor a lamentation.

21 For death has come through our windows,
Has entered our palaces,
To kill off the children—*no longer to be*
outside!
And the young men—*no longer* on the streets!

22 Speak, "Thus says the LORD:
   'Even the carcasses of men shall fall as refuse
     on the open field,
   Like cuttings after the harvester,
   And no one shall gather *them.*'"

Jer. 9:17–22

Weeping in public is decidedly out of style these days. At best it is considered to be a dreadful sign of weakness. Winston Churchill took pains to create a "macho" image to his public. He felt he needed it because of his habit of crying in public. "I'm a blubberer," he cheerfully would confess to friends. Imagine! One of the century's greatest statesmen, a colossal figure of a man needing to apologize for tears to a culture that feels scandalized by them instead of blessed by them.

In this text, however, we find God encouraging more mourning. In ancient societies there were such things as professional mourners. *"Call for the mourning women . . . send for skillful wailing women"* (v. 17). There is even an urgency to the summons. *"Let them make haste"* (v. 18). They are even instructed to teach their children to mourn. Obviously it is a quality God wants to characterize His people.

"Conviction must of necessity precede conversion, a real sense of sin must come before there can be a true joy of salvation. . . . Those who are going to be converted and who wish to be truly happy and blessed are those who first of all mourn."[2]

Imagine the kind of comfort in store for Jeremiah who said, "Oh, that my head were waters, And my eyes a fountain of tears, That I might weep day and night For the slain of the daughter of my people!" (9:1). Imagine the comfort of Jesus of whom it was written, "For the joy that was set before Him, endured the cross and despised the shame."

AND HE SHALL BE COMFORTED

9:23 Thus says the LORD:
   "Let not the wise *man* glory in his wisdom,
   Let not the mighty *man* glory in his might,
   Nor let the rich *man* glory in his riches;

24 But let him who glories glory in this,
    That he understands and knows Me,
    That I *am* the LORD, exercising lovingkindness,
        judgment, and righteousness in the earth.
    For in these I delight," says the LORD.
25 "Behold, the days are coming," says the LORD,
"that I will punish all *who are* circumcised with the
uncircumcised—
26 "Egypt, Judah, Edom, the people of Ammon,
Moab, and all *who are* in the farthest corners, who
dwell in the wilderness. For all *these* nations *are* uncircumcised, and all the house of Israel *are* uncircumcised in the heart."

Jer. 9:23–26

Joy, as God wants us to understand it, is not some frivolous, giggly
kind of emotion. Actually it is quite serious business. It is also difficult business as well, hating sin while loving the sinner.

Isaiah, whose prophetic ministry was also characterized by
mourning, caught something brilliant about comfort when he wrote,
"The Spirit of the Lord GOD *is* upon Me, . . . He has sent Me
to heal the brokenhearted, . . . To comfort all who mourn, . . . To
give them beauty for ashes, The oil of joy for mourning, The garment
of praise for the spirit of heaviness" (Isa. 61:1–3). If he used the word
"beauty," then there must be some sense in which comfort is trans-
figuring; it is visible. Oil is soothing; it is used for anointing. A
garment is used for covering. Like the priestly garments of the tabernacle, they were "for beauty and for glory." The kind of comfort we
are invited to imagine so far transcends what this world can imagine
that it is quite literally "out of this world."

In his bright vision of comfort found in verses 23 and 24,
Jeremiah used the word "glory" repeatedly. He told us what it was
and what it was not. Perhaps you have a keen intellect and an im-
pressive education. Indeed, those are good things, but they are not
your glory. They will not be your ultimate source of comfort. Or
maybe you are heavily endowed with physical strength and a well-
exercised body. Maybe you are one of those born leaders who just
naturally exerts authority over others. These things are not your
glory. Ah, then it must be wealth. If you have everything that
money can buy, then of course it will comfort you. The world is

convinced that some combination of these conditions, preferably all of them, will constitute happiness. Jeremiah, however, said, *"Let not the wise man . . . let not the mighty man . . . nor let the rich man"* glory in these things (v. 23).

What could possibly be better than wisdom, power, and wealth? Jeremiah answered the question. *"Let him who glories glory in this, That he understands and knows Me"* (v. 24). That is not just knowing about God; that means knowing God. There was one central pleasure in the life of the prophet that eclipsed all of the pain and rejection and failure that were forced upon him. He had an intimacy with God. When he was doing what he was commissioned and designed to do, Jeremiah felt the pleasure of God. *"Blessed is he who mourns for he shall be comforted"* (Matt. 5:4).

NOTES

1. Stanley Hopper, *"The Book of Jeremiah: Exposition,"* in *The Interpreter's Bible*, vol. 5, ed. George A. Buttrick et al. (Nashville: Abingdon Press, 1956), 887.

2. D. Martyn Lloyd-Jones, *Studies in the Sermon on the Mount* (Grand Rapids, Mich.: Eerdmans, 1985), 55.

CHAPTER SEVEN

Learn Not the Way of the Gentiles

Jeremiah 10:1–11:17

IDOLS OF WOOD

10:1 Hear the word which the LORD speaks to you,
O house of Israel.
  2 Thus says the LORD:
    "Do not learn the way of the Gentiles;
    Do not be dismayed at the signs of heaven,
    For the Gentiles are dismayed at them.
  3 For the customs of the peoples *are* futile;
    For *one* cuts a tree from the forest,
    The work of the hands of the workman, with
      the ax.
  4 They decorate it with silver and gold;
    They fasten it with nails and hammers
    So that it will not topple.
  5 They *are* upright, like a palm tree,
    And they cannot speak;
    They must be carried,
    Because they cannot go *by themselves.*
    Do not be afraid of them,
    For they cannot do evil,
    Nor can they do any good."
  6 Inasmuch as *there is* none like You, O LORD
    (You *are* great, and Your name *is* great in
      might),
  7 Who would not fear You, O King of the nations?
    For this is Your rightful due,
    For among all the wise *men* of the nations,
    And in all their kingdoms,
    There is none like You.

8 But they are altogether dull-hearted and
     foolish;
   A wooden idol *is* a worthless doctrine.
9 Silver is beaten into plates;
   It is brought from Tarshish,
   And gold from Uphaz,
   The work of the craftsman
   And of the hands of the metalsmith;
   Blue and purple *are* their clothing;
   They *are* all the work of skillful *men.*
10 But the LORD *is* the true God;
   He *is* the living God and the everlasting King.
   At His wrath the earth will tremble,
   And the nations will not be able to endure His
     indignation.

Jer. 10:1–10

How easily we of all ages have fallen into the worship of intellect, of education, of power, and of wealth. In the process of losing the knowledge of and an intimacy with God, we do not lose the need for Him. So we fill the void with other things, things that ultimately do not satisfy the deepest cries of our hearts. Is it any wonder that Jeremiah's thoughts would turn to the wooden images he saw around him? These passages may well have been written during the time of Josiah's reforms and the purging of the temple when so many idols were paraded about in shame and dishonor.

This chapter offers a striking comparison between the worship of these idols and the worship of God. A comparison so animated that it even infuses the literary style. The prose moves back and forth between words calculated for satire to those of exuberant worship. The passage begins with a deuteronomic warning, *"Do not learn the way of the Gentiles"* (v. 1). This is followed by a description of their futile customs (vv. 1–5). A tree was cut from the forest and worked over with an axe in some vain attempt to disguise the fact that it was nothing but tree stock. It has to be hauled from the forest; it cannot go by itself nor can it speak for itself (v. 5). An apparatus was then contrived whereby it would stand up and be kept from falling (v. 4).

It stood rootless and without expression. Silver was imported from Tarshish. The people have gone all the way to Uphaz for gold. They bent the silver flat. The gold was fashioned by metalsmiths. With precious metals they decorated this impotent thing, hoping to give it worth. The folly was not yet over. They tailored costumes and dressed this tree stock in blue and purple, wishing to confer royalty upon it (v. 9). *"A wooden idol"* it remains and *"a worthless doctrine"* (v. 8).

The satire was not only cutting but also filled with pathos for a people who have lost their vision for God, but not Jeremiah! His vision was alive and well. His language of exuberant worship burst into the midst of these descriptions like a fountain splashing in a desert. The language of verses 6 and 7 is passionate. It was spoken directly to God as though He were alive and had a personality. *"There is none like You, O LORD"* (v. 6). The palpable reality of God is felt against the empty woodenness of the idols. "What I find so shocking, God," the prophet goes on, "is that anyone would want to settle for so little when there is so much to be had." That, I believe, is the essence of his cry of verse 7. Then the contrast shifts back again. *"But they are altogether dull-hearted and foolish"* (v. 8). After another burst of worship, he repeated this same idea, "Everyone is dull-hearted, without knowledge" (v. 14).

A GOD OF WONDER

10:11 Thus you shall say to them: "The gods that have not made the heavens and the earth shall perish from the earth and from under these heavens."
12 He has made the earth by His power,
He has established the world by His wisdom,
And has stretched out the heavens at His discretion.
13 When He utters His voice,
There is a multitude of waters in the heavens:
"And He causes the vapors to ascend from the ends of the earth.
He makes lightning for the rain,
He brings the wind out of His treasuries."
14 Everyone is dull-hearted, without knowledge;
Every metalsmith is put to shame by an image;
For his molded image *is* falsehood,
And *there is* no breath in them.

15 They *are* futile, a work of errors;
  In the time of their punishment they shall
    perish.
16 The Portion of Jacob *is* not like them,
  For He *is* the Maker of all *things,*
  And Israel *is* the tribe of His inheritance;
  The LORD of hosts *is* His name.
17 Gather up your wares from the land,
  O inhabitant of the fortress!
18 For thus says the LORD:
  "Behold, I will throw out at this time
  The inhabitants of the land,
  And will distress them,
  That they may find *it so.*"

Jer. 10:11–18

Yahweh is the true God; He is the living God and the everlasting King (v. 10). In that one sentence is a world of reality as to the nature of God. The prophet has moved from a revelation of the ridiculous to a revelation of the sublime. Exposing the idols and their vanity has pushed Jeremiah to the heights of his reverence for God. His worship knows no bounds. After having penetrated to the root of idolatry and its shocking forms of human defection, he now penetrates to the root of worship and its forms of divine perfection.

Those words "true" and "living" and "everlasting" designate God in the meaning of His name, Yahweh. They ascribe to Him a quality that He alone holds in this universe. He and He alone is self-existent. He alone can say, "I AM WHO I AM" (Exod. 3:14). We humans depend for origin and continuance upon forces outside of ourselves. This giant of a God, however, is the ground of His own existence, the living spring of His own energy and being. He is totally independent and of underived existence, without beginning and without end. The death of God is an impossibility.

One might expect a being this supreme and preeminent to be indifferent to the affairs of nations. "At His wrath the earth will tremble, And the nations will not be able to endure His indignation" (v. 10). This was anything but the language of indifference. What was it about God that caused Him to be so emotionally involved with the business of earth?

Not only is He self-existent by virtue of His name, He is also creative. *"He has made the earth by His power, He has established the world by His wisdom, And has stretched out the heavens at His discretion"* (v. 12). God has every right to exercise sovereign claim to the universe, and specifically over the politics and culture of the nations. Like the psalmist, Jeremiah was saying, *"It is He who has made us, and not we ourselves"* (Ps. 100:3).

THE WAY OF MAN IS NOT IN HIMSELF

10:19 Woe is me for my hurt!
　　　My wound is severe.
　　　But I say, "Truly this *is* an infirmity,
　　　And I must bear it."
　20 My tent is plundered,
　　　And all my cords are broken;
　　　My children have gone from me,
　　　And they *are* no more.
　　　There is no one to pitch my tent anymore,
　　　Or set up my curtains.
　21 For the shepherds have become dull-hearted,
　　　And have not sought the LORD;
　　　Therefore they shall not prosper,
　　　And all their flocks shall be scattered.
　22 Behold, the noise of the report has come,
　　　And a great commotion out of the north
　　　　country,
　　　To make the cities of Judah desolate, a den of
　　　　jackals.
　23 O LORD, I know the way of man *is* not in
　　　　himself;
　　　It is not in man who walks to direct his own
　　　　steps.
　24 O LORD, correct me, but with justice;
　　　Not in Your anger, lest You bring me to
　　　　nothing.
　25 Pour out Your fury on the Gentiles, who do
　　　　not know You,
　　　And on the families who do not call on Your
　　　　name;

95

For they have eaten up Jacob,
Devoured him and consumed him,
And made his dwelling place desolate.

Jer. 10:19–25

There is an enormous implication to this proclamation that is born out in the early chapters of Genesis where we find the undergirding structure of the universe. God spreads a lavish creation out before us, along with the bountiful command, "Be fruitful and multiply; fill the earth and subdue it; have dominion over the fish of the sea, over the birds of the air, and over every living thing that moves on the earth" (Gen. 2:28). Curiously enough, He did not invite us to have dominion over Himself. Our humanity was structured for His sovereignty, not our own. In the Hebrew tradition, the name of something was indicative of its nature. The person doing the naming was also the authority over the person named. Who named the animals? Adam. Yet who named Adam? God. For always it was His intention to be our King in the midst of His plenty. *"O LORD, I know the way of man is not in himself. It is not in man who walks to direct his own steps. O LORD, correct me, but with justice; Not in Your anger, lest You bring me to nothing"* (vv. 23–24).

Only the one who has made heaven and earth has a right to reign over it. "The gods that have not made the heavens and the earth shall perish from the earth and from under these heavens" (v. 11). The wooden idols we talked about earlier could not make anything, let alone the heavens and the earth. They could not even stand up by themselves. They could not even get from one place to another. In fashioning them to worship, men had made things less than even themselves, and then looked to them to fill the deepest of their needs. What a hollow contrivance. What a slander to the dignity and nature of God to substitute in His place not only something infinitely less than Himself but also something less than human, less that bestial even. "Everyone is dull-hearted, without knowledge; Every metalsmith is put to shame by an image; For his molded image *is* falsehood, And *there is* no breath in them. They *are* futile, a work of errors" (vv. 14, 15). Is it any wonder that God reacts in anger and judgment? The prophet agrees as he speaks of the coming captivity of Judah. "Gather up your wares from the land, . . . For thus says the LORD: 'Behold I will throw [you] out at this time'" (vv. 17, 18).

96

We need to notice something else in all of these passages. God reacted more to the idolatry found in His own people that to that found in the pagan nations. "Israel is the tribe of His inheritance" (v. 16). Clearly those of us with a revelation of God and of His nature are judged by a different standard than the rest of the world. The clarion cry goes out to all believers, "learn not the way of the Gentiles" (v. 1).

The language is so prophetic of what we are later to hear from the Apostle Paul: "You should no longer walk as the rest of the Gentiles walk, in the futility of their mind, having their understanding darkened, being alienated from the life of God, because of the ignorance that is in them, because of the blindness of their heart" (Eph. 4:17–18). If we are to understand anything at all it is that we are to be different from the world. In trying to summarize the sublime things he has said in his Epistle to the Romans, Paul implored his listeners with this plea, "Do not be conformed to this world, but be transformed by the renewing of your mind, that you may prove what is that good and acceptable and perfect will of God" (Rom. 12:2).

Unfortunately Judah was being so conformed to the world that the tireless work of the prophet seemed of no avail. Again he uttered a mourning that comes to characterize him as the weeping prophet. It was an attitude already touched upon in 8:21. Again he cried, "Woe is me for my hurt! My wound is severe. But I say, 'Truly this is an infirmity, And I must bear it'" (v. 19). He was coming to grips with the totality of prophetic ministry and with the sovereign claim of God upon his life, whether the tasks be pleasant or painful. This is not a grin-and-bear-it or stiff-upper-lip kind of mentality, but rather a steady life of confessing, accepting, and perseverance. What a witness this tenacity is to our instant society of today.

THE SHATTERED COVENANT

11:1 The word that came to Jeremiah from the LORD, saying,

2 "Hear the words of this covenant, and speak to the men of Judah and to the inhabitants of Jerusalem;

3 "and say to them, 'Thus says the LORD God of Israel: "Cursed is the man who does not obey the words of this covenant

4 "which I commanded your fathers in the day I brought them out of the land of Egypt, from the iron furnace, saying, 'Obey My voice, and do according to all that I command you; so shall you be My people, and I will be your God,'

5 "that I may establish the oath which I have sworn to your fathers, to give them 'a land flowing with milk and honey,' as *it is* this day."'" And I answered and said, "So be it, LORD."

6 Then the LORD said to me, "Proclaim all these words in the cities of Judah and in the streets of Jerusalem, saying: 'Hear the words of this covenant and do them.

7 'For I earnestly exhorted your fathers in the day I brought them up out of the land of Egypt, until this day, rising early and exhorting, saying, "Obey My voice."

8 'Yet they did not obey or incline their ear, but everyone followed the dictates of his evil heart; therefore I will bring upon them all the words of this covenant, which I commanded *them* to do, but *which* they have not done.'"

9 And the LORD said to me, "A conspiracy has been found among the men of Judah and among the inhabitants of Jerusalem.

10 "They have turned back to the iniquities of their forefathers who refused to hear My words, and they have gone after other gods to serve them; the house of Israel and the house of Judah have broken My covenant which I made with their fathers."

11 Therefore thus says the LORD: "Behold, I will surely bring calamity on them which they will not be able to escape; and though they cry out to Me, I will not listen to them.

12 "Then the cities of Judah and the inhabitants of Jerusalem will go and cry out to the gods to whom they offer incense, but they will not save them at all in the time of their trouble.

13 "For *according to* the number of your cities were your gods, O Judah; and *according to* the number of the streets of Jerusalem you have set up altars to *that* shameful thing, altars to burn incense to Baal.

14 "So do not pray for this people, or lift up a cry or prayer for them; for I will not hear *them* in the time that they cry out to Me because of their trouble.

15 "What has My beloved to do in My house,
Having done lewd deeds with many?
And the holy flesh has passed from you.
When you do evil, then you rejoice.

16 The LORD called your name,
Green Olive Tree, Lovely *and* of Good Fruit.
With the noise of a great tumult
He has kindled fire on it,
And its branches are broken.

17 "For the LORD of hosts, who planted you, has pronounced doom against you for the evil of the house of Israel and of the house of Judah, which they have done against themselves to provoke Me to anger in offering incense to Baal."

Jer. 11:1–17

In contrasting the wonder of God with the woodenness of idols, Jeremiah felt in his body the shock of that polarity more severely than the people to whom he was speaking. They were too "dull-hearted" (10:14). Another figure comes quickly to mind in thinking of the trauma of sin and the broken covenant.

Moses had fellowshiped with God for forty days. He had been wrapped in a celestial cloud of holiness on the top of Mount Sinai. Parting from that ineffable presence was made possible only by the wonderful thought of returning to his people and delivering to them, in the very handwriting of God, the covenant terms of their life together as it was to be in the "land of milk and honey." Picture the titanic figure of Moses, his flowing mane of white hair blowing in the breeze, descending the mountain, embracing in his strong arms the tablets of stone. Drawing closer and closer to his people, he could no longer hear the music of heaven. Instead another music struck his ears. It was harsh, dissonant, and lewd. The "sound of singing" (Exod. 32:18) was an accompaniment to the orgiastic dancing that was taking place around a golden calf. Even though God had warned him (Exod. 32:7–8), the shock was still more than Moses could bear. The contrast between God's perfection and Israel's perversion sent a rush of hot anger through his body. Lifting the tablets over his head, with massive and trembling arms, he dashed them against the rocky ground at the base of the mountain. They shattered.

We must understand that the breach of God's law—of which we are all guilty—is not a hair-line fracture, some easily remedied little hurt. Moses dramatized that they had shattered the covenant. Jeremiah, also aware of the enormity of the wound, cried out, "they have healed the hurt of the daughter of My people slightly" (Jer. 8:11). Both servants of God stand in complete agreement with His verdict. Jeremiah countersigned God's words to him in this chapter with a hearty, *"So be it, LORD"* (v. 5). What he delivered to the people captures the holiness of God, both in the dimension of His love and of His wrath. His love emerged strongly in these seventeen verses. It was very reminiscent of the blessings already dealt with in 2:1–8. (1) *"[God] brought them out of the land of Egypt, from the iron furnace"* (v. 4) He did not create a people to be tyrannized but a people to be governed. There is a difference. He created a people for work but not for the taskmaster. Someone said, "He didn't mean to burden us with work; He meant to bless us with it." (2) He made them free for service, not for self-serving. "Let My people go, that they may hold a feast for Me" (Exod. 5:1). In His service is perfect freedom. *"Obey My voice, and do according to all that I command you"* (v. 4; cf. vv. 6–7). (3) He had committed Himself by oath to bring them into bounty. *"I have sworn to your fathers, to give them 'a land flowing with milk and honey'"* (v. 5). The extravagance of His love was further reflected in the statement, *"The LORD called your name, Green Olive Tree, Lovely and of Good Fruit"* (v. 16). (4) Throughout their history He has been a "rising early" God, exhorting them and saying, "Obey My voice" (v. 7). The term "rising early" appears frequently in prophetic literature, both of God and of His spokesman. "The Lord is not slack concerning *His* promise, as some count slackness, but is longsuffering toward us, not willing that any should perish but that all should come to repentance" (2 Pet. 3:9). In addition to the love of God, Jeremiah brought out the theme of His wrath in these same verses.

1. *"Cursed is the man who does not obey the words of this covenant"* (v. 3). We find out how seriously God takes His love and also how seriously God takes His law. Any breach of it brings a curse. The strong language found here came originally from the Book of

the Law (Deut. 27:26). The word "curse" is loaded with calamity and blame. It carries bad news to those who are under the law, but good news today to those who are under the grace of Jesus Christ. He took the calamity of our condition and the blame of our disobedience upon Himself. "Christ has redeemed us from the curse of the law, having become a curse for us (for it is written 'Cursed is everyone who hangs on a tree')" (Gal. 3:13; cf. Deut. 21:23).

2. *"I will bring upon them all the words of this covenant, which I commanded them to do, but which they have not done"* (v. 8). The ultimate intention of God to vindicate His own holiness has never been so clear. Those people both today and then who insist on having only a God of love must settle up with these prophetic words. Because He is a powerful God, He cannot be a permissive God.

3. *"Though they cry out to Me, I will not listen to them. . . . I will not hear them in the time that they cry out to Me because of their trouble"* (vv. 11, 14). These two verses begin and end a clear teaching of God that although He is long-suffering, there is an end to His patience. When He lets go of His people, they are on their own with only their wooden idols to cling to. "Go ahead, go to the many altars you've set up in the streets of Jerusalem, burn all the incense to Baal you want, find out where those gods are when you really need them."

4. *"Do not pray for this people"* (v. 14). This shocking thing first appeared in 7:28 and was treated in that chapter. God has turned out the last light of their hope. For all the brilliant potential that they once had, it has come to this. *"For the LORD of hosts, who planted you, has pronounced doom against you"* (v. 17).

CHAPTER EIGHT

Why Do Good Things Happen to Bad People?

Jeremiah 11:18–12:17

THE CONSPIRACY

11:18 Now the LORD gave me knowledge *of it*, and I know *it*; for You showed me their doings.

19 But I *was* like a docile lamb brought to the slaughter; and I did not know that they had devised schemes against me, *saying*, "Let us destroy the tree with its fruit, and let us cut him off from the land of the living, that his name may be remembered no more."

20 But, O LORD of hosts,
You who judge righteously,
Testing the mind and the heart,
Let me see Your vengeance on them,
For to You I have revealed my cause.

21 "Therefore thus says the LORD concerning the men of Anathoth who seek your life, saying, 'Do not prophesy in the name of the LORD, lest you die by our hand'—

22 "therefore thus says the LORD of hosts: 'Behold, I will punish them. The young men shall die by the sword, their sons and their daughters shall die by famine;

23 'and there shall be no remnant of them, for I will bring catastrophe on the men of Anathoth, *even* the year of their punishment.'"

Jer. 11:18–23

After dealing with a shattered covenant, the prophet was now faced with a shattered relationship, one that radically affected his personal life. In chapter 4, we find that the stand he took against empty traditionalism was to prove to be costly. The priests themselves were implicated when Jeremiah's cry went out to the people: "Amend your ways and your doings" (7:3). They were working for a system that gave only lip service to the Lord, but beneath the surface it was blatant unbelief. God was "near in their mouth But far from their mind" (12:2). Since the famous temple sermon Jeremiah had continued to hammer courageously on the reality of that fact. Priests might possibly lose their jobs. A conspiracy formed, a plot thickened against Jeremiah's life.

So pure was the prophet's heart, so intent upon the work before him in exposing apostasy, that he had obviously never given much thought to his own safety. Anathoth had always been for him the soft sanctuary of his youth, the walled city of priests. Now it had become a sinister place of plotting. What was to prevent him from being blind-sided by the faction about to pounce on him? He was so unsuspecting, later confessing of himself, "I was like a docile lamb brought to the slaughter; and I did not know that they had devised schemes against me" (v. 19).

Remember the words God spoke when He commissioned Jeremiah as a young country boy? "Do not be afraid of their faces, For I am with you to deliver you" (1:8). Jeremiah is informed of the conspiracy by none other than God Himself. "Now the LORD gave me knowledge of it, and I know it" (v. 18). In the course of that revelation, God also allowed him to know the exact words of the conspirators as they revealed the blackness of their hearts. "Let us destroy the tree with its fruit, and let us cut him off from the land of the living, that his name may be remembered no more" (v. 19). Out of this episode in Jeremiah's life we learn three things about evil opposition.

1. Evil is deluded into believing it has power over God, that it can thwart His plan. The Pharisees, thinking they were so shrewd, believed they could eliminate the kingdom of which Jesus spoke by eliminating Him. Pharaoh was deluded into believing he could keep the deliverer of Israel out of Egypt by slaying all male babies. Herod was deluded into believing he could prevent the coming of the Messiah by ordering infanticide.

2. Evil fails to calculate for the danger involved in crossing God's sovereign plan. Unbelief is always unaware of peril. *"Behold, I will punish them. The young men shall die by the sword, their sons and their daughters shall die by famine"* (v. 22). Miriam and Aaron met with judgment when they criticized Moses. They failed to understand how dearly God loved and how carefully God protected him. God reminded them of this fact and then asked the question as they trembled before the tent of meeting with Him, "Why then were you not afraid To speak against My servant Moses?" (Num. 12:8).

3. Evil's tactics of intimidation are usually counterproductive. The conspiracy of evil fails to understand the tremendous force of courage that lives in the servant of God. They said to Jeremiah, *"Do not prophesy in the name of the* LORD, *lest you die by our hand"* (v. 21). Statements like that one made the prophet more resolute than ever and kept him in his forty-year ministry of faithfulness. The apostles Peter and John were threatened by the Sanhedrin, "not to speak at all nor teach in the name of Jesus" (Acts 4:18). They responded with more courage than they ever expressed before: "For we cannot but speak the things which we have seen and heard" (Acts 4:20).

THE PRAYER OF PUZZLEMENT

12:1 Righteous *are* You, O LORD, when I plead with
        You;
     Yet let me talk with You about *Your* judgments.
     Why does the way of the wicked prosper?
     Why are those happy who deal so
        treacherously?
  2 You have planted them, yes, they have taken root;
     They grow, yes, they bear fruit.
     You *are* near in their mouth
     But far from their mind.
  3 But You, O LORD, know me;
     You have seen me,
     And You have tested my heart toward You.
     Pull them out like sheep for the slaughter,
     And prepare them for the day of slaughter.
  4 How long will the land mourn,
     And the herbs of every field wither?

> The beasts and birds are consumed,
> For the wickedness of those who dwell there,
> Because they said, "He will not see our final
>   end."
>
> *Jer. 12:1-4*

According to the *Interpreter's Bible*, this passage is the earliest in Old Testament literature to raise the question, "Why do the wicked prosper?" (v. 1).[1] It comes on the heels of the personal hurt dealt to Jeremiah in discovering his very own relatives, his very own townsmen, were the ones seeking his life. It is prophetic of the injury dealt to the heart of Jesus in being betrayed not by a Roman, not by a Pharisee, but by the kiss of a friend, a member of His circle of trust and communion.

It is more then than just an intellectual or academic question. The plot and the shattered relationship it represented were the catalyst that brought this candid question before the throne of God. The prophet asks it with an aching heart. In the prayer eight things are disclosed about the prophet.

1. He took the force of this question to a private moment with God. We are to deal with our doubts and our puzzlements in private, not in public. *"Let me talk with You about Your judgments"* (v. 1).

2. He has a resolute commitment to the fact that God has the answer and will do right. *"Righteous are You, O LORD, when I plead with You"* (v. 1).

3. He was frustrated by the happiness of the wicked. What right have they to be happy? This is just as true today. The world is literally crashing up against the principles of God, violating them at every turn, yet this same world seems so happy. *"Why are those happy who deal so treacherously?"* (v. 1).

4. He has a resolute commitment to God's sovereignty. Not only are the wicked seemingly happy, but they are growing and they are bearing fruit (v. 2). Even this puzzling phenomenon is not outside of the power of God. *"You have planted them"* (v. 2). The prayer rests on that confession.

5. His own heart did not condemn him. He was conscious of nothing against himself. The steady obedience of the prophet has left him with a clean conscience. *"But You, O LORD, know me; You have seen me, And You have tested my heart toward You"* (v. 3).

105

6. His anger, therefore, was righteous anger, and it burned with a personal cause. Hometown security had been cut from him. He felt the sting of betrayal from those he considered his own, and more than ever he knew how God felt about the treachery of His "hometown" of Israel. *Pull them out like sheep for the slaughter, And prepare them for the day of slaughter"* (v. 3).

7. He was frustrated by God's timing. In the midst of his own maturity and his own obedience, he still knew puzzlement. In spite of his commitment to the righteousness and sovereignty of God, he was still frustrated over the fact that "His ways [are] past finding out" (Rom. 11:33). The question goes up, *"How long will the land mourn?"* (v. 4).

8. If he was ever naive before, he was certainly not now. Not only did he know the Word of God, but he also knew the words of His enemies. He knew their mind-set, their conversation, and their intentions. It was a savvy prophet who emerges from this puzzlement. "So this is actually what they think of You, God!" They say in the arrogance of their unbelief, *"He will not see our final end"* (v. 4).

THE ANSWER OF AUTHORITY

12:5 "If you have run with the footmen, and they
      have wearied you,
      Then how can you contend with horses?
      And *if* in the land of peace,
      In which you trusted, *they wearied you,*
      Then how will you do in the flood plain of the
      Jordan?

6 For even your brothers, the house of your
      father,
      Even they have dealt treacherously with you;
      Yes, they have called a multitude after you.
      Do not believe them,
      Even though they speak smooth words to you.

7 "I have forsaken My house, I have left My
      heritage;
      I have given the dearly beloved of My soul
      into the hand of her enemies.

8 My heritage is to Me like a lion in the forest;

       It cries out against Me;
       Therefore I have hated it.
9 My heritage *is* to Me *like* a speckled vulture;
       The vultures all around *are* against her.
       Come, assemble all the beasts of the field,
       Bring them to devour!
10 "Many rulers have destroyed My vineyard,
       They have trodden My portion underfoot;
       They have made My pleasant portion a desolate
         wilderness.
11 They have made it desolate;
       Desolate, it mourns to Me;
       The whole land is made desolate,
       Because no one takes *it* to heart.
12 The plunderers have come
       On all the desolate heights in the wilderness,
       For the sword of the LORD shall devour
       From *one* end of the land to the *other* end of the
         land;
       No flesh shall have peace.
13 They have sown wheat but reaped thorns;
       They have put themselves to pain *but* do not
         profit.
       But be ashamed of your harvest
       Because of the fierce anger of the LORD."

14 Thus says the LORD: "Against all My evil neighbors who touch the inheritance which I have caused My people Israel to inherit—behold, I will pluck them out of their land and pluck out the house of Judah from among them.

15 "Then it shall be, after I have plucked them out, that I will return and have compassion on them and bring them back, everyone to his heritage and everyone to his land.

16 "And it shall be, if they will learn carefully the ways of My people, to swear by My name, 'As the LORD lives,' as they taught My people to swear by Baal, then they shall be established in the midst of My people.

17 "But if they do not obey, I will utterly pluck up and destroy that nation," says the LORD.

                                   Jer. 12:5-17

Why do good things happen to bad people? "Why do the wicked prosper?" (v. 1). This was not a casual question. It was addressed to God out of the deepest human experience. He did not answer it directly, but He honored the question. In addressing Himself to it He gives the perceptive reader more understanding into His nature. His response to the prophet was fourfold.

1. He posed another question. Rather than answering directly why? and when? God took command of the interview and changed its whole dynamic with a question of His own that penetrated to the real issues. Job had the same experience when he assumed that he was going to reason with God. Instead he was flooded with questions that God proposed, so high, so ineffable as to leave Job with more of God and with more of His majesty than he had ever dreamed possible.

"If you have run with the footmen, and they have wearied you, Then how can you contend with horses?" (v. 5). On the surface, it seemed a cruel question, but underneath it were the everlasting arms and the everlasting heart that understands four things.

First, God understood that what gave rise to the question was a profound weariness. The footmen have wearied you; *"in the land of peace . . . they wearied you"* (v. 5). One can almost hear God say, "Jeremiah, I understand. You're bone tired." Second, He also understood that Jeremiah was hurt. The prophet was not some thick-skinned tough guy. The tender-hearted country boy had been dealt a severe blow. He had been rejected by his heartland. *"Your brothers, the house of your father, . . . have dealt treacherously with you. . . . [T]hey have called a multitude after you. . . . Even though they speak smooth words to you"* (v. 6). In the third place, God understood that the work was not yet finished. It would go on in spite of the weariness and in spite of the hurt. In essence He told Jeremiah that what he has done in and around Anathoth, in a land of relative peace under the reign of Josiah, has really been just the beginning. He has only "run with the footmen." He would one day "contend with horses," and not in the provincial setting, but rather *"in the flood plain of the Jordan"* (v. 5). The fourth thing God addressed was the nature of Jeremiah's work; it would grow in complexity. As it would grow in complexity, it would also grow in scope. Remember that his commission was not just as a prophet to the Southern Kingdom or the Northern Kingdom but "as a prophet to the nations" (1:5).

2. God confessed His own pain. Verses 7–9 form God's lament. He honored Jeremiah's original question with an intimate display of His own heart. One feels the closeness of the friendship between God and prophet, rather like the picture of John the Beloved resting his head on the bosom of Jesus. In essence He seems to have been saying, "You're not alone Jeremiah. The betrayal of your own Anathoth hurts. Having family and childhood friends turn against you is no small injury. It happened to me too."

First, *"I have forsaken My house, I have left My heritage; I have given the dearly beloved of My soul into the hand of her enemies"* (v. 7). This is reminiscent of what the Apostle Paul writes: "God gave them up to vile passions" (Rom. 1:26). Here, however, we find something of His heart in doing so, something of the hurt it caused Him.

Also, "My own hometown has cried out against me too." In essence this is what God shared with Jeremiah. Like a roaring lion in the forest, Judah had betrayed her God (v. 8).

A third anguish takes poetic form. *"My heritage is to Me like a speckled vulture; The vultures all around are against her. . . . Assemble all the beasts of the field, Bring them to devour [Me]"* (v. 9). In His lament God showed the prophet that the rejection he was suffering was in order for him to be more closely identified with the heart of His creator. Jeremiah would not always get the answers to his questions, but he would always have the God of the questions.

3. He described the fate of the betrayers. In verses 10–13, God dealt with the "desolate" condition that awaited the traitors. That word was repeated five times to create a sense of mournfulness. Never is God glad to deal out judgment.

4. He comforted with a vision. In answering Jeremiah, God questioned, He confided, He described, and then He comforted. The self-disclosing God ministered to the weary prophet. He did not meet Jeremiah's agenda. The prophet did not really need to know why or when. He simply needed to know who. The vision for his ministry had been eclipsed by a heartbreak, but out of that darkness, a light shone into the prophet's world. What he saw was found in verses 14–17.

First, a nation stands or falls by how it treats God's people. *"Against all My evil neighbors who touch the inheritance, . . . I will pluck them out of their land"* (v. 14). A return to the land awaited the true people of God. *"That I will . . . have compassion on them and bring them back"* (v. 15). The "new" people, living a "new" life in the land were to convert the Gentile nations to the Lord, just as those nations had first converted them to Baal (v. 16). A day would come when angel voices would proclaim, "The kingdoms of this world have become *the kingdoms* of our Lord and of His Christ, and He shall reign forever and ever!" (Rev. 11:15). This was Jeremiah's vision, and it gave him new energy in order to serve.

NOTE

1. Stanley Hopper, "The Book of Jeremiah: Exposition," in *The Interpreter's Bible,* vol. 5, ed. George A. Buttrick et al. (Nashville: Abingdon Press, 1956), 915.

CHAPTER NINE

Pride Goes before a Fall

Jeremiah 13:1–27

The wicked did indeed seem to be prospering in Jerusalem, not realizing that they were heading for a fall. In 609 B.C., Judah lost her
righteous king Josiah. With his death, she lost the restraining influence his reign exerted over the forces of pride against God. Josiah was
killed in the crossfire between Egypt and Assyria, in the inevitable
clash between the nations in their struggle for world dominance.

Exercising his prophetic ministry under Josiah's reign had been
difficult for Jeremiah. It was destined to become more difficult under
his successors, particularly in terms of their arrogant independence
from God. The country boy from Anathoth had been "running with
footmen." Now he would be "contending with horses." He would be
contending with internal power struggles for the throne, each con-
testant more wicked than the last.

The tiny kingdom of Judah looked at the configuration of powers
around her and pondered an alliance with Egypt. Jeremiah knew
that was wrong. The vision he had received of the boiling cauldron
spilling its fury from the north (1:13) told him that the real threat
would come from Babylon. Even Egypt could not stand against this
up-and-coming power. Seeing the future all alone, Jeremiah would
stand against the conceit of political decisions made entirely without
the council of God.

WHAT THE WELL-DRESSED PROPHET WAS WEARING

13:1 Thus the LORD said to me: "Go and get yourself
a linen sash, and put it around your waist, but do not
put it in water."

2 So I got a sash according to the word of the LORD, and put *it* around my waist.

3 And the word of the LORD came to me the second time, saying,

4 "Take the sash that you acquired, which *is* around your waist, and arise, go to the Euphrates, and hide it there in a hole in the rock."

5 So I went and hid it by the Euphrates, as the LORD commanded me.

6 Now it came to pass after many days that the LORD said to me, "Arise, go to the Euphrates, and take from there the sash which I commanded you to hide there."

7 Then I went to the Euphrates and dug, and I took the sash from the place where I had hidden it; and there was the sash, ruined. It was profitable for nothing.

8 Then the word of the LORD came to me, saying,

9 "Thus says the LORD: 'In this manner I will ruin the pride of Judah and the great pride of Jerusalem.

10 'This evil people, who refuse to hear My words, who follow the dictates of their hearts, and walk after other gods to serve them and worship them, shall be just like this sash which is profitable for nothing.

11 'For as the sash clings to the waist of a man, so I have caused the whole house of Israel and the whole house of Judah to cling to Me,' says the LORD, 'that they may become My people, for renown, for praise, and for glory; but they would not hear.'"

Jer. 13:1–11

In vain Jeremiah cried, "Hear and give ear: Do not be proud, For the LORD has spoken" (v. 15). *"I will ruin the pride of Judah and the great pride of Jerusalem"* (v. 9). Words were missing the mark with this resistant people so God chose to communicate His reality in a dramatic use of nonverbals. Jeremiah makes a public appearance in a shocking outfit. Instead of preaching a sermon, he is to be a sermon.

Once before Jeremiah had been a metaphor of the people by cutting off his hair on the barren heights where he was silhouetted between earth and heaven as a mournful image of Judah's lost glory. Now he was to make a foray into tempestuous Jerusalem wearing not

112

only the predictable prophet's garb but also a linen sash. Its ivory smoothness, the linen coming from the finest flax, was draped in stark contrast to his rugged robes. It clung to his waist, an odd and unexpected thing.

Linen was the fabric of the aristocracy, reserved for priestly vestments and the robes of kings.[1] The temple curtains were embroidered linen. The country boy again becomes a silent communicator for God. Through Jeremiah, God has this to say: *"I have caused the whole house of Israel and the whole house of Judah to cling to Me"* (v. 11). In essence He is saying, "You are a nation meant to carry the dignity of the divine out into the world of other nations." You were meant *"for renown, for praise, and for glory"* (v. 11).

Judah was to have a dignity above that of other nations, not an intrinsic dignity stemming from herself, but a higher dignity derived from God who had chosen to be identified with this people. The eyes of all the nations were to fall upon the kingdom of Judah and to see in her a pristine elegance, to be drawn to her beauty and to her glory.

Yet the ivory sash, bridal in its virtue, did not remain long on the waist of the prophet. He was soon instructed to journey to the town of Parah, about three miles northeast of Anathoth. (The Euphrates [Perath] was less likely to have been his destination since it was five hundred miles away.) There he was to hide the linen sash in a hole in a rock (v. 4).

After several days the prophet was to return to this place of hiding and retrieve the waistband. There he found that the glory that had clung to his waist—as the people were to have clung to their God—was now utterly ruined. *"It was profitable for nothing"* (v. 7). *"This evil people, who refuse to hear My words, who follow the dictates of their hearts, and walk after other gods to serve them and worship them, shall be just like this sash which is profitable for nothing"* (v. 10).

DIGNITY CAN'T BE PRESERVED IN ALCOHOL

13:12 "Therefore you shall speak to them this word:
'Thus says the LORD God of Israel: "Every bottle shall
be filled with wine."' And they will say to you, 'Do
we not certainly know that every bottle will be filled
with wine?'

13 "Then you shall say to them, 'Thus says the
LORD: "Behold, I will fill all the inhabitants of this
land—even the kings who sit on David's throne, the
priests, the prophets, and all the inhabitants of
Jerusalem—with drunkenness!

14 "And I will dash them one against another,
even the fathers and the sons together," says the
LORD. "I will not pity nor spare nor have mercy, but
will destroy them"'"

Jer. 13:12-14

Again Jeremiah is called upon to dramatize the message that God
will ruin the false pride of the people; they will suffer a profound
loss of dignity. This time he uses a parable of wine jars.

The people are likened to the jars. Both are filled with wine, but
when wine is poured into people, they become drunk. *"'And I will
dash them one against another, even the fathers and the sons together,'
says the LORD"* (v. 14). They suffer the loss of composure, of coordi-
nation, and of judgment. It is a sad commentary on the state of society when parents drink with their children to the point of mutual
inebriation. We who are parents are called to be examples of dignity
and sobriety, not of drunkenness.

Our public officials also are called upon to be examples. As a
nation we would not feel very comfortable about the state of the
union if we always saw our president, our representatives, and our
clergy drunk. Yet that was a common sight to Judah. *"I will fill all
the inhabitants of this land—even the kings who sit on David's throne,
the priests, the prophets, and all the inhabitants of Jerusalem—with
drunkenness"* (v. 13).

SIX FEATURES OF PRIDE

13:15 Hear and give ear:
        Do not be proud,
        For the LORD has spoken.
    16 Give glory to the LORD your God
        Before He causes darkness,
        And before your feet stumble
        On the dark mountains,

And while you are looking for light,
He turns it into the shadow of death
And makes *it* dense darkness.
17 But if you will not hear it,
My soul will weep in secret for *your* pride;
My eyes will weep bitterly
And run down with tears,
Because the LORD's flock has been taken
    captive.
18 Say to the king and to the queen mother,
"Humble yourselves;
Sit down,
For your rule shall collapse, the crown of your
    glory."
19 The cities of the South shall be shut up,
And no one shall open *them;*
Judah shall be carried away captive, all of it;
It shall be wholly carried away captive.
20 Lift up your eyes and see
Those who come from the north.
Where *is* the flock *that* was given to you,
Your beautiful sheep?
21 What will you say when He punishes you?
For you have taught them
To be chieftains, to be head over you.
Will not pangs seize you,
Like a woman in labor?
22 And if you say in your heart,
"Why have these things come upon me?"
For the greatness of your iniquity
Your skirts have been uncovered,
Your heels made bare.
23 Can the Ethiopian change his skin or the
    leopard its spots?
Then may you also do good who are
    accustomed to do evil.
24 "Therefore I will scatter them like stubble
That passes away by the wind of the
    wilderness.
25 This is your lot,
The portion of your measures from Me," says
    the LORD,

> "Because you have forgotten Me
> And trusted in falsehood.
> 26 Therefore I will uncover your skirts over your
>   face,
> That your shame may appear.
> 27 I have seen your adulteries
> And your *lustful* neighings,
> The lewdness of your harlotry,
> Your abominations on the hills in the fields.
> Woe to you, O Jerusalem!
> Will you still not be made clean?"
>
> *Jer. 13:15–27*

It has been said that pride hides a man's faults to himself and magnifies them to everyone else. Jerusalem had become a spectacle of pride. In the series of laments and warnings that make up the balance of this chapter Jeremiah makes us very aware of her faults while she herself remains blind to them. We learn the following.

1. What little light is left in the prideful heart can be turned off at any time. *"Give glory to the LORD your God Before He causes darkness"* (v. 16). Whenever God chooses, He can flick the switch. *"And while you are looking for light, He turns it into the shadow of death And makes it dense darkness"* (v. 16). Then He says to Judah that she will be left puzzled and wondering *"Why have these things come upon me?"* (v. 22).

2. It grieves the heart of God and those of the godly. Another cameo is given of the private agony of prophet and God. *"My soul will weep in secret for your pride; My eyes will weep bitterly And run down with tears"* (v. 17).

3. When present in its leaders, pride can cause a whole nation to fall. Verses 18 and 19 lament the brief reign of Jehoiachin who came to the throne at the age of eighteen. He and his mother, Nehushta, refused what little light was left to them. The golden crown fell and the stark humiliation of defeat pressed in upon Judah. Both they and all the skilled artisans of the nation were led captive to Babylon. *"Therefore I will scatter them like stubble That passes away by the wind of the wilderness"* (v. 24).

4. Pride can intensify to the point of becoming irreversible. *"Can the Ethiopian change his skin or the leopard its spots? Then may you also do good who are accustomed to do evil"* (v. 23). Jeremiah has become

116

famous in this Western culture for this saying. The chapter ends on this striking note, *"Woe to you, O Jerusalem! Will you still not be made clean?"* (v. 27).

5. All that pride hides will one day be exposed. *"Therefore I will uncover your skirts over your face, That your shame may appear"* (v. 26). *"Your skirts have been uncovered, Your heels made bare"* (v. 22).

6. Pride is under the constant scrutiny of God. *"I have seen your adulteries And your lustful neighings, The lewdness of your harlotry, Your abominations on the hills in the fields"* (v. 27). In the light of all of this pride, some kind of fall is in the wings. We should not then be surprised at the contents of our next chapter. The wicked prosper no longer.

NOTE

1. R. K. Harrison, *Jeremiah and Lamentations,* The Tyndale Old Testament Commentary (Downers Grove, Ill.: Inter-Varsity Press, 1973), 99.

CHAPTER TEN

Jerusalem: A Disaster Waiting to Happen

Jeremiah 14:1–15:21

THE DROUGHT

14:1 The word of the LORD that came to Jeremiah concerning the droughts.
> 2 "Judah mourns,
> And her gates languish;
> They mourn for the land,
> And the cry of Jerusalem has gone up.
> 3 Their nobles have sent their lads for water;
> They went to the cisterns *and* found no water.
> They returned with their vessels empty;
> They were ashamed and confounded
> And covered their heads.
> 4 Because the ground is parched,
> For there was no rain in the land,
> The plowmen were ashamed;
> They covered their heads.
> 5 Yes, the deer also gave birth in the field,
> But left because there was no grass.
> 6 And the wild donkeys stood in the desolate
> heights;
> They sniffed at the wind like jackals;
> Their eyes failed because *there was* no grass."
>
> *Jer. 14:1–6*

Drought in Palestine was certainly not unheard of. The description in this passage is poignant and suggests the parched spiritual condition that is as much a disaster as the natural one. Judah had brought it upon herself by hewing out cisterns of her own making and forsaking the fountains of the living water of God. In the forensic language of 2:13, Jeremiah had warned them against this most illogical decision. Now they contend with the consequences, with the fall that comes on the heels of pride. Throughout chapters 14 and 15, reference is made also to famine, sword, pestilence, and captivity (14:12; 15:1, 2). All of these afflictions are understood as the consequences of covenantal disobedience.

The heavens that once offered rain which they had taken for granted now stretched over their heads like bronze (Deut. 28:23). The earth, which once yielded its fruit, was now dry and cracked. No plow could turn its soil. The environment had undergone an upheaval of its natural course. The deer, renowned for their maternal instincts, abandoned their helpless newborn to die in a dry field. "The whole creation groans and labors with birth pangs together" (Rom. 8:22). All had fallen subject to this futility because of the pride of Judah.

WHEN THE GOING GETS TOUGH, THE TOUGH GET GOING

14:7 O LORD, though our iniquities testify against
     us,
     Do it for Your name's sake;
     For our backslidings are many,
     We have sinned against You.
   8 O the Hope of Israel, his Savior in time of
     trouble,
     Why should You be like a stranger in the land,
     And like a traveler *who* turns aside to tarry for
     a night?
   9 Why should You be like a man astonished,
     Like a mighty one *who* cannot save?
     Yet You, O LORD, *are* in our midst,
     And we are called by Your name;
     Do not leave us!
  10 Thus says the LORD to this people:
     "Thus they have loved to wander;
     They have not restrained their feet.

Therefore the LORD does not accept them;
He will remember their iniquity now,
And punish their sins."

11 Then the LORD said to me, "Do not pray for this people, for *their* good.

12 "When they fast, I will not hear their cry; and when they offer burnt offering and grain offering, I will not accept them. But I will consume them by the sword, by the famine, and by the pestilence."

13 Then I said, "Ah, Lord GOD! Behold, the prophets say to them, 'You shall not see the sword, nor shall you have famine, but I will give you assured peace in this place.'"

14 And the LORD said to me, "The prophets prophesy lies in My name. I have not sent them, commanded them, nor spoken to them; they prophesy to you a false vision, divination, a worthless thing, and the deceit of their heart.

15 "Therefore thus says the LORD concerning the prophets who prophesy in My name, whom I did not send, and who say, 'Sword and famine shall not be in this land'—'By sword and famine those prophets shall be consumed!

16 'And the people to whom they prophesy shall be cast out in the streets of Jerusalem because of the famine and the sword; they will have no one to bury them—them nor their wives, their sons nor their daughters—for I will pour their wickedness on them.'

17 "Therefore you shall say this word to them:
'Let my eyes flow with tears night and day,
And let them not cease;
For the virgin daughter of my people
Has been broken with a mighty stroke, with a
   very severe blow.

18 If I go out to the field,
Then behold, those slain with the sword!
And if I enter the city,
Then behold, those sick from famine!
Yes, both prophet and priest go about in a land
   they do not know.'"

19 Have You utterly rejected Judah?
Has Your soul loathed Zion?

120

Why have You stricken us so that *there is* no
healing for us?
We looked for peace, but *there was* no good;
And for the time of healing, and there was
trouble.
20 We acknowledge, O LORD, our wickedness
And the iniquity of our fathers,
For we have sinned against You.
21 Do not abhor *us,* for Your name's sake;
Do not disgrace the throne of Your glory.
Remember, do not break Your covenant with us.
22 Are there any among the idols of the nations
that can cause rain?
Or can the heavens give showers?
Are You not He, O LORD our God?
Therefore we will wait for You,
Since You have made all these.

15:1 Then the LORD said to me, "*Even* if Moses and
Samuel stood before Me, My mind *would* not *be* favorable toward this people. Cast *them* out of My sight,
and let them go forth.

2 "And it shall be, if they say to you, 'Where
should we go?' then you shall tell them, 'Thus says
the LORD:

"Such as *are* for death, to death;
And such as *are* for the sword, to the sword;
And such as *are* for the famine, to the famine;
And such as *are* for the captivity, to the
captivity."'

3 "And I will appoint over them four forms *of destruction,*" says the LORD: "the sword to slay, the dogs
to drag, the birds of the heavens and the beasts of
the earth to devour and destroy.

4 "I will hand them over to trouble, to all kingdoms of the earth, because of Manasseh the son of
Hezekiah, king of Judah, for what he did in Jerusalem.

5 "For who will have pity on you, O Jerusalem?
Or who will bemoan you?
Or who will turn aside to ask how you are
doing?
6 You have forsaken Me," says the LORD,
"You have gone backward.

121

> Therefore I will stretch out My hand against
>   you and destroy you;
> I am weary of relenting!
> 7 And I will winnow them with a winnowing
>   fan in the gates of the land;
> I will bereave *them* of children;
> I will destroy My people,
> *Since* they do not return from their ways.
> 8 Their widows will be increased to Me more
>   than the sand of the seas;
> I will bring against them,
> Against the mother of the young men,
> A plunderer at noonday;
> I will cause anguish and terror to fall on them
>   suddenly.
> 9 "She languishes who has borne seven;
> She has breathed her last;
> Her sun has gone down
> While *it was* yet day;
> She has been ashamed and confounded.
> And the remnant of them I will deliver to the
>   sword
> Before their enemies," says the LORD.
> *Jer. 14:7–15:9*

Not only did all of creation groan under the burden of the drought, but so did the prophet. The people mourned, but they did so because of the loss of their comfort and their pleasures, not the loss of their God. Jeremiah stands in the gap, pressing every energy to avert the oncoming judgment of God against Judah. He offered the prayer of puzzlement (Jer. 12:1–4) from out of the anguish of Anathoth's rejection of him. Now he offers three more prayers from out of the anguish of the drought. The going is getting tougher. No longer is he "running with footmen." Now he is "contending with horses." Tough issues call for tough people and their tough prayers.

1. *"Why should You be like a stranger in the land?"* (14:8). What a shock to hear the prophet talk to God like this. He has known an intimacy with God that has been his central comfort in life. How do we explain this sudden sense of estrangement that seems to have overtaken Jeremiah?

"O LORD, though our iniquities testify against us, . . . We have sinned against You" (14:7). Even though the sin of pride and the sin of idolatry have not been true of Jeremiah, he confesses them as though they were his own sins. The intercessor so completely identifies with those for whom he intercedes that he actually experiences the estrangement caused by the sin he confesses on their behalf. It is prophetic of the moment when Jesus cried from the cross, *"My God, My God, why have You forsaken Me?"* (Matt. 27:46). Jesus had literally become the Godforsaken derelict that sin has made of us all.

This first prayer of verses 7–9 receives a very direct and challenging answer in verses 10 and 11. Jeremiah has surrendered the sweetness of his communion with God in order to take on the results of Judah's apostasy. He experienced the dreadful scourge of separation from God that sin had caused. Loneliness from fellowship with men and from the routine joys of life was one thing, but this loneliness was infinitely worse, infinitely more desperate. God has an answer for him and one for his people.

To Jeremiah, God says again the startling thing we have found once before (Jer. 7:16): *"Do not pray for this people, for their good"* (v. 11). Are we so faithful in prayer, so doggedly persistent in it that we have to be told when to stop by God Himself? Most of us have long since grown weary of praying and of loving the unlovable, of standing in the gap.

To the people, God identifies the real stranger. *"I am not the stranger; it is you who have left me and not the other way around."* The sentiment of verse 10 continues. Not only have you wandered, but you have loved every minute of it. We too are world-class wanderers! We warm the church pews but not our hearts. Our acquaintance with God is such a casual one. We are so careless to know His word and His ways, yet so quick to complain.

I am reminded of a story about a man who operated a giant drawbridge. One day he took his young son with him in order to show him what it was he did every day. He led the young lad down into the cavernous workings of the bridge that they might marvel together over its powerful machinery. While down there the man received a phone call that a train, well ahead of schedule, was speeding toward the bridge. There was just enough time for him to race to the top of the tower and flip the switch to lower it into place. Patiently he instructed his son not to budge from his tight position of safety.

The father reached the tower with just enough time to lower the bridge. In that same split second he looked down to find that his son had moved into the jaws of the powerful machinery. He had to decide between the hundreds of lives speeding toward him in the train or the precious life of his only son. In great pain and anguish he flipped the switch. Down came the bridge, grinding the life out of his son. The train rushed by and as it did he could see people sitting there, in the comfort of their dining cars, chatting merrily with one another, totally oblivious to the enormous sacrifice that had just been made for their lives. Beating his fists on the tower window, the man screamed out against the stiff faces streaking past, a people for whom he had made so dear a sacrifice. "Don't you know that I gave my son for you?" "Don't you know that you are alive now because he yielded up his life?" "Does anybody care?"

God looks at the indifference of humanity rushing by Him, careless and unconcerned by the enormous cost of their salvation. We compound His anguish when we accuse Him of becoming the stranger when it is our own feet that have wandered. Is it any wonder that a time came when He said, *"Therefore the LORD does not accept them; He will remember their iniquity now, And punish their sins"* (v. 10).

2. They are victims of false teaching. Is it really their fault? This second question is hurled at God in verse 13. Catch the sigh in the prophet's voice as he perseveres in one last-ditch effort to intercede even when he has been told not to pray anymore and has been released from all such responsibilities. *"Ah, Lord GOD! Behold, the prophets say to them, 'You shall not see the sword, nor shall you have famine, but I will give you assured peace in this place'"* (v. 13). After Jeremiah has poured out his soul for the people, the other prophets come in and neutralize it; they snatch it away with their counter words of false comfort.

Again there is a twofold answer from God, one for the false prophets and one for those who listen to them. We may be shocked by what we hear. The false prophets have yielded to the temptation of telling the people what they want to hear, of preaching a popular gospel. Not only are they telling lies, but they are using God to endorse them. Have you ever experienced the embarrassment of misquoting someone and then discovering they were standing right there, listening to every word you were saying in their name? When we are conscious of the presence of the people we are quoting, we choose our words quite carefully lest we misrepresent them and scandalize ourselves in the process.

Not only have the false prophets betrayed their total ignorance of God's word, but worse they have betrayed their unbelief in His presence. In verses 14 and 15 God pronounces a fitting consequence upon them. They shall reap themselves the very dangers they refused to preach, so glibly discarding them in favor of their own more popular opinions.

Those who have listened to the false prophets are victims, but they are not innocent. We bear a responsibility for the kind of teaching we decide to listen to according to verses 16–18. *"And the people to whom they prophesy shall be cast out in the streets of Jerusalem"* (v. 16).

Today we have an education system running farther and farther away from the notion of moral absolutes. It is producing a generation of young people who have no respect for authority, who are encouraged to develop a morality that is right for each one of them in that time and in that situation. Ethics spring out of circumstances and not out of the rock-bed Judeo-Christian values upon which this culture has been built. According to God's answer to Jeremiah's prayer, we bear a responsibility for the kind of teaching we accept into our culture and we will reap a judgment.

3. Have You utterly rejected us? Verses 19–22 continue in a plea for mercy. Is there not just a pinprick of light and hope against this darkness? You may abhor us for our sins and our fathers for theirs, but what about "Your name's sake," "the throne of Your glory," "Your covenant?" (v. 21). In essence Jeremiah pleads, "will You save us to save face?"

Moses had prayed that way (Exod. 32:12, 13) and enjoyed the luxury of having that intercession succeed in averting the anger of God. Samuel stood in the gap for his people, and they finally gave heed. Jeremiah, however, has to endure the sting of failure, not because his prayers were not faithful enough, but because Judah's sin had been escalating in darkness; she had been failing to convert her generations.

It is conversion that transforms society and lack of conversion that leads to evil. *"I will hand them over to trouble . . . because of Manasseh"* (15:4). We have to convert every generation. Just because you have a generation of righteous leaders in a church or in a denomination does not mean you can rest on your laurels.

Hezekiah was a good king who purged the temple from the pollution of its idolatries. So was Josiah. Both of them, however, had unconverted sons. Manasseh was the unconverted son of Hezekiah, and look what God says about their fate because of him. The lack of conversions has caused a progressive decline in their society that no prayer can change now. *"Even if Moses and Samuel stood before Me, My mind would not be favorable toward this people"* (15:1).

Not only must we convert every generation, we must reach them when they are young. Josiah, the righteous king under whom Jeremiah began his prophetic ministry, came out of two generations of wickedness (Manasseh and Amon). At an early age he came under the influence of the prophetess Huldah, and because of this one man's conversion Judah enjoyed many years of opportunity to repent.

History affords us many illustrations of the radical impact one conversion can make upon a whole society. Lord Shaftesbury was a British statesman, converted as a child by his nanny. Throughout his life of social reform and philanthropy, he held her Bible as his dearest possession. In the wake of the preaching of Whitfield and Wesley, he led a movement to correct the conditions of the poor in England.

William Wilberforce led the fight against slavery in the British Empire. It was such a long-fought fight that he died two weeks before the Emancipation Bill became law in Britain. He had been converted by his aunt and uncle with whom he lived following the death of his father.

More than 80 percent of the people in any congregation who are committed, made their commitments before the age of twenty-one. That points out the folly of parents who say, "I'm not going to train my child in the way of the Lord. I'm going to let him grow up and decide for himself." If you do that you're looking for a Manasseh and for an Amon. Ultimately the judgment of God will fall on the society corrupted by this wicked leadership.

TWO PERSONAL PRAYERS

15:10 Woe is me, my mother,
     That you have borne me,
     A man of strife and a man of contention to the
       whole earth!

I have neither lent for interest,
Nor have men lent to me for interest.
Every one of them curses me.

11 The LORD said:
"Surely it will be well with your remnant;
Surely I will cause the enemy to intercede
with you
In the time of adversity and in the time of
affliction.

12 Can anyone break iron,
The northern iron and the bronze?

13 Your wealth and your treasures
I will give as plunder without price,
Because of all your sins,
Throughout your territories.

14 And I will make *you* cross over with your
enemies
Into a land *which* you do not know;
For a fire is kindled in My anger,
Which shall burn upon you."

15 O LORD, You know;
Remember me and visit me,
And take vengeance for me on my persecutors.
In Your enduring patience, do not take me
away.
Know that for Your sake I have suffered
rebuke.

16 Your words were found, and I ate them,
And Your word was to me the joy and
rejoicing of my heart;
For I am called by Your name,
O LORD God of hosts.

17 I did not sit in the assembly of the mockers,
Nor did I rejoice;
I sat alone because of Your hand,
For You have filled me with indignation.

18 Why is my pain perpetual
And my wound incurable,
Which refuses to be healed?
Will You surely be to me like an unreliable
stream,
As waters *that* fail?

19 Therefore thus says the LORD:
    "If you return,
    Then I will bring you back;
    You shall stand before Me;
    If you take out the precious from the vile,
    You shall be as My mouth.
    Let them return to you,
    But you must not return to them.
20 And I will make you to this people a fortified
        bronze wall;
    And they will fight against you,
    But they shall not prevail against you;
    For I *am* with you to save you
    And deliver you," says the LORD.
21 "I will deliver you from the hand of the
        wicked,
    And I will redeem you from the grip of the
        terrible."

Jer. 15:10–21

Among all the prophets, none has been more self-disclosing than Jeremiah, more willing to be transparent before God and the world. Unlike Moses and Samuel whose missions were successful, Jeremiah is singled out as part of a giant controversy, the focal point of a dispute between heaven and earth. It was ultimately settled, not in his lifetime but on a cross at Calvary.

In these prayers Jeremiah speaks not as a prophet but as a man staring into the abyss of his own despair. Others have stared over that same edge. Great achievers such as Goethe, Lincoln, Bismarck, Luther, Tolstoy, and Churchill have wrestled with depression.

"Woe is me, my mother, That you have borne me," Jeremiah confesses in his privacy with God (v. 10). The plea is to his mother, one of the last memories of human affection and approval. Few men in the sweep of human history carry such pathos yet stand so tall. More will be said about this form of depression in reference to 20:14 and following.

God's answer is recorded in verses 11–14. *"Can anyone break iron, The northern iron and the bronze?"* (v. 12). This has a double meaning. The force of the Babylonian power, sweeping in from the north, is now unbreakable. Yet Jeremiah, even in the midst of such black despair, is also unbreakable. God has made him "bronze walls against the whole land" (1:18). What we must remember when we face depression is that we are not our feelings and we are not to be overly impressed by their testimony, particularly when it is contrary to God's.

He goes on to acquaint Jeremiah with the events that will surround the defeat of Jerusalem. Foreign dignitaries will come to him for advice (v. 11). We will find the outworking of this in subsequent chapters. Remember that Jeremiah is not merely a provincial figure, a voice to the little kingdoms of Israel and Judah, but he is to be an international figure, "a prophet to the nations." This mission goes on in spite of his despair. Jeremiah rests his case in his next personal prayer; he places his discouragement and all it contains in the arms of God.

"O LORD, You know; Remember me and visit me, And take vengeance for me on my persecutors" (v. 15). In our own prayer life we need to lay hold of the prophet's three affirmations. This all-knowing God by His very nature remembers, visits, and avenges. He remembers even when I feel forgotten and forsaken. (Thank heavens I am not my feelings.) God has not forgotten that Jeremiah has suffered rebuke (v. 15), mockery (v. 17), and loneliness (v. 17). He still visits the prophet just as He did on the day of his call and commission. "The word of the LORD came to me" (1:4). This is the God who makes house calls. "Your word was to me the joy and rejoicing of my heart" (v. 16). Are we not today the visited planet whose time has been intersected by eternity because of God's visit to earth in the person of His son?

He takes vengeance for us on our persecutors (v. 15). Flashes of this weave through the life story of this prophet. People who come against him meet their demise. One such episode will be found in chapter 20 when Pashhur puts him in the stocks. Poor Pashhur.

The protective presence of God is only in the face of our obedience. The reassurance of it is found in verses 19–21. It should be a great encouragement to all preachers. "You must not compromise, Jeremiah," God is saying. "Let them return to you, But you must not return to them" (v. 19). If there is any turning to be done, the false prophets are to do it. Jeremiah is to stand his ground. It might be tempting to capitulate and end up preaching their message. Modern-day preachers give traditional language new meanings. They take the traditional concepts but do not mean the same things by them.

What Jeremiah is being told to do here is to never change the real meanings. When you do you are preaching worthlessness and you ultimately become worthless.

The encouragement to Jeremiah is to keep on uttering what is precious. Very often all you have to do to win is "to keep on keeping on." There is victory built into perseverance. I have heard it said that in order to win a fight all you've got to be is the last one standing.

"And I will make you to this people a fortified bronze wall; And . . . they shall not prevail against you" (v. 20). We communicators are impregnable and indomitable when we do not capitulate. God does not promise to visit and to take revenge when we play the coward. The champions that God has promised to be with are those that will hold fast the truth. Remember the words of Martin Luther: "Here I stand." And the history of the world was changed.

"I will deliver you from the hand of the wicked, And I will redeem you from the grip of the terrible" (v. 21). The servant of the Lord ultimately only has the Lord on whom to depend, not the wisdom and the subtlety of the world. When the system is wrong, and the leadership of the system is committed against you, and the Lord sends you to preach against the system, then you are going to have to allow Him to defend you. "It's you and me against the world," God says to that preacher. We need more leaders like that in the church today.

CHAPTER ELEVEN

Sermons Spoken and Sermons Lived

Jeremiah 16:1–17:27

FORBIDDEN TO MARRY, FORBIDDEN TO MOURN, FORBIDDEN TO MINGLE

16:1 The word of the LORD also came to me, saying,
2 "You shall not take a wife, nor shall you have sons or daughters in this place."
3 For thus says the LORD concerning the sons and daughters who are born in this place, and concerning their mothers who bore them and their fathers who begot them in this land:
4 "They shall die gruesome deaths; they shall not be lamented nor shall they be buried, *but* they shall be like refuse on the face of the earth. They shall be consumed by the sword and by famine, and their corpses shall be meat for the birds of heaven and for the beasts of the earth."
5 For thus says the LORD: "Do not enter the house of mourning, nor go to lament or bemoan them; for I have taken away My peace from this people," says the LORD, "lovingkindness and mercies.
6 "Both the great and the small shall die in this land. They shall not be buried; neither shall men lament for them, cut themselves, nor make themselves bald for them.
7 "Nor shall *men* break *bread* in the mourning for them, to comfort them for the dead; nor shall *men* give them the cup of consolation to drink for their father or their mother.

131

8 "Also you shall not go into the house of feasting
to sit with them, to eat and drink."

9 For thus says the LORD of hosts, the God of
Israel: "Behold, I will cause to cease from this place,
before your eyes and in your days, the voice of mirth
and the voice of gladness, the voice of the bridegroom and the voice of the bride.

10 "And it shall be, when you show this people all
these words, and they say to you, 'Why has the LORD
pronounced all this great disaster against us? Or
what is our iniquity? Or what is our sin that we have
committed against the LORD our God?'

11 "then you shall say to them, 'Because your fathers have forsaken Me,' says the LORD; 'they have
walked after other gods and have served them and
worshiped them, and have forsaken Me and not kept
My law.

12 'And you have done worse than your fathers,
for behold, each one follows the dictates of his own
evil heart, so that no one listens to Me.

13 'Therefore I will cast you out of this land into a
land that you do not know, neither you nor your fathers; and there you shall serve other gods day and
night, where I will not show you favor.'"

Jer. 16:1–13

A member of my congregation once made a very incisive statement about the difference between those communicating the pure
apostolic faith and those delivering a modern version with many of
the meanings changed. "The moderns," he said, "speak to the subject, but the gospel preacher speaks to the people."

Jeremiah speaks to the people. He bares his soul because he cares
about them. Others are just plying their trade, but they are not
reaching the people in any kind of penetrating manner. In the language of Jesus, those plying their trade are hirelings. Unlike the true
shepherd, they do not own the sheep. When they see a wolf coming,
they leave the sheep and flee. The wolf catches the sheep and scat-
ters them (John 10:12). The real shepherd pays the price. He lays
down his life for the sheep.

In 16:1–13 we find a further laying down of his life in order to
speak to the people. Already Jeremiah has said, "I sat alone because

of Your hand" (15:17). Now he is destined to become even more of a pariah. If the people will not regard what he says, then perhaps they will regard what he does. Again the prophet becomes a sermon by taking on three costly self-denials.

1. He is forbidden to marry (vv. 1–3). This is shocking in the light of the fact that God instituted marriage as one of the major provisions for fulfilling His command to all of creation: "Be fruitful and multiply; fill the earth and subdue it" (Gen. 1:28). One of the few maledictions pronounced by God in Scripture has to do with marriage. "*It is* not good that man should be alone" (Gen. 2:18). Up to this point God had surveyed everything that He had made and pronounced that "*it was* very good" (Gen. 1:31). Man being alone, however, was not good.

Yet Jeremiah was called to be alone in order to shock Jerusalem to her senses. There was to be no comfort of marriage for Jeremiah, no children's voices in his house. The children born to this city and the parents to whom they were born shall all die gruesome deaths (v. 4).

Not only does the prophet put his lifestyle on the line of his preaching, but he also describes the carnage in stirring language. A carnage of men, women, and children denied the dignity of burial. It is reminiscent of the language used by the Apostle Paul describing the stench of an open grave as it speaks of the universal depravity of man (Rom. 3:13).

2. He is forbidden to mourn (vv. 5–7). In order for God to illustrate "I have taken away my peace from this people," He takes away the prophet from their places of mourning. God forbids Jeremiah to participate in the cultural practices then customary in funeral observances. The self-inflicted wounds and the shaving of their heads were popular forms of grief, even though they were forbidden (Deut. 14:1). Jeremiah was to be conspicuous by his absence.

The bread in mourning and the cup of consolation (v. 7) were not to touch Jeremiah's lips. Does not this imagery invite us to ponder the Last Supper where the bread and the wine have the last word against sin and its destructive force?

3. He was forbidden to mingle (vv. 8–13). God had so long been in their midst as an unwelcome presence. Their hospitality toward Him had been so poor that now He would no longer come to their gatherings. He used the lifestyle of Jeremiah to illustrate that re-

fusal. *"You shall not go into the house of feasting to sit with them, to eat and drink"* (v. 8).

There will no longer be a festive ring to their gatherings. Imagine a wedding devoid of mirth and gladness, a bride without brightness, and a gloomy groom. The wedding in Cana of Galilee was graced with our Lord's presence and with His first miracle. Here, however, God is saying "don't grace any gathering with your presence, Jeremiah, because of their long-term forsaking." *"Your fathers have forsaken Me . . . And you have done worse than your fathers"* (vv. 11–12). "Since you have loved serving other Gods so much, go ahead and serve them, but not in this land will you serve, but in theirs, day and night, as much as you want. Go to it." This seems to be the essence of verses 10–13.

FACTS FROM THE FAR COUNTRY

16:14 "Therefore behold, the days are coming," says the LORD, "that it shall no more be said, 'The LORD lives who brought up the children of Israel from the land of Egypt,'

15 "but, 'The LORD lives who brought up the children of Israel from the land of the north and from all the lands where He had driven them.' For I will bring them back into their land which I gave to their fathers.

16 "Behold, I will send for many fishermen," says the LORD, "and they shall fish them; and afterward I will send for many hunters, and they shall hunt them from every mountain and every hill, and out of the holes of the rocks.

17 "For My eyes *are* on all their ways; they are not hidden from My face, nor is their iniquity hidden from My eyes.

18 "And first I will repay double for their iniquity and their sin, because they have defiled My land; they have filled My inheritance with the carcasses of their detestable and abominable idols."

19 O LORD, my strength and my fortress,
My refuge in the day of affliction,
The Gentiles shall come to You

From the ends of the earth and say,
"Surely our fathers have inherited lies,
Worthlessness and unprofitable *things.*"
20 Will a man make gods for himself,
Which *are* not gods?
21 "Therefore behold, I will this once cause them
to know,
I will cause them to know
My hand and My might;
And they shall know that My name *is* the LORD.
17:1 "The sin of Judah *is* written with a pen of iron;
With the point of a diamond *it is* engraved
On the tablet of their heart,
And on the horns of your altars,
2 While their children remember
Their altars and their wooden images
By the green trees on the high hills.
3 O My mountain in the field,
I will give as plunder your wealth, all your
treasures,
And your high places of sin within all your
borders.
4 And you, even yourself,
Shall let go of your heritage which I gave you;
And I will cause you to serve your enemies
In the land which you do not know;
For you have kindled a fire in My anger *which*
shall burn forever."
5 Thus says the LORD:
"Cursed *is* the man who trusts in man
And makes flesh his strength,
Whose heart departs from the LORD.
6 For he shall be like a shrub in the desert,
And shall not see when good comes,
But shall inhabit the parched places in the
wilderness,
In a salt land *which is* not inhabited.
7 "Blessed *is* the man who trusts in the LORD,
And whose hope is the LORD.
8 For he shall be like a tree planted by the
waters,
Which spreads out its roots by the river,

And will not fear when heat comes;
But its leaf will be green,
And will not be anxious in the year of
   drought,
Nor will cease from yielding fruit.
9 "The heart *is* deceitful above all *things,*
And desperately wicked;
Who can know it?
10 I, the LORD, search the heart,
I test the mind,
Even to give every man according to his ways,
According to the fruit of his doings.
11 "*As* a partridge that broods but does not hatch,
So *is* he who gets riches, but not by right;
It will leave him in the midst of his days,
And at his end he will be a fool."

Jer. 16:14–21; 17:1–11

Having told them He would give them over to the consequences of
their forsakings, God now discloses facts about the exile that they
soon face.

1. They will be cast out (16:16–18; 17:3, 4). The fact that Babylon
will overtake them and carry them away is not an accidental thing in
the life of Judah. God is Himself casting them out. Each person will
be hunted out of every hill and fished out of every hole in the rock
and sent into captivity (v. 16).

Nothing escapes God's scrutiny (16:17). They will be rounded up
and carried off. According to R. K. Harrison, they will be recom-
pensed in proportion to their offense. The word "double" of verse 18
would better be rendered "proportionate."[1]

2. They will be carried home (16:14, 15). After they have been
dealt with justly, in a witness to all the nations, they will then become participants in a second exodus. Once again, God's people will
be led from the land of their exile as they once were led from the
land of Egypt.

The most immediate fulfillment of this prophecy came during the
time of the Persian Empire when Nehemiah orchestrated the rebuild-
ing of the walls of Jerusalem around a people returning from their
place of exile.

3. They will attract the attention of other nations (vv. 19–20).

136

Jeremiah sees into the intention of God to bring the Gentiles into the kingdom by making the return of his people such a spectacle. In these verses, Jerusalem is representative of all wayward people, those who come to the Lord from the ends of the earth in confession and repentance. "You shall be witnesses to Me in Jerusalem, and in all Judea and Samaria, and to the end of the earth" (Acts 1:8).

The Gentiles that come into the kingdom will know the strength of the Lord and they will know His name. When Jesus said, "I am the good shepherd" (John 10:11), "I am the way, the truth, and the light" (John 14:6), "Before Abraham was, I am" (John 8:58), He was clearly declaring His name to be Yahweh, "I AM WHO I AM" (Exod. 3:14).

There are a variety of meditations in these verses. All of them pivot around the theme of the heart. Jeremiah uses the imagery of nature to depict two contrasting spiritual conditions.

1. The heart that departs from the Lord lives in the desert, the parched places in the wilderness (17:6). Other imagery is then employed to further describe this mind-set.

This heart is cursed (v. 5). People who make flesh their strength have denied the ultimate call of God upon their lives. The Apostle Paul says, "to be carnally minded *is* death, but to be spiritually minded *is* life and peace" (Rom. 8:6).

This heart is hard. Jeremiah refers to the "pen of iron" and the "diamond point" that are needed to etch into the hard heart of Judah and forever mark it with her sins (vv. 1–2). This condition ultimately meets with judgment. *"I will give as plunder your wealth, all your treasures"* (vv. 3–4).

"Th[is] heart is deceitful above all things, And desperately wicked" (v. 9). This line rings through Scripture as an expression of how incurably sick is the heart of unregenerate humankind.

This heart is unproductive. What a futile thing it is for a partridge to sit on eggs that never hatch (vv. 11–12). The unregenerate heart gets riches the wrong way. They are the kind that do not last and do not produce wisdom. The implication is that our professions, in the economy of God, are meant to be the arena in which we develop spiritually.

2. The heart that hopes in the Lord lives "like a tree planted by the waters." Instead of the parched, hard, unproductive condition of the mind-set of the flesh, this heart is borne from the fruitful condition of the mind-set on the spirit. It has distinctive characteristics.

137

This heart is blessed (v. 7). It spreads out its roots with the promise of becoming productive and of being refreshed. It does not fear (v. 8). Heat and drought are ever-present realities but need not be the undoing of the trusting heart. This is reminiscent of David's pastoral of Psalm 23: "He leads me beside the still waters. He restores my soul."

A GLORIOUS THRONE ON HIGH

17:12 A glorious high throne from the beginning
　　　 Is the place of our sanctuary.
　 13 O LORD, the hope of Israel,
　　　 All who forsake You shall be ashamed.
　　　 "Those who depart from Me
　　　 Shall be written in the earth,
　　　 Because they have forsaken the LORD,
　　　 The fountain of living waters."
　 14 Heal me, O LORD, and I shall be healed;
　　　 Save me, and I shall be saved,
　　　 For You *are* my praise.
　 15 Indeed they say to me,
　　　 "Where *is* the word of the LORD?
　　　 Let it come now!"
　 16 As for me, I have not hurried away from *being* a
　　　　 shepherd *who* follows You,
　　　 Nor have I desired the woeful day;
　　　 You know what came out of my lips;
　　　 It was right there before You.
　 17 Do not be a terror to me;
　　　 You *are* my hope in the day of doom.
　 18 Let them be ashamed who persecute me,
　　　 But do not let me be put to shame;
　　　 Let them be dismayed,
　　　 But do not let me be dismayed.
　　　 Bring on them the day of doom,
　　　 And destroy them with double destruction!
　　　　　　　　　　　　　　　　 Jer. 17:12–18

Jeremiah's sermons, both those that he has been speaking and those he has been living in his celibacy, are burdened more and more with a sense of impending doom. Descriptions of judgment and carnage are hurled upon a God-forsaken people who continue in their refusal to hear or to change.

The kind of data Jeremiah is being forced to deal with is sinking deep into his own consciousness and arousing all of his own instincts of self-preservation and of fear. Even when he is taking dictation from God, he continues to keep his own humanity, which is beginning to tremble in the face of this darkness and oncoming disaster.

What good news it is to notice that the fear and trembling do not have the last word. Breaking in upon them is this vision of the throne. Visions such as this one are beginning to flicker across the prophet's mind. They will rise to a crescendo in the next several chapters. Now they are gathering murmurs in a great orchestration toward a fuller awareness of the sovereignty of God.

Here the God of judgment is found also to be the God of refuge. His throne, the symbol of His reign and kingdom, is found to be a sanctuary. What might have mounted to panic has now been turned to peace for Jeremiah, who claims his safety in the purposes of God. Like the psalmist, the prophet can proclaim, "I will say of the LORD, 'He is my refuge and my fortress; My God, in Him I will trust'" (Ps. 91:2).

From out of the shelter of that sanctuary, he cries, "Heal me, O LORD, and I shall be healed; Save me, and I shall be saved, For You are my praise" (v. 14). He has both feet firmly planted in his obedience and his sense of God's faithfulness. Holding his head high, he affirms the vindication of God against his enemies.

He refers to a downward spiral of negatives that he firmly refuses to fall prey to, even though circumstances and popular opinion were converging to bring him down. The spiral of terror, shame, dismay, and doom will not strike him as their target but instead will strike his enemies (vv. 17–18). Jeremiah will be the last one standing because the throne of God has been his sanctuary. Boldly he calls down these judgments upon the heads of his enemies, inviting God to be the sovereign vindicator.

REMEMBER THE SABBATH DAY

17:19 Thus the LORD said to me: "Go and stand in the gate of the children of the people, by which the kings of Judah come in and by which they go out, and in all the gates of Jerusalem;

20 "and say to them, 'Hear the word of the LORD, you kings of Judah, and all Judah, and all the inhabitants of Jerusalem, who enter by these gates.

21 'Thus says the LORD: "Take heed to yourselves, and bear no burden on the Sabbath day, nor bring *it* in by the gates of Jerusalem;

22 "nor carry a burden out of your houses on the Sabbath day, nor do any work, but hallow the Sabbath day, as I commanded your fathers.

23 "But they did not obey nor incline their ear, but made their neck stiff, that they might not hear nor receive instruction.

24 "And it shall be, if you heed Me carefully," says the LORD, "to bring no burden through the gates of this city on the Sabbath day, but hallow the Sabbath day, to do no work in it,

25 "then shall enter the gates of this city kings and princes sitting on the throne of David, riding in chariots and on horses, they and their princes, accompanied by the men of Judah and the inhabitants of Jerusalem; and this city shall remain forever.

26 "And they shall come from the cities of Judah and from the places around Jerusalem, from the land of Benjamin and from the lowland, from the mountains and from the South, bringing burnt offerings and sacrifices, grain offerings and incense, bringing sacrifices of praise to the house of the LORD.

27 "But if you will not heed Me to hallow the Sabbath day, such as not carrying a burden when entering the gates of Jerusalem on the Sabbath day, then I will kindle a fire in its gates, and it shall devour the palaces of Jerusalem, and it shall not be quenched."'"

Jer. 17:19–27

This is a sermon spoken in a very powerful setting. Because Jerusalem was a walled city, all commerce in and out went through her gates. The gates therefore stood as great architectural symbols of the comings and goings of this city. Whatever passed through them came to characterize the city itself. In order to reinforce his message,

Jeremiah was speaking to the people using those gates for an unlawful Sabbath-day commerce.

There he would be again, standing against the prevailing culture of the day. Needless to say, he was not winning friends nor was he influencing people. They had a chance to make an extra buck by working on the seventh day. Jeremiah was a cosmic kill-joy as far as they were concerned.

Greed was rearing its ugly head as it had in the wilderness days when manna was rained down from heaven. Each person was to gather his daily supply of one omer. On the sixth day, he was to gather twice as much in order that he might rest on the Sabbath (Exod. 16:22). When the Sabbath came, instead of finding them resting, it found them out in search of more bread—but they found none (Exod. 16:27).

God cried out to them through Moses: "The Lord has given you the Sabbath" (Exod. 16:29). Making the same appeal to another unbelieving generation, Jesus said, "The Sabbath was made for man, and not man for the Sabbath" (Mark 2:27). In Nehemiah we find yet another picture of God's generosity and their perversity. They were treading their wine presses, bringing in their sheaves, loading their donkeys with grapes and figs, getting and spending at a furious rate on the Sabbath day. Nehemiah commanded that the gates be shut. He courageously legislated a stop to all the commerce. Merchants called his bluff by remaining outside the gates thinking that for sure he would relent, he would "go with the flow" of popular opinion. Nehemiah waited out those merchants who finally relented and left, knowing he meant business.

Jeremiah too means business. Standing there, buffeted by the harangues of angry greed, he raises his voice above the din of their commerce long enough to say some of the most important words the Lord's people could ever hear. He said them to deaf ears and stiff necks. Nonetheless, he said them.

If they would observe the Sabbath day, they would discover that God is not meaning to deprive them. He is meaning to give them more. He is meaning to show them an extravagant kingdom. *"Kings and princes sitting on the throne of David, riding in chariots and on horses"* would come parading through those gates left open for the Lord, for just one day of the week flung wide, exclusively for Him and not for petty commerce (v. 25).

If Jeremiah were to preach to our culture, he might be standing by a sports arena or a shopping mall. The message would be the same. We are the losers when we use up Sunday for mere recreation. We are not really re-created. We need to ask the question, has it blessed us spiritually? We have turned our Sunday into something other than what God intended. We go about our commerce in ways that do nothing to enhance our relationship with Him. In the process we violate our own humanity. Our days in the workplace are to be productive and personally fulfilling in the economy of God. On our Sabbath day we are to rest in those good works and rest in the God who made us for those works. He it is who has re-created us into the new humanity that we represent as believers. That act of re-creation is dramatized in the events of the next chapter.

NOTE

1. R. K. Harrison, *Jeremiah and Lamentations,* The Tyndale Old Testament Commentary (Downers Grove, Ill.: Inter-Varsity Press, 1973), 105.

CHAPTER TWELVE

The Sovereign Potter

Jeremiah 18:1–20:18

THE VESSEL HE MAKES

18:1 The word which came to Jeremiah from the LORD, saying:

2 "Arise and go down to the potter's house, and there I will cause you to hear My words."

3 Then I went down to the potter's house, and there he was, making something at the wheel.

4 And the vessel that he made of clay was marred in the hand of the potter; so he made it again into another vessel, as it seemed good to the potter to make.

5 Then the word of the LORD came to me, saying:

6 "O house of Israel, can I not do with you as this potter?" says the LORD. "Look, as the clay *is* in the potter's hand, so *are* you in My hand, O house of Israel!

7 "The instant I speak concerning a nation and concerning a kingdom, to pluck up, to pull down, and to destroy *it*,

8 "if that nation against whom I have spoken turns from its evil, I will relent of the disaster that I thought to bring upon it.

9 "And the instant I speak concerning a nation and concerning a kingdom, to build and to plant *it*,

10 "if it does evil in My sight so that it does not obey My voice, then I will relent concerning the good with which I said I would benefit it.

11 "Now therefore, speak to the men of Judah and to the inhabitants of Jerusalem, saying, 'Thus says the LORD: "Behold, I am fashioning a disaster and

143

devising a plan against you. Return now every one
from his evil way, and make your ways and your doings good."'"

Jer. 18:1–11

The content of these three chapters forms around the central
theme of the sovereignty of God. This theme permeates the life and
ministry of Jeremiah—"I formed you . . . I knew you . . . I sanctified you . . . I ordained you" (1:5). Jeremiah's understanding of this
relationship with God is irrevocable, and yet his is not a static understanding; it is subject to deeper and complex development.

Just as the word of God had come to him in the beginning when
Jeremiah was called and commissioned, so now it comes to the
prophet anew. Jeremiah responds as always to the divine initiative,
and this practice makes for his better understanding of the sovereignty of God. These next few verses offer brilliant revelations of
this doctrine, brighter than Jeremiah has yet discovered. A common
place becomes the scene of an uncommon revelation. God does more
than expound it; He takes Jeremiah to the potter's house where He
demonstrates it.

*"Arise and go down to the potter's house, and there I will cause you
to hear My words"* (v. 2). For Jeremiah, the "knowing" was in the
"going." Revelation follows obedience. He had to get up and go, and
so must all of us who wish for our spiritual lives to mature. We
cannot sit and stagnate. We must be obedient to the truth God gives.
Why should He give truth that will go unused? As a sovereign potter, God has six things to say about the vessel He has made.

1. God's work has a purpose. *"There he was, making something at
the wheel"* (v. 3). G. Campbell Morgan observed, "the potter was not
fooling with the clay, he was not playing with it, he was not amusing
himself! It was work, it was serious; there was purpose in it. I do not
know how that appeals to you, but as God is my witness, it has
problems, and pressure, with its oft-times agonies; God is not playing with me."[1] Just as the potter has a serious investment in his
product, so does God have a purpose in creating me. So also does
He have a purpose in creating nations.

2. Creation is a good thing gone bad. *"And the vessel that he made
of clay was marred in the hand of the potter"* (v. 4). Notice it does not
say that it was marred by the hand of the potter. It allows for the

agency of human responsibility. Applying this to national causes, Judah was marred. On the individual level, we have all sinned and fallen short of the glory of God. Can that marred clay possibly help itself? Does not its shape and its destiny from beginning to end rest in the hands of the potter?

3. The good thing gone bad has been re-created. *"So he made it again into another vessel"* (v. 4). In that split second, standing there in the potter's shop, with the smell of wet clay and the sound of it spinning in the potter's hands, Jeremiah tasted the powers of the age to come. He saw ahead into the sovereign intention of God to make out of the marred an entirely new humanity. It was moments like these, with their flashing vision, that kept him going.

4. The new creation was God's idea. *"As it seemed good to the potter to make"* (v. 4). First, in the act of redeeming a lost humanity, God pleased Himself. He satisfied His own vision. Notice that God did not call a townhall meeting and take a poll as to what this irretrievably marred clay thought should be done. Thank heaven! (and I mean that literally), for we could never have imagined the gleaming symmetry of a new creation like God could.

5. The potter has prerogative. *"'O house of Israel, can I not do with you as this potter?' says the LORD. 'Look, as the clay is in the potter's hand, so are you in My hand, O house of Israel!'"* (v. 6). Not only was the new vessel His vision and His execution, it becomes His possession to do with as He pleases.

Jeremiah was not the first to use imagery of the potter in reference to the sovereignty of God. The psalmist exclaimed, "But our God *is* in heaven; He does whatever He pleases" (Ps. 115:3). Isaiah too penetrated this reality: "Woe to him who strives with his Maker! . . . Shall the clay say to him who forms it, 'What are you making?'" (Isa. 45:9).

6. The vessel has responsibility. *"Now therefore, speak to the men of Judah . . . 'Behold, I am fashioning a disaster and devising a plan against you. Return now every one from his evil way, and make your ways and your doings good'"* (v. 11). Herein we encounter the interplay between the sovereignty of God and the responsibility of humankind, an issue that has been controversial in the Christian church throughout its history. The one claim we can make, however, from this text and the whole sweep of biblical revelation is that the God who has redeemed and recreated us holds us accountable for

our response to that singular act of grace and brilliance. *"If that nation against whom I have spoken turns from its evil, I will relent of the disaster that I thought to bring upon it"* (v. 8).

Hard Lessons for Hard Clay

18:12 And they said, "That is hopeless! So we will walk according to our own plans, and we will every one obey the dictates of his evil heart."
13 Therefore thus says the LORD:
"Ask now among the Gentiles,
Who has heard such things?
The virgin of Israel has done a very horrible thing.
14 Will *a man* leave the snow-water of Lebanon,
Which comes from the rock of the field?
Will the cold flowing waters be forsaken for strange waters?
15 "Because My people have forgotten Me,
They have burned incense to worthless idols.
And they have caused themselves to stumble in their ways,
From the ancient paths,
To walk in pathways and not on a highway,
16 To make their land desolate *and* a perpetual hissing;
Everyone who passes by it will be astonished
And shake his head.
17 I will scatter them as with an east wind before the enemy;
I will show them the back and not the face
In the day of their calamity."
Jer. 18:12–17

The sovereign potter desires to fashion Judah into a useful vessel, but she is no longer malleable. Instead she is brittle and set in her resistance to His purposes for her. Judah does answer His plea, but her answer is no. Jeremiah must have felt a distinct agony in receiving the hopeful vision in the potter's house, rushing to deliver its message of repentance, and then seeing only the faces of his hearers set in anger. *"That is hopeless!"* they say. *"So we will walk according to our own plans, and we will every one obey the dictates of his evil heart"* (v. 12). Self-avowed rebels, shaking their fists in the face of a sovereign God, are in for a lesson.

The lesson takes much the same form and content as one previously taught in 2:9–12. They both begin with a solemn "therefore." God is mustering all the powerful forces of His logic. One of them is right, and one of them is wrong. God goes on to point out two glaring inconsistencies just as He did in the earlier lesson. They are acting against common sense and against common practice. Even the pagan nations that have no revelation of God are not this bad. *"Ask now among the Gentiles, Who has heard such things?"* (v. 13). Anybody can see that Judah is a scandal. *"Everyone who passes by it will be astonished And shake his head"* (v. 16). Judah's stupidity is obvious to everyone but herself.

What a humiliation it is for Judah to lose her credibility. The body language of her public is so well described, hissing and wagging heads instead of the glory and honor for which she was designed. Judah has also violated common practice. In this passage the reference is to the *"snow-water of Lebanon"* (v. 14). No one in his right mind would turn his back upon such a sure and refreshing water source. *"Will the cold flowing waters be forsaken for strange waters?"* (v. 14). The answer is yes. *"They have caused themselves to stumble in their ways, . . . To walk in pathways and not on a highway"* (v. 15). Judah has violated her own humanity, her own logic, even her own destiny.

CHARACTER ASSASSINATION

18:18 Then they said, "Come and let us devise plans against Jeremiah; for the law shall not perish from the priest, nor counsel from the wise, nor the word from the prophet. Come and let us attack him with the tongue, and let us not give heed to any of his words."

19 Give heed to me, O LORD,
    And listen to the voice of those who contend
       with me!

20 Shall evil be repaid for good?
    For they have dug a pit for my life.

> Remember that I stood before You
> To speak good for them,
> To turn away Your wrath from them.
> 21 Therefore deliver up their children to the
>   famine,
> And pour out their *blood*
> By the force of the sword;
> Let their wives *become* widows
> And bereaved of their children.
> Let their men be put to death,
> Their young men *be* slain
> By the sword in battle.
> 22 Let a cry be heard from their houses,
> When You bring a troop suddenly upon them;
> For they have dug a pit to take me,
> And hidden snares for my feet.
> 23 Yet, LORD, You know all their counsel
> Which is against me, to slay *me*.
> Provide no atonement for their iniquity,
> Nor blot out their sin from Your sight;
> But let them be overthrown before You.
> Deal *thus* with them
> In the time of Your anger.
>
> *Jer. 18:18–23*

Is it any wonder that another conspiracy formed against Jeremiah? The last one was formed around the shattered relationship between the prophet and his hometown of Anathoth. This time he has a somewhat different set of adversaries. Priests, wise men, and prophets are all referred to in verse 18. They combine the weight of their professions and their intellects in a scheme to slander Jeremiah and find him guilty of some heresy. This dynamic suggests the one Jesus found Himself in toward the end of His ministry when the scribes and Pharisees were seeking to trap Him and find something by which to accuse Him.

In the light of this conspiracy, the prophet prays as he had done during the first conspiracy. Then he had raised the question "why do the wicked prosper?" (12:1). Now, however, he offers the bitterest prayer for vengeance found in the whole book. Those from whom he had expected the most help and understanding were the very ones who turned on him.

Any communicator of God's truth, living on the front line, attempting to change the spirit of the age, is forced to deal with high doses of rejection. We keep on going, but the hurt sinks down deep into the human spirit. When it begins to fester, we are surprised at the power of these negative emotions, mostly repressed and thought to be under control. When they erupt, they seem to take on a life of their own. Jeremiah does the best he can do with them. He submits them to the final tribunal rather than lashing out in an ugly skirmish with the offenders.

With great pathos he proclaims his role as an intercessor for the very people who *"have dug a pit for my life. . . . I stood before You To speak good for them"* (v. 20). What a thankless task it was feeling like now! The vengeful language of Scripture is hardest to understand and presents difficulties for the communicator, but there are times when it is indeed the language of our own wounded humanity. There are times when our anger shouts out to God, "Don't forgive them! Don't blot out their sin!" Jeremiah's candor before God is healthy, perhaps purgative for the prophet's spirit that must press on, that must release the load. *"Deal thus with them In the time of Your anger"* (v. 23).

THE VESSEL HE BREAKS

19:1 Thus says the LORD: "Go and get a potter's earthen flask, and *take* some of the elders of the people and some of the elders of the priests.

2 "And go out to the Valley of the Son of Hinnom, which *is* by the entry of the Potsherd Gate; and proclaim there the words that I will tell you,

3 "and say, 'Hear the word of the LORD, O kings of Judah and inhabitants of Jerusalem. Thus says the LORD of hosts, the God of Israel: "Behold, I will bring such a catastrophe on this place, that whoever hears of it, his ears will tingle.

4 "Because they have forsaken Me and made this an alien place, because they have burned incense in it to other gods whom neither they, their fathers, nor the kings of Judah have known, and have filled this place with the blood of the innocents

5 "(they have also built the high places of Baal, to burn their sons with fire *for* burnt offerings to Baal, which I did not command or speak, nor did it come into My mind),

6 "therefore behold, the days are coming," says the LORD, "that this place shall no more be called Tophet or the Valley of the Son of Hinnom, but the Valley of Slaughter.

7 "And I will make void the counsel of Judah and Jerusalem in this place, and I will cause them to fall by the sword before their enemies and by the hands of those who seek their lives; their corpses I will give as meat for the birds of the heaven and for the beasts of the earth.

8 "I will make this city desolate and a hissing; everyone who passes by it will be astonished and hiss because of all its plagues.

9 "And I will cause them to eat the flesh of their sons and the flesh of their daughters, and everyone shall eat the flesh of his friend in the siege and in the desperation with which their enemies and those who seek their lives shall drive them to despair."

10 "Then you shall break the flask in the sight of the men who go with you,

11 "and say to them, 'Thus says the LORD of hosts: "Even so I will break this people and this city, as *one* breaks a potter's vessel, which cannot be made whole again; and they shall bury *them* in Tophet till *there is* no place to bury.

12 "Thus I will do to this place," says the LORD, "and to its inhabitants, and make this city like Tophet.

13 "And the houses of Jerusalem and the houses of the kings of Judah shall be defiled like the place of Tophet, because of all the houses on whose roofs they have burned incense to all the host of heaven, and poured out drink offerings to other gods."'"

14 Then Jeremiah came from Tophet, where the LORD had sent him to prophesy; and he stood in the court of the Lord's house and said to all the people,

15 "Thus says the LORD of hosts, the God of Israel: 'Behold, I will bring on this city and on all her towns all the doom that I have pronounced against

it, because they have stiffened their necks that they
might not hear My words.'"

A lesser man would have kept a low profile, knowing that he is
being scrutinized for heresy. Jeremiah instead took the lesson from
the potter's house and went forward to another painful public demonstration. In privacy with his sovereign potter, he learned that a
new vessel would be made but not until the resistant, brittle one was
broken. On the strength of this, he went forward to Tophet.

Recently he had stood at the Benjamin gate to preach against their
Sabbath-day commerce. Now he stood at the Potsherd Gate, having
invited his audience of secular and religious dignitaries to follow
him out there. Never let us accuse God of failing to dramatize His
word. He infused Jeremiah with a strong sense of drama, with an
understanding that atmosphere impacts the message. The setting for
the sermon is important.

This gate was probably the place where broken pottery was de-
posited. Perhaps he stood near the rubble. It led down into the valley of Ben-Hinnom, south of Jerusalem, which was used for burning
garbage and cremating the bodies of criminals. Need we spell out
the implications of location to message? I doubt that these dignitaries
particularly appreciated following the prophet to this setting, and
surely they were not going to appreciate what he was about to say.
They watched him there, silhouetted against the gate, holding in one
hand a costly earthen flask. All eyes upon him narrowed in hostility.
News of this moment will travel to one named Pashhur. He is the
one who will harden the mounting conspiracy into the first instance
of physical harm to Jeremiah. All ears wait to catch him in some
treasonous statement. They tingle with tension, waiting for a reason
to pounce.

*"Behold, I will bring such a catastrophe on this place, that whoever
hears of it, his ears will tingle"* (v. 3). This statement was like pouring
gasoline onto a burning fire. Jeremiah, however, does not stop there
and run for cover. Instead he lists the grievances of which they are
guilty. They have burned incense upon the altars they have built to
Baal. Worse than that, they have burned their own children as sacrifices to this false deity. Perhaps someone standing there would recall the dying screams of his own child, sacrificed in such fire. The

very ground to which Jeremiah had brought them was stained with the blood of innocents. They had been brought to the scene of their crime, caught red-handed in their guilt.

We too are spilling the blood of innocents, every day in abortion facilities across the country. The bomb that was dropped on Hiroshima killed seventy-five thousand people. We are destroying that many unborn children every seventeen days. We need to heed the message preached that day, to watch the hand of Jeremiah and what it is about to do with the costly flask it holds.

Lifting it high for all to see, he smashed it against the Potsherd Gate. His voice rises above the hollow burst of sound. *"Thus says the LORD of hosts: 'Even so I will break this people and this city, as one breaks a potter's vessel, which cannot be made whole again; and they shall bury them in Tophet till there is no place to bury'"* (v. 11). They shall receive the burying place of criminals. How fitting! Yet how offensive to their self-righteousness!

Notice that Jeremiah spares no detail but offends the physical senses with imagery of death and destruction. Indeed their ears were tingling and their hearts were raging against him in the Valley of Slaughter. He moves on from that valley and preaches that same sermon in a yet more dangerous setting. Standing now in the temple courts, he clashed head-on with their priestly supposition that their temple was inviolable.

The indictment against them is that they move from the valley of slaughtering their children up into the precincts of their temple, expecting some kind of immunity from and benediction upon their disgrace. As dramatic as the demonstration was, it was equally as costly for the prophet when it came to the attention of Pashhur.

POOR PASHHUR

20:1 Now Pashhur the son of Immer, the priest who *was* also chief governor in the house of the LORD, heard that Jeremiah prophesied these things.

2 Then Pashhur struck Jeremiah the prophet, and put him in the stocks that *were* in the high gate of Benjamin, which *was* by the house of the LORD.

3 And it happened on the next day that Pashhur brought Jeremiah out of the stocks. Then Jeremiah said

to him, "The LORD has not called your name Pashhur, but Magor-Missabib.

4 "For thus says the LORD: 'Behold, I will make you a terror to yourself and to all your friends; and they shall fall by the sword of their enemies, and your eyes shall see *it*. I will give all Judah into the hand of the king of Babylon, and he shall carry them captive to Babylon and slay them with the sword.

5 'Moreover I will deliver all the wealth of this city, all its produce, and all its precious things; all the treasures of the kings of Judah I will give into the hand of their enemies, who will plunder them, seize them, and carry them to Babylon.

6 'And you, Pashhur, and all who dwell in your house, shall go into captivity. You shall go to Babylon, and there you shall die, and be buried there, you and all your friends, to whom you have prophesied lies.'"

Jer. 20:1–6

Pashhur ben Immer was the chief officer of the temple at the close of the monarchy and was apparently in office during the reign of Jehoiakim. Pashhur was therefore the immediate subordinate of the high priest, in charge of his police force.

"*Then Pashhur struck Jeremiah the prophet, and put him in the stocks that were in the high gate of Benjamin, which was by the house of the* LORD" (v. 2). Why do I say poor Pashhur? Shouldn't I be saying poor Jeremiah? After all it is his body that was wracked in the pain of forty lashes. It is his dignity that is being accused of common criminality in those rough wooden stocks. Pashhur has made Jeremiah the symbol of how costly it is to go against the prevailing system. In the economy of God, however, the tables turn. Jeremiah makes Pashhur the symbol of the universal terror soon to grip Judah. The name Pashhur, otherwise obscure, acquires a place in history along with that of Judas Iscariot. Each man enjoyed a moment's success before paying the ultimate and eternal price.

It was almost as though Pashhur realized the consequences of his action against Jeremiah, as though he felt God's anger burning. "*And it happened on the next day that Pashhur brought Jeremiah out of the stocks*" (v. 3). The action was too little and far too late. The lashes and the stocks were designed to make Jeremiah weaker, but the idea backfired. The prophet was energized with righteous indignation. He had the last word. *"The LORD has not called your name Pashhur, but Magor-Missabib ['Fear on Every Side'],"* (v. 3), which is descriptive of the fear soon to overtake Judah. Wherever he goes, Pashhur will be a walking symbol of the advancing catastrophe, forced to live in the context of constant panic without comfort.

"You shall go to Babylon, and there you shall die, and be buried there, you and all your friends, to whom you have prophesied lies" (v. 6). Because of the mention of Babylon, we can assume that the meaning of the battle of Carchemish (605 B.C.), which unseated Egyptian and Assyrian power, was clear to the occupants of the Fertile Crescent— they were witnesses to a new arrival on the world arena, spectators to the emerging force of a new empire.

CONFESSIONS OF A PROPHET TO A SOVEREIGN GOD

20:7   O LORD, You induced me, and I was persuaded;
           You are stronger than I, and have prevailed.
           I am in derision daily;
           Everyone mocks me.
   8   For when I spoke, I cried out;
           I shouted, "Violence and plunder!"
           Because the word of the LORD was made to me
           A reproach and a derision daily.
   9   Then I said, "I will not make mention of Him,
           Nor speak anymore in His name."
           But *His word* was in my heart like a burning
               fire
           Shut up in my bones;
           I was weary of holding *it* back,
           And I could not.
  10   For I heard many mocking:
           "Fear on every side!"
           "Report," *they say,* "and we will report it!"
           All my acquaintances watched for my
               stumbling, *saying,*
           "Perhaps he can be induced;

> Then we will prevail against him,
> And we will take our revenge on him."

11 But the LORD *is* with me as a mighty, awesome
>   One.
> Therefore my persecutors will stumble, and
>   will not prevail.
> They will be greatly ashamed, for they will
>   not prosper.
> *Their* everlasting confusion will never be
>   forgotten.

12 But, O LORD of hosts,
> You who test the righteous,
> *And* see the mind and heart,
> Let me see Your vengeance on them;
> For I have pleaded my cause before You.

13 Sing to the LORD! Praise the LORD!
> For He has delivered the life of the poor
> From the hand of evildoers.

14 Cursed *be* the day in which I was born!
> Let the day not be blessed in which my mother
>   bore me!

15 Let the man *be* cursed
> Who brought news to my father, saying,
> "A male child has been born to you!"
> Making him very glad.

16 And let that man be like the cities
> Which the LORD overthrew, and did not relent,
> Let him hear the cry in the morning
> And the shouting at noon,

17 Because he did not kill me from the womb,
> That my mother might have been my grave,
> And her womb always enlarged *with me.*

18 Why did I come forth from the womb to see
>   labor and sorrow,
> That my days should be consumed with
>   shame?

Jer. 20:7–18

More than any of the other prophets, Jeremiah is most willing to disclose himself, to open his memoirs and reveal the naked emotions that lie there. He can tell God anything and does. It is an outpouring that rings with authenticity but never violates sovereignty.

To paraphrase verses 7 and 8, we hear the prophet say, "I am in this mess because of You, God, and because You are stronger than I am." If Jeremiah had gone the way of the prevailing culture, he would have followed his own urgings. If he had, he might never have had to suffer the mockery and derision that public ministry brought upon him—but then he would not ever have known the sovereign potter so personally.

We hear him say that he tried not to preach, but that was worse (v. 9). It would have been much easier not to go to the Benjamin Gate and preach against their Sabbath disobedience. It would certainly have been easier not to have preached at the Potsherd Gate. Obedience is hard. In the long run, however, disobedience is harder! If Jeremiah had not delivered the word of the Sovereign, it would be left burning in his bones.

"For I heard many mocking: . . . All my acquaintances watched for my stumbling" (v. 10). He rehearses the sounds of the conspiracies against him. They are hard to shake from his mind and keep getting in the way of his communion with the Lord. The niggling thoughts do not have the last word. About his persecutors he says, *"Let me see Your vengeance on them; For I have pleaded my cause before You"* (v. 12).

We can hear the prophet sigh, "Praise the Lord, yet I wish I'd never been born." What an odd mingling of the height and depth reflected in verses 13–18. But they resonate with the sound and emotion of our humanity. Has there ever been a more perfect expression of human inconsistency? Does your own prayer life seem riddled with contradictions? Then join the crowd of the saints who have gone before us. We are in good company. These are the unabridged confessions of one of the best of them. The bottom line is that he is not seeking happiness, but rather he is seeking obedience. Jeremiah could be so candid because he knew God to be so sovereign.

NOTE

1. G. Campbell Morgan, *Studies in the Prophecy of Jeremiah* (Old Tappan, N.J.: Fleming H. Revell, 1969), 116.

CHAPTER THIRTEEN

Leaders Who Fleece and Leaders Who Feed

Jeremiah 21:1–23:40

OUT OF THE STOCKS AND INTO THE PALACE

21:1 The word which came to Jeremiah from the LORD when King Zedekiah sent to him Pashhur the son of Melchiah, and Zephaniah the son of Maaseiah, the priest, saying,

2 "Please inquire of the LORD for us, for Nebuchadnezzar king of Babylon makes war against us. Perhaps the LORD will deal with us according to all His wonderful works, that *the king* may go away from us."

3 Then Jeremiah said to them, "Thus you shall say to Zedekiah,

4 'Thus says the LORD God of Israel: "Behold, I will turn back the weapons of war that *are* in your hands, with which you fight against the king of Babylon and the Chaldeans who besiege you outside the walls; and I will assemble them in the midst of this city.

5 "I Myself will fight against you with an outstretched hand and with a strong arm, even in anger and fury and great wrath.

6 "I will strike the inhabitants of this city, both man and beast; they shall die of a great pestilence.

7 "And afterward," says the LORD, "I will deliver Zedekiah king of Judah, his servants and the people, and such as are left in this city from the pestilence and the sword and the famine, into the hand of Nebuchadnezzar king of Babylon, into the hand of their enemies,

157

and into the hand of those who seek their life; and he shall strike them with the edge of the sword. He shall not spare them, or have pity or mercy."'

8 "Now you shall say to this people, 'Thus says the LORD: "Behold, I set before you the way of life and the way of death.

9 "He who remains in this city shall die by the sword, by famine, and by pestilence; but he who goes out and defects to the Chaldeans who besiege you, he shall live, and his life shall be as a prize to him.

10 "For I have set My face against this city for adversity and not for good," says the LORD. "It shall be given into the hand of the king of Babylon, and he shall burn it with fire."'

Jer. 21:1–10

The last chapter closed with poignant expressions of frustration poured out to a sovereign God to whom Jeremiah remained fiercely loyal. Pashhur, the policeman, tried to silence the voice of prophecy by throwing Jeremiah into the stocks. Little did he know, he had taken a tiger by the tail, and now that tiger was loose again and stronger than ever. A new Pashhur came upon the scene, this one seeking the voice of God on behalf of the king, Zedekiah. God always turns the tables on rebellion.

Jeremiah emerged from the attempted scandal not only with more credibility but with more courage and readiness to go. Zedekiah, now on the throne, was the last monarch to reign over Jerusalem in her dying years. The mention of Babylon four times in the preceding chapter is indicative of the impending doom. Babylon had broken the grip that Assyria had held for centuries. The great capital of Nineveh had fallen in 612 B.C., and by 605 B.C. the fate of the Egyptians had been sealed by the battle of Carchemish. Momentum was now solidly in the hands of Nebuchadnezzar.

Only Jeremiah chose to face this reality. Jerusalem chose to shake her fist in the face of this monarch and to join neighboring nations in posturing for independence from him. She naively thought that Egypt would rise to her rescue. Zedekiah was breaking covenant with Nebuchadnezzar when he endorsed this national move, and he was breaking council with Jeremiah who all along had urged that Jerusalem make peace with Babylon and quit placing her hopes in Egypt.

Babylon, the mighty power, was now encamped around the walls of Jerusalem and ready to swallow her alive. Zedekiah only then sought the council of the man he had scorned. A frightened king turned to a faithful prophet through his emissary Pashhur.

The personal interaction between prophet and king reveals who was stronger and who was weaker. It was not as the world would think. Josephus, the historian, described the vacillating king: "Now as to Zedekiah himself, while he heard the prophet speak, he believed him, and agreed to everything as true, and supposed it was for his advantage; but then his friends perverted him, and dissuaded him from what the prophet advised and obliged him to do what they pleased."[1] A nation would burn because of this tragic flaw, and Jeremiah must watch it happen.

Poised now on the brink of this disaster, Zedekiah said, *"Perhaps the LORD will deal with us according to all His wonderful works"* (v. 2). If he really thought the Lord's work was so wonderful, why had he crossed Him at every turn? This false piety did nothing but insult Jeremiah's intelligence. The fearsome Nebuchadnezzar was encamped around Jerusalem, burning with anger at Zedekiah who had broken covenant with him. (The Babylonian monarch had called Zedekiah to the throne of Judah and had received a promise of loyalty.)

Now Zedekiah expressed to the prophet the naive hope that Nebuchadnezzar "will go away." Here was a man, trembling in his boots, about to reap the consequences of his many sinful judgment calls, standing on nothing but false piety and naive hope. The last chapter of a tyrant's life is indeed a tragic one. Zedekiah strained to hear comfortable words when none could be pronounced upon the style of leadership he had exhibited. He may have guessed that Jeremiah's answer would not be good. He could not have guessed how bad it really would be.

A fearsome enemy was outside the walls. Zedekiah was no match for Nebuchadnezzar, but a far more fearsome enemy was inside the walls. *"I Myself will fight against you with an outstretched hand and with a strong arm, even in anger and fury and great wrath"* (v. 5). A hostile Babylon was the least of his worries. Zedekiah has fallen into the hands of an angry God. Jeremiah forecasted a famine and a pestilence that would attack the city from within (vv. 6–7). Imagine being weak from hunger, wracked with disease, and at the same time having to fight a war. Josephus's description of the fall of Jerusalem confirmed this prophecy.

Furthermore, as the prophet went on, Zedekiah would not be allowed to die of the pestilence. Nor would he have the nobility of dying in battle. Instead he would be captured by Nebuchadnezzar and put to death as a prisoner of war; he who had all his reign been a prisoner of pride (v. 7). Again Josephus's historical account supports this detail, now uttered prophetically.

Jeremiah summarized for Zedekiah his present options. *"Behold, I set before you the way of life and the way of death. He who remains in this city shall die by the sword, by famine, and by pestilence; but he who goes out and defects to the Chaldeans who besiege you, he shall live, and his life shall be as a prize to him"* (vv. 8–9). The king was left with two unsavory possibilities—death or defection.

It is amazing how sin narrows our options in life. Instead of bringing the liberty it advertises, it brings deeper and deeper bondage. Now Zedekiah was being told, "Pick your poison." Much as he would like, there was no third option. Nebuchadnezzar was not going "to go away." Neither was God. The tragic ruins of Jerusalem tell of the choice Zedekiah made by not believing Jeremiah's council. History tells how costly it was for the prophet to deliver that unheeded council.

From now on, Jeremiah would be persecuted as a turncoat for espousing surrender to Babylon. Let no one accuse prophecy of being impractical. Jeremiah was no pie-in-the-sky theorist. He stuck with the events until they were reduced to the issue of death or surrender. Being the lover of life that he was as a man of God, he and God would rather have seen Judah march out of her walls and fall into the hands of Nebuchadnezzar than into the hands of death's finality. Jeremiah knew he would pay another price for this rock-bed practicality, but he did not know when or what it would be. Suffering at the hands of conspiracy just goes with the business of being *contra mundum.* Would he ever get used to it? Would it ever quit hurting?

A City for Fame or a City for Shame?

21:11 "And concerning the house of the king of Judah,
    say, 'Hear the word of the LORD,

12 'O house of David! Thus says the LORD:
"Execute judgment in the morning;
And deliver *him who is* plundered
Out of the hand of the oppressor,
Lest My fury go forth like fire
And burn so that no one can quench *it*,
Because of the evil of your doings.

13 "Behold, I *am* against you, O inhabitant of the
valley,
And rock of the plain," says the LORD,
"Who say, 'Who shall come down against us?
Or who shall enter our dwellings?'

14 But I will punish you according to the fruit of
your doings," says the LORD;
"I will kindle a fire in its forest,
And it shall devour all things around it."'"

22:1 Thus says the LORD: "Go down to the house of
the king of Judah, and there speak this word,

2 "and say, 'Hear the word of the LORD, O king
of Judah, you who sit on the throne of David, you
and your servants and your people who enter these
gates!

3 'Thus says the LORD: "Execute judgment and
righteousness, and deliver the plundered out of the
hand of the oppressor. Do no wrong and do no violence to the stranger, the fatherless, or the widow,
nor shed innocent blood in this place.

4 "For if you indeed do this thing, then shall enter
the gates of this house, riding on horses and in chariots, accompanied by servants and people, kings who
sit on the throne of David.

5 "But if you will not hear these words, I swear by
Myself," says the LORD, "that this house shall become
a desolation."'"

6 For thus says the LORD to the house of the king
of Judah:
"You *are* Gilead to Me,
The head of Lebanon;
Yet I surely will make you a wilderness,
Cities *which* are not inhabited.

7 I will prepare destroyers against you,
Everyone with his weapons;

> They shall cut down your choice cedars
> And cast *them* into the fire.
>
> 8 "And many nations will pass by this city; and
> everyone will say to his neighbor, 'Why has the LORD
> done so to this great city?'
>
> 9 "Then they will answer, 'Because they have for-
> saken the covenant of the LORD their God, and wor-
> shiped other gods and served them.'"
>
> *Jer. 21:11–22:9*

Two oracles are contained in these verses. They were spoken at
different times but say the same thing, one of those things that bears
repeating. Since they were issued to the kings who followed Josiah,
they came before the episode between Jeremiah and Zedekiah that
was just recounted. In essence, God said through Jeremiah that oppression and injustice would have to cease. If Judah did not deal
with the dreadful cases of social injustice presently in her midst,
then she would have to deal with the dreadful case of an angry God
(21:11; 22:3).

Should she face the issues and correct them, an extravagant award
would be waiting at her gates. *"Then shall enter the gates of this house,
riding on horses and in chariots, accompanied by servants and people,
kings who sit on the throne of David"* (v. 4). Having been born and
raised in England, I have an acquired taste for pageantry. Here it is
in its highest form. God wanted Jerusalem to be famous for righteousness.

She must make the choice. Some people would rather die than
change. So also would some cities. God promised to destroy Jerusalem if she refused to change. *"And many nations will pass by this
city; and everyone will say to his neighbor, 'Why has the LORD done so to
this great city?' Then they will answer, 'Because they have forsaken the
covenant of the LORD their God, and worshiped other gods and served
them'"* (vv. 8–9).

We must ask ourselves a question. Are we trying to make our city
famous for God? My church is nestled in a suburb of Pittsburgh. I am
glad to say that many men and women in this city care to answer "yes"
to that question. In 1955, a clergyman by the name of Sam Shoemaker
formed the Pittsburgh Experiment. It was an organization designed to
bring spiritual renaissance into the business community of this city. It

remains still faithful to its early vision to make Pittsburgh, in the words of its founder, "a city under God, as famous for God as it is for steel." Yours can be a city for fame or a city for shame, depending on the strength of righteous leadership. The two oracles affirm the benefits of good leadership and the scandal of oppressive leadership.

The Kings Who Think They Are God

22:10 Weep not for the dead, nor bemoan him;
  Weep bitterly for him who goes away,
  For he shall return no more,
  Nor see his native country.

11 For thus says the LORD concerning Shallum the son of Josiah, king of Judah, who reigned instead of Josiah his father, who went from this place: "He shall not return here anymore,

12 "but he shall die in the place where they have led him captive, and shall see this land no more.

13 "Woe to him who builds his house by unrighteousness
  And his chambers by injustice,
  Who uses his neighbor's service without wages
  And gives him nothing for his work,

14 Who says, 'I will build myself a wide house
   with spacious chambers,
  And cut out windows for it,
  Paneling *it* with cedar
  And painting *it* with vermilion.'

15 "Shall you reign because you enclose *yourself* in
   cedar?
  Did not your father eat and drink,
  And do justice and righteousness?
  Then *it was* well with him.

16 He judged the cause of the poor and needy;
  Then *it was* well.
  Was not this knowing Me?" says the LORD,

17 "Yet your eyes and your heart *are* for nothing
   but your covetousness,
  For shedding innocent blood,
  And practicing oppression and violence."

18 Therefore thus says the LORD concerning Jehoiakim the son of Josiah, king of Judah:

"They shall not lament for him,
Saying, 'Alas, my brother!' or 'Alas, my sister!'
They shall not lament for him,
Saying, 'Alas, master!' or 'Alas, his glory!'

19 He shall be buried with the burial of a donkey,
Dragged and cast out beyond the gates of
Jerusalem.

20 "Go up to Lebanon, and cry out,
And lift up your voice in Bashan;
Cry from Abarim,
For all your lovers are destroyed.

21 I spoke to you in your prosperity,
But you said, 'I will not hear.'
This *has been* your manner from your youth,
That you did not obey My voice.

22 The wind shall eat up all your rulers,
And your lovers shall go into captivity;
Surely then you will be ashamed and
humiliated
For all your wickedness.

23 O inhabitant of Lebanon,
Making your nest in the cedars,
How gracious will you be when pangs come
upon you,
Like the pain of a woman in labor?

24 "*As* I live," says the LORD, "though Coniah the son of Jehoiakim, king of Judah, were the signet on My right hand, yet I would pluck you off;

25 "and I will give you into the hand of those who seek your life, and into the hand *of those* whose face you fear—the hand of Nebuchadnezzar king of Babylon and the hand of the Chaldeans.

26 "So I will cast you out, and your mother who bore you, into another country where you were not born; and there you shall die.

27 "But to the land to which they desire to return, there they shall not return.

28 "Is this man Coniah a despised, broken idol—
A vessel in which *is* no pleasure?

Why are they cast out, he and his descendants,
And cast into a land which they do not know?
29 O earth, earth, earth,
Hear the word of the LORD!
30 Thus says the LORD:
'Write this man down as childless,
A man *who* shall not prosper in his days;
For none of his descendants shall prosper,
Sitting on the throne of David,
And ruling anymore in Judah.'"

Jer. 22:10-30

A parade of wicked kings followed Josiah, three are his sons and one his grandson. Although Zedekiah was the last, he was the first to be mentioned in these chapters concerning leadership. Perhaps the chronology was shifted in order to capture the irony of the two Pashhurs. Now Jeremiah made specific predictions to the three sons of Josiah who followed their father's righteous reign with their own tyrannies.

1. *To Jehoahaz, otherwise called Shallum* (vv. 10–12)

This king "did evil in the sight of the LORD" (2 Kings 23:32). In her fit of mourning Josiah, Jerusalem placed one of his younger son's upon the throne. It was not a move of God's choosing. Jehoahaz had reigned only three months and ten days when Pharaoh Neco of Egypt called him to come to the city of Hamath. He rode right into a trap. Neco then carried this twenty-three-year-old king off to Egypt, where he died without the comfort of his homeland.

In prophesying this king's fate, Jeremiah instructed the people not to weep over the death of Josiah but rather to weep over the life of Jehoahaz. When a righteous man dies, he is embraced by the kingdom he has served. The Apostle Paul could say, "there is laid up for me the crown of righteousness" (2 Tim. 4:8). Josiah had fought the good fight and was now reaping its rewards. That is a matter for rejoicing not for weeping.

The real matter for weeping was the scarcity of righteous leadership. Jehoahaz reigned for only three months. *"He shall return no more"* (v. 10; cf. v. 11). The words are twice given in a mournful strain that reflects Jeremiah's own love for his homeland and the shame of dying in exile. To die in dignity at home was the highest honor to be conferred upon a life well lived.

Josiah sustained a mortal wound at the battle of Megiddo but requested that his chariot carry him home, that his last breath might be drawn in the country of his love, surrounded by the people he had served for thirty of his thirty-eight years. How can we not be reminded of the gospel message? It calls us to quit the service of this world, to not be conformed to its Egypts and its Babylons. It calls us to be found serving the kingdom of God so that when death comes, it will carry us home to the Lord. Jeremiah's prophetic consciousness reached for this comforting truth, hence his preoccupation not only with the way these kings lived but also with the way they died.

2. *To Jehoiakim* (vv. 13–23)

This older brother of Jehoahaz was more pleasing to the likes of Neco, who placed him on the throne of Jerusalem which was to suffer his reign for eleven years. There was also a clash between his spirit and Jeremiah's during that time as well. The prophet watched his beloved homeland grow progressively weaker and visionless. No wonder his prophecy to this king was so impassioned!

"Woe to him who builds his house by unrighteousness And his chambers by injustice, . . . Who says, 'I will build myself a wide house with spacious chambers, And cut out windows for it, Paneling it with cedar and painting it with vermilion'" (vv. 13–14). At the most critical time in his nation's history, Jehoiakim built a palatial monument to his ego. Jeremiah cited the intense orange-red color that stood out against the landscape as a metaphor of tyranny and oppression. No expense was spared on the palace. Yet no wages were paid to the laborers whom Jeremiah watched struggle under the burning sun. He was not impressed by the palace. It bore no likeness to the kingdom he served. It was nothing but an ego trip for a wicked king, sucking the life out of his people.

Memories of Josiah rushed back to the prophet. He struggled with the contrasts. All of that king's needs had been met without the lavish fanfare. *"Did not your father eat and drink, And do justice and righteousness? Then it was well with him. He judged the cause of the poor and needy; Then it was well,"* (vv. 15–16). There was something soothing in the repetition of "Then it was well" as though the prophet was pronouncing a benediction that struck against the spacious palace, making it a sinister symbol of corruption and greed.

Jeremiah, however, did not stop with this exposure. He went on to predict the style of Jehoiakim's death and burial. What irony! He who had enclosed himself in cedar (v. 15) would now receive *"the burial of a donkey"* (v. 19). When will we learn that God has the last word?

"Dragged and cast out beyond the gates of Jerusalem" (v. 19), Jehoiakim would receive no accolades from his public. *"They shall not lament for him, . . . They shall not lament for him"* (v. 18). Again the repetitious literary style strikes a mournful note over the king who had a chance to serve the same kingdom that his father Josiah had served. *"I spoke to you in your prosperity, But you said, 'I will not hear.' This has been your manner from your youth"* (v. 21). He never chose the noble life. He died in infamy.

3. *To Jehoiachin* (vv. 24–30)

Jeremiah uses the shortened form of his name—Coniah—in addressing this prophecy to the son of Jehoiakim who most likely died early during the Babylonian siege of Jerusalem. A teenager on the throne of a toppling nation was hardly cause for comfort. The city was so relieved to be rid of the tyrannies of Jehoiakim that she placed her hopes in his eighteen-year-old son who had reigned only three months before he was carried away captive to Babylon. The false prophets encouraged this hope with pleasant predictions of his early return. Whereas Jeremiah affirmed that not only would Jehoiakim not return any time soon, he would not return at all. Zedekiah was given the reigns of government even though many of Jerusalem's citizens continued to look to Jehoiachin as the king. They continued to chase moonbeams of their own wishful thinking while Jeremiah continued to "tell it like it was."

With each address Jeremiah made to the sons (and grandson) of Josiah, there was a preoccupation with the style and circumstances of each one's death until they became a collection of follies that ended in infamy. He began this final pronouncement with striking words. *"As I live, says the LORD"* (v. 24), the infinite, speaking to the finite, pronounced its final judgment.

"Though Coniah . . . were the signet on My right hand, yet I would pluck you off" (v. 24). There was no king now who could forestall the coming doom of Jerusalem. *"So I will cast you out, and your mother who bore you, into another country where you were not born; and there you shall die"* (v. 26). This prediction was literally fulfilled.

A young man so ready to be deified by his public would become instead *"a despised, broken idol—A vessel in which is no pleasure"* (v. 28). He would die under two indignities, or so they were considered by that culture. He would be childless and live in a land of exile.

THE KING WHO IS GOD

23:1 "Woe to the shepherds who destroy and scatter the sheep of My pasture!" says the LORD.

2 Therefore thus says the LORD God of Israel against the shepherds who feed My people: "You have scattered My flock, driven them away, and not attended to them. Behold, I will attend to you for the evil of your doings," says the LORD.

3 "But I will gather the remnant of My flock out of all countries where I have driven them, and bring them back to their folds; and they shall be fruitful and increase.

4 "I will set up shepherds over them who will feed them; and they shall fear no more, nor be dismayed, nor shall they be lacking," says the LORD.

5 "Behold, *the* days are coming," says the LORD,
"That I will raise to David a Branch of
    righteousness;
A King shall reign and prosper,
And execute judgment and righteousness in
    the earth.

6 In His days Judah will be saved,
And Israel will dwell safely;
Now this *is* His name by which He will be
    called:
THE LORD OUR RIGHTEOUSNESS.

7 "Therefore, behold, *the* days are coming," says the LORD, "that they shall no longer say, 'As the LORD lives who brought up the children of Israel from the land of Egypt,'

8 but, 'As the LORD lives who brought up and led the descendants of the house of Israel from the north country and from all the countries where I had driven them.' And they shall dwell in their own land."

Jer. 23:1–8

The sight of this king came to Jeremiah at the time he most needed it. The first wave of the attack had hit Jerusalem. Zedekiah was king, watching the nation disintegrate before his eyes. The line of kings before him had left this legacy of hopelessness. How could a man of such tender spirit as Jeremiah sustain so much bad news? We need to remember this when darkness falls around our own lives, when burn-out and spiritual fatigue threaten to obscure all hope. Times such as these provide God His finest hour and the prophet his finest vision.

Jeremiah looked through this long, dark tunnel into the light of a new age. There are two facets to this prophetic vision.

1. *"I will gather the remnant of My flock out of all [the] countries where I have driven them, and bring them back to their folds; and they shall be fruitful and increase"* (v. 3). At this time, only the first exiles had been carried off, but soon the entire city would be carried off to Babylon. Against this darkness came the prediction of repatriation, a prediction that was fulfilled in 446 B.C. when Nehemiah was authorized by the Persian monarch to return to Jerusalem and rebuild her broken walls. This return from exile is again referred to in 23:7, 8 when Jeremiah makes the staggering claim that the enterprise would rival the fame of the Exodus from Egypt under Moses, an event buried in the heart of every Jew.

2. *"I will raise to David a Branch of righteousness, A King shall reign and prosper, And execute judgment and righteousness in the earth"* (v. 5). This second facet of light shines past the repatriation under Nehemiah and into the gospel age. It shines on the coming of the real King. For all his unrequited love of country, for all his thankless labor, Jeremiah was given the refreshment of seeing God fulfill His own intention, of becoming the King of His own people. The reality of this breaks through all prophetic literature. As a matter of fact, all sixty-six books of Scripture are united by a common theme—the kingdom of God.

John the Baptist broke the four hundred years of silence that lay between the Old and New Testaments. He renewed the prophetic voice with the words, "Repent, for the kingdom of heaven is at hand!" (Matt. 3:2). What Jeremiah saw prophetically, John's age saw actually. They could strike up the music then, "O come all ye faithful, joyful and triumphant, O come ye, O come ye to Bethlehem; come and behold him, born the King of angels . . ."

"'I will set up shepherds over them who will feed them; and they shall fear no more, nor be dismayed, nor shall they be lacking,' says the Lord" (v. 4). After his courageous prophecies to the wicked shepherd kings and to their infamy, Jeremiah could now rejoice in the shepherds referred to here.

When Jesus, the Good Shepherd, laid down His life for the sheep, He left a legacy of bold leadership in the apostles and disciples. The carnal kings had fleeced the flock. These shepherds would feed the flock.

When he uttered these words, it was almost as though Jeremiah stood in the gospel age, side by side with those apostles who had the privilege of witnessing Jesus' ascension into heaven. Squinting up into the brilliance of the cloud that received Him out of their sight, they were present at the supreme political event of the universe—the coronation of Christ as King. When He sat down at the right hand of the Father, He was righteousness for a race of fallen humanity. Jeremiah's voice rings out, proclaiming His name to the age in which he spoke: Yahweh Tsidkenu, the Lord our Righteousness! On this and only this vision could the prophet rest his heart and receive consolation concerning the wreckage around him. It was not the final word.

A PROPHET LOOKS AT HIS PROFESSION

23:9 My heart within me is broken
Because of the prophets;
All my bones shake.
I am like a drunken man,
And like a man whom wine has overcome,
Because of the LORD,
And because of His holy words.
10 For the land is full of adulterers;
For because of a curse the land mourns.
The pleasant places of the wilderness are dried
up.
Their course of life is evil,
And their might *is* not right.
11 "For both prophet and priest are profane;
Yes, in My house I have found their
wickedness," says the LORD.

170

12 "Therefore their way shall be to them
　　Like slippery *ways;*
　　In the darkness they shall be driven on
　　And fall in them;
　　For I will bring disaster on them,
　　The year of their punishment," says the LORD.

13 "And I have seen folly in the prophets of
　　　　Samaria:
　　They prophesied by Baal
　　And caused My people Israel to err.

14 Also I have seen a horrible thing in the
　　　　prophets of Jerusalem:
　　They commit adultery and walk in lies;
　　They also strengthen the hands of evildoers,
　　So that no one turns back from his
　　　　wickedness.
　　All of them are like Sodom to Me,
　　And her inhabitants like Gomorrah.

15 "Therefore thus says the LORD of hosts
　　　　concerning the prophets:
　　'Behold, I will feed them with wormwood,
　　And make them drink the water of gall;
　　For from the prophets of Jerusalem
　　Profaneness has gone out into all the land.'"

16 Thus says the LORD of hosts:
　　"Do not listen to the words of the prophets
　　　　who prophesy to you.
　　They make you worthless;
　　They speak a vision of their own heart,
　　Not from the mouth of the LORD.

17 They continually say to those who despise Me,
　　'The LORD has said, "You shall have peace"';
　　And to everyone who walks according to the
　　　　dictates of his own heart,
　　'No evil shall come upon you.'"

18 For who has stood in the counsel of the LORD,
　　And has perceived and heard His word?
　　Who has marked His word and heard *it?*

19 Behold, a whirlwind of the LORD has gone
　　　　forth in fury—
　　A violent whirlwind!
　　It will fall violently on the head of the wicked.

20 The anger of the LORD will not turn back
    Until He has executed and performed the
      thoughts of His heart.
    In the latter days you will understand it
      perfectly.
21 "I have not sent these prophets, yet they ran.
    I have not spoken to them, yet they
      prophesied.
22 But if they had stood in My counsel,
    And had caused My people to hear My words,
    Then they would have turned them from their
      evil way
    And from the evil of their doings.
23 *Am* I a God near at hand," says the LORD,
    "And not a God afar off?
24 Can anyone hide himself in secret places,
    So I shall not see him?" says the LORD;
    "Do I not fill heaven and earth?" says the
      LORD.
25 "I have heard what the prophets have said who prophesy lies in My name, saying, 'I have dreamed, I have dreamed!'
26 "How long will *this* be in the heart of the prophets who prophesy lies? Indeed *they are* prophets of the deceit of their own heart,
27 "who try to make My people forget My name by their dreams which everyone tells his neighbor, as their fathers forgot My name for Baal.
28 "The prophet who has a dream, let him tell a
    dream;
    And he who has My word, let him speak My
      word faithfully.
    What *is* the chaff to the wheat?" says the LORD.
29 "*Is* not My word like a fire?" says the LORD,
    "And like a hammer *that* breaks the rock in
      pieces?
30 "Therefore behold, I *am* against the prophets," says the LORD, "who steal My words every one from his neighbor.
31 "Behold, I *am* against the prophets," says the LORD, "who use their tongues and say, 'He says.'
32 "Behold, I *am* against those who prophesy false

dreams," says the LORD, "and tell them, and cause My people to err by their lies and by their recklessness. Yet I did not send them or command them; therefore they shall not profit this people at all," says the LORD.

33 "So when these people or the prophet or the priest ask you, saying, 'What is the oracle of the LORD?' you shall then say to them, 'What oracle?' I will even forsake you," says the LORD.

34 "And *as for* the prophet and the priest and the people who say, 'The oracle of the LORD!' I will even punish that man and his house.

35 "Thus every one of you shall say to his neighbor, and every one to his brother, 'What has the LORD answered?' and, 'What has the LORD spoken?'

36 "And the oracle of the LORD you shall mention no more. For every man's word will be his oracle, for you have perverted the words of the living God, the LORD of hosts, our God.

37 "Thus you shall say to the prophet, 'What has the LORD answered you?' and, 'What has the LORD spoken?'

38 "But since you say, 'The oracle of the LORD!' therefore thus says the LORD: 'Because you say this word, "The oracle of the LORD!" and I have sent to you, saying, "Do not say, 'The oracle of the LORD!'"

39 'therefore behold, I, even I, will utterly forget you and forsake you, and the city that I gave you and your fathers, and *will cast you* out of My presence.

40 'And I will bring an everlasting reproach upon you, and a perpetual shame, which shall not be forgotten.'"

Jer. 23:9-40

To this point, Jeremiah had focused on the leadership of kings. Now he turned his attention to the quality of leadership coming from his own profession. Standing at the apex of his own career, he took moral inventory of the prophetic vocation as a whole. What he saw was shocking to his system. *"My heart within me is broken . . . All my bones shake. I am like a drunken man"* (v. 9). Suppose a member of today's ecclesiastical world wrote an article entitled "A

Clergyman Looks at the Ministry," and then the article began with this same opening sentence. How would it be received?

Prophecy, like the leadership of kings, was supposed to result in the furthering of righteousness. Theirs, however, produced depravity. *"The land is full of adulterers; . . . both prophet and priest are profane"* (vv. 10–11). The Word of the Lord was a holy, transcendent thing to Jeremiah. Yet the professional prophets had no such reverence. As a result, their ways had become "slippery" and would ultimately lead to disaster (v. 12).

As was typical of Jeremiah, he used a comparison between the Northern and Southern Kingdoms. Jerusalem's prophets have become more sophisticated in their deceit. They were adulterers because they professed loyalty to God but practiced loyalty to other deities. The end result of their professional ethics furthered the cause of evil rather than diminishing it (v. 14). Instead of being part of the solution, they had become part of the problem. They had actually caused an epidemic. *"Profaneness has gone out into all the land"* (v. 15). There was now no reverence, no sense of the sacred. It was into this societal crudeness that Jeremiah must take his holy warning. *"They make you worthless"* (v. 16). Let this be a caution to us. Who and what we listen to is important. We will become what we listen to. Remember that the next time you choose what movie you want to see, what magazine you choose to read, or what you let your children watch on television. This principle runs through the messages of Jeremiah and bears repeating. It was behind the forsaking of the fountain for cisterns that held no water (2:13).

The listening audience of these professional prophets was now identified as *"those who despise"* the Lord (v. 17). They all hated God but loved to use His name. They sanctified their lies with the preface, *"The LORD has said"* (v. 17). Then they went on to deliver a false hope: *"'You shall have peace'; . . . 'No evil shall come upon you'"* (v. 17). Instead of offering a moral challenge to a generation in danger, they anesthetized that generation with lies. Meanwhile a mighty storm was brewing against them, a *"whirlwind of the Lord"* (v. 19).

These professionals plied their trade with vigor. They ran with it like important messengers. Yet they were never sent (v. 21). Had they carried the right message with their swift feet, they would have changed the spirit of their age. They would have converted the society and saved the city (v. 22).

Such thoughts might have sent a lesser man into a state of despair. How could he possibly run cross-current to this wave of apostasy that threatened to swallow up his authentic prophetic voice? Then came that familiar voice: *"Am I a God near at hand . . . And not a God afar off?"* (v. 23). None of these false members of the profession could hide from the scrutiny of a God who fills heaven and earth (v. 24).

God was as near in this moment as in the day he touched the mouth of the country boy. Now Jeremiah stood like a bronze wall, the only man in the universe so strong, yet so alone. To paraphrase the word of God to Jeremiah, "Let the prophets tell their little made-up dreams. What is that to you and Me Jeremiah?" *"What is the chaff to the wheat? . . . Is not My word like a fire?"* (vv. 28–29) that will ultimately burn the chaff.

Three times God assured Jeremiah. *"Behold, I am against the prophets"* (vv. 30, 31, 32). God stepped in and took full responsibility for them. *"So when these people . . . ask you, saying, 'What is the oracle of the Lord?' you shall then say to them, 'What oracle?'"* (v. 33). No longer was Jeremiah to waste his energy preaching to them when they only wanted to plagiarize his words to their own ends and mount a conspiracy against him.

"And the oracle of the Lord you shall mention no more" (v. 36). They would end up manufacturing their own oracles, writing fictions for their own listening public, telling their own dreams. *"For every man's word will be his oracle"* (v. 36). It was no longer to be Jeremiah's concern. What a liberating word to the frustrated prophet, so embarrassed for the state of his profession and so angered by its abuse of him.

NOTE

1. Flavius Josephus, *Antiquities of the Jews,* 3 vols. (Grand Rapids, Mich.: Baker Book House, 1984), 3:68.

CHAPTER FOURTEEN

A Prophet to the Nations

Jeremiah 24:1–25:38

WHICH KIND OF BASKET CASE ARE YOU?

24:1 The LORD showed me, and there were two baskets of figs set before the temple of the LORD, after Nebuchadnezzar king of Babylon had carried away captive Jeconiah the son of Jehoiakim, king of Judah, and the princes of Judah with the craftsmen and smiths, from Jerusalem, and had brought them to Babylon.

2 One basket *had* very good figs, like the figs *that are* first ripe; and the other basket *had* very bad figs which could not be eaten, they were so bad.

3 Then the LORD said to me, "What do you see, Jeremiah?" And I said, "Figs, the good figs, very good; and the bad, very bad, which cannot be eaten, they are so bad."

4 Again the word of the LORD came to me, saying,

5 "Thus says the LORD, the God of Israel: 'Like these good figs, so will I acknowledge those who are carried away captive from Judah, whom I have sent out of this place for *their own* good, into the land of the Chaldeans.

6 'For I will set My eyes on them for good, and I will bring them back to this land; I will build them and not pull *them* down, and I will plant them and not pluck *them* up.

7 'Then I will give them a heart to know Me, that I *am* the LORD; and they shall be My people, and I will be their God, for they shall return to Me with their whole heart.

8 'And as the bad figs which cannot be eaten, they are so bad'—surely thus says the LORD—'so will I give up Zedekiah the king of Judah, his princes, the residue of Jerusalem who remain in this land, and those who dwell in the land of Egypt.

9 'I will deliver them to trouble into all the kingdoms of the earth, for *their* harm, *to be* a reproach and a byword, a taunt and a curse, in all places where I shall drive them.

10 'And I will send the sword, the famine, and the pestilence among them, till they are consumed from the land that I gave to them and their fathers.'"

Jer. 24:1–10

Let the professional prophets continue to ply their trade. Let them go ahead and tell their dreams. Jeremiah was renewed in his own prophetic mission to send the world the authentic word from the Lord and let Him care for its consequences. With this burst of comfort and encouragement, Jeremiah published a bold statement about two baskets of figs that became a metaphor of two kinds of people and their response to suffering.

Because his name meant "God hurls," so he has been sent against the world to reach it in time with a message of repentance. Because his name meant "God exalts," so he has been lifted above the conspiracies and threats upon this mission. If God brought him out of Pashhur's stocks and into Zedekiah's palace, what more might He do?

Chapters 24 and 25 elaborate Jeremiah's career development. A new and bold prophecy swiftly elevated him out of the merely domestic arena and into the international, according to the intention of the God who said, "I have this day set you over the nations" (1:10). A radical political crisis gave rise to this message, which is equally radical and bears a shocking truth about the economy of God.

In this title, I have used our own jargon to paraphrase imagery from the ancient Near East. Jeremiah saw two baskets of figs. One basket held *very good* figs and the other *very bad* (v. 3). These were two different results from the same event. Everyone would be sent into Babylonian exile. Some would profit from that suffering and would become well seasoned by it. Others would not profit from it and would become bitter and rotten from the very same event.

177

This event took place during the reign of Jeconiah, the eighteen-year-old successor to Jehoiakim's tyrannies. This young man's only claim to fame, or should we say infamy, was to be ruler of Judah during an early deportation of Jerusalem's elite to Babylon. Along with them went treasures from the temple and treasures from the palace. Supposing we were to wake up one morning to discover that all of our public officials, our medical personnel, our social servants, our law enforcement officials were simply gone. Shock waves would run through the media—what media there would be left to cover the story.

Emphasis is not on the shock of the event itself but on what it tells us about our response to suffering and God's use of that response. Those who were carried away captive in this first wave of exile typify one kind of response to suffering. It has three encouraging characteristics.

1. A willingness to believe that good can come out of it. *"For I will set My eyes on them for good, and I will bring them back to this land; I will build them and not pull them down, and I will plant them and not pluck them up"* (v. 6).

2. A teachable heart. *"I will give them a heart to know Me, that I am the LORD"* (v. 7). In spite of the disaster being suffered, something redemptive is happening inside the sufferer.

3. A higher form of obedience. *"And they shall be My people, and I will be their God, for they shall return to Me with their whole heart"* (v. 7). Instead of the suffering separating them from God, it serves to bring them yet closer to Him than they had been in their leisure and in their comfort. This is the attitude of heart that God does not give up on like He does with the bad figs. *"So will I give up Zedekiah the king of Judah, his princes, the residue of Jerusalem who remain in this land"* (v. 8).

Being given up on might not seem so bad until it was further explained. *"I will deliver them to trouble, . . . to be a reproach . . . in all places where I shall drive them"* (v. 9). Jeremiah suggested that those earlier sufferers, carried off in the first wave of exile, had the potential for redemption because they were not set in their hardness. They were carried off before they were able to become too entrenched against the purposes of God. Yielding early to suffering gave them the threefold potential for redemption. Those who remained tight jawed and stiff necked under the next reign, which was the reign of Zedekiah, lost their teachability and the redemptive dimension to suffering.

Notice also that there were only two baskets. There was not a third basket filled with middle-of-the-road figs. Suffering is common to our humanity. It is bound to come our way. We are all "basket cases" in this respect. Do we want to let it mature us and produce in us something usable and good? Or do we want to stiffen against it, and become bitter and utterly useless?

How Are Good Prophets like Pagan Kings?

25:1 The word that came to Jeremiah concerning all the people of Judah, in the fourth year of Jehoiakim the son of Josiah, king of Judah (which *was* the first year of Nebuchadnezzar king of Babylon),

2 which Jeremiah the prophet spoke to all the people of Judah and to all the inhabitants of Jerusalem, saying:

3 "From the thirteenth year of Josiah the son of Amon, king of Judah, even to this day, this *is* the twenty-third year in which the word of the LORD has come to me; and I have spoken to you, rising early and speaking, but you have not listened.

4 "And the LORD has sent to you all His servants the prophets, rising early and sending *them*, but you have not listened nor inclined your ear to hear.

5 "They said, 'Repent now everyone of his evil way and his evil doings, and dwell in the land that the LORD has given to you and your fathers forever and ever.

6 'Do not go after other gods to serve them and worship them, and do not provoke Me to anger with the works of your hands; and I will not harm you.'

7 "Yet you have not listened to Me," says the LORD, "that you might provoke Me to anger with the works of your hands to your own hurt.

8 "Therefore thus says the LORD of hosts: 'Because you have not heard My words,

9 'behold, I will send and take all the families of the north,' says the LORD, 'and Nebuchadnezzar the

king of Babylon, My servant, and will bring them
against this land, against its inhabitants, and against
these nations all around, and will utterly destroy
them, and make them an astonishment, a hissing,
and perpetual desolations.

10 'Moreover I will take from them the voice of
mirth and the voice of gladness, the voice of the bridegroom and the voice of the bride, the sound of the
millstones and the light of the lamp.

11 'And this whole land shall be a desolation *and*
an astonishment, and these nations shall serve the
king of Babylon seventy years.

12 'Then it will come to pass, when seventy years
are completed, *that* I will punish the king of Babylon
and that nation, the land of the Chaldeans, for their
iniquity,' says the LORD; 'and I will make it a perpetual desolation.

13 'So I will bring on that land all My words which
I have pronounced against it, all that is written in this
book, which Jeremiah has prophesied concerning all
the nations.

14 '(For many nations and great kings shall be
served by them also; and I will repay them according
to their deeds and according to the works of their own
hands.)'"

Jer. 25:1–14

Jeremiah had sounded a warning about the crisis of deportation.
This present text was spoken seven years before the crisis, when
Jehoiakim had reigned four years. The person who was to master-
mind the deportation and the final siege of Jerusalem came to the
throne of Babylon. It was that event that inspired this shocking
prophecy.

Jeremiah looked to Nebuchadnezzar, remembered the vision of the
boiling cauldron spilling its violence from the north, and knew that
his beloved Jerusalem had not long to live. Egypt would not help her
because she had lost her bid for power at the battle of Carchemish.

The new political configuration and its danger to Jerusalem went
unheeded by Jehoiakim who was more interested in his vermilion
palace than in his needy people. It did not go unheeded by Jeremiah
who saw the mighty Nebuchadnezzar in a way that no one else did.

A good prophet looked at a pagan king and saw a striking similarity. Each, in his own way, was a servant of God.

1. The prophet as a servant of God is profiled in verses 3–8. For twenty-three years Jeremiah had stayed faithful to his vocation. *"I have spoken to you, rising early and speaking"* (v. 3; cf. v. 4). This reference to the patience and style that characterized the ministry of all the prophets was repeated twice. Jeremiah also issued a brief form of the prophetic message of repentance and new life (vv. 5, 6). We are not at all surprised that prophets should be called servants of God. The imagery is consistent with their serving, long-suffering nature.

2. The pagan king is also called a servant of God in verse 9. The same judgment that the prophets were told to utter, the pagan king was told to execute. In so doing that godless monarch was acting as an instrument of God. Secular history tells us how Nebuchadnezzar came against Jerusalem. Prophetic history gives us another dimension to that event. The verbs are unequivocal. God "took" all the families of the north and "sent" them against Jerusalem (v. 9).

As humans we only see the earthly version of history. Here a curtain is drawn aside for us to see the heavenly version and to be staggered by its implications. Yahweh was not merely a provincial deity for a little band of people nestled in the Fertile Crescent. He is a world God! He determines the affairs of all nations regardless of whether they own Him or not. He owns them! He has sovereign use of any pagan tyrant at any time. His authority does not stop there. He also has the sovereign right to judge that tyrant. *"Then it will come to pass, when seventy years are completed, that I will punish the king of Babylon and that nation, the land of the Chaldeans, for their iniquity,' says the* LORD; *'and I will make it a perpetual desolation'"* (v. 12).

By specifying seventy years, Jeremiah informed Jerusalem that a whole generation of life would be spent away from home. It is a determinate God who rules over all the nations of this world! This conviction set Jeremiah's philosophy of history, his whole world-view.

Even though this message was so exact, it was not stated in a clinical way. There was more here than statistics. There were poignant emotions on the page with them. As the first wave of hostages to Babylon was led out of their homeland, they might have remembered back seven years to the hearing of these words. If so, they would have known then and there that only their children and grandchildren would see the beloved mountains of Jerusalem again.

Sounds of gladness, sounds of singing, sounds of celebration would forever leave the land. *"Moreover I will take from them the voice of mirth and the voice of gladness, the voice of the bridegroom and the voice of the bride"* (v. 10). No longer would millstones grind the good wheat of the land. No longer would lamp light flicker on contented evenings. No one mourned harder than Jeremiah and the God he served.

"So I will bring on that land all My words which I have pronounced against it, all that is written in this book, which Jeremiah has prophesied concerning all the nations" (v. 13). In the face of such crisis, Jeremiah kept on writing, perhaps never suspecting that he was handing down a living legacy to Western civilization. The Hebrews became known in the secular histories of the Near East, not for their contribution to industry, to architecture, or to warfare. They became known as the people of "the book." We must remember that the work we do for the kingdom may seem insignificant at the time, but it has an enduring and eternal value.

SET OVER THE NATIONS

25:15 For thus says the LORD God of Israel to me: "Take this wine cup of fury from My hand, and cause all the nations, to whom I send you, to drink it.

16 "And they will drink and stagger and go mad because of the sword that I will send among them."

17 Then I took the cup from the LORD's hand, and made all the nations drink, to whom the LORD had sent me:

18 Jerusalem and the cities of Judah, its kings and its princes, to make them a desolation, an astonishment, a hissing, and a curse, as *it is* this day;

19 Pharaoh king of Egypt, his servants, his princes, and all his people;

20 all the mixed multitude, all the kings of the land of Uz, all the kings of the land of the Philistines (namely, Ashkelon, Gaza, Ekron, and the remnant of Ashdod);

21 Edom, Moab, and the people of Ammon;

22 all the kings of Tyre, all the kings of Sidon, and the kings of the coastlands which *are* across the sea;

23 Dedan, Tema, Buz, and all *who are* in the farthest corners;

24 all the kings of Arabia and all the kings of the mixed multitude who dwell in the desert;

25 all the kings of Zimri, all the kings of Elam, and all the kings of the Medes;

26 all the kings of the north, far and near, one with another; and all the kingdoms of the world which *are* on the face of the earth. Also the king of Sheshach shall drink after them.

27 "Therefore you shall say to them, 'Thus says the LORD of hosts, the God of Israel: "Drink, be drunk, and vomit! Fall and rise no more, because of the sword which I will send among you."'

28 "And it shall be, if they refuse to take the cup from your hand to drink, then you shall say to them, 'Thus says the LORD of hosts: "You shall certainly drink!

29 "For behold, I begin to bring calamity on the city which is called by My name, and should you be utterly unpunished? You shall not be unpunished, for I will call for a sword on all the inhabitants of the earth," says the LORD of hosts.'

30 "Therefore prophesy against them all these words, and say to them:

'The LORD will roar from on high,
And utter His voice from His holy habitation;
He will roar mightily against His fold.
He will give a shout, as those who tread *the grapes*,
Against all the inhabitants of the earth.

31 A noise will come to the ends of the earth—
For the LORD has a controversy with the nations;
He will plead His case with all flesh.
He will give those *who are* wicked to the sword,' says the LORD."

32 Thus says the LORD of hosts:
"Behold, disaster shall go forth
From nation to nation,
And a great whirlwind shall be raised up
From the farthest parts of the earth.

33 "And at that day the slain of the LORD shall be
from *one* end of the earth even to the *other* end of
the earth. They shall not be lamented, or gathered, or
buried; they shall become refuse on the ground.

34 "Wail, shepherds, and cry!
Roll about *in the ashes,*
You leaders of the flock!
For the days of your slaughter and your
    dispersions are fulfilled;
You shall fall like a precious vessel.

35 And the shepherds will have no way to flee,
Nor the leaders of the flock to escape.

36 A voice of the cry of the shepherds,
And a wailing of the leaders to the flock *will*
    be heard.
For the LORD has plundered their pasture,

37 And the peaceful dwellings are cut down
Because of the fierce anger of the LORD.

38 He has left His lair like the lion;
For their land is desolate
Because of the fierceness of the Oppressor,
And because of His fierce anger."

Jer. 25:15–38

The prophet must move now from being tender to being tough, for
both are dimensions of God's character. He moved also from being a
voice to Jerusalem, to being a voice to the world. Again the deliber-
ateness of God is seen in the language He uses. "See, I have this day
set you over the nations and over the kingdoms, To root out and to
pull down, To destroy and to throw down, To build and to plant"
(1:10). On the very day when God touched the mouth of the young
country boy, He could see this moment in the life of what was now a
veteran prophet.

*"Take this wine cup of fury from My hand, and cause all the nations, to
whom I send you, to drink it"* (v. 15). The dynamic was not tender. The
mission was awesome—but then so was the response! No longer did
Jeremiah sigh, "Ah, Lord GOD" (1:6). No longer did he say, "I cannot
speak, for I *am* a youth" (1:6). This was no Johnny-come-lately writing. *"Then I took the cup from the LORD's hand, and made all the nations
drink, to whom the LORD had sent me"* (v. 17). Because of his early

184

resolve, courage now had become a consistent thing. "Do not be afraid of their faces" (1:8). And Jeremiah wasn't! There are staggering results when we take courage and stay obedient.

Jeremiah had just now stepped into a new dimension of his vocation. His ministry to foreign nations becomes the subject of subsequent chapters. As an introduction to this, he names them all now in verses 15-29. The intoxicating cup, here a symbol of God's wrath, was given first to Jerusalem, then to Egypt, and then to the surrounding nations here named. The message was not clothed in the language of diplomacy. *"Drink, be drunk, and vomit! Fall and rise no more"* (v. 27). Terse and sharp, it was hurled like a sword against the nations by a prophet who no longer "fears their faces."

"For the LORD *has a controversy with the nations; He will plead His case with all flesh"* (v. 31). Two more images struck terror in the hearts of unbelieving nations. One was of a great noise that will roar from the heavens as it came down upon a rebellious people. Anyone who has ever witnessed the force of a hurricane or a tornado will understand this great whirlwind, and will remember the noise that heralds its coming. A second noise was described, not of a roar but of a wail. A chorus of voices would be heard across the land (vv. 34-38). They were the voices of leaders and of false shepherds moaning over a fate they could no longer reverse, over lost opportunities to repent. Jeremiah did not hesitate to use any sensual imagery necessary to strike the ears of the nations.

SECTION TWO

Experiences and Relationships of the Prophet

Jeremiah 26:1–45:5; 52:1–34

CHAPTER FIFTEEN

Caution: Preaching Can Be Hazardous

Jeremiah 26:1–29:32

Jehoiakim's ascendance to the throne of Judah changed the whole dynamic of the city and of Jeremiah's prophetic ministry. Josiah's presence and popularity maintained some form of righteousness and provided sanction for the prophet. Jehoiakim, however, was nothing like his father, a fact that became palpably real as Jeremiah continued to preach to a people now encouraged by their king to be hostile to God. What follows in these chapters is a series of such hostilities. They help us to understand the ambiance in which Jeremiah had now to conduct his ministry.

DO NOT DIMINISH A WORD OF WHAT I TELL YOU TO SAY

26:1 In the beginning of the reign of Jehoiakim the son of Josiah, king of Judah, this word came from the LORD, saying,

2 "Thus says the LORD: 'Stand in the court of the LORD's house, and speak to all the cities of Judah, which come to worship *in* the LORD's house, all the words that I command you to speak to them. Do not diminish a word.

3 'Perhaps everyone will listen and turn from his evil way, that I may relent concerning the calamity which I purpose to bring on them because of the evil of their doings.'

4 "And you shall say to them, 'Thus says the LORD:

189

"If you will not listen to Me, to walk in My law which I have set before you,

5 "to heed the words of My servants the prophets whom I sent to you, both rising up early and sending *them* (but you have not heeded),

6 "then I will make this house like Shiloh, and will make this city a curse to all the nations of the earth."'"

7 So the priests and the prophets and all the people heard Jeremiah speaking these words in the house of the LORD.

8 Now it happened, when Jeremiah had made an end of speaking all that the LORD had commanded *him* to speak to all the people, that the priests and the prophets and all the people seized him, saying, "You will surely die!

9 "Why have you prophesied in the name of the LORD, saying, 'This house shall be like Shiloh, and this city shall be desolate, without an inhabitant'?" And all the people were gathered against Jeremiah in the house of the LORD.

10 When the princes of Judah heard these things, they came up from the king's house to the house of the LORD and sat down in the entry of the New Gate of the LORD's *house*.

11 And the priests and the prophets spoke to the princes and all the people, saying, "This man deserves to die! For he has prophesied against this city, as you have heard with your ears."

12 Then Jeremiah spoke to all the princes and all the people, saying: "The LORD sent me to prophesy against this house and against this city with all the words that you have heard.

13 "Now therefore, amend your ways and your doings, and obey the voice of the LORD your God; then the LORD will relent concerning the doom that He has pronounced against you.

14 "As for me, here I am, in your hand; do with me as seems good and proper to you.

15 "But know for certain that if you put me to death, you will surely bring innocent blood on yourselves, on this city, and on its inhabitants; for truly

the LORD has sent me to you to speak all these words in your hearing."

16 So the princes and all the people said to the priests and the prophets, "This man does not deserve to die. For he has spoken to us in the name of the LORD our God."

17 Then certain of the elders of the land rose up and spoke to all the assembly of the people, saying:

18 "Micah of Moresheth prophesied in the days of Hezekiah king of Judah, and spoke to all the people of Judah, saying, 'Thus says the LORD of hosts:

"Zion shall be plowed *like* a field,
Jerusalem shall become heaps of ruins,
And the mountain of the temple
Like the bare hills of the forest."'

19 "Did Hezekiah king of Judah and all Judah ever put him to death? Did he not fear the LORD and seek the LORD's favor? And the LORD relented concerning the doom which He had pronounced against them. But we are doing great evil against ourselves."

20 Now there was also a man who prophesied in the name of the LORD, Urijah the son of Shemaiah of Kirjath Jearim, who prophesied against this city and against this land according to all the words of Jeremiah.

21 And when Jehoiakim the king, with all his mighty men and all the princes, heard his words, the king sought to put him to death; but when Urijah heard *it,* he was afraid and fled, and went to Egypt.

22 Then Jehoiakim the king sent men to Egypt: Elnathan the son of Achbor, and *other* men *who went* with him to Egypt.

23 And they brought Urijah from Egypt and brought him to Jehoiakim the king, who killed him with the sword and cast his dead body into the graves of the common people.

24 Nevertheless the hand of Ahikam the son of Shaphan was with Jeremiah, so that they should not give him into the hand of the people to put him to death.

Jer. 26:1–24

As a prophet it would be very tempting to compromise his message out of the instinct of self-preservation. Yet when God told him to stand in the temple court for this sermon, He also said, *"Do not diminish a word"* (v. 2). It was in this place that Jeremiah had cried against them once before: "The temple of the LORD, the temple of the LORD, the temple of the LORD" (7:4). It was an anguished plea for them to quit worshiping the temple and start worshiping the Lord of the temple. They had not taken well to Jeremiah then, and that was under Josiah's righteous reign. What would be their response under an anything-goes kind of leadership?

The message came right in the beginning of Jehoiakim's reign (v. 1). Jeremiah stood boldly in the temple court among its unbelieving masses and issued a threat: *"If you will not listen to Me, . . . then I will make this house like Shiloh, and will make this city a curse to all the nations of the earth"* (vv. 4–6). In that permissive culture you could say anything as long as it was not against the temple or against the city. After all, the court was filled with religious and political officials whose lives and livelihoods were built around the temple system and the city, both of which were thriving at the time.

To march onto their turf and start talking about Shiloh was an invitation to trouble. Before the establishment of the kingdom, Shiloh had been the center of worship for the tribal confederacies, the home of the ark of the covenant. Shiloh, however, was destroyed by the Philistines and left in ruins. No one wanted to be reminded of this punishment of disobedience. The mere mention of the heap of ruins brought back bad memories. It brought convictions they did not want to entertain. It was one of those unmentionable subjects that only a courageous prophet would dare to preach about, and then only under the solemn authorization of a Holy God.

After only a few words, Jeremiah had already touched raw nerves. He could see faces set in anger against him. Should he cut short his message? *"Now it happened, when Jeremiah had made an end of speaking all that the LORD had commanded him to speak to all the people, that the priests and the prophets and all the people seized him"* (v. 8). He did not bring the hard words to a premature end. He spoke all that was given to him, even though he knew it might be getting him off to a bad start with the king, the city's dignitaries, and members of his own profession.

One always wants the approval of members of his own profession. Preachers are no exception. We desire concord among our ranks. Yet Jeremiah faced the priests and delivered the whole truth, letting the "chips fall where they may." He was seized right there in the precincts of his own profession by priests and prophets shouting in unison, *"You will surely die!"* (v. 8). They lost all their demeanor and resorted to violence.

The commotion that followed must have been what attracted the princes of Judah from the palace (v. 10). This kind of disorderly conduct was somewhat shocking, so they assembled in *"the entry of the New Gate of the LORD's house"* (v. 10). Now Jeremiah had their attention in a way he might never have expected. His life hung in the balance between an angry mob of priests and a group of concerned princes. *"This man deserves to die! For he has prophesied against this city"* (v. 11). Their theology looked at God as merely a national deity who took their side against other nations. Prophecy directed against others was fine, but prophecy directed against them was shocking and unpatriotic.

By mentioning the city and not the temple, they were obviously trying to incite the princes to join them in their anger and thereby gain momentum for their cause. The gaze of all public officials came to rest on Jeremiah. It was their hour to decide the question, "Is he for real?" One of the themes of these great chapters is that the hour of decision comes to every man.

What defense of himself would Jeremiah give them in this hour? His brilliance lay in the fact that he did not become defensive at all. *"The LORD sent me to prophesy against this house and against this city with all the words that you have heard"* (v. 12). In essence, Jeremiah said, "I am only delivering a message. The real issue is between you and God." He bluntly addressed the princes, *"Amend your ways; . . . then the LORD will relent concerning the doom that He has pronounced against you"* (v. 13).

The hearts of the princes were struck by the integrity of this solitary man and his behavior under stress. He did not tremble, or cower, or plead. *"As for me, here I am, in your hand; do with me as seems good and proper to you. But know for certain that if you put me to death, you will surely bring innocent blood on yourselves"* (vv. 14–15). A man as composed as this was a rare sight in that culture. He credited them with the capacity to make *"good and proper"* judgments.

They must have conferred for some time with one another before they spoke. *"This man does not deserve to die. For he has spoken to us in the name of the LORD our God"* (v. 16). They had taken the side of the prophet and not that of the priests. Jeremiah remembered God's words: "Do not be dismayed before their faces, Lest I dismay you before them" (1:17). God cannot honor cowardice, but, oh, how He loves to honor courage!

Certain of the elders rose to speak (v. 17). Some of them may have been senior enough to remember the day Micah prophesied during the reign of Hezekiah and said essentially what Jeremiah had just said. *"Did Hezekiah king of Judah and all Judah ever put him to death?"* (v. 19). The Lord relented of their doom. Why then should they do any differently? They would only be bringing a great evil against themselves (v. 19). They recognized that Micah's message was authenticated by the test of time. He had spoken the word of God. If Jeremiah was saying the same thing, then he too must be an authentic prophet. Jeremiah walked away, a free man, free to continue his dangerous mission.

Among those elders is a figure worthy of our attention. *"Nevertheless the hand of Ahikam the son of Shaphan was with Jeremiah, so that they should not give him into the hand of the people to put him to death"* (v. 24). Ahikam had been part of an earlier delegation, one that must have affected the course of his life and certainly affected his intercession here on behalf of Jeremiah. When the Book of the Law was found, Josiah sent a delegation to the prophetess Huldah asking her to interpret the alarming passages on judgment. Ahikam was in that party (2 Kings 22:12–14). He heard her solemn pronouncement against Jerusalem. He also heard her words to the anxious king, "because your heart was tender, and you humbled yourself before the LORD . . . your eyes shall not see all of the calamity" (2 Kings 22:19–20). Ahikam learned in that moment to prize a tender and humble heart. Therefore his later years would be lived with a wisdom that came to be prized by his associates. It was the intervention and the authority of this unsung hero that helped to save the life of Jeremiah and assure the continuation of his prophetic ministry. When God called him, Jeremiah had cried, "I'm too young" (1:6). Many of us today say, "I'm too old." The life of Ahikam, however, has something more wonderful to say about the value of growing wiser as we grow older. Senior

194

citizens can be a valuable commodity to society, one of its dearest treasures.

Another character is mentioned in this narrative. Urijah also prophesied faithfully against the city. *"And when Jehoiakim the king, with all his mighty men and all the princes, heard his words, the king sought to put him to death"* (v. 21). We would never have found something like this said about Josiah. Urijah was unlike Jeremiah. He did not stand his ground, but instead fled to Egypt where he was overtaken and slain. Obviously there was strong momentum against righteous prophecy. Jeremiah's escape therefore was not an inconsiderable thing. It was a tribute to his courage, to Ahikam's wisdom, and to the Lord's honoring of those virtues.

BRING YOUR NECKS UNDER THE YOKE OR UNDER THE SWORD

27:1 In the beginning of the reign of Jehoiakim the son of Josiah, king of Judah, this word came to Jeremiah from the LORD, saying,

2 "Thus says the LORD to me: 'Make for yourselves bonds and yokes, and put them on your neck,

3 'and send them to the king of Edom, the king of Moab, the king of the Ammonites, the king of Tyre, and the king of Sidon, by the hand of the messengers who come to Jerusalem to Zedekiah king of Judah.

4 'And command them to say to their masters, "Thus says the LORD of hosts, the God of Israel— thus you shall say to your masters:

5 'I have made the earth, the man and the beast that *are* on the ground, by My great power and by My outstretched arm, and have given it to whom it seemed proper to Me.

6 'And now I have given all these lands into the hand of Nebuchadnezzar the king of Babylon, My servant; and the beasts of the field I have also given him to serve him.

7 'So all nations shall serve him and his son and his son's son, until the time of his land comes; and then many nations and great kings shall make him serve them.

195

8 'And it shall be, *that* the nation and kingdom which will not serve Nebuchadnezzar the king of Babylon, and which will not put its neck under the yoke of the king of Babylon, that nation I will punish,' says the LORD, 'with the sword, the famine, and the pestilence, until I have consumed them by his hand.

9 'Therefore do not listen to your prophets, your diviners, your dreamers, your soothsayers, or your sorcerers, who speak to you, saying, "You shall not serve the king of Babylon."

10 'For they prophesy a lie to you, to remove you far from your land; and I will drive you out, and you will perish.

11 'But the nations that bring their necks under the yoke of the king of Babylon and serve him, I will let them remain in their own land,' says the LORD, 'and they shall till it and dwell in it.'"'

12 I also spoke to Zedekiah king of Judah according to all these words, saying, "Bring your necks under the yoke of the king of Babylon, and serve him and his people, and live!

13 "Why will you die, you and your people, by the sword, by the famine, and by the pestilence, as the LORD has spoken against the nation that will not serve the king of Babylon?

14 "Therefore do not listen to the words of the prophets who speak to you, saying, 'You shall not serve the king of Babylon,' for they prophesy a lie to you;

15 "for I have not sent them," says the LORD, "yet they prophesy a lie in My name, that I may drive you out, and that you may perish, you and the prophets who prophesy to you."

16 Also I spoke to the priests and to all this people, saying, "Thus says the LORD: 'Do not listen to the words of your prophets who prophesy to you, saying, "Behold, the vessels of the LORD's house will now shortly be brought back from Babylon"; for they prophesy a lie to you.

17 'Do not listen to them; serve the king of Babylon, and live! Why should this city be laid waste?

196

18 'But if they *are* prophets, and if the word of the LORD is with them, let them now make intercession to the LORD of hosts, that the vessels which are left in the house of the LORD, *in* the house of the king of Judah, and at Jerusalem, do not go to Babylon.'

19 "For thus says the LORD of hosts concerning the pillars, concerning the Sea, concerning the carts, and concerning the remainder of the vessels that remain in this city,

20 "which Nebuchadnezzar king of Babylon did not take, when he carried away captive Jeconiah the son of Jehoiakim, king of Judah, from Jerusalem to Babylon, and all the nobles of Judah and Jerusalem—

21 "yes, thus says the LORD of hosts, the God of Israel, concerning the vessels that remain in the house of the LORD, and in the house of the king of Judah and of Jerusalem:

22 'They shall be carried to Babylon, and there they shall be until the day that I visit them,' says the LORD. 'Then I will bring them up and restore them to this place.'"

Jer. 27:1–22

Jeremiah delivered this message some twelve years after the temple skirmish that had strengthened his resolve and had given the poise we see in him here. In the temple sermon, he had warned that they would become like Shiloh. Now Jehoiakim's reign was over. He had brought them to the very brink of Shiloh. Zedekiah had been placed on the throne of Judah by Nebuchadnezzar, who had also carried off the first wave of hostages and had threatened total destruction of the city if it resisted his control any further.

Delegates from neighboring nations had arrived in Jerusalem desiring with Zedekiah to plan a revolt against Babylon. Jeremiah knew that would be the final undoing of his beloved city. With pressure like this mounting, he decided once again to do something radical. The country boy, now grown older, would much prefer solitude, but he had decided on a life of obedience and not a life of comfort, so he forayed into the midst of this conference, into the very hub of its insanity. Perhaps I should not say insanity. Their fourfold reasoning sounded quite logical. Nebuchadnezzar was eight hundred miles away. They would recruit the help of Egypt. Nebuchadnezzar was preoccupied with civil problems, and he was conducting a military movement to the east and would not be watching the west.[1] The thinking was iron clad—except for one thing: it made no allowance for God.

Jeremiah was all alone in what he believed. Not only did he think differently, but that day he looked different from all the delegates milling about. Over his rough robes, he wore something even rougher. If a picture is worth a thousand words, then Jeremiah was eloquent that day. Wearing a wooden yoke across his tired shoulders, he was willing to become a laughing stock if it meant saving Jerusalem. Are we willing to wear our hearts on our shoulders like this? Do we go public with our protests against the dangerous trends in our society? The title for this unit expresses in capsule form the choices he envisioned in this final hour, before Jerusalem would become another Shiloh. This seemingly unpatriotic platform was their only hope. The same council was delivered to three audiences with a profound sensitivity for their different perspectives.

1. *To the foreign delegates* (vv. 1–11). The tone of this presentation was commanding. Jeremiah was not just making diplomatic suggestions to Edom, Moab, the Ammonites, Tyre, and Sidon, all referred to in verse 3. Standing before them under a rough wooden yoke he said, *"Make for yourselves bonds and yokes, and put them on your neck"* (v. 2). With all the force of his personality, Jeremiah insisted that these delegates go back to their kings not with plans of revolt, but instead wearing yokes that symbolized their acceptance of Babylonian power over their nations. He insisted that they shock these little monarchs, posturing for war, with the facts about the real monarch. *"Thus says the LORD of hosts, . . . 'I have made the earth, the man and the beast that are on the ground, by My great power and by My outstretched arm, and have given it to whom it seemed proper to Me'"* (vv. 4–5).

Nebuchadnezzar's present power over them was a *fait accompli*. *"All nations shall serve him and his son and his son's son, until the time of his land comes"* (v. 7). Not only had God determined who they would now serve, but He had also determined how long. All of the summit conferences in the world were not going to change that. All of the dreamers' dreams, the diviners' incantations, the sorcerers' "tea leaves" were not going to change that (v. 9).

The only thing they could change now was whether they lived in the land or died by the sword of Nebuchadnezzar. They had no political options, only the option of life or death. His strong face, framed with a mane of white hair, tightened with conviction as Jeremiah asked these delegates the only questions that had any meaning: Do you want to stay in your homeland? Do you want to till its soil? (v. 11). Then put on the yoke of Babylon and wear it before your kings. It was the final sanity, the only sanity left to a defeated people.

2. *To Zedekiah* (vv. 12–15). The great versatility and range of prophetic utterance is found in the way Jeremiah delivered the same message but tailored it to the needs of the hearer. Zedekiah was indecisive. He vacillated between different opinions without the courage to seize the truth and stand with it. He had made an oath of loyalty to Nebuchadnezzar. In return, Nebuchadnezzar had given him the throne of Judah. He could not, however, seem to stand with that oath. Josephus described him as "a despiser of justice and of his duty."[2]

The seasoned prophet looked into the eyes of the twenty-year-old king and condensed his logic to one sentence: Why would you choose death when you could choose survival? (v. 13). Granted they were enduring a substandard of living and they had lost many important members of society, but at least they had their lives, their city, and their temple. Jeremiah cut through all of the confusion around the king, now swarmed with delegates from neighboring nations and lying prophets. We have a tendency to divorce the prophetic from the practical. Here Jeremiah was both prophetic and practical. You have heard of people "who are so spiritual that they are no earthly good." Jeremiah was spiritual in a way that makes him more earthly good than anyone else.

3. *To the priests and all the people* (vv. 16–22). To this audience, Jeremiah had yet a third mode of approach with the same message. The nations needed a commanding presence, but not from a tribal deity. Rather they could find that presence in Almighty God. The weak king needed practical logic condensed to its most basic and understandable form. The priests and the people needed to be rescued from widespread heresy. *"The vessels of the LORD's house will now shortly be brought back from Babylon"* (v. 16).

Jeremiah focused on the temple vessels knowing that they would incite the people's interest because the temple was their central preoccupation, particularly the priests. Unfortunately, they were not

199

preoccupied with the God of the vessels nor with the truth for which the vessels stood, but they respected only the vessels themselves and the rituals for which they were used. The ritualistic void was being filled by the false prophets, those who told the people just what they wanted to hear. They loved to believe that the vessels carried off in the first wave of the great deportation would soon be restored to them.

Jeremiah had to penetrate this false comfort. It bred a dangerous naïveté about how bad things really were. It was leading them to consider a revolt that would be their downfall. As with the king, Jeremiah was very direct. He shouted one sentence that delivered a punch to their fuzzy thinking: *"Serve the king of Babylon, and live! Why should this city be laid waste?"* (v. 17). Why should they continue in a naïveté that would ultimately cost them everything?

Again the vessels of the temple were mentioned. This time it was not the vessels carried away, but rather those that still remained. The prophet admonished them to quit crying over spilled milk. The bronze pillars could still be saved and so could the carts (v. 19). With a light touch of sarcasm, Jeremiah added, *"if the word of the LORD is with [your prophets], let them now make intercession . . . that the vessels which are left in the house of the LORD, . . . do not go to Babylon"* (v. 18). It was a tongue-in-cheek way of saying that nothing but submission to Babylon could now save them.

AND MAY THE BEST MAN WIN

28:1 And it happened in the same year, at the beginning of the reign of Zedekiah king of Judah, in the fourth year *and* in the fifth month, *that* Hananiah the son of Azur the prophet, who *was* from Gibeon, spoke to me in the house of the LORD in the presence of the priests and of all the people, saying,

2 "Thus speaks the LORD of hosts, the God of Israel, saying: 'I have broken the yoke of the king of Babylon.

3 'Within two full years I will bring back to this place all the vessels of the LORD's house, that Nebuchadnezzar king of Babylon took away from this place and carried to Babylon.

4 'And I will bring back to this place Jeconiah the son of Jehoiakim, king of Judah, with all the captives of Judah who went to Babylon,' says the LORD, 'for I will break the yoke of the king of Babylon.'"

5 Then the prophet Jeremiah spoke to the prophet Hananiah in the presence of the priests and in the presence of all the people who stood in the house of the LORD,

6 and the prophet Jeremiah said, "Amen! The LORD do so; the LORD perform your words which you have prophesied, to bring back the vessels of the LORD's house and all who were carried away captive, from Babylon to this place.

7 "Nevertheless hear now this word that I speak in your hearing and in the hearing of all the people:

8 "The prophets who have been before me and before you of old prophesied against many countries and great kingdoms—of war and disaster and pestilence.

9 "As for the prophet who prophesies of peace, when the word of the prophet comes to pass, the prophet will be known as one whom the LORD has truly sent."

10 Then Hananiah the prophet took the yoke off the prophet Jeremiah's neck and broke it.

11 And Hananiah spoke in the presence of all the people, saying, "Thus says the LORD: 'Even so I will break the yoke of Nebuchadnezzar king of Babylon from the neck of all nations within the space of two full years.'" And the prophet Jeremiah went his way.

12 Now the word of the LORD came to Jeremiah, after Hananiah the prophet had broken the yoke from the neck of the prophet Jeremiah, saying,

13 "Go and tell Hananiah, saying, 'Thus says the LORD: "You have broken the yokes of wood, but you have made in their place yokes of iron."

14 'For thus says the LORD of hosts, the God of Israel: "I have put a yoke of iron on the neck of all these nations, that they may serve Nebuchadnezzar king of Babylon; and they shall serve him. I have given him the beasts of the field also."'"

15 Then the prophet Jeremiah said to Hananiah

the prophet, "Hear now, Hananiah, the LORD has not
sent you, but you make this people trust in a lie.

16 "Therefore thus says the LORD: 'Behold, I will
cast you from the face of the earth. This year you
shall die, because you have taught rebellion against
the LORD.'"

17 So Hananiah the prophet died the same year in
the seventh month.

Jer. 28:1–17

This kind of prophetic courage has its hazards. Within the year,
Jeremiah was challenged by an angry prophet who did not like being criticized. He did not like his credibility—and along with it, his
livelihood—damaged. Two men squared off against each other in
the temple, surrounded by a crowd of people and priests (v. 1).
They focused intensely upon one another. Hananiah, a prophet and
the son of a prophet, addressed Jeremiah. It became clear that this
was a battle of wits; the false was challenging the real. Scripture is
woven through with stories like this: Pharaoh's magicians faced off
against Moses; Goliath thundered at young David with his sling-
shot; Haman laid a trap for Mordecai; the Pharisees, Levites, and
scribes seemed to confront Jesus almost daily; and the list goes on.
Yet God said with confidence, "May the best man win, the man
after My heart."

"Thus speaks the LORD of hosts, the God of Israel" (v. 2). Hananiah
used this solemn prophetic preface to endorse the words of his own
imagining. He seemed sincere. Have you ever heard it said that it
doesn't matter what you believe as long as you are sincere? This
story proves the lie in that. Hananiah was sincerely wrong as he
goes on to quote God as saying, *"I have broken the yoke of the king of
Babylon. Within two full years I will bring back to this place all the
vessels of the LORD's house, that Nebuchadnezzar king of Babylon took
away from this place and carried to Babylon"* (vv. 2–3). The people
were left to decide how God could make two statements that stand
in opposition to each other. Jeremiah said, "Take the yoke of Babylon." Hananiah said, "Don't take the yoke." Jeremiah said, "The vessels will stay seventy years." Hananiah said, "Within two years the
temple's relics will be returned." Jeremiah said that Jeconiah would
die in Babylon (22:26). Hananiah said, *"I will bring back to this place*

Jeconiah" (v. 4). Who are you going to believe? We must all decide among the many voices we hear.

"Then the prophet Jeremiah spoke to the prophet Hananiah" (v. 5). I can imagine a silence falling over the whole scene of debate between these two forces. *"Amen! The LORD do so; the LORD perform your words which you have prophesied"* (v. 6). Jeremiah confessed that he too would love to believe these words. Does anyone think for one minute that he enjoyed prophesying doom? Do they think it was fun being a social outcast and weeping all alone? We are not at liberty, however, to believe anything we want to believe. Just as Jeremiah wore the yoke in the presence of his opponent, so also he was wearing a mind-set that was bound to that which the Lord said was true and not according to what others wanted to think was true. The confrontation between these two men is a confrontation that must take place within every one of us. There is a vast difference between faith and wishful thinking, as vast as the difference between Jeremiah and Hananiah.

The issue must be settled. So Jeremiah spoke again, looking squarely into the eyes of his opponent: *"The prophets who have been before me and before you of old prophesied against many countries and great kingdoms—of war and disaster and pestilence. As for the prophet who prophesies of peace, when the word of the prophet comes to pass, the prophet will be known as one whom the LORD has truly sent"* (vv. 8–9). We must take responsibility for what we say, Hananiah. The acid test of a prophet is whether his words come true. There is a payday.

Jeremiah kept his cool as he delivered these words into the face of Hananiah. *"Then Hananiah the prophet took the yoke off the prophet Jeremiah's neck and broke it"* (v. 10). In the midst of this tantrum of anger, Hananiah reiterated his prophecy, insisting on its truth (v. 11). The curtain went down on this scene with Hananiah strutting the stage, all sound and fury. He did not, however, have the last word. The curtain rose again, a short time later, when Jeremiah had heard from the Lord and had this to say: *"You have broken the yokes of wood, but you have made in their place yokes of iron"* (v. 13). Whenever we insist on wishful thinking over against God's facts we ultimately get "out of the frying pan and into the fire."

Early in their confrontation, it may have looked like two equal powers facing off. Yet that is never the case when the lie faces the truth. Jeremiah now had the momentum. He now had the solemn authority to make this pronouncement. *"Hear now, Hananiah, the LORD has not sent you, but you make this people trust in a lie. Therefore thus says the LORD: 'Behold, I will cast you from the face of the earth. This year you shall die, because you have taught rebellion against the LORD'"* (vv. 15–16). Not only was Jeremiah's prophecy bold, it was specific. The acid test was whether it came true. *"So Hananiah the prophet died the same year in the seventh month"* (v. 17).

The death of Hananiah the prophet was God's clear statement as to which of these men was delivering the truth and which the counterfeit. The exiles in Babylon did not have access to this drama. They ran the risk of becoming victims of the Hananiahs that rose up in their midst, lulling them with false promises.

A LETTER TO THE EXILES

29:1 Now these *are* the words of the letter that Jeremiah the prophet sent from Jerusalem to the remainder of the elders who were carried away captive—to the priests, the prophets, and all the people whom Nebuchadnezzar had carried away captive from Jerusalem to Babylon.

2 (This happened after Jeconiah the king, the queen mother, the eunuchs, the princes of Judah and Jerusalem, the craftsmen, and the smiths had departed from Jerusalem.)

3 *The letter was sent* by the hand of Elasah the son of Shaphan, and Gemariah the son of Hilkiah, whom Zedekiah king of Judah sent to Babylon, to Nebuchadnezzar king of Babylon, saying,

4 Thus says the LORD of hosts, the God of Israel, to all who were carried away captive, whom I have caused to be carried away from Jerusalem to Babylon:

5 Build houses and dwell *in them*; plant gardens and eat their fruit.

6 Take wives and beget sons and daughters; and take wives for your sons and give your daughters to husbands, so that they may bear sons and daughters—that you may be increased there, and not diminished.

7 And seek the peace of the city where I have caused you to be carried away captive, and pray to the LORD for it; for in its peace you will have peace.

8 For thus says the LORD of hosts, the God of Israel: Do not let your prophets and your diviners who are in your midst deceive you, nor listen to your dreams which you cause to be dreamed.

9 For they prophesy falsely to you in My name; I have not sent them, says the LORD.

10 For thus says the LORD: After seventy years are completed at Babylon, I will visit you and perform My good word toward you, and cause you to return to this place.

11 For I know the thoughts that I think toward you, says the LORD, thoughts of peace and not of evil, to give you a future and a hope.

12 Then you will call upon Me and go and pray to Me, and I will listen to you.

13 And you will seek Me and find *Me*, when you search for Me with all your heart.

14 I will be found by you, says the LORD, and I will bring you back from your captivity; I will gather you from all the nations and from all the places where I have driven you, says the LORD, and I will bring you to the place from which I cause you to be carried away captive.

15 Because you have said, "The LORD has raised up prophets for us in Babylon"—

16 therefore thus says the LORD concerning the king who sits on the throne of David, concerning all the people who dwell in this city, and concerning your brethren who have not gone out with you into captivity—

17 thus says the LORD of hosts: Behold, I will send on them the sword, the famine, and the pestilence, and will make them like rotten figs that cannot be eaten, they are so bad.

18 And I will pursue them with the sword, with famine, and with pestilence; and I will deliver them to trouble among all the kingdoms of the earth—to be a curse, an astonishment, a hissing,

and a reproach among all the nations where I have driven them,

19 because they have not heeded My words, says the LORD, which I sent to them by My servants the prophets, rising up early and sending *them*; neither would you heed, says the LORD.

20 Therefore hear the word of the LORD, all you of the captivity, whom I have sent from Jerusalem to Babylon.

21 Thus says the LORD of hosts, the God of Israel, concerning Ahab the son of Kolaiah, and Zedekiah the son of Maaseiah, who prophesy a lie to you in My name: Behold, I will deliver them into the hand of Nebuchadnezzar king of Babylon, and he shall slay them before your eyes.

22 And because of them a curse shall be taken up by all the captivity of Judah who *are* in Babylon, saying, "The LORD make you like Zedekiah and Ahab, whom the king of Babylon roasted in the fire";

23 because they have done disgraceful things in Israel, have committed adultery with their neighbors' wives, and have spoken lying words in My name, which I have not commanded them. Indeed I know, and *am* a witness, says the LORD.

24 You shall also speak to Shemaiah the Nehelamite, saying,

25 Thus speaks the LORD of hosts, the God of Israel, saying: You have sent letters in your name to all the people who *are* at Jerusalem, to Zephaniah the son of Maaseiah the priest, and to all the priests, saying,

26 "The LORD has made you priest instead of Jehoiada the priest, so that there should be officers *in* the house of the LORD over every man *who* is demented and considers himself a prophet, that you should put him in prison and in the stocks.

27 Now therefore, why have you not rebuked Jeremiah of Anathoth who makes himself a prophet to you?

28 For he has sent to us *in* Babylon, saying, 'This *captivity is* long; build houses and dwell *in them,* and plant gardens and eat their fruit.'"

29 Now Zephaniah the priest read this letter in the hearing of Jeremiah the prophet.

30 Then the word of the LORD came to Jeremiah, saying:

31 Send to all those in captivity, saying, Thus says the LORD concerning Shemaiah the Nehelamite: Because Shemaiah has prophesied to you, and I have not sent him, and he has caused you to trust in a lie—

32 therefore thus says the LORD: Behold, I will punish Shemaiah the Nehelamite and his family: he shall not have anyone to dwell among this people, nor shall he see the good that I will do for My people, says the LORD, because he has taught rebellion against the LORD.

Jer. 29:1–32

This letter has been considered one of the most important documents of the Old Testament. Undaunted by the eight hundred miles that separated him from his mission field, Jeremiah wrote and arranged for the letter to be delivered by Elasah and Gemariah, members of Zedekiah's delegation to Babylon—a delegation seeking to pacify a monarch who may have heard of the intended revolt. The fact that they were allowed to deliver such a letter indicates that Nebuchadnezzar was not oppressing the Hebrews but rather was allowing them a reasonable existence. Craftsmen, smiths, and other talented professionals may even have been exalted to fairly significant opportunities because they had been selectively deported as human resources in the aggrandizement of Nebuchadnezzar and of Babylon.

It was Ahikam's hand that had saved the life of Jeremiah from the angry mob of priests. It was now Elasah's hand that delivered this letter. They were the brother and the son of Shaphan, the priest who had found the scroll of the Law during the temple restoration. We must not forget the power that one God-fearing family can have on history, even when they stand in such a painful minority. Our churches ought to be nurturing families such as these, fathers like

Shaphan, discovering the scroll of God's word for their lives and sending out their Ahikams and Elasahs into the mainstream of society. This is the way we change the world and win the culture for Christ.

The letter was a comfort to those broken with homesickness and confusion. Its every word, read and circulated among them, must have brought to mind vivid pictures of Jeremiah himself and of all the ways he had tried to reach them with the truth. Perhaps they remembered when he cut off his dark curls in a mournful moment, silhouetted on the barren heights, or the time he wore the linen sash over his prophet's robes. Who could forget the sound of the clay pot breaking against the Potsherd Gate as he preached on their brokenness, or the way he bore the unjust scandal of Pashhur's stocks? This colorful figure would not let them go.

Eight hundred miles away from him now, with a whole new set of circumstances, they read his words with new ears. He had five things to say to them.

1. Settle down in Babylon and prepare for the long haul. *"Build houses and dwell in them; plant gardens and eat their fruit. Take wives and beget sons and daughters"* (vv. 5–6). Anyone thinking he was going to be back home in two years might not make these kinds of commitments. Here they were being told to roll up their sleeves and get to the business of living; theirs was going to be a long exile. As the saying goes, "bloom where you are planted." They were to be just as active, as fruitful, as industrious as if they were not in captivity. God never condones indigence under any circumstance. It was always His desire that His people be *"increased . . . and not diminished"* (v. 6).

2. Be good citizens. Become involved in making that place better for your having been there. *"Seek the peace of the city, . . . pray to the LORD for it"* (v. 7). Rather than becoming detached and passive, they were actively to be bringing down the grace of God into that pagan city. In much the same way, Christians are to be instruments of peace in the midst of a secular culture. When Jesus prayed for his disciples before his arrest in Gethsemane, He said, "I do not pray that You should take them out of the world, but that You should keep them from the evil *one.* They are not of the world, just as I am not of the world" (John 17:15–16). Jesus was clearly speaking of the way disciples were to live on earth, even though they were citizens

of heaven. Earlier, He had said to them, "Render to Caesar the things that are Caesar's, and to God the things that are God's" (Mark 12:17). We are to be law-abiding citizens within the secular culture, all the while knowing that this is not the culture to which we ultimately belong. Heaven is our real home. This earth is only the land of our exile, but it is a land nonetheless for which we are to pray and for which we are to seek peace.

3. Do not let yourselves be deceived. The land of their exile was not only filled with all the pagan gods of Babylon; it was also filled with their own false prophets. It was the latter about which Jeremiah was most concerned. How like this present world for the Christian. We can more easily detect many of the dangers of the secular system but not so easily do we detect heresies in the midst of those professing the faith.

Paul wrote passionately to the Galatians who were being led astray by a false doctrine. "There are some who trouble you and want to pervert the gospel of Christ" (Gal. 1:7). Centuries earlier, Jeremiah, operating out of those same protective instincts, said, *"Do not let your prophets and your diviners . . . deceive you, . . . I have not sent them, says the LORD"* (vv. 8–9). They were perverting the pure words of guidance coming to them from the Lord, words that were their only hope in the land of their exile.

4. In spite of how it may seem, you have a future and a hope. Many of those who heard the news concerning the length of exile, would have lots of reason to feel utterly hopeless. They would never live to see the promise fulfilled, *"I will visit you and perform My good word toward you, and cause you to return to this place"* (v. 10). About the only comfort they could draw from those words would be that possibly their children or their grandchildren might reap that blessing. Jeremiah, however, could have been describing something that reached beyond the return from Babylon, beyond any point in time; something that referred to the eternal destiny of all those who honor the Lord with their earthly lives.

The words that follow reach into the gospel age and bring further reality to Jeremiah's vision of what life can be like, even in the land of our exile. *"And you will seek Me and find Me, when you search for Me with all your heart"* (v. 13). Not only will they come back home to Jerusalem, they will come back home to the Lord, to the intimacy of heart that is described here. This is the intimacy available to us in the gospel age. Just as they read Jeremiah's words like a letter from home, so also should we read all of Scripture like a letter from home, the kind that will keep us from falling away in the land of exile and will sustain us until we come into the new Jerusalem.

5. The false prophets' teaching shall soon be disproved (vv. 15–23). Jeremiah had already told them not to be deceived by people directly contradicting his message to them. He seemed to be addressing, as a pastor, that unspoken question, "How shall we know who to believe?" He answered with a prophecy against the false prophets, Zedekiah, and the people remaining in Jerusalem, all of whom were partners in the deception. *"I will send on them the sword, the famine, and the pestilence, and will make them like rotten figs that cannot be eaten, they are so bad"* (v. 17). Because of their refusal to learn a lesson from the adversity of the first wave of deportees, they indeed would fight a losing battle when their city came under siege. Those who did not die then, died from the famine or the disease that struck the city prior to the attack by Nebuchadnezzar.

Not only were they given this general prophecy, they were given a specific prophecy in which two people were called by name. Most scholars agree on the historical accuracy of this account. Ahab and Zedekiah (not the king) were prophesying lies in the Lord's name. God said through Jeremiah, *"I will deliver them into the hand of Nebuchadnezzar king of Babylon, and he shall slay them before your eyes"* (v. 21). Jeremiah gave the deportees a very specific event to look for that would document his words. He could have told them the story of Hananiah and his fate. Instead he cited two more false prophets, ones right in their midst so that the drama of this fulfillment would have its fullest impact. He was not asking them to be gullible, to believe merely what he was telling them without some endorsement of his words. He was not asking them to violate their intellects. He instead gave them hard evidence for trusting the credibility of his prophecy, because it would color the next seventy years of their existence.

It was therefore no accident that he says that *"he shall slay them before your eyes."* No one will be allowed to say they had not heard or had not seen the fulfillment of Jeremiah's words. He gave them clear reason to believe him. As a matter of fact, Zedekiah and Ahab became infamous figures. There was no one who did not know who they were and what happened to them. One could say, "The Lord make you like Zedekiah and Ahab," and everyone would know what that meant. Jeremiah made it easy for them to believe him rather than the false prophets. He could never be accused of not giving them sufficient evidence.

False prophets are a dime a dozen. The Jeremiahs of the world are few and far between. They are a rare breed of obedient and persevering stock. Another false prophet was addressed personally in this letter. Shemaiah had written the high priest, Zephaniah, in Jerusalem saying that Jeremiah was a lunatic and that he ought to be thrown in prison. Again the protective hand of the Lord intervened. Instead of heeding Shemaiah's council, *"Zephaniah the priest read this letter in the hearing of Jeremiah the prophet"* (v. 29). Now all of the people of the deportation could read about Shemaiah's scheme and could then read Jeremiah's rebuke.

Jeremiah's letter, a word from home, was powerful. It seemed to read their minds, to answer their questions, to tell them some hard truth about the length of their stay, but then it overcame the sound of rebuke with good news about changed hearts and intimacy with God.

NOTES

1. William J. Petersen, *Jeremiah: The Prophet Who Wouldn't Quit* (Wheaton, Ill.: Victor Books, 1984), 107.
2. Flavius Josephus, *Antiquities of the Jews*, 3 vols. (Grand Rapids, Mich.: Baker Book House, 1984), 3:68.

CHAPTER SIXTEEN

The Book of Comfort

Jeremiah 30:1–33:26

Jeremiah 26–29 were largely narrative accounts of the prophet's experiences with both friend and foe—mostly foe. Jeremiah had resigned himself to a life of few friendships. Alone, he wept over the destiny of his people and over the doom he had to warn them of continually. The texture of his writing is largely foreboding and sorrowful. For this reason these next two chapters provide much refreshment. They are a mini-book of comfort set against a dark landscape. They are filled with joyous revelations concerning the restoration of Israel and Judah and of their restored unity. Some scholars maintain that this material is a collection of reflections written during Josiah's reign, but there is no historic note to that effect. The next two chapters are clearly in the reign of Zedekiah. In agreement with G. Campbell Morgan, I place them among the meditations penned by Jeremiah from his prison cell during the time that Jerusalem suffered her final siege.[1]

Because Jeremiah was so lonely and misunderstood, he lavished all the affairs of his heart on God. How many of us could make the staggering claim that God is our best friend? In turn, God lavished the affairs of His heart on Jeremiah according to His economy. The darker it got in Jerusalem, the brighter came the vision of restoration to the prophet's heart. Human nature tends to grow more despondent with bad news. Here, however, we find an operation of a nature quite higher than human nature.

THY WILL BE DONE ON EARTH

30:1 The word that came to Jeremiah from the LORD, saying,

2 "Thus speaks the LORD God of Israel, saying: 'Write in a book for yourself all the words that I have spoken to you.

3 'For behold, the days are coming,' says the LORD, 'that I will bring back from captivity My people Israel and Judah,' says the LORD. 'And I will cause them to return to the land that I gave to their fathers, and they shall possess it.'"

4 Now these *are* the words that the LORD spoke concerning Israel and Judah.

5 "For thus says the LORD:
'We have heard a voice of trembling,
Of fear, and not of peace.

6 Ask now, and see,
Whether a man is ever in labor with child?
So why do I see every man *with* his hands on
   his loins
Like a woman in labor,
And all faces turned pale?

7 Alas! For that day *is* great,
So that none *is* like it;
And it *is* the time of Jacob's trouble,
But he shall be saved out of it.

8 'For it shall come to pass in that day,'
Says the LORD of hosts,
'*That* I will break his yoke from your neck,
And will burst your bonds;
Foreigners shall no more enslave them.

9 But they shall serve the LORD their God,
And David their king,
Whom I will raise up for them.

10 'Therefore do not fear, O My servant Jacob,'
   says the LORD,
'Nor be dismayed, O Israel;
For behold, I will save you from afar,
And your seed from the land of their captivity.
Jacob shall return, have rest and be quiet,
And no one shall make *him* afraid.

11 For I *am* with you,' says the LORD, 'to save
   you;
Though I make a full end of all nations where
   I have scattered you,

Yet I will not make a complete end of you.
But I will correct you in justice,
And will not let you go altogether
    unpunished.'
12 "For thus says the LORD:
'Your affliction *is* incurable,
Your wound *is* severe.
13 *There is* no one to plead your cause,
That you may be bound up;
You have no healing medicines.
14 All your lovers have forgotten you;
They do not seek you;
For I have wounded you with the wound of an
    enemy,
With the chastisement of a cruel one,
For the multitude of your iniquities,
Because your sins have increased.
15 Why do you cry about your affliction?
Your sorrow *is* incurable.
Because of the multitude of your iniquities,
Because your sins have increased,
I have done these things to you.
16 'Therefore all those who devour you shall be
    devoured;
And all your adversaries, every one of them,
    shall go into captivity;
Those who plunder you shall become plunder,
And all who prey upon you I will make a prey.
17 For I will restore health to you
And heal you of your wounds,' says the LORD,
'Because they called you an outcast *saying:*
"This *is* Zion;
No one seeks her."'
18 "Thus says the LORD:
'Behold, I will bring back the captivity of
    Jacob's tents,
And have mercy on his dwelling places;
The city shall be built upon its own mound,
And the palace shall remain according to its
    own plan.
19 Then out of them shall proceed thanksgiving
And the voice of those who make merry;

I will multiply them, and they shall not
    diminish;
I will also glorify them, and they shall not be
    small.
20 Their children also shall be as before,
And their congregation shall be established
    before Me;
And I will punish all who oppress them.
21 Their nobles shall be from among them,
And their governor shall come from their
    midst;
Then I will cause him to draw near,
And he shall approach Me;
For who *is* this who pledged his heart to
    approach Me?' says the LORD.
22 'You shall be My people,
And I will be your God.'"
23 Behold, the whirlwind of the LORD
Goes forth with fury,
A continuing whirlwind;
It will fall violently on the head of the wicked.
24 The fierce anger of the LORD will not return
    until He has done it,
And until He has performed the intents of His
    heart.
In the latter days you will consider it.

Jer. 30:1-24

Jeremiah spent forty years in the prophetic ministry despairing of
human nature, of its proclivity to sin and idolatry, and of its blind
refusal to be changed. Fallen nature is willful. It exalts itself against
God. Yet here Jeremiah saw so clearly that fallen nature did not have
the last word. *"You shall be My people, And I will be your God"* (v. 22).
Israel sought to own herself, to be her own master when God never
intended her for that kind of management. He would restore her to
His management. Her will brought destruction. His will brought reconstruction. This is seen here in eight promises.

1. *"'I will bring back from captivity My people Israel and Judah,'*
. . . *'And I will cause them to return to the land that I gave to their
fathers, and they shall possess it'"* (v. 3). This same promise occurs
again in verses 10 and 18. Like soldiers returning from the

215

battlefield, expatriates would see their homeland with the new eyes of appreciation. The poignance and joy of this homecoming would be even more striking by their comparison with the days of pain and labor and fear described in verses 5–7.

Men labor as a woman does in childbirth. Their voices tremble. Their faces pale in fear. Just as a man cannot possibly bring forth a child, neither can humanity bring forth its own redemption. Finally in pain and futility we cry, "Alas!" Here Jeremiah uses the biggest little word in all of Scripture—"but." *"But he shall be saved out of it"* (v. 7).

2. *"I will break his yoke from your neck, And will burst your bonds"* (v. 8). Judah and Israel had tried so hard to avoid all yokes, to pursue their own willful course. The more they searched for this so-called freedom the more bondage they found. Their harlotry and stolen pleasures did not produce happiness at all. Their options became narrower and narrower as the yoke of Babylon tightened around them as a giant symbol of their slavery to sin. Then one day, centuries later, a man named Jesus entered His hometown of Nazareth, climbed the synagogue steps, looked into the faces of His congregation, and made this staggering proclamation: "The Spirit of the LORD is upon Me, Because He has anointed Me . . . To proclaim liberty to the captives" (Luke 4:18; cf. Isa. 61:1–2). The God who gave His "I wills" to Isaiah and to Jeremiah had now come to execute them.

Liberty from captivity did not mean being free to go and do their own thing. It meant being free for something much higher, namely, the service of the Lord. *"Foreigners shall no more enslave them. But they shall serve the LORD their God"* (vv. 8–9). The whole idea is echoed in God's word to Pharaoh before the Exodus: "Let my people go that they may serve Me."

3. *"And David their king, Whom I will raise up for them"* (v. 9). Not only will He give them hearts to serve Him, but He will give them a righteous king to serve. Gone would be the woeful shepherds and the pageant of wicked kings whom Jeremiah lamented and for whom he wept bitter tears.

Seventeen generations after Jeremiah wrote this promise, it appeared again, almost word for word, on the lips of Zacharias, the father of John the Baptist. Knowing that his son was the forerunner of the kingdom that was now at hand, Zacharias all but sang these words: "Blessed *is* the Lord God of Israel, For He . . . has raised

up a horn of salvation for us In the house of His servant David"
(Luke 1:69). The genealogies in both Luke's and Matthew's Gospels
establish Jesus' descent from David.

4. *"Though I make a full end of all nations where I have scattered
you, Yet I will not make a complete end of you"* (v. 11). Nations would
come and nations would go; they would strut their stuff across the
stage of human history. Israel, however, was different from all of
them. She would come, but she would never go. Yes, she would be
punished and developed by wars and tribulations. She would look
like any other nation, but unlike any other nation she was under the
preserving hand of the Almighty.

Babylon was destroyed, never to rise again as a world power,
never to be anything more than a saga in a history book. The Jews,
however, rallied from this captivity and repatriated during the Persian Empire. They have been rallying ever since through the purgative tumults of their history. Another repatriation occurred after the
Second World War. In 1948, they gained the status of a modern
nation, while giant Babylon has long since slipped into obscurity.

5. *"I will correct you in justice, And will not let you go altogether
unpunished"* (v. 11). Having a destiny unique among the nations did
not mean being immune to their sufferings. God shepherded Israel
through the affairs of the world, using them to punish her and to
correct. "Whom the LORD loves He chastens, And scourges every son
whom He receives" (Heb. 12:6). The punishment was in perfect proportion to the crime. In punishment, God is just. In reconciliation,
God is extravagant.

6. *"And all who prey upon you I will make a prey"* (v. 16). Those
nations whom God used to punish Israel would themselves be punished as a final vindication of the mark He had placed on His people. Yes, they plunder; yes, they devour; but God has the last
word—*"All those who devour you shall be devoured; . . . Those who
plunder you shall become plunder"* (v. 16). He writes the final chapter
on all the earth's histories. The tyrant and his tribal deity have their
season. They force their "I wills" upon the world and upon the nation of Israel. Nevertheless it is the great Ego, I AM WHO I AM, to
whom they will all answer.

7. *"I will restore health to you And heal you of your wounds"*
(v. 17). The Great Physician then gave His reason. Notice that He
did not say, "I will heal you because you are so sick." He said, "I will

heal because they called you an outcast." The emphasis was not upon their need but upon God's honor for having invested in them.

When He described their incurable wound, He was really describing the disease of sin and its attendant loss of dignity. *"Your affliction is incurable, Your wound is severe. There is no one to plead your cause, That you may be bound up; You have no healing medicines"* (vv. 12–13). Would you like your doctor to be leaning over your hospital bed telling you that? Listen again, there is good news here. There may be no earthly physician with a cure, but there is a heavenly physician. "You have no healing medicine," He said, but "I will restore you to health."

Like Israel, all humanity is sick with sin. There is no health in us. What we thought would make us happy has in fact make us miserable. *"All your lovers have forgotten you"* (v. 14). Our misplaced affections will ultimately wound us because we were designed for God and for the health that He alone can give.

8. *"Then out of them shall proceed thanksgiving And the voice of those who make merry; I will multiply them, and they shall not diminish; I will also glorify them, and they shall not be small"* (v. 19). A song that began with the *"voice of trembling"* (v. 5) now ended with the voice of merrymaking. It was a song of grand reversals, of yokes being broken, of predators becoming prey, of wounds becoming emblems of health, of the dirge becoming shouts of joy.

Jeremiah sang from his prison cell. He sang with a nature other than that of his humanity. Years later another song was heard when Paul and Silas were arrested in Philippi. They were badly beaten. Their feet were fastened with iron clamps and anchored to the dark wall of an inner cell, the place for the most dangerous criminals. Their bodies were throbbing with pain, but two voices rose against the silence of the jail. Inmates heard songs of praise, sung not by human nature but by God's nature being expressed through humans. This is the nature that makes ordinary people do extraordinary things.

This was the nature that promised to bring Israel home, to set her free to serve, to give her a righteous king to serve and a unique destiny. She would be disciplined by God and yet vindicated by God. She would be healed and finally enlarged by joy. Now Jeremiah went on to reflect upon the nature of God's everlasting love.

Oh Love That Will Not Let Me Go

31:1 "At the same time," says the LORD, "I will be the
God of all the families of Israel, and they shall be
My people."
> 2 Thus says the LORD:
> "The people who survived the sword
> Found grace in the wilderness—
> Israel, when I went to give him rest."
> 3 The LORD has appeared of old to me, *saying:*
> "Yes, I have loved you with an everlasting
> love;
> Therefore with lovingkindness I have drawn
> you.
> 4 Again I will build you, and you shall be
> rebuilt,
> O virgin of Israel!
> You shall again be adorned with your
> tambourines,
> And shall go forth in the dances of those who
> rejoice.
> 5 You shall yet plant vines on the mountains of
> Samaria;
> The planters shall plant and eat *them* as
> ordinary food.
> 6 For there shall be a day
> *When* the watchmen will cry on Mount
> Ephraim,
> 'Arise, and let us go up *to* Zion,
> To the LORD our God.'"
> 7 For thus says the LORD:
> "Sing with gladness for Jacob,
> And shout among the chief of the nations;
> Proclaim, give praise, and say,
> 'O LORD, save Your people,
> The remnant of Israel!'
> 8 Behold, I will bring them from the north
> country,
> And gather them from the ends of the earth,
> *Among* them the blind and the lame,
> The woman with child

And the one who labors with child, together;
A great throng shall return there.
9 They shall come with weeping,
And with supplications I will lead them.
I will cause them to walk by the rivers of
waters,
In a straight way in which they shall not
stumble;
For I am a Father to Israel,
And Ephraim *is* My firstborn.
10 "Hear the word of the LORD, O nations,
And declare *it* in the isles afar off, and say,
'He who scattered Israel will gather him,
And keep him as a shepherd *does* his flock.'
11 For the LORD has redeemed Jacob,
And ransomed him from the hand of one
stronger than he.
12 Therefore they shall come and sing in the
height of Zion,
Streaming to the goodness of the LORD—
For wheat and new wine and oil,
For the young of the flock and the herd;
Their souls shall be like a well-watered
garden,
And they shall sorrow no more at all.
13 "Then shall the virgin rejoice in the dance,
And the young men and the old, together;
For I will turn their mourning to joy,
Will comfort them,
And make them rejoice rather than sorrow.
14 I will satiate the soul of the priests with
abundance,
And My people shall be satisfied with My
goodness, says the LORD."
15 Thus says the LORD:
"A voice was heard in Ramah,
Lamentation *and* bitter weeping,
Rachel weeping for her children,
Refusing to be comforted for her children,
Because they *are* no more."
16 Thus says the LORD:
"Refrain your voice from weeping,

220

And your eyes from tears;
For your work shall be rewarded, says the
   LORD,
And they shall come back from the land of the
   enemy.
17 There is hope in your future, says the LORD,
That *your* children shall come back to their
   own border.
18 "I have surely heard Ephraim bemoaning
      himself:
'You have chastised me, and I was chastised,
Like an untrained bull;
Restore me, and I will return,
For You *are* the LORD my God.
19 Surely, after my turning, I repented;
And after I was instructed, I struck myself on
   the thigh;
I was ashamed, yes, even humiliated,
Because I bore the reproach of my youth.'
20 *Is* Ephraim My dear son?
Is he a pleasant child?
For though I spoke against him,
I earnestly remember him still;
Therefore My heart yearns for him;
I will surely have mercy on him, says the
   LORD.
21 "Set up signposts,
Make landmarks;
Set your heart toward the highway,
The way in *which* you went.
Turn back, O virgin of Israel,
Turn back to these your cities.
22 How long will you gad about,
O you backsliding daughter?
For the LORD has created a new thing in the
   earth—
A woman shall encompass a man."
23 Thus says the LORD of hosts, the God of Israel:
"They shall again use this speech in the land of Judah
and in its cities, when I bring back their captivity:
'The LORD bless you, O home of justice, *and* mountain
of holiness!'

24 "And there shall dwell in Judah itself, and in all
its cities together, farmers and those going out with
flocks.

25 "For I have satiated the weary soul, and I have
replenished every sorrowful soul."

26 After this I awoke and looked around, and my
sleep was sweet to me.

Jer. 31:1–26

God's ultimate intention for Israel is expressed in the "I wills." We
should remember them when we share our faith with the Jews and
when we consider our foreign policy in today's global struggles. His
love for them is not to be taken lightly. Like the words of the hymn,
it is a love that will not let them go.

Verses 1–7 expand the theme of everlasting love. It is not a theme
we could have discovered on our own. The reason we have any
record of it at all, or any way of talking about it, is because God
visited us with it. *"The LORD has appeared of old to me"* (v. 3).
Jeremiah made it clear that we are the visited planet and he was the
visited prophet. We have been given extraordinary news that
reaches beyond our borders of time and space and into a new dimension. All of creation should hang in suspended animation waiting for the sound of these words: *"Yes, I have loved you with an
everlasting love"* (v. 3). The fact that they survived Pharaoh's sword
in Egypt was proof of this love. That they found grace in the
wilderness with Moses was another proof. God documented His
statement with these historical facts.

Again He keeps love from being an abstract concept. *"I will build
you, and you shall be rebuilt"* (v. 4). Israel was to have a concrete,
architectural reality. *"You shall again be adorned with your tambour-
ines, And shall go forth in the dances of those who rejoice"* (v. 4). The
physical imagery of sound and sight promised a palpable, bodily experience of His love. The transcendent reality of God's everlasting
love was translated into the language of our humanity. When the
Jews repatriated during the time of the Persian Empire they rebuilt
the walls of Jerusalem. Nehemiah was their project manager. Then
with all manner of music, they went forth upon those walls in a pro-
cessional of joy bursting with color and sound that was witnessed by
the incredulous world around them.

From his prison cell, Jeremiah prophetically heard the cry of the watchman from the mountain tops: *"Arise, and let us go up to Zion, To the LORD our God"* (v. 6). He anticipated a new infusion of zeal, of get-up-and-go enthusiasm into the now dark and dry hearts of a people dead in their sins.

Not only was the imagery physical, it was very personal. Jeremiah did not just say, "Sing with gladness for the Jews." He said, "Sing with gladness for Jacob" (v. 7). All of the people were spoken to through the history of this one man, the father of the twelve tribes and symbol of the chosen nation. God likes the specific. He also likes the spectacular.

"I will . . . gather them from the ends of the earth . . . A great throng shall return" (v. 8). Remember his council in the letter to the exiles, "that you may be increased . . . and not diminished" (29:6). This was a class act, a cast-of-thousands production because the producer and director is an extravagant God. Jews will return not just from one direction but from every direction. They would not just trickle into Jerusalem; they would come *"Streaming to the goodness of the LORD"* (v. 12). They would not come silently but with a great noise of singing. They would come home not with mourning and slumped shoulders but with great rejoicing (v. 13). It would not just be the strong members of their lot but *"the blind and the lame, The woman with child And the one who labors with child"* (v. 8). They would not come limping as if they were barely making it. Heavens no! *"Their souls shall be like a well-watered garden"* (v. 12). Remember the priests who caused Jeremiah such grief? Look at them now. *"I will satiate the soul of the priests with abundance"* (v. 14). To the derelict and restless people who could never find contentment He says, *"and My people shall be satisfied with My goodness"* (v. 14).

Jeremiah returned to the use of personal names in pronouncing a benediction upon the Northern Kingdom in verses 15–22, which he identified as Ephraim. Ephraim was a son of Joseph and therefore a grandson of Jacob and Rachel. He was the one upon whom Jacob chose to confer the birthright. Hence he came to symbolize all those who were destined to return to the Lord from the world of sin. Because of his tribal location in the north, he also came to symbolize the whole Northern Kingdom, which was carried into exile by the Assyrians one hundred years prior to the fall of the Southern Kingdom.

"A voice was heard in Ramah . . . Rachel weeping for her children, Refusing to be comforted for her children, Because they are no more"

223

(v. 15). Rachel, the wife whom Jacob loved, died giving birth to Benjamin. She was buried in Ramah. She never lived to see her beloved Joseph become ruler of Egypt, nor to see him sold into slavery. She never lived to see his son Ephraim and to be present at the family gathering in which her beloved husband blessed their grandchild. Yet with a mother's heart she held on to her children and to their children, even in eternity. Jeremiah's language suggested that she wept from her grave. What a model of tenacity! A mother's heart never gives up. It is to such hearts that God has this to say: *"Refrain your voice from weeping . . . For your work shall be rewarded . . . And they shall come back from the land of the enemy"* (v. 16). If Rachel, in all her human frailty, cared that much, how much more does a perfect God care? What pains has He taken to illustrate that love, using personal stories of people just like us? This is a lesson to all who desire to make our communication of His word as powerful and compelling as we possibly can. Make it personal. Tell a story that casts it in the flesh-and-blood experience of our humanity.

Verses 18 and 19 refer to the repentant spirit with which Ephraim returns from the land of exile. Like the prodigal son, he now turns toward the home to which he had once turned his back. He has set his heart *"toward the highway"* (v. 21). His reasoning is much like that of the prodigal. "I was ashamed, yes, even humiliated, because I bore the reproach of my youth" (30:19). Like the extravagant father of the prodigal, God says, *"Is Ephraim My dear son? Is he a pleasant child? . . . I will surely have mercy on him"* (v. 20). Ephraim, a representative of all repentant people, finds this everlasting love compelling.

Jeremiah used another strange metaphor, like the metaphor of the man in labor. Only this time he used his metaphor to illustrate something exceedingly good. *"For the LORD has created a new thing in the earth—A woman shall encompass a man"* (v. 22). Most scholars seem puzzled over this language and offer mostly awkward and meaningless interpretations. I find myself in agreement with Matthew Henry who sees this new thing as the incarnation of Christ. A woman encloses in her womb "the mighty one," for this is the meaning of the word used here.[2]

In verses 23–26, Jeremiah speaks to the Southern Kingdom. Once again, unbelievable as it seemed, particularly during this dark hour of destruction, people would stand within the city walls under a new restoration and say, *"The LORD bless you, O home of justice, and mountain of holiness"* (v. 23). At the moment, the city was anything but a home of justice. It was riddled with lies and compromise. This city was anything but a mountain of holiness; it was filled with the stench of harlotry. Jeremiah was given a vision beyond this into a day that was to come.

BEHOLD, THE DAYS ARE COMING

31:27 "Behold, the days are coming, says the LORD, that I will sow the house of Israel and the house of Judah with the seed of man and the seed of beast.

28 "And it shall come to pass, *that* as I have watched over them to pluck up, to break down, to throw down, to destroy, and to afflict, so I will watch over them to build and to plant, says the LORD.

29 "In those days they shall say no more:
'The fathers have eaten sour grapes,
And the children's teeth are set on edge.'

30 "But every one shall die for his own iniquity; every man who eats the sour grapes, his teeth shall be set on edge.

31 "Behold, the days are coming, says the LORD, when I will make a new covenant with the house of Israel and with the house of Judah—

32 "not according to the covenant that I made with their fathers in the day *that* I took them by the hand to lead them out of the land of Egypt, My covenant which they broke, though I was a husband to them, says the LORD.

33 "But this *is* the covenant that I will make with the house of Israel after those days, says the LORD: I will put My law in their minds, and write it on their hearts; and I will be their God, and they shall be My people.

34 "No more shall every man teach his neighbor, and every man his brother, saying, 'Know the LORD,' for they all shall know Me, from the least of them to the greatest of them, says the LORD. For I will forgive their iniquity, and their sin I will remember no more."

35 Thus says the LORD,
Who gives the sun for a light by day,

The ordinances of the moon and the stars for a
    light by night,
Who disturbs the sea,
And its waves roar
(The LORD of hosts *is* His name):
36 "If those ordinances depart
From before Me, says the LORD,
Then the seed of Israel shall also cease
From being a nation before Me forever."
37 Thus says the LORD:
"If heaven above can be measured,
And the foundations of the earth searched out
    beneath,
I will also cast off all the seed of Israel
For all that they have done, says the LORD.
38 "Behold, the days are coming, says the LORD,
that the city shall be built for the LORD from the
Tower of Hananel to the Corner Gate.
39 "The surveyor's line shall again extend straight
forward over the hill Gareb; then it shall turn toward
Goath.
40 "And the whole valley of the dead bodies and
of the ashes, and all the fields as far as the Brook
Kidron, to the corner of the Horse Gate toward the
east, *shall be* holy to the LORD. It shall not be plucked
up or thrown down anymore forever."

Jer. 31:27–40

The words in this title preface three revelations concerning the
restoration of Judah and the everlasting love of God. It is possible
that Jeremiah experienced them in the form of dreams. At the very
least, these visions came out of a great serenity. "After this I awoke
and looked around, and my sleep was sweet to me" (v. 26).

1. *"Behold, the days are coming, says the LORD, that I will sow the
house of Israel and the house of Judah with the seed of man and the seed
of beast"* (v. 27). He continued by speaking of building and planting,
images long familiar to the prophet from his early days in Anathoth
when the Lord called and commissioned him. In these coming days,
the dynamic would not be destructive, but rather constructive.
There would be a reversal of their verbal confession. They would
quit complaining that they were suffering unjustly for the sins of

their predecessors. No more would they say, *"The fathers have eaten sour grapes, And the children's teeth are set on edge"* (v. 29). Perhaps this is the origin of the expression, "crying sour grapes," often used to describe belligerent people. Then under the reversal brought about by the new days, they would be aware of perfect justice and of individual moral responsibility. They would have no one to blame but themselves; then they would be able to say, *"But every one shall die for his own iniquity; every man who eats the sour grapes, his teeth shall be set on edge"* (v. 30). They would understand justice. They would proclaim it with the same lips that had once served all manner of injustice. The ideal of Israel would yet be realized.

2. *"Behold, the days are coming, . . . when I will make a new covenant with the house of Israel and with the house of Judah—"* (v. 31). God distinguished this covenant from the one He had given them at the time of the Exodus. The terms of that covenant were written on tablets of stone. They were broken. This new covenant would be written directly upon their hearts (v. 33). *"I will forgive their iniquity, and their sin I will remember no more"* (v. 34). It is the forgiveness that washes away the barrier between humanity and God, and sets up a dynamic of intimate knowing.

God wants to give assurance of this reality. The sun never fails to give light by day, nor is the night completely dark because it is sprinkled with the lights of the moon and the stars. We never sit here on planet Earth doubting this fact. We never loose sleep worrying about the reliability of these natural ordinances. Neither are we to worry about the reliability of God's promises concerning Israel. *"If those ordinances depart From before Me, . . . Then the seed of Israel shall also cease From being a nation before Me forever"* (v. 36). God has used Babylon "to root out," but He will again "build and plant" (1:10). Like skywriting from an extravagant God, the sun and the moon testify to the sureness of His word. They cry out, "I have loved you with an everlasting love" (v. 3). Can the heavens be measured? Can we assign a number to infinity? Can we search out the foundations of the earth? If we can do that, then God can cast off Israel. His forsaking them is not improbable—it is impossible. The day was coming when everyone will know this, "from the least of them to the greatest."

3. *"Behold, the days are coming, says the LORD, that the city shall be built for the LORD from the Tower of Hananel to the Corner Gate"* (v. 38). The first of these announcements related to planting; the third

related to building. There is nothing abstract about this imagery. It is an architectural reality as well as a spiritual reality. These and two other proper names refer to the northeast and northwest, the southeast and southwest corners of the city. The fulfillment of this promise would be so tangible that "the surveyor's line" can touch it. It shall be "holy to the Lord." *"It shall not be plucked up or thrown down anymore forever"* (v. 40). Jeremiah was so sure of these realities that he decided to walk out on them in the radical way recounted in the next chapter.

PUTTING YOUR MONEY WHERE YOUR MOUTH IS

32:1 The word that came to Jeremiah from the LORD in the tenth year of Zedekiah king of Judah, which was the eighteenth year of Nebuchadnezzar.

2 For then the king of Babylon's army besieged Jerusalem, and Jeremiah the prophet was shut up in the court of the prison, which *was in* the king of Judah's house.

3 For Zedekiah king of Judah had shut him up, saying, "Why do you prophesy and say, 'Thus says the LORD: "Behold, I will give this city into the hand of the king of Babylon, and he shall take it;

4 "and Zedekiah king of Judah shall not escape from the hand of the Chaldeans, but shall surely be delivered into the hand of the king of Babylon, and shall speak with him face to face, and see him eye to eye;

5 "then he shall lead Zedekiah to Babylon, and there he shall be until I visit him," says the LORD; "though you fight with the Chaldeans, you shall not succeed"'?"

6 And Jeremiah said, "The word of the LORD came to me, saying,

7 'Behold, Hanamel the son of Shallum your uncle will come to you, saying, "Buy my field which *is* in Anathoth, for the right of redemption *is* yours to buy *it.*"'

8 "Then Hanamel my uncle's son came to me in the court of the prison according to the word of the

LORD, and said to me, 'Please buy my field that *is* in Anathoth, which *is* in the country of Benjamin; for the right of inheritance *is* yours, and the redemption yours; buy *it* for yourself.' Then I knew that this was the word of the LORD.

9 "So I bought the field from Hanamel, the son of my uncle who *was* in Anathoth, and weighed *out to* him the money—seventeen shekels of silver.

10 "And I signed the deed and sealed *it,* took witnesses, and weighed the money on the scales.

11 "So I took the purchase deed, *both* that which was sealed *according* to the law and custom, and that which was open;

12 "and I gave the purchase deed to Baruch the son of Neriah, son of Mahseiah, in the presence of Hanamel my uncle's *son,* and in the presence of the witnesses who signed the purchase deed, before all the Jews who sat in the court of the prison.

13 "Then I charged Baruch before them, saying,

14 'Thus says the LORD of hosts, the God of Israel: "Take these deeds, both this purchase deed which is sealed and this deed which is open, and put them in an earthen vessel, that they may last many days."

15 'For thus says the LORD of hosts, the God of Israel: "Houses and fields and vineyards shall be possessed again in this land."'

16 "Now when I had delivered the purchase deed to Baruch the son of Neriah, I prayed to the LORD, saying:

17 'Ah, Lord GOD! Behold, You have made the heavens and the earth by Your great power and outstretched arm. There is nothing too hard for You.

18 '*You* show lovingkindness to thousands, and repay the iniquity of the fathers into the bosom of their children after them—the Great, the Mighty God, whose name *is* the LORD of hosts.

19 '*You are* great in counsel and mighty in work, for your eyes *are* open to all the ways of the sons of men, to give everyone according to his ways and according to the fruit of his doings.

20 'You have set signs and wonders in the land of Egypt, to this day, and in Israel and among *other*

men; and You have made Yourself a name, as it is
this day.

21 'You have brought Your people Israel out of the
land of Egypt with signs and wonders, with a strong
hand and an outstretched arm, and with great terror;

22 'You have given them this land, of which You
swore to their fathers to give them—"a land flowing
with milk and honey."

23 'And they came in and took possession of it, but
they have not obeyed Your voice or walked in Your
law. They have done nothing of all that You commanded them to do; therefore You have caused all
this calamity to come upon them.

24 'Look, the siege mounds! They have come to the
city to take it; and the city has been given into the
hand of the Chaldeans who fight against it, because
of the sword and famine and pestilence. What You
have spoken has happened; there You see *it!*

25 'And You have said to me, O Lord GOD, "Buy
the field for money, and take witnesses"!—yet the
city has been given into the hand of the Chaldeans.'"

26 Then the word of the LORD came to Jeremiah,
saying,

27 "Behold, I *am* the LORD, the God of all flesh. Is
there anything too hard for Me?

28 "Therefore thus says the LORD: 'Behold, I will
give this city into the hand of the Chaldeans, into the
hand of Nebuchadnezzar king of Babylon, and he
shall take it.

29 'And the Chaldeans who fight against this city
shall come and set fire to this city and burn it, with the
houses on whose roofs they have offered incense to
Baal and poured out drink offerings to other gods,
to provoke Me to anger;

30 'because the children of Israel and the children
of Judah have done only evil before Me from their
youth. For the children of Israel have provoked Me
only to anger with the work of their hands,' says the
LORD.

31 'For this city has been to Me *a provocation of* My
anger and My fury from the day that they built it, even
to this day; so I will remove it from before My face

32 'because of all the evil of the children of Israel and the children of Judah, which they have done to provoke Me to anger—they, their kings, their princes, their priests, their prophets, the men of Judah, and the inhabitants of Jerusalem.

33 'And they have turned to Me the back, and not the face; though I taught them, rising up early and teaching *them*, yet they have not listened to receive instruction.

34 'But they set their abominations in the house which is called by My name, to defile it.

35 'And they built the high places of Baal which *are* in the Valley of the Son of Hinnom, to cause their sons and their daughters to pass through *the fire* to Molech, which I did not command them, nor did it come into My mind that they should do this abomination, to cause Judah to sin.'

36 "Now therefore, thus says the LORD, the God of Israel, concerning this city of which you say, 'It shall be delivered into the hand of the king of Babylon by the sword, by the famine, and by the pestilence':

37 'Behold, I will gather them out of all countries where I have driven them in My anger, in My fury, and in great wrath; I will bring them back to this place, and I will cause them to dwell safely.

38 'They shall be My people, and I will be their God;

39 'then I will give them one heart and one way, that they may fear Me forever, for the good of them and their children after them.

40 'And I will make an everlasting covenant with them, that I will not turn away from doing them good; but I will put My fear in their hearts so that they will not depart from Me.

41 'Yes, I will rejoice over them to do them good, and I will assuredly plant them in this land, with all My heart and with all My soul.'

42 "For thus says the LORD: 'Just as I have brought all this great calamity on this people, so I will bring on them all the good that I have promised them.

43 'And fields will be bought in this land of which

you say, *"It is* desolate, without man or beast; it has
been given into the hand of the Chaldeans."

44 'Men will buy fields for money, sign deeds and
seal *them,* and take witnesses, in the land of Benjamin, in the places around Jerusalem, in the cities of
Judah, in the cities of the mountains, in the cities
of the lowland, and in the cities of the South; for I
will cause their captives to return,' says the LORD."

Jer. 32:1–44

In Zedekiah's tenth year, Nebuchadnezzar besieged Jerusalem
(vv. 1–2). Jeremiah was *"shut up in the court of the prison, which was
in the king of Judah's house"* (v. 2). The Book of Comfort was written
from the confines of this prison; it was a great triumph of a prophet
and his God over circumstances. Jeremiah had learned a new song,
one that utterly transcended the darkness. He was called to "put
his money where his mouth was," to make a financial investment in
the vision of the reconstruction of Jerusalem. When spiritual reality
reaches our wallet, we then know for sure that it has reached our
heart and has become more than lip service.

Before he recounted this strange turn of events, Jeremiah explained the atmosphere in which it happened. Verses 3–5 find king
and prophet in a revealing confrontation. Zedekiah simply could not
understand what made Jeremiah tick. "Why do you prophesy that
the city will fall to Babylon?" he asked Jeremiah (v. 3). "Why do you
say that I will be captured by Nebuchadnezzar, that we will meet
each other face to face and eye to eye?" (v. 4). "Why do you say that
no matter how hard we fight, we're going to lose?" (v. 5). This was all
such horrible, discouraging news. Zedekiah did not care about what
was true. He cared about what was pleasant. People like that simply
do not understand the Jeremiahs of the world who are committed to
obedience, truth, and moral absolutes regardless of how uncomfortable they might make us.

People living resolute lives are dangerous to those who are only
seeking pleasure. Zedekiah kept the prophet imprisoned in the
palace, where he could keep an eye on him. That did not stop
the business of the real kingdom from continuing. It never does.
The Book of Comfort was produced for the future enrichment of
civilization and for the building up of the body of Christ, but
Zedekiah thought he was containing the prophet. Out of this same

imprisonment God produced a heart-warming story that called Jeremiah to make a radical financial investment. Straight past Zedekiah and all his posted guards came the word of the Lord to Jeremiah: *"Behold, Hanamel the son of Shallum your uncle will come to you, saying, 'Buy my field which is in Anathoth, for the right of redemption is yours to buy it'"* (v. 7). If Jeremiah's past obediences had gotten him into prison, what kind of trouble would his future obediences bring him? God knew that he needed confirmation for this next radical assignment. Even though he had been seasoned by almost forty years of prophetic ministry, he still needed tokens of God's presence and nudges into faithfulness.

The day that his cousin Hanamel walked into the prison and spoke the words almost exactly as God had said he would, something happened for Jeremiah. *"Then I knew that this was the word of the LORD"* (v. 8). Once the confirmation came, there was no time wasted. *"So I bought the field from Hanamel"* (v. 9). Instant obedience is a rare quality, the kind that leaves the consequences to the Lord and does the task closest at hand. Jeremiah described the details of the transaction, the weighing out of the money, the amount of it, the signing of the deed, the sealing of it, and the presence of witnesses. It was all done *"according to the law and custom"* (v. 11). Then he turned to his secretary and faithful friend, Baruch, handing him the purchase deed in the presence of his cousin, the witnesses, and all the Jews in the court of the prison. *"Then I charged Baruch before them, saying, . . . 'Take these deeds . . . and put them in an earthen vessel, that they may last many days'"* (vv. 13–14). Jeremiah, with all the substance of his being, both physical and financial, took a stand on God's word. *"Houses and fields and vineyards shall be possessed again in this land"* (v. 15). Jeremiah knew that he would not live to see the day, but the deed would be there to prove that God had said it would happen. He had literally bought into the promises of God and invested in their future. Do we make investments in the kingdom? Are we this sure of its promises?

I'm not at all sure that this obedience was easy for Jeremiah. As a matter of fact, he prayed to understand it. Notice that he did not pray before the obedience, but rather afterward. We find a sigh similar to the one when God called him from Anathoth: *"Ah, Lord GOD! Behold, You have made the heavens and the earth by Your great power and outstretched arm. There is nothing too hard for You"* (v. 17).

Jeremiah continues in this praise and in a rehearsal of God's mighty deeds in Israel's history for seven verses. At the end of his praise, he offers one little verse from his humanity because as far as his eye can see there were nothing but siege mounds in and around Jerusalem. *"You have said to me, O Lord GOD, 'Buy the field for money, and take witnesses'! —yet the city has been given into the hand of the Chaldeans'"* (v. 25). He offered seven parts of praise to one part of puzzlement. With that he rested his case.

To me this embodies the reality of the faith life. It is not carefree nor is it blind to circumstances. Faith looks squarely at the circumstances, admits a fear, and keeps on going. It is this kind of faith life that God answers with His assurance in verses 21–44. He began His answer by keying on the first thing Jeremiah had said, asking the question, *"Is there anything too hard for Me?"* (v. 27).

A city lying in charred and smoking ruins may be hard for the tribal deities to restore, but the task was not difficult for the God of heaven and earth. He confirms the destruction and the reason for it in verses 28–36. Then He verifies the reconstruction and describes it, summarizing with the words, *"Just as I have brought all this great calamity on this people, so I will bring on them all the good that I have promised them"* (v. 42). Finally He gives Jeremiah the understanding he had prayed for, why it was that he had been asked to buy the field. The whole process of owning real estate, its laws and customs, would again be restored to Israel. Countless times God had issued the promise that they would possess the land. In order to illustrate that this was not just so much Jewish poetry, God called Jeremiah to take a big risk.

God has sealed His word with the ordinances of the sun, the moon, and the stars. Now He sealed it by purchasing real estate through his prophet. May they never accuse Him of not confirming His promises. What more could He say or do, this God of everlasting love?

RISKTAKERS, CARETAKERS, AND UNDERTAKERS

33:1 Moreover the word of the LORD came to Jeremiah a second time, while he was still shut up in the court of the prison, saying,

2 "Thus says the LORD who made it, the LORD who formed it to establish it (the LORD *is* His name):

3 'Call to Me, and I will answer you, and show you great and mighty things, which you do not know.'

4 "For thus says the LORD, the God of Israel, concerning the houses of this city and the houses of the kings of Judah, which have been pulled down *to fortify* against the siege mounds and the sword:

5 'They come to fight with the Chaldeans, but *only* to fill their places with the dead bodies of men whom I will slay in My anger and My fury, all for whose wickedness I have hidden My face from this city.

6 'Behold, I will bring it health and healing; I will heal them and reveal to them the abundance of peace and truth.

7 'And I will cause the captives of Judah and the captives of Israel to return, and will rebuild those places as at the first.

8 'I will cleanse them from all their iniquity by which they have sinned against Me, and I will pardon all their iniquities by which they have sinned and by which they have transgressed against Me.

9 'Then it shall be to Me a name of joy, a praise, and an honor before all nations of the earth, who shall hear all the good that I do to them; they shall fear and tremble for all the goodness and all the prosperity that I provide for it.'

10 "Thus says the LORD: 'Again there shall be heard in this place—of which you say, "It *is* desolate, without man and without beast"—in the cities of Judah, in the streets of Jerusalem that are desolate, without man and without inhabitant and without beast,

11 'the voice of joy and the voice of gladness, the voice of the bridegroom and the voice of the bride, the voice of those who will say:

"Praise the LORD of hosts,
For the LORD *is* good,
For His mercy *endures* forever"—

and of those *who will* bring the sacrifice of praise into the house of the LORD. For I will cause the captives of the land to return as at the first,' says the LORD.

12 "Thus says the LORD of hosts: 'In this place which is desolate, without man and without beast, and in all its cities, there shall again be a dwelling place of shepherds causing *their* flocks to lie down.

13 'In the cities of the mountains, in the cities of the lowland, in the cities of the South, in the land of Benjamin, in the places around Jerusalem, and in the cities of Judah, the flocks shall again pass under the hands of him who counts *them*,' says the LORD.

14 'Behold, the days are coming,' says the LORD, 'that I will perform that good thing which I have promised to the house of Israel and to the house of Judah:

15 'In those days and at that time
I will cause to grow up to David
A Branch of righteousness;
He shall execute judgment and righteousness in
the earth.

16 In those days Judah will be saved,
And Jerusalem will dwell safely.
And this *is the name* by which she will be
called:
THE LORD OUR RIGHTEOUSNESS.'

17 "For thus says the LORD: 'David shall never lack a man to sit on the throne of the house of Israel;

18 'nor shall the priests, the Levites, lack a man to offer burnt offerings before Me, to kindle grain offerings, and to sacrifice continually.'"

19 And the word of the LORD came to Jeremiah, saying,

20 "Thus says the LORD: 'If you can break My covenant with the day and My covenant with the night, so that there will not be day and night in their season,

21 'then My covenant may also be broken with David My servant, so that he shall not have a son to reign on his throne, and with the Levites, the priests, My ministers.

22 'As the host of heaven cannot be numbered, nor the sand of the sea measured, so will I multiply the

descendants of David My servant and the Levites who minister to Me.'"

23 Moreover the word of the LORD came to Jeremiah, saying,

24 "Have you not considered what these people have spoken, saying, 'The two families which the LORD has chosen, He has also cast them off'? Thus they have despised My people, as if they should no more be a nation before them.

25 "Thus says the LORD: 'If My covenant is not with day and night, and if I have not appointed the ordinances of heaven and earth,

26 'then I will cast away the descendants of Jacob and David My servant, so that I will not take any of his descendants to be rulers over the descendants of Abraham, Isaac, and Jacob. For I will cause their captives to return, and will have mercy on them.'"

Jer. 33:1–26

As a pastor, I am often asked to preach at the ordination of seminary graduates. It is an honor to which I respond with enthusiasm because it presents the opportunity to call new ministries to courage. Often I use the threefold description of leadership style referred to in this title. When he bought the field in Anathoth, Jeremiah showed his style as a risktaker. He was willing to stake all on the fact that God intended to make good on His promises. Jeremiah stood out from the crowd, a one-man resistance movement against the status quo. Zedekiah exhibited the caretaker leadership, merely trying to maintain what was there, never urging it on to reformation, never challenging the sinful condition of the people. It was no wonder then that Zedekiah soon became an undertaker and witnessed the demise of a people led astray by weak leadership. Is there really such a thing as the status quo? When we simply try to stay the same are we not in all honesty regressing? God does not call us to be static. He calls us to be fruitful, to multiply, to fill the earth and subdue it. When we decide on caretaker leadership, we are like the servant who received one talent and buried it in the ground, while the other two took their talents and built upon them and produced more. The caretaker talent owner was finally made accountable, "You wicked and lazy servant" (Matt. 25:26).

It is only to risk-taking leaders that God makes the bountiful offer found in verse 3: *"Call to Me, and I will answer you, and show you great and mighty things, which you do not know."* Why should God give more revelation to someone not willing to act on revelation already given? Caretaker leadership does not take advantage of the opportunity handed to Jeremiah in his prison cell. God stood ready to burst upon the prophet with great and mighty things that had been previously inaccessible. Right within the prison walls, Jeremiah was handed this expansive good news.

Many of us find ourselves to be prisoners of certain circumstances. Instead of feeling shut up by them we can be like Jeremiah and allow that prison to be the very place where God whispers His holy secrets into our hearts. Perhaps I should not say secrets; God means for us to share what it is we learn inside those walls of difficulty and despair. He means for us to be risktakers and to act out the promises He gives us. Each time the risk being taken is more costly, but the revelation being given is more precious.

God addresses Jeremiah in line with his immediate circumstances, reading the trouble of his heart over the real estate investment he had just made. *"For thus says the LORD, the God of Israel, concerning the houses of this city and the houses of the kings of Judah, which have been pulled down to fortify against the siege mounds and the sword"* (v. 4). Who in their right mind would buy land in such wreckage? Babylon had built siege mounds against them. In counter measure, Judah had torn down houses that stood near the walls in order to make it possible for soldiers to maneuver more easily around the walls. It was a last-ditch effort destined for futility. What a sense of irony. Judah, who refused to tear down altars to Baal, ends up tearing down her own houses. By then, however, it was too little, too late. There was no healing she could bring to her own condition.

At this moment, Jerusalem is hardly a *"name of joy, . . . an honor before all nations of the earth"* (v. 9). Yet that is what she would one day be, as Jeremiah went on to describe the healing (v. 6), the repatriation (v. 7), the cleansing from sin (v. 8), and the restored reputation (v. 9) that Jerusalem would enjoy.

He returned to the familiar imagery of the voice of the bridegroom and the voice of the bride (v. 11). This was the music that Jeremiah never knew as his own, but he used it so poignantly as the music of their restoration. The desolate wasteland they were becoming would once again hear the soft bleating of sheep and the voices of good shepherds (v. 12). We know they are good shepherds because *"the flocks shall again pass under the hands of him who counts them"* (v. 13). If only ninety-nine were counted, then the shepherd would go in search for the one that was lost and restore it to the fold under the gospel economy Jesus used in the parables of Luke 16.

Such visions of future restoration, its sights, sounds, and textures, were inaccessible to the natural mind. Jeremiah was entrusted with them centuries before their fulfillment. He knew that their fulfillment was wrapped up in a person whom he ventured to name Yahweh Tsidkenu, *"THE LORD OUR RIGHTEOUSNESS"* (v. 16). How it must have astonished him to entertain the idea that one person's righteousness could restore a race of humanity that had lost theirs— this person would come from the throne of David and execute judgment in such a way that He could actually become righteousness for us in a substitutionary way. Indeed God had shown him *"great and mighty things"* (v. 3).

It seemed so hard to believe that one greater than David would one day rule the throne. Jeremiah had suffered through his years in the prophetic ministry with one wicked king after another, and all that remained now was Zedekiah, a puny and compromising figure of hopelessness. Jeremiah had a choice to make. He could believe what things looked like or he could believe what God's word was assuring him. The call to the life of faith begs this same choice of us all. God laid before Jeremiah the logic of faith, and we all do well to listen: *"If you can break My covenant with the day and My covenant with the night, so that there will not be day and night in their season, then My covenant may also be broken with David My servant"* (vv. 20–21). We look at the laws of the universe concerning day and night and sun and moon as irrevocable. That was just how irrevocable God's promise was concerning a coming king and concerning His intention to restore His people.

Are we willing to live as Jeremiahs in this present world? Are we willing to invest financially in the work of the kingdom? Are we willing to look at the sun and the moon as promises of God's faithfulness to fulfill His word? Are we willing to live risk-taking lives for Jesus?

NOTES

1. G. Campbell Morgan, *Studies in the Prophecy of Jeremiah* (Old Tappan, N.J.: Fleming H. Revell, 1969), 160.

2. Matthew Henry, *Commentary on the Whole Bible*, ed. Leslie F. Church (Grand Rapids, Mich.: Zondervan Publishing House, 1961), 994.

CHAPTER SEVENTEEN

A Study in Contrasts

Jeremiah 34:1–36:32

DOING THE RIGHT THING FOR THE WRONG REASON

34:1 The word which came to Jeremiah from the LORD, when Nebuchadnezzar king of Babylon and all his army, all the kingdoms of the earth under his dominion, and all the people, fought against Jerusalem and all its cities, saying,

2 "Thus says the LORD, the God of Israel: 'Go and speak to Zedekiah king of Judah and tell him, "Thus says the LORD: 'Behold, I will give this city into the hand of the king of Babylon, and he shall burn it with fire.

3 'And you shall not escape from his hand, but shall surely be taken and delivered into his hand; your eyes shall see the eyes of the king of Babylon, he shall speak with you face to face, and you shall go to Babylon.'"'

4 "Yet hear the word of the LORD, O Zedekiah king of Judah! Thus says the LORD concerning you: 'You shall not die by the sword.

5 'You shall die in peace; as in the ceremonies of your fathers, the former kings who were before you, so they shall burn incense for you and lament for you, *saying*, "Alas, lord!" For I have pronounced the word, says the LORD.'"

6 Then Jeremiah the prophet spoke all these words to Zedekiah king of Judah in Jerusalem,

7 when the king of Babylon's army fought against Jerusalem and all the cities of Judah that were left,

against Lachish and Azekah; for *only* these fortified cities remained of the cities of Judah.

8 *This is* the word that came to Jeremiah from the LORD, after King Zedekiah had made a covenant with all the people who *were* at Jerusalem to proclaim liberty to them:

9 that every man should set free his male and female slave—a Hebrew man or woman—that no one should keep a Jewish brother in bondage.

10 Now when all the princes and all the people, who had entered into the covenant, heard that everyone should set free his male and female slaves, that no one should keep them in bondage anymore, they obeyed and let *them* go.

11 But afterward they changed their minds and made the male and female slaves return, whom they had set free, and brought them into subjection as male and female slaves.

12 Therefore the word of the LORD came to Jeremiah from the LORD, saying,

13 "Thus says the LORD, the God of Israel: 'I made a covenant with your fathers in the day that I brought them out of the land of Egypt, out of the house of bondage, saying,

14 "At the end of seven years let every man set free his Hebrew brother, who has been sold to him; and when he has served you six years, you shall let him go free from you." But your fathers did not obey Me nor incline their ear.

15 'Then you recently turned and did what was right in My sight—every man proclaiming liberty to his neighbor; and you made a covenant before Me in the house which is called by My name.

16 'Then you turned around and profaned My name, and every one of you brought back his male and female slaves, whom he had set at liberty, at their pleasure, and brought them back into subjection, to be your male and female slaves.'

17 "Therefore thus says the LORD: 'You have not obeyed Me in proclaiming liberty, every one to his brother and every one to his neighbor. Behold, I proclaim liberty to you,' says the LORD—'to the sword, to

pestilence, and to famine! And I will deliver you to trouble among all the kingdoms of the earth.

18 'And I will give the men who have transgressed My covenant, who have not performed the words of the covenant which they made before Me, when they cut the calf in two and passed between the parts of it—

19 'the princes of Judah, the princes of Jerusalem, the eunuchs, the priests, and all the people of the land who passed between the parts of the calf—

20 'I will give them into the hand of their enemies and into the hand of those who seek their life. Their dead bodies shall be for meat for the birds of the heaven and the beasts of the earth.

21 'And I will give Zedekiah king of Judah and his princes into the hand of their enemies, into the hand of those who seek their life, and into the hand of the king of Babylon's army which has gone back from you.

22 'Behold, I will command,' says the LORD, 'and cause them to return to this city. They will fight against it and take it and burn it with fire; and I will make the cities of Judah a desolation without inhabitant.'"

Jer. 34:1–22

We move back now from the Book of Comfort to the Jerusalem of 588 B.C. which was anything but comfortable. *"Nebuchadnezzar king of Babylon and all his army, all the kingdoms of the earth under his dominion, and all the people, fought against Jerusalem and all its cities"* (v. 1). Everything that Jeremiah had predicted now came upon them, incited by Zedekiah's rebellion which the prophet had tried to prevent when he crashed the summit conference wearing a wooden yoke. Now Jeremiah was yoked by the words that he had to deliver to Zedekiah, disquieting as they were and similar to those spoken a year before and recorded in 32:3–5. *"Thus says the LORD, 'Behold, I will give this city into the hand of the king of Babylon, and he shall burn it with fire"* (v. 2). Jeremiah's words burned Zedekiah's heart as he heard his own destiny described: *"You shall not die by the sword"* (v. 4). Instead Zedekiah was told of a face-to-face encounter with Nebuchadnezzar, the monarch with whom he had once made a league of mutual assistance. Now this ruler came as conqueror and he would hold Zedekiah accountable for breaking the treaty.

Josephus recorded the encounter: "When he was come, Nebuchadnezzar began to call him a wicked wretch, and a covenant-breaker, and one that had forgotten his former words, when he promised to keep the country for him. He also reproached him for his ingratitude." Listen now to the strange words Josephus recorded as coming from Nebuchadnezzar: "God is great who hateth that conduct of thine, and hath brought thee under us."[1] Even the pagan monarch could see the hand of God working against Zedekiah's broken promises.

Jeremiah was even more specific in referring to this face-to-face confrontation: *"Your eyes shall see the eyes of the king of Babylon"* (v. 3). This was more than a rhetorical device for heightening intensity, it provided specific reference to the form of punishment the angry monarch of Babylon would visit upon Zedekiah. Josephus went on to describe what was also found in 2 Kings 25:7. Zedekiah was forced to watch the slaughter of his sons and his friends and then to have his eyes put out. He was destined to stand in darkness with those terrifying images left to haunt him. Anyone under these circumstances would look for a way to avert the terrible demise.

When he learned the actual way he would die, it possibly gave him further encouragement toward reform. *"You shall die in peace . . . so they shall burn incense for you and lament for you, saying, 'Alas, lord!'"* (v. 5). The dignity promised him in his death may have heightened his awareness of all human dignity and of the fact that this had been violated by the slave practices in Jerusalem. Having contemplated his own mortality, he looked upon his fellowman with new eyes, eyes that were not destined to see much longer. Zedekiah issued a royal proclamation *"that every man should set free his male and female slave—a Hebrew man or woman—that no one should keep a Jewish brother in bondage"* (v. 9). It was the right thing, but it was done with mixed motives. William J. Petersen cited two more reasons that this move was expedient. First, feeding the slaves was getting more expensive than freeing them because the price of food was growing daily. Second, if Nebuchadnezzar did attack, freemen would fight more heartily than slaves.[2]

All of the people obeyed Zedekiah's proclamation and conceded—at least intellectually and for whatever reason—that the practice of enslaving their own Hebrew brothers and sisters was scandalous.

The terms of God's covenant had allowed service of one Hebrew to another, but never slavery. God also specified a six-year limitation to that service; the seventh year was to be a jubilee release from all further obligation. Finally, the king and the people agreed to the letter of the law by freeing the slaves, but they missed the spirit of the law.

History explains why the reformation was so short lived. At this point in the siege, news arrived that the Egyptians had come with their armies to relieve Judah. The Babylonians were forced to suspend their attack in order to turn and face the Egyptians—whom they soundly defeated. Judah looked at the brief respite and jumped to the conclusion that God was favoring them for the release of the slaves. Now that the skies seemed fair again and the friendship of God was now presumed, the slave-owning citizens of Judah *"changed their minds and made the male and female slaves return"* (v. 11). What a mis-understanding of God's grace and mercy to think that it comes so cheap, to think that our half-hearted, short-lived reforms could ever pay the costly ransom needed to redeem us. There had never been a real change of heart. No one knew that better than God, whom they thought they had fooled.

"You recently turned and did what was right in My sight. . . . Then you turned around and profaned My name" (vv. 15–16). He sees their fair-weather friendship as an insult to His dignity and goes on to describe the way He sees their promise-making ceremonies: *"They cut the calf in two and passed between the parts of it—the princes . . . , the eunuchs, the priests, and all the people"* (vv. 18–19). They went through the motions traditional to the ratification of a covenant, but it was only body language—it was all promise and no performance. For so many years Jeremiah had been trying to convince them that empty ceremonies would get them nowhere, that they were nothing but an offense to God. Now they would find out another way. Warnings they would never heed now take the form of events. *"I will give them into the hand of their enemies and into the hand of those who seek their life. Their dead bodies shall be for meat for the birds of the heaven and the beasts of the earth"* (v. 20).

Jeremiah's message made a significant play on words. Judah had dishonored the whole concept of liberty by first granting it to their slaves and then taking it away. *"'Behold, I proclaim liberty to you,' says the LORD—'to the sword, to pestilence, and to famine!'"* (v. 17). Those

245

who thought they were free to do their own thing, to trifle with the things of God, now found themselves free only to experience a dreadful punishment.

RECHABITE FAITH AND JUDAHITE FOLLY

35:1 The word which came to Jeremiah from the LORD in the days of Jehoiakim the son of Josiah, king of Judah, saying,

2 "Go to the house of the Rechabites, speak to them, and bring them into the house of the LORD, into one of the chambers, and give them wine to drink."

3 Then I took Jaazaniah the son of Jeremiah, the son of Habazziniah, his brothers and all his sons, and the whole house of the Rechabites,

4 and I brought them into the house of the LORD, into the chamber of the sons of Hanan the son of Igdaliah, a man of God, which *was* by the chamber of the princes, above the chamber of Maaseiah the son of Shallum, the keeper of the door.

5 Then I set before the sons of the house of the Rechabites bowls full of wine, and cups; and I said to them, "Drink wine."

6 But they said, "We will drink no wine, for Jonadab the son of Rechab, our father, commanded us, saying, 'You shall drink no wine, you nor your sons, forever.

7 'You shall not build a house, sow seed, plant a vineyard, nor have *any of these*; but all your days you shall dwell in tents, that you may live many days in the land where you are sojourners.'

8 "Thus we have obeyed the voice of Jonadab the son of Rechab, our father, in all that he charged us, to drink no wine all our days, we, our wives, our sons, or our daughters,

9 "nor to build ourselves houses to dwell in; nor do we have vineyard, field, or seed.

10 "But we have dwelt in tents, and have obeyed and done according to all that Jonadab our father commanded us.

11 "But it came to pass, when Nebuchadnezzar king of Babylon came up into the land, that we said, 'Come, let us go to Jerusalem for fear of the army of the Chaldeans and for fear of the army of the Syrians.' So we dwell at Jerusalem."

12 Then came the word of the LORD to Jeremiah, saying,

13 "Thus says the LORD of hosts, the God of Israel: 'Go and tell the men of Judah and the inhabitants of Jerusalem, "Will you not receive instruction to obey My words?" says the LORD.

14 "The words of Jonadab the son of Rechab, which he commanded his sons, not to drink wine, are performed; for to this day they drink none, and obey their father's commandment. But although I have spoken to you, rising early and speaking, you did not obey Me.

15 "I have also sent to you all My servants the prophets, rising up early and sending *them*, saying, 'Turn now everyone from his evil way, amend your doings, and do not go after other gods to serve them; then you will dwell in the land which I have given you and your fathers.' But you have not inclined your ear, nor obeyed Me.

16 "Surely the sons of Jonadab the son of Rechab have performed the commandment of their father, which he commanded them, but this people has not obeyed Me."'

17 "Therefore thus says the LORD God of hosts, the God of Israel: 'Behold, I will bring on Judah and on all the inhabitants of Jerusalem all the doom that I have pronounced against them; because I have spoken to them but they have not heard, and I have called to them but they have not answered.'"

18 And Jeremiah said to the house of the Rechabites, "Thus says the LORD of hosts, the God of Israel: 'Because you have obeyed the commandment of Jonadab your father, and kept all his precepts and done according to all that he commanded you,

19 'therefore thus says the LORD of hosts, the God of Israel: "Jonadab the son of Rechab shall not lack a man to stand before Me forever."'"

Jer. 35:1–19

In stark contrast to the lore of the Judahites stands the story of the Rechabites, placed here for the sake of drawing comparisons even though the living parable took place in the days of Jehoiakim. It obviously had a profound impression on Jeremiah who was starved to see examples of obedience in human lives when all he ever saw were broken promises and empty ceremonies.

The Rechabites were a sect living in the uplands of Judah. They had been founded some three hundred years earlier by Jonadab, the son of Rechab, for the fanatic worship of Yahweh and the violent expulsion of Baal worship. They were a Puritan-like group, much like the Nazirites in that they had separated themselves from wine and other strong drink. They were committed to a nomadic way of life that scorned the more permanent agrarian culture of the day. The *Interpreter's Bible* makes an interesting contrast between Rechabite theology and the theology of God's prophets. Rechabites believed that nothing was right about the culture, so their cry was "Return to the desert." The prophets, however, believed that the culture could be redeemed, so their cry was "Return to the Lord."[3] Therefore, Jeremiah was not endorsing Rechabite theology, but he was endorsing the faithfulness with which they held it. When the nomadic sect came inside the walls of Jerusalem for protection, Jeremiah wasted no time in capitalizing on their peculiar appearance and doggedly faithful ways. He used them as an object lesson for his unteachable mission field. God is the producer and director of this drama. He told Jeremiah to take the Rechabite leader—Jaazaniah—and the whole sect into a certain chamber in the house of the Lord where they would be noticed widely. The lesson would attain maximum significance. The chamber location and its jurisdiction is specified in verse 4.

"Then I set before the sons of the house of the Rechabites bowls full of wine, and cups; and I said to them, 'Drink wine'" (v. 5). Imagine the contrast between these indomitable nomads, looking so peculiar, and the sophisticated society of the temple elite as they stared at one another over the tempting bowls of wine. The Rechabites could have reasoned among themselves "when in Rome do as the Romans do." They could have rationalized disobedience under these extenuating circumstances. Instead, they answered, *"We will drink no wine, for Jonadab the son of Rechab, our father, commanded us, saying, 'You shall drink no wine, you nor your sons, forever'"* (v. 6). They give a vigorous

confession of their faith in verses 8–10. Judahites had the word of the mighty and sovereign God of all creation. Rechabites had nothing but the word of a mere mortal, yet they were more faithful to the miniword than Judah was to the Mighty Word. The Rechabites proved themselves faithful in all seasons, under great temptations, and with no prophets coming to remind them.

Jeremiah used this living parable to plead with his people. Seeing the long prophetic line that had gone before him, Jeremiah cried out in language now familiar for its many repetitions: *"I have also sent to you all My servants the prophets, rising up early and sending them. . . . But you have not inclined your ear, nor obeyed me"* (v. 15). The many mornings that Jeremiah had risen early and made his forays into Jerusalem had come to naught. *"Surely the sons of Jonadab the son of Rechab have performed the commandment of their father, which he commanded them, but this people has not obeyed Me"* (v. 16).

Each group would now receive rewards proportionate to the degree of faith expressed in their lives over the many chances given them to express it. *"Behold, I will bring on Judah . . . all the doom that I have pronounced against them; because I have spoken to them but they have not heard, and I have called to them but they have not answered"* (v. 17). God promised the Rechabites, *"Jonadab the son of Rechab shall not lack a man to stand before Me forever"* (v. 19). Do we want to get to the end of the line and find that our lives are nothing but a colossal embarrassment by comparison to those who have received less revelation and yet have done so much more with it?

THE KING WHO REPENTS AND THE
KING WHO RESENTS

36:1 Now it came to pass in the fourth year of Jehoiakim the son of Josiah, king of Judah, *that* this word came to Jeremiah from the LORD, saying:

2 "Take a scroll of a book and write on it all the words that I have spoken to you against Israel, against Judah, and against all the nations, from the day I spoke to you, from the days of Josiah even to this day.

3 "It may be that the house of Judah will hear all the adversities which I purpose to bring upon them,

249

that everyone may turn from his evil way, that I may forgive their iniquity and their sin."

4 Then Jeremiah called Baruch the son of Neriah; and Baruch wrote on a scroll of a book, at the instruction of Jeremiah, all the words of the LORD which He had spoken to him.

5 And Jeremiah commanded Baruch, saying, "I *am* confined, I cannot go into the house of the LORD.

6 "You go, therefore, and read from the scroll which you have written at my instruction, the words of the LORD, in the hearing of the people in the LORD's house on the day of fasting. And you shall also read them in the hearing of all Judah who come from their cities.

7 "It may be that they will present their supplication before the LORD, and everyone will turn from his evil way. For great *is* the anger and the fury that the LORD has pronounced against this people."

8 And Baruch the son of Neriah did according to all that Jeremiah the prophet commanded him, reading from the book the words of the LORD in the LORD's house.

9 Now it came to pass in the fifth year of Jehoiakim the son of Josiah, king of Judah, in the ninth month, *that* they proclaimed a fast before the LORD to all the people in Jerusalem, and to all the people who came from the cities of Judah to Jerusalem.

10 Then Baruch read from the book the words of Jeremiah in the house of the LORD, in the chamber of Gemariah the son of Shaphan the scribe, in the upper court at the entry of the New Gate of the LORD's house, in the hearing of all the people.

11 When Michaiah the son of Gemariah, the son of Shaphan, heard all the words of the LORD from the book,

12 he then went down to the king's house, into the scribe's chamber; and there all the princes were sitting—Elishama the scribe, Delaiah the son of Shemaiah, Elnathan the son of Achbor, Gemariah the son of Shaphan, Zedekiah the son of Hananiah, and all the princes.

13 Then Michaiah declared to them all the words

that he had heard when Baruch read the book in the hearing of the people.

14 Therefore all the princes sent Jehudi the son of Nethaniah, the son of Shelemiah, the son of Cushi, to Baruch, saying, "Take in your hand the scroll from which you have read in the hearing of the people, and come." So Baruch the son of Neriah took the scroll in his hand and came to them.

15 And they said to him, "Sit down now, and read it in our hearing." So Baruch read *it* in their hearing.

16 Now it happened, when they had heard all the words, that they looked in fear from one to another, and said to Baruch, "We will surely tell the king of all these words."

17 And they asked Baruch, saying, "Tell us now, how did you write all these words—at his instruction?"

18 So Baruch answered them, "He proclaimed with his mouth all these words to me, and I wrote *them* with ink in the book."

19 Then the princes said to Baruch, "Go and hide, you and Jeremiah; and let no one know where you are."

20 And they went to the king, into the court; but they stored the scroll in the chamber of Elishama the scribe, and told all the words in the hearing of the king.

21 So the king sent Jehudi to bring the scroll, and he took it from Elishama the scribe's chamber. And Jehudi read it in the hearing of the king and in the hearing of all the princes who stood beside the king.

22 Now the king was sitting in the winter house in the ninth month, with *a fire* burning on the hearth before him.

23 And it happened, when Jehudi had read three or four columns, *that the king* cut it with the scribe's knife and cast *it* into the fire that *was* on the hearth, until all the scroll was consumed in the fire that *was* on the hearth.

24 Yet they were not afraid, nor did they tear their garments, the king nor any of his servants who heard all these words.

25 Nevertheless Elnathan, Delaiah, and Gemariah implored the king not to burn the scroll; but he would not listen to them.

26 And the king commanded Jerahmeel the king's son, Seraiah the son of Azriel, and Shelemiah the son of Abdeel, to seize Baruch the scribe and Jeremiah the prophet, but the LORD hid them.

27 Now after the king had burned the scroll with the words which Baruch had written at the instruction of Jeremiah, the word of the LORD came to Jeremiah, saying:

28 "Take yet another scroll, and write on it all the former words that were in the first scroll which Jehoiakim the king of Judah has burned.

29 "And you shall say to Jehoiakim king of Judah, 'Thus says the LORD: "You have burned this scroll, saying, 'Why have you written in it that the king of Babylon will certainly come and destroy this land, and cause man and beast to cease from here?'"

30 'Therefore thus says the LORD concerning Jehoiakim king of Judah: "He shall have no one to sit on the throne of David, and his dead body shall be cast out to the heat of the day and the frost of the night.

31 "I will punish him, his family, and his servants for their iniquity; and I will bring on them, on the inhabitants of Jerusalem, and on the men of Judah all the doom that I have pronounced against them; but they did not heed."'"

32 Then Jeremiah took another scroll and gave it to Baruch the scribe, the son of Neriah, who wrote on it at the instruction of Jeremiah all the words of the book which Jehoiakim king of Judah had burned in the fire. And besides, there were added to them many similar words.

Jer. 36:1–32

The episode recounted in this chapter concerning the scroll paints a portrait of Jehoiakim that is shocking for its contrast to Josiah, his father, under whose reign Jeremiah began his prophetic ministry. We earlier reconstructed the moment that the scroll of the Law was found during the restoration of the temple. Shaphan, the king's chancellor and scribe, rushed it to Josiah, where the Book of the Law was read in his presence. "When the king heard the words of the Book of the Law, . . . he tore his clothes" (2 Kings 22:11). The present account involves Jehoiakim and his response to a similar reading of the word of God. Josiah tore his clothes in repentance; Jehoiakim tore the word in resentment. Therein lies the great difference. Their respective attitudes toward the authority of God were characteristic of their leadership styles.

The drama takes place in the fourth year of Jehoiakim's reign when Jeremiah was instructed by God to set down in writing all the prophetic content he had been delivering from the beginning of his ministry (vv. 1–2). God's desire was to provide His people with a document that would reinforce the spoken word and provide the house of Judah with a chance to turn around and be forgiven (v. 3). God wants to do more than convict; He wants to convert. The lengths to which He will go in that purpose are most striking.

"Then Jeremiah called Baruch the son of Neriah; and Baruch wrote on a scroll of a book, at the instruction of Jeremiah, all the words of the LORD which He had spoken to him" (v. 4). This is precious information given here because it is the only description in the Old Testament concerning the actual mechanics of recording prophetic literature. A new dimension opened in Jeremiah's ministry as well. Now he was more than an orator. He was also a writer whose work was to be read in public. As the political scene intensified in danger so also does Jeremiah's image to the public.

Momentous events took place in the spring of 605 B.C. when Nebuchadnezzar defeated the Egyptians in the battle of Carchemish. Now the Babylonians were the dominant world power. Judah stood bereft of her protection from Egypt. The new configuration threatened her safety and stirred the prophet to even more aggressive ways to warn her. Of all times to be confined and unable to go into the house of the Lord (v. 5). We are not sure just what this confinement amounted to for he was not yet in prison. Perhaps his temple address recorded in chapter 26 had brought about this restriction.

Baruch takes his place as one of those few people who chose to be a friend to the controversial personage of Jeremiah. It was a costly choice. "You go, therefore, and read from the scroll which you have written at my instruction, the words of the LORD, in the hearing of the people in the LORD's house on the day of fasting. And you shall also read them in *the hearing of all Judah who come from their cities"* (v. 6). Just when the king thought he had eliminated the voice of Jeremiah, up pops the voice of Baruch. You can't keep a good man down—or the God of the good man. Together they will forge a way. The messages were delivered to three audiences.

1. *"Then Baruch read from the book the words of Jeremiah in the house of the LORD, in the chamber of Gemariah the son of Shaphan the scribe, in the upper court at the entry of the New Gate of the LORD's house, in the hearing of all the people"* (v. 10). Baruch's first congregation was the largest, all of the people who had assembled for a fast in the ninth month of Jehoiakim's fifth year (v. 9). Since the ancient Hebrews had very few fixed days of fasting, this might have been one proclaimed out of the impending Babylonian threat.

Around the temple itself and within its courts there were chambers used as storerooms or residences and open to the public. We remember Shaphan reading the deuteronomic scroll to Josiah. This reading took place in the chambers of his son, Gemariah, who perhaps had endorsed this auspicious occasion and maybe even assembled the listeners. One very important listener was his own son, Michaiah, Shaphan's grandson. *"When Michaiah . . . heard all the words of the LORD from the book, he then went down to the king's house, into the scribe's chamber; and there all the princes were sitting. . . . Then Michaiah declared to them all the words that he had heard when Baruch read the book in the hearing of the people"* (vv. 11–13).

We must pause for a look at Michaiah's bravado and where it came from. Notice his family history. His grandfather Shaphan had a son, Ahikam, who interceded for Jeremiah against an angry mob that was about to lynch him (26:17). He had another son, Gemariah, who here provides the chamber and the congregation for Baruch's reading and whose heroism for God will be found again in later chapters. What a family! One might almost miss them in the crowd of events taking place here. Yet God would never miss them. Families such as these are the very substance of His kingdom and should be the substance of our own aspirations for our own families.

2. *"Therefore all the princes sent Jehudi . . . to Baruch, saying, 'Take in your hand the scroll from which you have read in the hearing of the people, and come"* (v. 14). Because of Michaiah's zeal and his willingness to use his reputation and his social status in the service of

254

the Lord, he secured for Baruch an audience with the princes. I am fortunate to have in my parish many men and women who have reached outstanding levels of achievement within their respective professions. It is so very gratifying to see them using the credibility they have with the world to influence others for the kingdom. They are the Michaiahs of this generation. Notice another thing about Michaiah. He declared all the words he had heard when Baruch read, making himself a communicator of sorts, working his own mind with the content of God's word, not merely looking to someone else to do it. My guess is that his enthusiasm was so infectious that the princes decided to invite Baruch.

First there was Jeremiah who received the word. Then there was Baruch who recorded it and read it. Then there was Michaiah who repeated what he heard in such an inviting way that others wanted to hear. Do we not see here the various ministries of communicating the word of God and how all of us are called to some aspect of them?

Michaiah's mission field was the princes. Perhaps he knew exactly which ones to approach because he assembled a selection of those who actually had ears to hear. These kinds of people were growing more and more scarce under the reign of Jehoiakim. *"Now it happened, when they had heard all the words, that they looked in fear from one to another, and said to Baruch, 'We will surely tell the king of all these words'"* (v. 16). The words that Jehoiakim had thought to stifle had come full circle from the people to the princes and back to him all because of the corporate ministry of obedient servants like you and me. The corporate body enlarged from Jeremiah to Baruch to Gemariah to Michaiah and now to these princes who took up with a different ministry. They became painfully aware of the danger to the word and to Jeremiah and Baruch.

Elnathan, one of the princes, was responsible for the extradition of Urijah the prophet whom Jehoiakim executed (26:20–23). If Jehoiakim did not like Urijah, he was going to hate Baruch and hate the scroll he carried. Elnathan and the other princes were caught in a tension between the authority of the scroll and the authority of the king. *"Then the princes said to Baruch, 'Go and hide, you and Jeremiah; and let no one know where you are'"* (v. 19). These princes knew the power of the scroll, that in its safety was the safety of their city. If only Jehoiakim were more like his father Josiah, who had wept over the powerful words. They had to approach this volatile king with the greatest finesse.

3. *"And they went to the king, into the court; but they stored the scroll in the chamber of Elishama the scribe, and told all the words in the hearing of the king"* (v. 20). Why didn't they take the scroll with them? Could they have been afraid for its safety? After hearing their commentary, Jehoiakim asked that the scroll be brought to him. On that winter day as he warmed himself before a brazier, his anger similarly burned in his heart.

"And it happened, when Jehudi had read three or four columns, that the king cut it with the scribe's knife and cast it into the fire that was on the hearth, until all the scroll was consumed in the fire that was on the hearth" (v. 23). As those flames licked around the parchment containing God's word, they would similarly consume the very walls of Jerusalem whose fate was being settled that very moment by Jehoiakim's show of defiance. The princes who *"stood beside the king"* (v. 21) also stood beside his treatment of God's authority. *"They were not afraid, nor did they tear their garments, the king nor any of his servants who heard all these words"* (v. 24).

In those moments when dreadful history was being written by dreadful deeds, there were three who stood against it. *"Nevertheless Elnathan, Delaiah, and Gemariah implored the king not to burn the scroll; but he would not listen to them"* (v. 25). The frustration and shattering disappointment these men felt then were but a touch of what the prophet Jeremiah lived with for more than forty years of ministry. If you were there, on which side would you be found? Would you be beside the king, acquiescing to him? Or would you be beside the three who chose for all eternity to please the Lord? This is not some incidental little story from the archives of ancient history. It is a story for every person and a story of the call upon every life. For whom are you living?

You can't keep a good man down. Seeing his life and labor go up in smoke does not stop the Jeremiahs of the world nor the Baruchs. After the king burned the scroll, God said to the prophet, *"Take yet another scroll, and write on it all the former words that were in the first scroll"* (v. 28). The famous team not only recorded all that had been on the first scroll but also added more to the weight and substance of this most awesome document (v. 32).

256

God has the last word. When will we learn that? He goes on to pronounce the demise of Jehoiakim and the demise of Jerusalem. A whole city went down with the king. May we never underestimate the importance of righteous leadership.

NOTES

1. Flavius Josephus, *Antiquities of the Jews,* 3 vols. (Grand Rapids, Mich.: Baker Book House, 1984), 3:72.

2. William J. Petersen, *Jeremiah: The Prophet Who Wouldn't Quit* (Wheaton, Ill.: Victor Books, 1984) 130.

3. Stanley Hopper, "The Book of Jeremiah: Exposition," in *The Interpreter's Bible,* vol. 5, ed. George A. Buttrick et al. (Nashville: Abingdon Press, 1956), 1059.

CHAPTER EIGHTEEN

To Root Out and Destroy

Jeremiah 37:1–39:18; 52:1–34

The mournful events of the next three chapters lead up to and include the fall of Jerusalem. When God first called Jeremiah, He said that He would use him "to root out and to pull down, to destroy and to throw down" (1:10). All the while, however, God was "watching over His word to perform it." Now was the time for that inexorable word to be fulfilled. The painful process had reached its climax. The forces of Babylon, moved by the Almighty hand, had opened their siege on Jerusalem. Young Zedekiah, now in the ninth year of his eleven-year reign, was caught between the forces of his military advisers, his princes, and his prophet. Tragic history was made by the interplay of these personalities.

THE CAPTAIN AGAINST THE PROPHET

37:1 Now King Zedekiah the son of Josiah reigned instead of Coniah the son of Jehoiakim, whom Nebuchadnezzar king of Babylon made king in the land of Judah.

2 But neither he nor his servants nor the people of the land gave heed to the words of the LORD which He spoke by the prophet Jeremiah.

3 And Zedekiah the king sent Jehucal the son of Shelemiah, and Zephaniah the son of Maaseiah, the priest, to the prophet Jeremiah, saying, "Pray now to the LORD our God for us."

4 Now Jeremiah was coming and going among the people, for they had not *yet* put him in prison.

5 Then Pharaoh's army came up from Egypt; and when the Chaldeans who were besieging Jerusalem heard news of them, they departed from Jerusalem.

6 Then the word of the LORD came to the prophet Jeremiah, saying,

7 "Thus says the LORD, the God of Israel, 'Thus you shall say to the king of Judah, who sent you to Me to inquire of Me: "Behold, Pharaoh's army which has come up to help you will return to Egypt, to their own land.

8 "And the Chaldeans shall come back and fight against this city, and take it and burn it with fire."'

9 "Thus says the LORD: 'Do not deceive yourselves, saying, "The Chaldeans will surely depart from us," for they will not depart.

10 'For though you had defeated the whole army of the Chaldeans who fight against you, and there remained *only* wounded men among them, they would rise up, every man in his tent, and burn the city with fire.'"

11 And it happened, when the army of the Chaldeans left *the siege* of Jerusalem for fear of Pharaoh's army,

12 that Jeremiah went out of Jerusalem to go into the land of Benjamin to claim his property there among the people.

13 And when he was in the Gate of Benjamin, a captain of the guard *was* there whose name *was* Irijah the son of Shelemiah, the son of Hananiah; and he seized Jeremiah the prophet, saying, "You are defecting to the Chaldeans!"

14 Then Jeremiah said, "False! I am not defecting to the Chaldeans." But he did not listen to him. So Irijah seized Jeremiah and brought him to the princes.

15 Therefore the princes were angry with Jeremiah, and they struck him and put him in prison in the house of Jonathan the scribe. For they had made that the prison.

16 When Jeremiah entered the dungeon and the cells, and Jeremiah had remained there many days,

17 then Zedekiah the king sent and took him *out*. The king asked him secretly in his house, and said,

"Is there *any* word from the LORD?" And Jeremiah said, "There is." Then he said, "You shall be delivered into the hand of the king of Babylon!"

18 Moreover Jeremiah said to King Zedekiah, "What offense have I committed against you, against your servants, or against this people, that you have put me in prison?

19 "Where now *are* your prophets who prophesied to you, saying, 'The king of Babylon will not come against you or against this land?'

20 "Therefore please hear now, O my lord the king. Please, let my petition be accepted before you, and do not make me return to the house of Jonathan the scribe, lest I die there."

21 Then Zedekiah the king commanded that they should commit Jeremiah to the court of the prison, and that they should give him daily a piece of bread from the bakers' street, until all the bread in the city was gone. Thus Jeremiah remained in the court of the prison.

Jer. 37:1–21

Verses 1 and 2 of this chapter quickly move us from the reign of Jehoiakim to the latter days of Zedekiah's reign. They also refer to the interruption in the line of succession. Coniah, the son of Jehoiakim, was removed after a brief three months' reign. Zedekiah, the brother of Jehoiakim, took the throne, thus fulfilling the prophet's words concerning Jehoiakim: "He shall have no one to sit on the throne of David" (36:30). Matters concerning this upset have already been recounted in our discussion of 22:24–30. A final glimpse of Coniah (Jehoiachin) is given in the closing verses of the book (52:31–34). Such details of Jeremiah's predictions must not go unnoticed. To the careful observer they heap credibility upon the prophet and help that observer know which voice to listen to in times of confusion and calamity. The God who calls us to exercise discernment does not ask us to do so without facts.

Zedekiah, his captain, and his princes live in a palpable tension with each other concerning the fate of Jeremiah. *"But neither he nor his servants nor the people of the land gave heed to the words of the LORD which He spoke by the prophet Jeremiah"* (v. 2). Baruch, who faithfully rewrote the scroll that Jehoiakim had burned, made this comment. Zedekiah flirted with the word of God. His captain, Irijah, fought with it and with the prophet whom he perceived as his arch enemy. A deputation from the king was sent to seek the council of Jeremiah, asking him to *"Pray now to the LORD our God for us"* (v. 3). Under the then-present stress it seemed wise for Zedekiah to cover his bases. Look for help from Egypt—that would please Irijah and all his princes who wanted to throw off the yoke of Babylon. Just in case, though, try a little prayer. That would please Jeremiah who continued to warn of coming judgment. When compromising thinking like this prevails, the man who stands against it will ultimately find himself in danger. *"Now Jeremiah was coming and going among the people, for they had not yet put him in prison"* (v. 4). His warnings had been sounded out to the listening ears of frightened people who were beginning to agree that defection to Babylon was their only hope.

At this point a curious thing happened that seemed to answer Zedekiah's every dream. *"Then Pharaoh's army came up from Egypt; and when the Chaldeans who were besieging Jerusalem heard news of them, they departed from Jerusalem"* (v. 5). What a sight for sore eyes: oncoming Egyptians and retreating Babylonians! The sense of relief was overwhelming. Did it mean that this brief respite would spell permanent relief for the city? When the Babylonian siege mounds were lifted and Nebuchadnezzar's attacks became less frequent, the captain and the princes wanted to believe that Jeremiah's predictions of doom had been discredited, that there would really be no judgment. How easily we believe those things we wish.

Jeremiah, however, continued to hammer at the truth, in spite of how it seemed to be discredited. The Egyptian army that had come to help would prove to be no help at all. Furthermore the Babylonian army would return to finish the destruction it had started (vv. 6–10). *"Do not deceive yourselves"* (v. 9), cries the prophet.

The secular world accuses the church of being a pie-in-the-sky Pollyanna in its outlook on life. In actuality it is the secular mind-set that is running away from the truth, and it is the Christian world-view that looks squarely into the face of hard realities. The Bible never minimizes distress. Instead it presents a real God who has come to meet us in a real world and in the real storms of life. When Peter got out of the boat to walk on the water toward Jesus, the storm raged around him. Today's mass media are forced to report on the storms of life: rapes, robberies, AIDS, wars and rumors of wars, and scandals in high places. Often, after they have packaged the whole thing, they will end with a facile piece of news or a little quip that seems designed to lighten the whole load and give it a cast of unreality. Zedekiah here was probably wishing for such a quip to come from the prophet, one that would lighten the whole load.

Jeremiah did not like the prognosis any better than Zedekiah, but he looked at it with an honest eye and called it just as he saw it. Like it or not, Judah must surrender to Babylon. Irijah, however, was determined to prevent Jeremiah's preaching this message. Standing by the Gate of Benjamin, his eyes scanned the crowds leaving the city. They had been pent up within the walls so long and were now delirious over the lifting of the siege. With evil intent, Irijah looked for one man. He was not disappointed. *"And it happened, when the army of the Chaldeans left the siege of Jerusalem for fear of Pharaoh's army, that Jeremiah went out of Jerusalem to go into the land of Benjamin to claim his property there among the people"* (vv. 11–12). Perhaps the prophet yearned for one last look at the hill country of his youth; he might have wanted to reconstruct distant memories of comfort and feed on them during this evil time.

That was all Irijah needed to seize Jeremiah and accuse him, *"You are defecting to the Chaldeans!"* (v. 13). Jeremiah must have struggled against him emotionally and physically. From out of the dust stirred up by their scuffle, Jeremiah's voice rose defensively: *"False! I am not defecting to the Chaldeans"* (v. 14). When you have laid down your life for the saving of a city, it hurts to be called a traitor. There was no one on the face of the universe more loyal to his country—no king, no prince, no priest, no prophet. He had come that they might have light, but his people preferred darkness. In that darkness their perceptions were so warped that they saw him not as a savior but as a traitor, just as the Lord was executed as a common criminal at the hands of the twisted people He had come to save.

Naturally the gathering of princes to which Irijah brought the prophet were of like mind. We find confederacies of belief and unbelief among the princes in these narratives. There were the Gemariah and Ahikam gatherings who sought to defend Jeremiah, and the Irijah and Jonathan gatherings who sought to defeat him. We need to ask ourselves what kind of crowd we are in, because the company we keep will affect the crucial decisions we make about the relevance of God's word in today's society.

Jonathan, the scribe who offered his house as Jeremiah's prison, may have done so with the best of intentions. He most likely believed he was protecting his city from a traitor—a sincere belief. God calls us, however, to a higher standard than sincerity; He calls us to discernment. Both Irijah and Jonathan had access to the prophecies of Jeremiah that had already been fulfilled, that documented his voice over the many other voices in the culture. Babylon was at their gates (as predicted), Jehoiakim's son did not succeed him (as predicted), the captives had not returned (as predicted), the life of Hananiah the false prophet had been cut short (as predicted). Against this mounting evidence of the credibility of Jeremiah, they still choose to cast him into prison.

"Then Zedekiah the king sent and took him out" (v. 17). The system trying to work against Jeremiah was actually working against itself. The princes put him in prison; the king took him out behind their backs. The left hand did not know what the right hand was doing. God used the confusion as a means of extricating Jeremiah.

Again Zedekiah appealed to Jeremiah, this time in secret: *"'Is there any word from the LORD?' And Jeremiah said, 'There is'"* (v. 17), knowing that the king wanted him to change his story, to make up some good news. *"You shall be delivered into the hand of the king of Babylon!"* (v. 17). The bronze wall stood against the vacillating king at a time when pleasant news might have created pleasant circumstances. Zedekiah had been playing with the prophet, hoping that enough torture would force him to change his word; after all, everyone had a price. He quickly discovered that Jeremiah was not for sale. Jeremiah challenged the king with brazen strength. *"What offense have I committed against you, against your servants, or against this people, that you have put me in prison?"* (v. 18). If anyone should have been in prison, it should have been the false prophets. *"Where now are your prophets who prophesied to you, saying, 'The king of Babylon will not come against you or against this land?'"* (v. 19). Now that they were needed, they had vanished. The iron pillar who had not forsaken the king, who was still around when the going got tough, appealed for his own life. *"'Please hear now, O my lord the king. . . . do not make me return to the house of Jonathan the scribe, lest I die there.' Then Zedekiah the king commanded that they should commit Jeremiah to the court of the prison, and that they should give him daily a piece of bread from the bakers' street, until all the bread in the city was gone. Thus Jeremiah remained in the court of the prison"* (vv. 20–21).

Through this cast of characters—Zedekiah, Irijah, Jonathan, and the princes—we see the crumbling of a system at cross-purposes with itself, floundering against the hard realities instead of facing them, wanting to believe that Egypt had actually saved them, that their own engines of war would ultimately triumph over the inexorable judgments of God. The gaunt look of famine was pressing in on the city, the prophet remained in prison, receiving each day his daily bread. "I *am* with you to deliver you" (1:8). Those were the words he must remember as the next conspiracy began to mount against him, promising to be worst than the last. The captain and the princes were after his death, to root out and destroy him—yet God was after theirs.

THE PRINCES AGAINST THE PROPHET

38:1 Now Shephatiah the son of Mattan, Gedaliah the son of Pashhur, Jucal the son of Shelemiah, and Pashhur the son of Malchiah heard the words that Jeremiah had spoken to all the people, saying,

2 "Thus says the LORD: 'He who remains in this city shall die by the sword, by famine, and by pestilence; but he who goes over to the Chaldeans shall live; his life shall be as a prize to him, and he shall live.'

3 "Thus says the LORD: 'This city shall surely be given into the hand of the king of Babylon's army, which shall take it.'"

4 Therefore the princes said to the king, "Please, let this man be put to death, for thus he weakens the hands of the men of war who remain in this city, and the hands of all the people, by speaking such words to them. For this man does not seek the welfare of this people, but their harm."

5 Then Zedekiah the king said, "Look, he *is* in your hand. For the king can *do* nothing against you."

6 So they took Jeremiah and cast him into the dungeon of Malchiah the king's son, which *was* in the court of the prison, and they let Jeremiah down with ropes. And in the dungeon *there was* no water, but mire. So Jeremiah sank in the mire.

7 Now Ebed-Melech the Ethiopian, one of the eunuchs, who was in the king's house, heard that they had put Jeremiah in the dungeon. When the king was sitting at the Gate of Benjamin,

8 Ebed-Melech went out of the king's house and spoke to the king, saying:

9 "My lord the king, these men have done evil in all that they have done to Jeremiah the prophet, whom they have cast into the dungeon, and he is likely to die from hunger in the place where he is. For *there is* no more bread in the city."

10 Then the king commanded Ebed-Melech the Ethiopian, saying, "Take from here thirty men with you, and lift Jeremiah the prophet out of the dungeon before he dies."

11 So Ebed-Melech took the men with him and went into the house of the king under the treasury, and took from there old clothes and old rags, and let them down by ropes into the dungeon to Jeremiah.

12 Then Ebed-Melech the Ethiopian said to Jeremiah, "Please put these old clothes and rags under your armpits, under the ropes." And Jeremiah did so.

13 So they pulled Jeremiah up with ropes and lifted him out of the dungeon. And Jeremiah remained in the court of the prison.

14 Then Zedekiah the king sent and had Jeremiah the prophet brought to him at the third entrance of the house of the LORD. And the king said to Jeremiah, "I will ask you something. Hide nothing from me."

15 Jeremiah said to Zedekiah, "If I declare *it* to you, will you not surely put me to death? And if I give you advice, you will not listen to me."

16 So Zedekiah the king swore secretly to Jeremiah, saying, "*As* the LORD lives, who made our very souls, I will not put you to death, nor will I give you into the hand of these men who seek your life."

17 Then Jeremiah said to Zedekiah, "Thus says the

LORD, the God of hosts, the God of Israel: 'If you surely surrender to the king of Babylon's princes, then your soul shall live; this city shall not be burned with fire, and you and your house shall live.

18 'But if you do not surrender to the king of Babylon's princes, then this city shall be given into the hand of the Chaldeans; they shall burn it with fire, and you shall not escape from their hand.'"

19 And Zedekiah the king said to Jeremiah, "I am afraid of the Jews who have defected to the Chaldeans, lest they deliver me into their hand, and they abuse me."

20 But Jeremiah said, "They shall not deliver *you.* Please, obey the voice of the LORD which I speak to you. So it shall be well with you, and your soul shall live.

21 "But if you refuse to surrender, this *is* the word that the LORD has shown me:

22 'Now behold, all the women who are left in the king of Judah's house *shall be* surrendered to the king of Babylon's princes, and those *women* shall say:

"Your close friends have set upon you
And prevailed against you;
Your feet have sunk in the mire,
And they have turned away again."

23 'So they shall surrender all your wives and children to the Chaldeans. You shall not escape from their hand, but shall be taken by the hand of the king of Babylon. And you shall cause this city to be burned with fire.'"

24 Then Zedekiah said to Jeremiah, "Let no one know of these words, and you shall not die.

25 "But if the princes hear that I have talked with you, and they come to you and say to you, 'Declare to us now what you have said to the king, and also what the king said to you; do not hide *it* from us, and we will not put you to death,'

26 "then you shall say to them, 'I presented my request before the king, that he would not make me return to Jonathan's house to die there.'"

27 Then all the princes came to Jeremiah and asked him. And he told them according to all these words

that the king had commanded. So they stopped speaking with him, for the conversation had not been heard.

28 Now Jeremiah remained in the court of the prison until the day that Jerusalem was taken. And he was *there* when Jerusalem was taken.

Jer. 38:1–28

Irijah had failed to silence the voice of Jeremiah. Now a new deputation comes before Zedekiah with the same obsession. The four are named in verse 1. They had caught the indecisive nature of the king and were working it for all it was worth, determined to cast Jeremiah back into prison. Another group, appearing later in the chapter, was equally determined to pull him out. These opposing forces tugged at Zedekiah in the closing days of Jerusalem's struggle for survival.

Of the four men named, three of them were not entirely strangers to the sad drama of the last days. Gedeliah may be son of the Pashhur who put Jeremiah in the stocks. If so, he had inherited his father's conviction that Jeremiah was a traitor. Jucal was a member of an earlier deputation that Zedekiah had sent to the prophet with the request for prayer (37:3). He would therefore have had a private audience with Jeremiah and witnessed his integrity, the strength of his conviction, and the powers of his being in prayer. It was that very power and its persuasiveness that Jucal found threatening to the cause of the alliance with Egypt and the fight against Babylon. Pashhur we should well remember as the leader of the first deputation to Jeremiah after he had escaped from the stocks. He, like Jucal, would fear the influence Jeremiah held in a society trembling and on the verge of collapse.

It was to that society that Jeremiah had been saying, "He who remains in this city shall die; . . . but he who goes over to the Chaldeans shall live" (v. 2). Siege mounds were again built around Jerusalem. Egypt had not held the Babylonians for long. Now people had even more reason to believe that the prophet knew what he was talking about. The thud of the battering ram would soon be heard against the walls of Jerusalem. She fought not only against that but also against famine and disease within her own walls. The people around Jeremiah listened night and day to his persuasive logic.

"The princes said to the king, 'Please, let this man be put to death, for *thus he weakens the hands of the men of war who remain in this city, and the hands of all the people, by speaking such words to them. For this man does not seek the welfare of this people, but their harm'"* (v. 4). Their line of thinking seemed so logical, so patriotic. They were trying to save their city from the Babylonians. What could be wrong with that? If the Babylonian siege mounds outside Jerusalem represented the judgment of God, then they were pitting their engines of war against the divine anger. They wanted only a God of mercy and not a God of justice. This is similar to Peter's refusal to believe that judgment for human sin would come upon the perfection of Jesus. He rebuked Jesus saying, "Far be it from You, Lord; this shall not happen to You!" (Matt. 16:22). There were in his words a resistance to the concept of the wrath of God, His judgment, and His punishment of sin. When Jesus turned to Peter, He made a statement that might apply also to the mind-set of this deputation appearing for the moment so patriotic. "Get thee behind Me, Satan! You are . . . not mindful of the things of God, but of the things of men" (Matt. 16:23).

Jeremiah was mindful of the things of God. He saw that God had chosen Babylon in order to chastise Judah. The prophet was acting out of a higher form of patriotism. All that would save them was repentance and righteousness, not their own military devices. There is a world of people to this day who refuse the concept of the wrath of God and want only a loving God. They are mindful only of the things of the world. They make decisions only on the basis of present circumstances and never on the basis of moral absolutes. The many prophecies of Jeremiah, already fulfilled, spoke eloquently of moral absolutes. His enemies thought to destroy them by destroying Jeremiah.

Zedekiah's weak response was a sad commentary: *"Look, he is in your hand. For the king can do nothing against you"* (v. 5). What a tragic thing to see a king capitulate to cowardice, to become a toy in the hands of his court. I once heard it said, "There are three kinds of people, those who make things happen, those who let things happen, and those who say 'what happened?'" Zedekiah lingers somewhere between the latter two, and in so doing he lost command of the situation.

"So they took Jeremiah and cast him into the dungeon of Malchiah . . . which was in the court of the prison, and they let Jeremiah down with ropes. And in the dungeon there was no water, but mire. So

Jeremiah sank in the mire" (v. 6). It was a cistern, hewn out for catching water during the winter months when it rained. In August, however, it contained nothing but brackish sediment, sucking Jeremiah to a slow but sure death. How reminiscent of the broken cisterns of his early sermons (2:13). Jerusalem had forsaken the fountain of living water and had hewn cisterns of her own making. She had sold out on the precious and bought into the worthless. The betrayal of truth was never so shocking as in this moment when the prophet of God was cast into the mire. The most valuable person in human society, one who should have been exalted, was instead lowered into a pit. The exchange of virtue for vice can reach no lower point than this. This was too crude a treatment for the man guilty only of loving them too much.

Psalm 69 has been hailed as one of the great Messianic songs:

> I sink in deep mire,
> Where *there is* no standing;
> I have come into deep waters,
> Where the floods overflow me . . .
> Let not the pit shut its mouth on me. . . .
> Reproach has broken my heart,
> And I am full of heaviness;
> I looked for someone to take pity.
> *Ps. 69:2, 15, 20*

From the darkness of the cistern came a plea for escape, for someone to understand. One lone figure answered that cry. He was neither king nor prince. He was a heathen, an Ethiopian servant by the name of Ebed-Melech. Mark him well in your memory. See his dark-skinned figure running to the Gate of Benjamin in search of the king. *"My Lord the king, these men have done evil in all that they have done to Jeremiah the prophet, whom they have cast into the dungeon, and he is likely to die from hunger in the place where he is"* (v. 9). The name Ebed-Melech means simply "the king's servant." We do not even know the proper name of this gentile who had the courage to confront the king and stand against the princes for the life of Jeremiah. He blew the whistle on the prevailing insanity.

Remember the heathen harlot who hid Joshua's men under the flax on her roof when they came to spy out the land of Jericho? Rahab was forever immortalized in the genealogy of the Lord for this singular act of heroism that began her life of faith and her eternal link to the Savior of the World. Challenged to act honorably by the Ethiopian, Zedekiah stepped out of character for a moment and acted decisively. *"Take from here thirty men with you, and lift Jeremiah the prophet out of the dungeon before he dies"* (v. 10). Thus began a life-saving adventure that Baruch told with gusto. Would you have been among those thirty men that day had you been there? In spite of the weakness from famine and disease that plagued Jerusalem, these men found strength for their highest priorities. They were not given a lot of time to think about it. A crisis forces us to make an urgent choice. It will reveal the true cut of our heart.

The grit and grime of this heroic enterprise was recorded with authenticity. Old clothes and rags, hastily tied together and dangled into the deep stench of the cistern, formed the ragged ladder between Jeremiah and life itself. Hearts beat in hope that death had not sucked him under. Would he still have enough strength to follow Ebed-Melech's orders that echoed down into the cavernous bowl of mire: *"Please put these old clothes and rags under your armpits, under the ropes"* (v. 12)? They were careful of his comfort, of how fragile he had become. Thirty-one men, who valued the priceless life at the bottom of that pit, prepared to pull for all they were worth. We must ask ourselves who we are pulling for among the voices of this present society. Do we have heroes? Do we care what happens to them?

Jeremiah was reinstated to the court of the prison where he remained until the walls of Jerusalem were finally breached. What God had in store for Ebed-Melech is found in the next chapter. Jeremiah was summoned again by the restless king whose weakness had sent him to the cistern. Now he begged, *"I will ask you something. Hide nothing from me"* (v. 14). Zedekiah keeps coming back to the only man whom he could trust. The only really trustworthy people in the world are those who hold themselves accountable to God. Jeremiah looked into the face of a pitiful man. He asked a very legitimate question, *"If I declare it to you, will you not surely put me to death? And if I give you advice, you will not listen to me"* (v. 15). He had hidden nothing from Zedekiah all along and look at what he had gotten in return: prison, beatings, and the polluted cistern. It is costly to stick to the truth. This was the last encounter these two men ever had. Soon the walls would be breached and the end would come. Each man would be carried to his destiny. Zedekiah vowed not to betray Jeremiah. *"As the LORD lives, who made our very souls"* (v. 16). There seems to be more integrity in these last words than ever before.

Once again Jeremiah advised that there was still time to surrender. *"Then your soul shall live; this city shall not be burned with fire, and you and your house shall live"* (v. 17). One senses that Zedekiah was convinced of the truth of these words but was crippled by fear and unable to act upon them. *"I am afraid of the Jews who have defected to the Chaldeans, lest they deliver me into their hand, and they abuse me"* (v. 19). He had good reason to fear reprisals, but he had better reason to trust the prophet's answer. *"They shall not deliver you. Please, obey the voice of the LORD which I speak to you. So it shall be well with you, and your soul shall live"* (v. 20). Who are you going to believe, Zedekiah? The choice was between his fears and God's facts, as ever it is in the life of faith. This same choice now facing Zedekiah would later face the refugees in chapter 42.

There is a twist of irony in the vision Jeremiah reveals. The people who Zedekiah did not trust were not the ones who would deceive him. Instead, his close friends would be those who would deceive him. Jeremiah described a vision. The women of the palace were pictured being carried away to the princes of Babylon. They set up a chorus of derision to the king, one that should have pierced his pride.

> *Your close friends have set upon you*
> *And prevailed against you;*
> *Your feet have sunk in the mire,*
> *And they have turned away again.*
> v. 22

Those who he had thought were his close friends were not at all. As a matter of fact, the closest friend Zedekiah ever had was the one pleading with him now. The king was sinking in the mire of his own wrong choices. It was a life-and-death matter.

Jeremiah thought of Zedekiah's wives and of his children. He pled on the basis of their lives with great compassion, as a man who had yearned for a family of his own but had surrendered it for the higher call. Now he was exercising that higher call with all the energies

271

of his being. He could not bear to think of women brutalized and of children tortured. He was stirred to his most direct eloquence. *"And you shall cause this city to be burned with fire"* (v. 23). This was Zedekiah's last chance to save the city, its walls, its warriors, its women and children. All he had to do was trust the prophet, to lift his head high, take up the flag of truce, walk past the princes and out to the Chaldean armies. This simple act of contrition would have saved the city. Zedekiah, however, was more worried about the princes and about their discovering this clandestine consultation. He made Jeremiah promise not to discuss their conversation when the princes interrogated him, even dictating the words he was to use (vv. 25–26). The prophet accommodated those trepidations, perhaps hoping Zedekiah would at last do the right thing. At peace with himself and with his prophetic mission, Jeremiah *"remained in the court of the prison until the day that Jerusalem was taken"* (v. 28), a day he had tried to prevent with all the powers of his being.

A BATTERING RAM AGAINST THE WALL

39:1 In the ninth year of Zedekiah king of Judah, in the tenth month, Nebuchadnezzar king of Babylon and all his army came against Jerusalem, and besieged it.

2 In the eleventh year of Zedekiah, in the fourth month, on the ninth *day* of the month, the city was penetrated.

3 Then all the princes of the king of Babylon came in and sat in the Middle Gate: Nergal-Sharezer, Samgar-Nebo, Sarsechim, Rabsaris, Nergal-Sarezer, Rabmag, with the rest of the princes of the king of Babylon.

4 So it was, when Zedekiah the king of Judah and all the men of war saw them, that they fled and went out of the city by night, by way of the king's garden, by the gate between the two walls. And he went out by way of the plain.

5 But the Chaldean army pursued them and overtook Zedekiah in the plains of Jericho. And when they had captured him, they brought him up to Nebuchadnezzar king of Babylon, to Riblah in the

land of Hamath, where he pronounced judgment on him.

6 Then the king of Babylon killed the sons of Zedekiah before his eyes in Riblah; the king of Babylon also killed all the nobles of Judah.

7 Moreover he put out Zedekiah's eyes, and bound him with bronze fetters to carry him off to Babylon.

8 And the Chaldeans burned the king's house and the houses of the people with fire, and broke down the walls of Jerusalem.

9 Then Nebuzaradan the captain of the guard carried away captive to Babylon the remnant of the people who remained in the city and those who defected to him, with the rest of the people who remained.

10 But Nebuzaradan the captain of the guard left in the land of Judah the poor people, who had nothing, and gave them vineyards and fields at the same time.

11 Now Nebuchadnezzar king of Babylon gave charge concerning Jeremiah to Nebuzaradan the captain of the guard, saying,

12 "Take him and look after him, and do him no harm; but do to him just as he says to you."

13 So Nebuzaradan the captain of the guard sent Nebushasban, Rabsaris, Nergal-Sharezer, Rabmag, and all the king of Babylon's chief officers;

14 then they sent *someone* to take Jeremiah from the court of the prison, and committed him to Gedaliah the son of Ahikam, the son of Shaphan, that he should take him home. So he dwelt among the people.

15 Meanwhile the word of the LORD had come to Jeremiah while he was shut up in the court of the prison, saying,

16 "Go and speak to Ebed-Melech the Ethiopian, saying, 'Thus says the LORD of hosts, the God of Israel: "Behold, I will bring My words upon this city for adversity and not for good, and they shall be *performed* in that day before you.

17 "But I will deliver you in that day," says the LORD, "and you shall not be given into the hand of the men of whom you *are* afraid.

18 "For I will surely deliver you, and you shall not

273

fall by the sword; but your life shall be as a prize to you, because you have put your trust in Me,' says the LORD.'"

52:1 Zedekiah *was* twenty-one years old when he became king, and he reigned eleven years in Jerusalem. His mother's name *was* Hamutal the daughter of Jeremiah of Libnah.

2 He also did evil in the sight of the LORD, according to all that Jehoiakim had done.

3 For because of the anger of the LORD *this* happened in Jerusalem and Judah, till He finally cast them out from His presence. Then Zedekiah rebelled against the king of Babylon.

4 Now it came to pass in the ninth year of his reign, in the tenth month, on the tenth *day* of the month, *that* Nebuchadnezzar king of Babylon and all his army came against Jerusalem and encamped against it; and *they* built a siege wall against it all around.

5 So the city was besieged until the eleventh year of King Zedekiah.

6 By the fourth month, on the ninth day of the month, the famine had become so severe in the city that there was no food for the people of the land.

7 Then the city wall was broken through, and all the men of war fled and went out of the city at night by way of the gate between the two walls, which *was* by the king's garden, even though the Chaldeans *were* near the city all around. And they went by way of the plain.

8 But the army of the Chaldeans pursued the king, and they overtook Zedekiah in the plains of Jericho. All his army was scattered from him.

9 So they took the king and brought him up to the king of Babylon at Riblah in the land of Hamath, and he pronounced judgment on him.

10 Then the king of Babylon killed the sons of Zedekiah before his eyes. And he killed all the princes of Judah in Riblah.

11 He also put out the eyes of Zedekiah; and the king of Babylon bound him in bronze fetters, took

him to Babylon, and put him in prison till the day of his death.

12 Now in the fifth month, on the tenth *day* of the month (which *was* the nineteenth year of King Nebuchadnezzar king of Babylon), Nebuzaradan, the captain of the guard, *who* served the king of Babylon, came to Jerusalem.

13 He burned the house of the LORD and the king's house; all the houses of Jerusalem, that is, all the houses of the great, he burned with fire.

14 And all the army of the Chaldeans who *were* with the captain of the guard broke down all the walls of Jerusalem all around.

15 Then Nebuzaradan the captain of the guard carried away captive *some* of the poor people, the rest of the people who remained in the city, the defectors who had deserted to the king of Babylon, and the rest of the craftsmen.

16 But Nebuzaradan the captain of the guard left *some* of the poor of the land as vinedressers and farmers.

17 The bronze pillars that *were* in the house of the LORD, and the carts and the bronze Sea that *were* in the house of the LORD, the Chaldeans broke in pieces, and carried all their bronze to Babylon.

18 They also took away the pots, the shovels, the trimmers, the bowls, the spoons, and all the bronze utensils with which the priests ministered.

19 The basins, the firepans, the bowls, the pots, the lampstands, the spoons, and the cups, whatever *was* solid gold and whatever *was* solid silver, the captain of the guard took away.

20 The two pillars, one Sea, the twelve bronze bulls which *were* under *it, and* the carts, which King Solomon had made for the house of the LORD—the bronze of all these articles was beyond measure.

21 Now *concerning* the pillars: the height of one pillar *was* eighteen cubits, a measuring line of twelve cubits could measure its circumference, and its thickness *was* four fingers; *it was* hollow.

22 A capital of bronze *was* on it; and the height of one capital *was* five cubits, with a network and

pomegranates all around the capital, all of bronze. The second pillar, with pomegranates was the same.

23 There were ninety-six pomegranates on the sides; all the pomegranates, all around on the network, *were* one hundred.

24 The captain of the guard took Seraiah the chief priest, Zephaniah the second priest, and the three doorkeepers.

25 He also took out of the city an officer who had charge of the men of war, seven men of the king's close associates who were found in the city, the principal scribe of the army who mustered the people of the land, and sixty men of the people of the land who were found in the midst of the city.

26 And Nebuzaradan the captain of the guard took these and brought them to the king of Babylon at Riblah.

27 Then the king of Babylon struck them and put them to death at Riblah in the land of Hamath. Thus Judah was carried away captive from its own land.

28 These *are* the people whom Nebuchadnezzar carried away captive: in the seventh year, three thousand and twenty-three Jews;

29 in the eighteenth year of Nebuchadnezzar he carried away captive from Jerusalem eight hundred and thirty-two persons;

30 in the twenty-third year of Nebuchadnezzar, Nebuzaradan the captain of the guard carried away captive of the Jews seven hundred and forty-five persons. All the persons *were* four thousand six hundred.

31 Now it came to pass in the thirty-seventh year of the captivity of Jehoiachin king of Judah, in the twelfth month, on the twenty-fifth *day* of the month, *that* Evil-Merodach king of Babylon, in the first *year* of his reign, lifted up the head of Jehoiachin king of Judah and brought him out of prison.

32 And he spoke kindly to him and gave him a more prominent seat than those of the kings who *were* with him in Babylon.

33 So Jehoiachin changed from his prison garments, and he ate bread regularly before the king all the days of his life.

34 And as for his provisions, there was a regular
ration given him by the king of Babylon, a portion
for each day until the day of his death, all the days of
his life.

Jer. 39:1-18; 52:1-34

I include chapter 52 here because its narrative parallels the events
described in this chapter. *"In the eleventh year of Zedekiah, in the
fourth month, on the ninth day of the month, the city was penetrated"*
(39:2; cf. 52:5). The battering ram took its last run at the walls. Darts
from the enemy siege mounds arched into the midnight sky and
struck their mark in flames. Famine had already claimed many lives
inside the walls. Five Babylonian princes marched through the
streets of Jerusalem, their faces illuminated by the flames of destruction. Josephus named the hour; Baruch named the princes or at least
five of the more formidable ones that came and sat in the Middle
Gate (39:3).

*"So it was, when Zedekiah the king of Judah and all the men of war saw
them, that they fled and went out of the city by night"* (39:4). Now
Zedekiah would know what it felt like to be hunted by his enemies.
Jeremiah had lived the last several years of his prophetic ministry in
this dynamic. He clung to the words of God, "I will defend you."
Zedekiah had no such consolation; *"All his army was scattered from
him"* (52:8). Under the cover of darkness, he left the city through a
gate in his garden, one that was between two walls, hoping that the
hills and the darkness would grant him refuge (52:7). *"But the
Chaldean army pursued them and overtook Zedekiah in the plains of Jericho"* (39:5; cf. 52:8). The face-to-face encounter with Nebuchadnezzar was to take place in Riblah, approximately 150 miles north of the
city. It was there that judgment would be pronounced upon him in
the form of a military trial (39:5; 52:9). What a dark journey that must
have been for Zedekiah, his sons, and his nobles. They marched toward judgment, hopelessly surrounded by the Chaldean army and by
the inexorable prophecies, but it was now too late to heed.

*"Then the king of Babylon killed the sons of Zedekiah before his eyes in
Riblah; the king of Babylon also killed all the nobles of Judah"* (39:6; cf.
52:10). Zedekiah was forced to watch the blood bath. The choices
given to him earlier by Jeremiah must have run through his mind now
as a litany of lost opportunities. "He who goes over to the Chaldeans

shall live; his life shall be as a prize to him, and he shall live" (38:2). *"Moreover he put out Zedekiah's eyes, and bound him with bronze fetters to carry him off to Babylon. And the Chaldeans burned the king's house and the houses of the people with fire, and broke down the walls of Jerusalem"* (39:7–8; cf. 52:11). The temple was also burned; the two bronze pillars that had been commissioned by Solomon were carried away along with many sacred vessels of gold and silver. Zedekiah's conscience would burn with even greater pain than the burning in the sockets of his eyes and in the walls of Jerusalem. Might he have remembered the words of the prophet, "Do not deceive yourselves, saying, 'The Chaldeans will surely depart from us,' for they will not depart" (37:9). Now the price was being paid.

The citizens also paid the price for Zedekiah's unbelief. *"Then Neb-uzaradan the captain of the guard carried away captive to Babylon the remnant of the people who remained in the city and those who defected to him, with the rest of the people who remained"* (39:9). F. B. Meyer describes it in this way:

> It was indeed a subject for an artist to depict, the long march of the exiles on the way to their distant home. Delicate women and little children forced to travel day after day, irrespective of fatigue and suffering; prophets and priests mingled together in the overthrow they had done so much to bring about; rich and poor marching side by side, manacled, and urged forward by the spear-point or scourge. All along the valley of the Jordan, past Damascus, and then for thirty days through the inhospitable wilderness . . . whilst all the nations round clapped their hands.[1]

"But Nebuzaradan the captain of the guard left in the land of Judah the poor people, who had nothing, and gave them vineyards and fields at the same time" (39:10). Could this possibly refer to the slaves who had been treated with such injustice? Were they now being given the land by a pagan monarch that their own king and princes were too greedy to give? Not only did they have vineyards and fields of their own, but now they had those of their cruel masters as well.

Nebuchadnezzar's orders concerning Zedekiah had been to blind him and to bind him. Listen now to his orders concerning Jeremiah: *"Take him and look after him, and do him no harm; but do to him just as he says to you"* (39:12). What a brilliant picture of a sovereign

278

God executing His purposes through the agency of pagan kings and captains.

Four of the highest officials of the land, named in verse 13, were accompanied by not just a few but *all the king of Babylon's chief officers* (39:13). The scene would put a Hollywood spectacular to shame. All of this pageantry in the march toward a Jewish prophet in his little prison. The name of Jeremiah means "God exalts." My, how He exalts when He wants to say "well done, good and faithful servant."

"Then they sent someone to take Jeremiah from the court of the prison, and committed him to Gedaliah the son of Ahikam, the son of Shaphan, that he should take him home. So he dwelt among the people" (39:14). What could be more honoring than a delegation of Babylonian nobles or more comforting than the sight of one of his best friends come to take him home? It would seem to be like a preview of heaven. Think of the joy among those people in seeing him restored to them who had run the race so well. Released from prison and restored to his friends, the prophet had new work to do. *"Go and speak to Ebed-Melech the Ethiopian"* (39:16). The words had come while Jeremiah was still shut up in the prison, before he could yet act upon them. God's word is stronger than the circumstances in which we find ourselves. Obviously Jeremiah maintained through the siege an attitude of heart that enabled the word to visit him. Obviously he was not so preoccupied with the distress that he could not see beyond it nor so self-involved that he could not think of others. His behavior in prison describes the posture of faith for all believers.

God read the heart of his obedient servant Ebed-Melech who had run through the streets of Jerusalem, who had publicly encountered Zedekiah with an insistence that Jeremiah be saved from the cistern, knowing all the while that raw heroism might one day cost him his life. As a servant in the courts of the king, Ebed-Melech had perhaps heard the princes counseling together. He had secretly exalted over the freeing of the slaves, had secretly loved the prophet for his passion for justice and human dignity. The day came that those secret loyalties had to go public in order to save Jeremiah's life which was moment by moment ebbing away in the cistern's miry and suffocating darkness. See in this drama a lesson for us all. We cannot live on private loyalties to God as "secret service" Christians. A time comes when we must go public, when like Jeremiah and Ebed-Melech we must nail our colors to the mast, knowing all the while that it was sure to draw the enemy's fire. Here, through the prophet Jeremiah, God assured the heart of Ebed-Melech, *"I will deliver you in that day . . . and you shall not be given into the hand of the men of whom you are afraid"* (39:17).

Because he feared God more than he feared his enemies, this Ethiopian servant was told, *"your life shall be as a prize to you"* (39:18). Zedekiah, however, feared his enemies more than he feared the word of God, and his life became a prize to Nebuchadnezzar, the property of his belligerent conqueror. We need to ask ourselves, "What are our lives the property of?" Ebed-Melech received himself back only because he had first given himself away to the Lord who used his courage. His personality, his sense of identity and purpose became more fully orbed as he gave himself away than ever they would have been had he stayed quiet and minded his own business. Would that name ever have been recorded for all posterity had he not acted on his beliefs? Do you want God to be proud of you and to prize your life? "He who receives a prophet [as Ebed-Melech did] shall receive a prophet's reward" (Matt. 10:41).

This final drama of the fall of Jerusalem is a telling one. It shows who God considered to be the real heroes. They were not those whom the world would have chosen. As Jeremiah looked out over broken gates and blackened ruins, all that would keep him going was the remembrance of those words "I have . . . set you over the nations and over the kingdoms, [not only] to pull down, [but also] to build and to plant" (1:10).

NOTE

1. F. B. Meyer, *Jeremiah* (Fort Washington, Pa.: Christian Literature Crusade, 1980), 139.

CHAPTER NINETEEN

To Build and to Plant

Jeremiah 40:1–42:22

TO BUILD WITH GEDALIAH

40:1 The word that came to Jeremiah from the LORD after Nebuzaradan the captain of the guard had let him go from Ramah, when he had taken him bound in chains among all who were carried away captive from Jerusalem and Judah, who were carried away captive to Babylon.

2 And the captain of the guard took Jeremiah and said to him: "The LORD your God has pronounced this doom on this place.

3 "Now the LORD has brought *it*, and has done just as He said. Because you *people* have sinned against the LORD, and not obeyed His voice, therefore this thing has come upon you.

4 "And now look, I free you this day from the chains that *were* on your hand. It if seems good to you to come with me to Babylon, come, and I will look after you. But if it seems wrong for you to come with me to Babylon, remain here. See, all the land *is* before you; wherever it seems good and convenient for you to go, go there."

5 Now while Jeremiah had not yet gone back, *Nebuzaradan said,* "Go back to Gedaliah the son of Ahikam, the son of Shaphan, whom the king of Babylon has made governor over the cities of Judah, and dwell with him among the people. Or go wherever it seems convenient for you to go." So the captain of the guard gave him rations and a gift and let him go.

6 Then Jeremiah went to Gedaliah the son of Ahikam, to Mizpah, and dwelt with him among the people who were left in the land.

7 And when all the captains of the armies who *were* in the fields, they and their men, heard that the king of Babylon had made Gedaliah the son of Ahikam governor in the land, and had committed to him men, women, children, and the poorest of the land who had not been carried away captive to Babylon,

8 then they came to Gedaliah at Mizpah—Ishmael the son of Nethaniah, Johanan and Jonathan the sons of Kareah, Seraiah the son of Tanhumeth, the sons of Ephai the Netophathite, and Jezaniah the son of a Maachathite, they and their men.

9 And Gedaliah the son of Ahikam, the son of Shaphan, took an oath before them and their men, saying, "Do not be afraid to serve the Chaldeans. Dwell in the land and serve the king of Babylon, and it shall be well with you.

10 "As for me, I will indeed dwell at Mizpah and serve the Chaldeans who come to us. But you, gather wine and summer fruit and oil, put *them* in your vessels, and dwell in your cities that you have taken."

11 Likewise, when all the Jews who *were* in Moab, among the Ammonites, in Edom, and who *were* in all the countries, heard that the king of Babylon had left a remnant of Judah, and that he had set over them Gedaliah the son of Ahikam, the son of Shaphan,

12 then all the Jews returned out of all places where they had been driven, and came to the land of Judah, to Gedaliah at Mizpah, and gathered wine and summer fruit in abundance.

13 Moreover Johanan the son of Kareah and all the captains of the forces that *were* in the fields came to Gedaliah at Mizpah,

14 and said to him, "Do you certainly know that Baalis the king of the Ammonites has sent Ishmael the son of Nethaniah to murder you?" But Gedaliah the son of Ahikam did not believe them.

15 Then Johanan the son of Kareah spoke secretly to Gedaliah in Mizpah, saying, "Let me go, please, and I will kill Ishmael the son of Nethaniah, and no

one will know *it*. Why should he murder you, so that
all the Jews who are gathered to you would be scattered, and the remnant in Judah perish?"
16 But Gedaliah the son of Ahikam said to Johanan
the son of Kareah, "You shall not do this thing, for you
speak falsely concerning Ishmael."

Jer. 40:1–16

When Jeremiah was called and commissioned, the Lord put forth
His hand and touched his mouth. From that moment on, the words
Jeremiah spoke prophetically would have power over the nations. It
was a double-edged power, "to root out and pull down" or "to build
and to plant." One comes before the other. As the prophet warned of
coming judgment, so God did pull down the very walls of Jerusalem
through the armies of Babylon. As he predicted an ultimate restoration, so God did begin to build and to plant them anew in the torn
land under the leadership of Gedaliah. The short life of this new
government did not come close to fulfilling the visions of restoration, but it did prefigure that refreshment. It was a faith flicker of
the building and planting God intends to do.

Nebuchadnezzar began to organize the newly conquered territories. The decision to make Gedaliah governor of conquered Judah
may well have been influenced by Jeremiah, who probably recom-
mended him to the new sovereign with the assurance that Gedaliah's
leadership style would be trustworthy and his word sure. A now
cooperative people would begin to build again. We know from the
dignity of the delegation sent to Jeremiah in the prison that he was
highly respected by the Babylonians, who wished him no harm. As a
matter of fact, they seemed to be moving heaven and earth to protect
the prophet who may well have been suffering physically from the
imprisonments and abuses dealt him by his own brethren. Verse 1
refers to a time when Jeremiah was taken in chains along with the
other captives. This had obviously been a mistake. In order to rectify
it, Nebuzaradan, the king's captain, was sent to the prophet. There is
a note of irony in this historic confrontation. A man whose name
means "chief of slaughterers," acts tenderly toward Jeremiah.

The *Interpreter's Bible* is quick to point out that a man as perceptive as Nebuchadnezzar would certainly have been aware of the
work and words of Jeremiah and of their international influence.

The prophet's voice in some ways favored Nebuchadnezzar's cause because it encouraged cooperation with him instead of resistance. Nebuchadnezzar and Jeremiah were easily among the greatest leaders of their time.[1] Granted each man hailed from a different sphere of sovereignty, their careers merge here in a mutual respect that is articulated by Nebuchadnezzar's captain of the guard. Speaking to Jeremiah, he says, *"The LORD your God has pronounced this doom on this place . . . Because you people have sinned against the LORD, and not obeyed His voice"* (vv. 2–3). How strange to hear such God-fearing language from a pagan. It was spoken not out of personal commitment, but out of political awareness. This pagan had been listening to the voices of the cultures he had conquered. He was as abreast of current events as any effective leader should be. An unassuming Jewish prophet, from an insignificant speck of land, had gained international attention. The concept of the universality of God's word was sooner grasped by this heathen than by the Hebrews.

Nebuchadnezzar and Jeremiah shared a more expansive vision than the rest of the world. One was a shrewd observer, analyzing the political, social, and religious currents of his world; the other a shrewd listener to the voice of God, holding those currents in the palm of His hand.

"Go back to Gedaliah" (v. 5), came the captain's words. It was indeed in the interest of Babylon to have the new governor reinforced by the presence and the council of Jeremiah. It was also in their interest to have the prophet's favor: *"Or go wherever it seems convenient for you to go"* (v. 5). His own people had made him a prisoner; an enemy nation granted him freedom. "When a man's ways please the LORD, He makes even his enemies to be at peace with him" (Prov. 16:7). *"So the captain of the guard gave him rations and a gift and let him go"* (v. 5). Naturally Jeremiah headed straight for Gedaliah *"and dwelt with him among the people who were left in the land"* (v. 6).

The prophet used extravagant language to describe Gedaliah's administration and to strike a contrast to the famine of Zedekiah's land. There was a peaceful, almost poetic, turn to Gedaliah's instruction to his people: *"Gather wine and summer fruit and oil, and put them in your vessels, and dwell in your cities that you have taken"* (v. 10). The new governor intended for his people to be fruitful in the land, to replenish it, and to live in peace with each other and with Babylon.

His intentions were like those of God Himself for the poor left in the land. "Blessed *are* the poor in spirit For theirs is the kingdom of heaven" (Matt. 5:3).

It is important to note that Gedaliah was appointed governor and not king. Zedekiah was the last king and the last of the line of David. There had been twenty-one kings; together they had reigned 514 years, 6 months, and 10 days as recorded in the histories of Josephus.[2] There would not be another king of the line of David until Jesus came with the words "the kingdom of heaven is among you." No wonder Matthew, in writing his kingdom gospel, was so excited to announce "The book of the genealogy of Jesus Christ, the Son of David" (Matt. 1:1). Filled with wonder, Matthew noticed that "So all the generations from Abraham to David *are* fourteen generations, from David until the captivity in Babylon *are* fourteen generations, and from the captivity in Babylon until the Christ *are* fourteen generations" (Matt. 1:17).

The Babylonian captivity and the governorship of Gedaliah stood at a pivotal point in God's orchestration of human history. They marked the end of an era. Short lived and ill fated as it was, the term of Gedaliah with its wine, summer fruit, and oil, prefigured the Great Administration yet to come. It was characterized by blessing and bounty. People gravitated to it. *"And when all the captains of the armies who were in the fields, they and their men, heard that the king of Babylon had made Gedaliah . . . governor in the land, . . . then they came to Gedaliah at Mizpah"* (vv. 7–8). People will respond to strong leadership.

The leaders of the Jewish forces are named. They came in from their various fields of independence and saw the new governor take *"an oath before them and their men, saying, 'Do not be afraid to serve the Chaldeans. Dwell in the land and serve the king of Babylon, and it shall be well with you'"* (v. 9). Beginning with a show of integrity, Gedaliah proved his ability to consolidate forces, to restore unity, to gain trust from frightened, defensive people. His heart and his very language were like those of the prophet. A new credibility rested upon them now that all of the prophetic utterances had been fulfilled to the letter. Yet one of those named was only giving lip service to Gedaliah. Ishmael had no intention of serving the king of Babylon nor of serving Gedaliah. So much credibility and momentum was bound to arouse jealousy, especially from an ambitious warrior of the line of David who thought that he should have been appointed king. Ishmael was just such a man. He formed an alliance with Baalis, the king of the Ammonites, their common ground being their mutual hatred of Gedaliah and of his success. Like brush fire, news of their plans to murder the good governor spread. *"Johanan the son of Kareah and all the captains of the forces that were in the fields came to Gedaliah at Mizpah, and said to him, 'Do you certainly know that Baalis . . . has sent Ishmael . . . to murder you?"* (vv. 13–14). Gedaliah should have listened to that breathless band of loyalists who had rushed such news to him. Perhaps naïveté was his tragic flaw; *"But Gedaliah the son of Ahikam did not believe them"* (v. 14). Those who are summoned to serve the kingdom are told to be "harmless as doves" and "wise as serpents." They are warned "I send you out as sheep in the midst of wolves" (Matt. 10:16). Gedaliah was guilty of an enormous miscalculation. He trusted human nature; he failed to be as wise as a serpent. When Jesus was in Jerusalem for the Passover, many believed in His name. "But Jesus did not commit Himself to them, because He knew all *men*" (John 2:24). Johanan kept urging Gedaliah, *"Let me go, please, and I will kill Ishmael . . . and no one will know it"* (v. 15). Perhaps his violent solution was wrong, but his perception of the problem and its implications was right. *"Why should he murder you, so that all the Jews who are gathered to you would be scattered, and the remnant in Judah perish?"* (v. 15).

I love Johanan for his zeal, for hating to see the cause of peace and unity be threatened again. Gedaliah should also have loved that zeal, but instead he scolded it: *"You shall not do this thing, for you speak falsely concerning Ishmael"* (v. 16).

CONCERNING ISHMAEL

41:1 Now it came to pass in the seventh month *that* Ishmael the son of Nethaniah, the son of Elishama, of the royal family and of the officers of the king, came with ten men to Gedaliah the son of Ahikam, at Mizpah. And there they ate bread together in Mizpah.

2 Then Ishmael the son of Nethaniah, and the ten men who were with him, arose and struck Gedaliah the son of Ahikam, the son of Shaphan, with the

sword, and killed him whom the king of Babylon had made governor over the land.

3 Ishmael also struck down all the Jews who were with him, *that is,* with Gedaliah at Mizpah, and the Chaldeans who were found there, the men of war.

4 And it happened, on the second day after he had killed Gedaliah, when as yet no one knew *it,*

5 that certain men came from Shechem, from Shiloh, and from Samaria, eighty men with their beards shaved and their clothes torn, having cut themselves, with offerings and incense in their hand, to bring *them* to the house of the LORD.

6 Now Ishmael the son of Nethaniah went out from Mizpah to meet them, weeping as he went along; and it happened as he met them that he said to them, "Come to Gedaliah the son of Ahikam!"

7 So it was, when they came into the midst of the city, that Ishmael the son of Nethaniah killed them *and cast them* into the midst of a pit, he and the men who were with him.

8 But ten men were found among them who said to Ishmael, "Do not kill us, for we have treasures of wheat, barley, oil, and honey in the field." So he desisted and did not kill them among their brethren.

9 Now the pit into which Ishmael had cast all the dead bodies of the men whom he had slain, because of Gedaliah, *was* the same one Asa the king had made for fear of Baasha king of Israel. Ishmael the son of Nethaniah filled it with *the* slain.

10 Then Ishmael carried away captive all the rest of the people who *were* in Mizpah, the king's daughters and all the people who remained in Mizpah, whom Nebuzaradan the captain of the guard had committed to Gedaliah the son of Ahikam. And Ishmael the son of Nethaniah carried them away captive and departed to go over to the Ammonites.

11 But when Johanan the son of Kareah and all the captains of the forces that *were* with him heard of all the evil that Ishmael the son of Nethaniah had done,

12 they took all the men and went to fight with Ishmael the son of Nethaniah; and they found him by the great pool that *is* in Gibeon.

13 So it was, when all the people who *were* with
Ishmael saw Johanan the son of Kareah, and all the
captains of the forces who *were* with him, that they
were glad.

14 Then all the people whom Ishmael had carried
away captive from Mizpah turned around and came
back, and went to Johanan the son of Kareah.

15 But Ishmael the son of Nethaniah escaped from
Johanan with eight men and went to the Ammonites.

16 Then Johanan the son of Kareah, and all the
captains of the forces that were with him, took from
Mizpah all the rest of the people whom he had re-
covered from Ishmael the son of Nethaniah after he
had murdered Gedaliah the son of Ahikam—the
mighty men of war and the women and the children
and the eunuchs, whom he had brought back from
Gibeon.

17 And they departed and dwelt in the habitation
of Chimham, which is near Bethlehem, as they went
on their way to Egypt,

18 because of the Chaldeans; for they were afraid
of them, because Ishmael the son of Nethaniah had
murdered Gedaliah the son of Ahikam, whom the
king of Babylon had made governor in the land.

Jer. 41:1–18

Unfortunately Johanan had not spoken falsely concerning Ishmael.
The political climate easily bred insurrection. It was hardly the time
for naïveté on the part of Gedaliah, who was forewarned but not
forearmed. Hindsight makes it easy to identify Ishmael as a potential
terrorist with whom it would have been impossible to negotiate. He
was next in line for the throne from the line of David, waiting his
turn to reign. Yet he was passed over in favor of Gedaliah. Therefore, he resented both Gedaliah and the Babylonian government that
seated him in power. Perhaps he was passed over because of a pro-
Egyptian loyalty.[3] His anger was compounded by the slaughter of
Zedekiah's sons. Violence had become the law of the land. He found
a similar mind in Baalis, the Ammonite king who did not want to see
a strong Judah rise again. His savage intentions must have been disguised for a time as Ishmael and ten of his men visited Gedaliah,
where *"they ate bread together in Mizpah"* (v. 1).

They waited until after the meal. *"Then Ishmael the son of Nethaniah, and the ten men who were with him, arose and struck Gedaliah the son of Ahikam, the son of Shaphan, with the sword, and killed him whom the king of Babylon had made governor over the land"* (v. 2). The last hope for peace and unity died there in that room with Gedaliah. Everything that Johanan had feared came to pass—and even more than he had feared. The savagery continued. *"Ishmael also struck down all the Jews who were with him, that is, with Gedaliah at Mizpah, and the Chaldeans who were found there, the men of war"* (v. 3).

For two days the rest of the world knew nothing of this blood bath. Satellites would have globalized the news within minutes in our current information society. This two-day information lag cost the lives of seventy men who were journeying toward Jerusalem, *"with their beards shaved and their clothes torn, having cut themselves, with offerings and incense in their hand, to bring them to the house of the LORD"* (v. 5). The gruesome events of war and desolation had brought them to a spirit of repentance. They yearned for a last look at the mountain of holiness that was Jerusalem, even at the charred and broken walls, to mourn there and pay their last respects. In their grief, they hardly anticipated terrorism. That is one thing that colors terrorism so darkly: it is rarely expected. It strikes when we are least prepared for it. Its victims are defenseless.

"Now Ishmael the son of Nethaniah went out from Mizpah to meet them, weeping as he went along" (v. 6). Was nothing sacred to this man? He had violated oriental custom by murdering Gedaliah while partaking of his hospitality. Now he violated the Jewish custom concerning mourning. He made a mockery of the tenderest human emotions. Without any conscience he laid a trap for these next victims. *"Come to Gedaliah the son of Ahikam!"* (v. 6), he invited. A wolf in sheep's clothing, Ishmael would stop at nothing to vent his anger upon the world, to make it worse for his having been here instead of better. *"So it was, when they came into the midst of the city, that Ishmael the son of Nethaniah killed them and cast them into the midst of a pit, he and the men who were with him"* (v. 7).

There was nonetheless a note of hope to be found in this carnage. All but ten of the mourners died, but they died after first expressing repentant sorrow for their own and the corporate lifestyle that had led to the demise of Jerusalem, assuming, of course, that this action was more than ceremonial. We never know when our hour is at hand.

It often comes swiftly and unexpectedly. These seventy men—with shaven faces, torn clothes, and incense in their hands—died in what was then the customary posture of mourning over sin.

Recently we conducted a funeral service in our church for a couple who had been happily living out the senior years of their lives. They went out for ice cream one hot summer evening. They never returned home because of a drunken driver. It made no sense. We all loved them so and demonstrated that love by packing the church to honor their lives and shed our tears. The central comfort that came, in spite of all our grief and outrage, was that they belonged to Jesus. Like those seventy whose lives were cut short by violence, our friends were Home, and we were consoled.

Like all the Ishmaels of the world, this murdering band was without reverence for human life. They slung their seventy victims into a pit and were ready to slaughter the remaining ten, but the victims cried out, *"Do not kill us, for we have treasures of wheat, barley, oil, and honey in the field"* (v. 8). The only thing that spoke to Ishmael was the potential for survival in a famine-struck land. If he could eat a meal at Gedaliah's table before murdering him, he could certainly listen to this plea with the ears of his own self-interest. In return for their food supplies, Ishmael spared those ten lives.

"Then Ishmael carried away captive all the rest of the people who were in Mizpah, the king's daughters and all the people who remained in Mizpah, whom Nebuzaradan the captain of the guard had committed to Gedaliah the son of Ahikam. And Ishmael the son of Nethaniah carried them away captive and departed to go over to the Ammonites" (v. 10). Suddenly all of the people who had trusted in the peaceful reign of Gedaliah found themselves in the hands of a radical. Once again they were being led out as exiles to yet another pagan power. Jeremiah and Baruch most likely were among the captives, all the while grieving the loss of Gedaliah, their friend and their hope for peace.

Baruch described the heroic rescue effort mounted by Johanan in league with the other captains who had come to trust the government of Gedaliah. Great companies of angry armies pressed after Ishmael the terrorist in an effort to rescue his hostages. *"And they found him by the great pool that is in Gibeon"* (v. 12). The town of Gibeon was built on the slope of a hill that overlooked a wide and fertile valley. Deep down in the rock on the eastern side of the hill a clear spring sends its refreshing waters into a large rectangular pool, seventy-two feet long and forty-two feet wide.[4] These tranquil waters reflected the confrontation between the rescue forces of Johanan and the terrorist forces of Ishmael, who had paused there in their flight to Ammon. *"So it was, when all the people who were with Ishmael saw Johanan the son of Kareah, and all the captains of the forces who were with him, that they were glad"* (v. 13). The hostages seized this chance; they *"turned around and came back, and went to Johanan"* (v. 14). Ishmael was outnumbered; his only option was to flee. He escaped with eight men and went to the Ammonites.

Jeremiah and Baruch long remembered the men of war coming over to the side of Johanan, the women, the children, and all who had been victims of Ishmael's bid for power. They must have been a crazed and emotionally exhausted company of people with so much terror and tragedy behind them and so much uncertainty before them. They could not afford to linger at the pool of Gibeon. It offered them no refuge; nothing did in their world of lawlessness and power struggles. *"And they departed and dwelt in the habitation of Chimham, which is near Bethlehem, as they went on their way to Egypt, because of the Chaldeans"* (vv. 17–18). Johanan must have feared that the Chaldeans would take revenge on anyone they could find who had ever been associated with Ishmael. They might not wait for an explanation, never again trust a Hebrew. His mind must have been straining for the right strategy as he headed his company of fugitives toward Egypt and settled them in Chimham near Bethlehem. God intended to build and to plant—but not in Egypt. What was Jeremiah thinking as he looked over this pitiful band of itinerants under the leadership of Johanan heading in the wrong direction? Would this new self-appointed leader decide to settle things with his fists or with his faith?

To Plant with Johanan

42:1 Now all the captains of the forces, Johanan the son of Kareah, Jezaniah the son of Hoshaiah, and all the people, from the least to the greatest, came near
2 and said to Jeremiah the prophet, "Please, let our petition be acceptable to you, and pray for us to

the LORD your God, for all this remnant (since we are left *but* a few of many, as you can see),

3 "that the LORD your God may show us the way in which we should walk and the thing we should do."

4 Then Jeremiah the prophet said to them, "I have heard. Indeed, I will pray to the LORD your God according to your words, and it shall be, *that* whatever the LORD answers you, I will declare *it* to you. I will keep nothing back from you."

5 So they said to Jeremiah, "Let the LORD be a true and faithful witness between us, if we do not do according to everything which the LORD your God sends us by you.

6 "Whether *it is* pleasing or displeasing, we will obey the voice of the LORD our God to whom we send you, that it may be well with us when we obey the voice of the LORD our God."

7 And it happened after ten days that the word of the LORD came to Jeremiah.

8 Then he called Johanan the son of Kareah, all the captains of the forces which *were* with him, and all the people from the least even to the greatest,

9 and said to them, "Thus says the LORD, the God of Israel, to whom you sent me to present your petition before Him:

10 'If you will still remain in this land, then I will build you and not pull *you* down, and I will plant you and not pluck *you* up. For I relent concerning the disaster that I have brought upon you.

11 'Do not be afraid of the king of Babylon, of whom you are afraid; do not be afraid of him,' says the LORD, 'for I *am* with you, to save you and deliver you from his hand.

12 'And I will show you mercy, that he may have mercy on you and cause you to return to your own land.'

13 "But if you say, 'We will not dwell in this land,' disobeying the voice of the LORD your God,

14 "saying, 'No, but we will go to the land of Egypt where we shall see no war, nor hear the sound of the trumpet, nor be hungry for bread, and there we will dwell'—

15 "Then hear now the word of the LORD, O remnant of Judah! Thus says the LORD of hosts, the God
of Israel: 'If you wholly set your faces to enter Egypt,
and go to dwell there,

16 'then it shall be *that* the sword which you feared
shall overtake you there in the land of Egypt; the
famine of which you were afraid shall follow close
after you there *in* Egypt; and there you shall die.

17 'So shall it be with all the men who set their
faces to go to Egypt to dwell there. They shall die by
the sword, by famine, and by pestilence. And none
of them shall remain or escape from the disaster that
I will bring upon them.'

18 "For thus says the LORD of hosts, the God of
Israel: "As My anger and My fury have been poured
out on the inhabitants of Jerusalem, so will My fury
be poured out on you when you enter Egypt. And
you shall be an oath, an astonishment, a curse, and a
reproach; and you shall see this place no more.'

19 "The LORD has said concerning you, O remnant
of Judah, 'Do not go to Egypt!' Know certainly that I
have admonished you this day.

20 "For you were hypocrites in your hearts when
you sent me to the LORD your God, saying, 'Pray for
us to the LORD our God, and according to all that the
LORD your God says, so declare to us and we will
do *it.*'

21 "And I have this day declared *it* to you, but you
have not obeyed the voice of the LORD your God, or
anything which He has sent you by me.

22 "Now therefore, know certainly that you shall
die by the sword, by famine, and by pestilence in the
place where you desire to go to dwell."

Jer. 42:1–22

*"Now all the captains of the forces, Johanan the son of Kareah, Jezaniah
the son of Hoshaiah, and all the people, from the least to the greatest,
came near and said to Jeremiah the prophet, 'Please, let our petition be
acceptable to you, and pray for us to the LORD your God, for all this
remnant, . . . that the LORD your God may show us the way in which
we should walk and the thing we should do'"* (vv. 1–3). Notice that they

said *"the LORD your God."* They had forfeited the right to claim Him
as their own, but they came as confessing "outsiders." If Jeremiah
ever wanted to say "I told you so," now was his chance. Or he could
have said, "I am much too tired; I am ending my prophetic ministry.
You're on your own." Instead he allowed his heart to be encouraged
by their seemingly sincere desire to know the way they should go
and walk in it. Once again he embraced an unworthy people with a
pledge to them. In essence he promised to pray and then to tell them
the whole truth and nothing but the truth. Feel the immense steadi-
ness and consistency of the prophet, always committed to the full
counsel of God's word, no matter what his circumstances or who his
petitioners. Whether he doubts their sincerity or not, he keeps about
his prophetic mission, about the long haul of consistent obedience.

He was the "fortified city," the "iron pillar," the "bronze wall" that
God had called him to be (1:18). The people were still "broken
cisterns that [could] hold no water" (2:13). They were full of promises, but they leaked. *"Let the LORD be a true and faithful witness between us, if we do not do according to everything which the LORD your
God sends us by you"* (v. 5). Jeremiah may have felt a painful reminiscence of the day when all released their slaves with a great show of
magnanimity (34:10). That action was borne only out of fear, not out
of true repentance.

Perhaps they sensed his misgivings because they continued to
make promises. *"Whether it is pleasing or displeasing, we will obey the
voice of the LORD our God to whom we send you, that it may be well with
us when we obey the voice of the LORD our God"* (v. 6). Even in their
darkness they have the sense to know that obedience to the word of
God does create well being. Spiritual darkness is not total ignorance.
We have seen that it does indeed know where to go for light. They
seemed to know instinctively that Jeremiah was the man whose
prayers they should seek. Their knees were knocking, and they did
not know how to kneel in prayer. The man they had ignored and
ridiculed was the man they approached for prayer because he kept
the light alive in himself and let it be a beacon on troubled waters.

God's response to Jeremiah was not instant. *"And it happened after
ten days that the word of the LORD came to Jeremiah"* (v. 7). Immediately the prophet called for Johanan, the captains, and the people,
regardless of their rank or status. The answer was ready to be delivered. It would not be the one for which they secretly hoped. *"If*

you will still remain in this land, then I will build you and not pull you down, and I will plant you and not pluck you up" (v. 10). God wished to be the building-and-the-planting God of His promises. They had already been pulled down and plucked up. *"For I relent concerning the disaster that I have brought upon you"* (v. 10). He is ready for the work of restoration, but they must choose to stay in the land and not flee to Egypt. They must choose not to yield to their fear of the Chaldeans and their possible reprisals. *"Do not be afraid of the king of Babylon, of whom you are afraid; do not be afraid of him . . . for I am with you, to save you and deliver you from his hand"* (v. 11).

Their knees had been knocking, and through Jeremiah's intercessions, they had knelt on them. The answers to our prayers do not always come in the form we wish. Often we are called to act on those answers when it is not easy, when everything around us is frightening, and when disobedience seems safer and easier. Do not think for a moment that God does not understand your dilemma, that He underestimates what you are up against. Hear His words to the fugitives: *"For I am with you, to save you and deliver you from his hand"* (v. 11). Think of the memories that would have rushed into Jeremiah's thoughts as he delivered these words, the same words delivered to him at the time of his call (1:8). Truly he had experienced deliverance: from Pashhur's stocks, from Hananiah's accusations, from prison, from the mire of the cistern, and from Babylonian anger, but most of all he had been delivered from the temptation to compromise. No wonder there was such a resonance of faith in the words themselves as they flow on.

"And I will show you mercy, that he may have mercy on you and cause you to return to your own land" (v. 12). Another picture of God's sovereignty is seen here. He promised to so regulate the heart of Nebuchadnezzar that he would choose not to blame them for Gedaliah's assassination. Instead Nebuchadnezzar would choose to return them to their own land. God had read their minds and settled their fears with these promises. At this point one would expect them to be cheering, "If God *is* for us, who *can be* against us?" (Rom. 8:31). The battle for their minds, however, was still going on and God read their remaining misgivings with laserlike precision. *"But if you say, 'We will not dwell in the land . . . but we will go to the land of Egypt where we shall see no war, nor hear the sound of the trumpet, nor be hungry for bread,' . . . Then hear now the word of the LORD, O remnant*

of Judah!" (vv. 13–15). Obedience is not always comfortable. Not only were they asked to step out over their fears of Babylon but also over their fears of famine and over their dreadful memories of war. In Egypt they would at least have food, and they would be in new surroundings that might possibly drown the sound of the trumpets that blasted like a nightmare in their memories. Going to Egypt was their solution. Staying at home was God's. There were consequences to both choices.

"If you wholly set your faces to enter Egypt, and go to dwell there, then it shall be that the sword which you feared shall overtake you there in the land of Egypt; the famine of which you were afraid shall follow close after you there in Egypt; and there you shall die" (vv. 15–16). There were rather awesome implications to these words from a Holy God. Their fears would become real if they ignored God's instruction. God will never honor faithlessness, nor will He honor cowardice. Jeremiah well remembered the day God said to him, "Do not be dismayed before their faces, Lest I dismay you before them" (1:17). Now that same principle was applied to Jeremiah's people. God means business. Should they choose fear instead of faith, this was what they were told to expect: *"As My anger and My fury have been poured out on the inhabitants of Jerusalem, so will My fury be poured out on you when you enter Egypt. And you shall be an oath, an astonishment, a curse, and a reproach; and you shall see this place no more"* (v. 18). This was straight talk. They could never say that God's answer was not clear. *"Do not go to Egypt! Know certainly that I have admonished you this day"* (v. 19).

When Jeremiah promised to give them the whole truth and nothing but the truth, he was not posturing. His council to them was uncompromising. Often today we compromise the council we give others. We hedge around the clear teaching of Scripture, trying to make it more palatable, more relevant. Not long ago a woman came to me confessing an extramarital relationship that was developing in intimacy. She was paying for council from two different, supposedly Christian sources. Neither of those counselors encouraged her to terminate the relationship. The way was getting fuzzier and fuzzier until I said, "Don't waste any more of your money on that kind of council. Get out of that relationship. Run for your life." With tears in her eyes, she thanked me and went home in the energy of a new obedience.

Unfortunately the same cannot be said for the remnant of Judah. Jeremiah called it like it was: *"For you were hypocrites in your hearts when you sent me to the LORD your God"* (v. 20). He protested the use they made of him and of his prayers. More than that, though, he protested the abuse they made of the faithful word of God. "Have it your way," he might have said. God set before them building and planting at home, but they chose famine and death in Egypt. The wreckage around them with its hideous nightmares had taught them no lesson at all.

NOTES

1. Stanley Hopper, "The Book of Jeremiah: Exposition," in *The Interpreter's Bible*, vol. 5, ed. George A. Buttrick et al. (Nashville: Abingdon Press, 1956), 1083.

2. Flavius Josephus, *Antiquities of the Jews*, 3 vols. (Grand Rapids, Mich.: Baker Book House, 1984), 3:74.

3. Hopper, "The Book of Jeremiah," 1086–87.

4. Alfred Edersheim, *Old Testament Bible History* (Grand Rapids, Mich.: Eerdman's Publishing Co., 1977), 4:155.

CHAPTER TWENTY

Episodes in Egypt

Jeremiah 43:1–45:5

WHY PRAY WHEN YOU CAN WORRY?

43:1 Now it happened, when Jeremiah had stopped speaking to all the people all the words of the LORD their God, for which the LORD their God had sent him to them, all these words,

2 that Azariah the son of Hoshaiah, Johanan the son of Kareah, and all the proud men spoke, saying to Jeremiah, "You speak falsely! The LORD our God has not sent you to say, 'Do not go to Egypt to dwell there.'

3 "But Baruch the son of Neriah has set you against us, to deliver us into the hand of the Chaldeans, that they may put us to death or carry us away captive to Babylon."

4 So Johanan the son of Kareah, all the captains of the forces, and all the people would not obey the voice of the LORD, to remain in the land of Judah.

5 But Johanan the son of Kareah and all the captains of the forces took all the remnant of Judah who had returned to dwell in the land of Judah, from all nations where they had been driven—

6 men, women, children, the king's daughters, and every person whom Nebuzaradan the captain of the guard had left with Gedaliah the son of Ahikam, the son of Shaphan, and Jeremiah the prophet and Baruch the son of Neriah.

7 So they went to the land of Egypt, for they did not obey the voice of the LORD. And they went as far as Tahpanhes.

8 Then the word of the LORD came to Jeremiah in Tahpanhes, saying,

9 "Take large stones in your hand, and hide them in the sight of the men of Judah, in the clay in the brick courtyard which *is* at the entrance to Pharaoh's house in Tahpanhes;

10 "and say to them, 'Thus says the LORD of hosts, the God of Israel: "Behold, I will send and bring Nebuchadnezzar the king of Babylon, My servant, and will set his throne above these stones that I have hidden. And he will spread his royal pavilion over them.

11 "When he comes, he shall strike the land of Egypt *and deliver* to death *those appointed* for death, and to captivity *those appointed* for captivity, and to the sword *those appointed* for the sword.

12 "I will kindle a fire in the houses of the gods of Egypt, and he shall burn them and carry them away captive. And he shall array himself with the land of Egypt, as a shepherd puts on his garment, and he shall go out from there in peace.

13 "He shall also break the sacred pillars of Beth Shemesh that *are* in the land of Egypt; and the houses of the gods of the Egyptians he shall burn with fire."'"

Jer. 43:1–13

Johanan was a real hero when he rescued the fugitives from Ishmael the terrorist. The waters of the pool of Gibeon reflected many happy faces that day. Worry about Babylonian reprisals took hold of Johanan. He headed the procession off toward Egypt. Before advancing very far, the company decided to solicit the prayers of Jeremiah to know the way to walk and the thing to do (42:3). They even vowed to be obedient regardless of whether the answer they received was pleasing or not (42:6). At the time they made that vow, they did not realize that secretly they preferred worry to prayer. They had not calculated the dark infidelities hidden deep within that would threaten their act of faith. They did not care to see that dark side of themselves. Admitting that they hated the unpleasant would be a confession of weakness. So rather than accuse themselves, they choose instead to accuse the word of God.

"*Azariah the son of Hoshaiah, Johanan the son of Kareah, and all the proud men spoke, saying to Jeremiah, 'You speak falsely! The LORD our God has not sent you to say, 'Do not go to Egypt to dwell there'*" (v. 2). Suddenly all the fulfilled prophecy, all the credibility that had been Jeremiah's was thrown to the winds. To have believed the prophet would mean having to obey the prophecy. It would mean ceasing to worry. It would involve the unpleasant business of staying put and not fleeing. The word itself would have to be discredited or else it would discredit them. That is the secret agenda behind much of today's unbelief, behind much of today's tampering with the authority of Scripture. Their grounds for discrediting Jeremiah's word from the Lord was to suggest that Baruch had poisoned his mind. "*Baruch . . . has set you against us, to deliver us into the hand of the Chaldeans*" (v. 3). Jeremiah was perceived as a cosmic kill-joy, out to spoil their plans at every turn. There are people who see God this way, who think of Him only in terms of that of which He deprives them. To them He is only a negative reality. Such people go ahead and do exactly as they have predetermined and deny the contradiction they receive from the word of God.

"*So they went to the land of Egypt, for they did not obey the voice of the LORD. And they went as far as Tahpanhes*" (v. 7). What a far cry from the people who had been asking God to show the way. "*Every person whom Nebuzaradan . . . had left with Gedaliah*" (v. 6) went headlong and headstrong in the opposite direction. "*Men, women, children, the king's daughters, and every person*" were caught up in the drama of willful disobedience. It was a mini-version of Jeremiah's whole prophetic ministry as he and Baruch were carried off with them.

He had already warned them that fleeing to Egypt meant certain death (42:22). What more could he have done? Was it perhaps time now just to "go with the flow," to live out his days in silence? The Jeremiahs of the world never really do that. They continue to hear the word of God no matter where they are. This time Jeremiah was in Tahpanhes, a frontier town at the easternmost mouth of the Nile River in the Delta. Pharaoh's palace was in this very important city. At the entrance to the royal house was a terrace paved in brick. An area like this was uncovered by a nineteenth-century excavation that further documents this story and its setting.[1]

Jeremiah ascended this platform, which represented all the powers of Egypt. The men of Judah stood watching and probably wondering. After all, this was the man who gave had given public demonstrations before—smashing a vessel at the Potter's Gate, wearing a yoke to an international summit conference. What next? Stooping down, Jeremiah picked up a large stone in each of his massive hands. Carefully, he set those stones right into the clay of Pharaoh's palace, until they were almost hidden. Then with a strong and resonant voice, the prophet proclaimed, *"Behold, I will send and bring Nebuchadnezzar the king of Babylon, My servant, and will set his throne above these stones that I have hidden"* (v. 10). The refugees had hoped to get a feeling of solidarity from Egypt, to be free from their worries. The Sphinx of granite strength from among the pyramids would surely grant them refuge. Not only were they fleeing Babylon, they were fleeing God. In this demonstration, Jeremiah promised that God was in pursuit of them, using the armies of Babylon. *"And he will spread his royal pavilion over them"* (v. 10). Lavish language to describe a conquering God Whom it is impossible to flee.

For each individual watching Jeremiah that day there were but two alternatives. God would strike and deliver death to *"those appointed for death, and to captivity those appointed for captivity"* (v. 11). They had gone after the gods of Egypt, paltry little saviors that they were. *"I will kindle a fire in the houses of the gods of Egypt, and he shall burn them and carry them away captive"* (v. 12). Those paltry little deities who could not move themselves would be carried away as surely as the idols were carried out of Josiah's temple. *"He shall also break the sacred pillars of Beth Shemesh that are in the land of Egypt; and the houses of the gods of the Egyptians he shall burn with fire"* (v. 13).

Inscriptions on fragments found in excavations record that Nebuchadnezzar did invade Egypt in 568/567 B.C.[2] So Jeremiah stood on Pharaoh's pavilion, a stronger pillar than even those of Beth Shemesh.

JEREMIAH'S LAST WORDS

44:1 The word that came to Jeremiah concerning all the Jews who dwell in the land of Egypt, who dwell at Migdol, at Tahpanhes, at Noph, and in the country of Pathros, saying,

2 "Thus says the LORD of hosts, the God of Israel: 'You have seen all the calamity that I have brought on Jerusalem and on all the cities of Judah; and behold, this day they *are* a desolation, and no one dwells in them,

3 'because of their wickedness which they have committed to provoke Me to anger, in that they went to burn incense *and* to serve other gods whom they did not know, they nor you nor your fathers.

4 'However I have sent to you all My servants the prophets, rising early and sending *them*, saying, "Oh, do not do this abominable thing that I hate!"

5 'But they did not listen or incline their ear to turn from their wickedness, to burn no incense to other gods.

6 'So My fury and My anger were poured out and kindled in the cities of Judah and in the streets of Jerusalem; and they are wasted *and* desolate, as it is this day.'

7 "Now therefore, thus says the LORD, the God of hosts, the God of Israel: 'Why do you commit *this* great evil against yourselves, to cut off from you man and woman, child and infant, out of Judah, leaving none to remain,

8 'in that you provoke Me to wrath with the works of your hands, burning incense to other gods in the land of Egypt where you have gone to dwell, that you may cut yourselves off and be a curse and a reproach among all the nations of the earth?

9 'Have you forgotten the wickedness of your fathers, the wickedness of the kings of Judah, the wickedness of their wives, your own wickedness, and the wickedness of your wives, which they committed in the land of Judah and in the streets of Jerusalem?

10 'They have not been humbled, to this day, nor have they feared; they have not walked in My law or in My statutes that I set before you and your fathers.'

11 "Therefore thus says the LORD of hosts, the God of Israel: 'Behold, I will set My face against you for catastrophe and for cutting off all Judah.

12 'And I will take the remnant of Judah who have set their faces to go into the land of Egypt to dwell

there, and they shall all be consumed *and* fall in the land of Egypt. They shall be consumed by the sword *and* by famine. They shall die, from the least to the greatest, by the sword and by famine; and they shall be an oath, an astonishment, a curse and a reproach!

13 'For I will punish those who dwell in the land of Egypt, as I have punished Jerusalem, by the sword, by famine, and by pestilence,

14 'so that none of the remnant of Judah who have gone into the land of Egypt to dwell there shall escape or survive, lest they return to the land of Judah, to which they desire to return and dwell. For none shall return except those who escape.'"

15 Then all the men who knew that their wives had burned incense to other gods, with all the women who stood by, a great multitude, and all the people who dwelt in the land of Egypt, in Pathros, answered Jeremiah, saying:

16 *"As for* the word that you have spoken to us in the name of the LORD, we will not listen to you!

17 "But we will certainly do whatever has gone out of our own mouth, to burn incense to the queen of heaven and pour out drink offerings to her, as we have done, we and our fathers, our kings and our princes, in the cities of Judah and in the streets of Jerusalem. For *then* we had plenty of food, were well-off, and saw no trouble.

18 "But since we stopped burning incense to the queen of heaven and pouring out drink offerings to her, we have lacked everything and have been consumed by the sword and by famine."

19 *The women also said,* "And when we burned incense to the queen of heaven and poured out drink offerings to her, did we make cakes for her, to worship her, and pour out drink offerings to her without our husbands' *permission?"*

20 Then Jeremiah spoke to all the people—the men, the women, and all the people who had given him *that* answer—saying:

21 "The incense that you burned in the cities of Judah and in the streets of Jerusalem, you and your fathers, your kings and your princes, and the people

303

of the land, did not the LORD remember them, and did it *not* come into His mind?

22 "So the LORD could no longer bear *it*, because of the evil of your doings *and* because of the abominations which you committed. Therefore your land is a desolation, an astonishment, a curse, and without an inhabitant, as *it is* this day.

23 "Because you have burned incense and because you have sinned against the LORD, and have not obeyed the voice of the LORD or walked in His law, in His statutes or in His testimonies, therefore this calamity has happened to you, as *at* this day.'

24 Moreover Jeremiah said to all the people and to all the women, "Hear the word of the LORD, all Judah who *are* in the land of Egypt!

25 "Thus says the LORD of hosts, the God of Israel, saying: 'You and your wives have spoken with your mouths and fulfilled with your hands, saying, "We will surely keep our vows that we have made, to burn incense to the queen of heaven and pour out drink offerings to her." You will surely keep your vows and perform your vows!'

26 "Therefore hear the word of the LORD, all Judah who dwell in the land of Egypt: 'Behold, I have sworn by My great name,' says the LORD, 'that My name shall no more be named in the mouth of any man of Judah in all the land of Egypt, saying, "The Lord GOD lives."

27 'Behold, I will watch over them for adversity and not for good. And all the men of Judah who *are* in the land of Egypt shall be consumed by the sword and by famine, until there is an end to them.

28 'Yet a small number who escape the sword shall return from the land of Egypt to the land of Judah; and all the remnant of Judah, who have gone to the land of Egypt to dwell there, shall know whose words will stand, Mine or theirs.

29 'And this *shall be* a sign to you,' says the LORD, 'that I will punish you in this place, that you may know that My words will surely stand against you for adversity.'

30 "Thus says the LORD: 'Behold, I will give Pharaoh Hophra king of Egypt into the hand of his

enemies and into the hand of those who seek his life,
as I gave Zedekiah king of Judah into the hand of
Nebuchadnezzar king of Babylon, his enemy who
sought his life.'"

Jer. 44:1-30

Jeremiah's life in Egypt was marked by two events, the first of
which was found in chapter 43. He had to demonstrate publicly to
the Jews who had fled there for refuge that they really were not safe
at all. No Pharaoh in the world could protect them from a God whose
justice was pursuing them for their arrogance and disobedience.

After his stand at Pharaoh's palace, Jeremiah issued a formal statement addressed not simply to the Jews who saw the public demonstration but to all the Jews scattered over various parts of Egypt. The
migration had begun almost a hundred years before, following
the fall of Samaria. He named the specific colonies to which his message was targeted, being fully aware of the geographic distribution
of his people in the land of the Sphinx. The motionless limestone
figure, half-king, half-beast, cast an eerie smile over the landscape
to which they had fled. A smile utterly incapable of comforting
them.

These would be the last words Jeremiah would speak. The country
boy from the hill country of Judea had come a long way in his
prophetic career. Never could he have dreamed that its closing hours
would be spent in Egypt, that his last words would ring out across
the land of the pyramids. A civilization of master builders had con-
structed these titanic monuments, but they could do nothing to save
the tiny band of refugees to whom Jeremiah made his last formal
address. He made it in the name of the Master Builder who would
still be standing, long after the pyramids were "rolled up as a garment." The years of long obedience equipped him well for this. He
could lift his head high and sing the Lord's song in a strange and
foreign land. Would that they could have been words of comfort,
issued to a people who had learned from their mistakes. Instead
they were words of warning, issued to a people determined to re-
peat the mistakes. *"Thus says the LORD of hosts, the God of Israel: ' You
have seen all the calamity that I have brought on Jerusalem and on
all the cities of Judah'"* (v. 2). The memories were all too painful, the
gaunt faces of little children struggling against famine, flaming

torches catapulted over the walls striking their mark, burning their homes, the dreadful sight of the battering ram breaking through the walls they thought impenetrable, the twisted faces of barbaric captains storming the streets of their defeated city. The stench of burning flesh, the sound of helpless cries, the sight of such calamity they bore forever in their memories.

Jeremiah was reasoning with them along the lines of this strong imagery. There was a reason for it all. *"Because of their wickedness which they have committed to provoke Me to anger, in that they went to burn incense and to serve other gods whom they did not know, they nor you nor your fathers"* (v. 3). The greatest trauma to strike Jeremiah's heart was the realization that all of this suffering and loss had gone to waste. The people had learned nothing from it and had in fact gone back to burning incense, now in the land of Egypt.

"Why do you commit this great evil against yourselves?" (v. 7). Not only had they sinned against God, but they had sinned against their own humanity which was not intended for foreign gods. God looked at the land of Judah where He had asked them to remain and, seeing it empty, described it poignantly, *"cut off from you man and woman, child and infant, out of Judah, leaving none to remain"* (v. 7). They had cut themselves off from their land, from their God, and from themselves. It was a total estrangement. Jeremiah must have remembered earlier years of his prophetic ministry, the time he was told to climb one of the nearby hills and there to cut off his long dark curls and cast them into the wind for all to see. He was to become a mournful warning of the desolation that comes when we cut ourselves off from home. Now he stood in Egypt. His hair was silver now. He passed the final indictment: *"They have not been humbled, to this day, nor have they feared; they have not walked in My law or in My statutes that I set before you and your fathers"* (v. 10).

As a result of this indictment, God passed judgment. Those who had fled to Egypt against His pleading and against His council would be destroyed by sword and by famine (vv. 11–14). By virtue of their own choices, they had nothing to look forward to but more of the same. What had their idolatry done for them? Their incense to the queen of heaven had permeated the air of Egypt. *"The incense that you burned in the cities of Judah and in the streets of Jerusalem . . . did not the LORD remember them, and did it not come into His mind?"* (v. 21). If God had hated it in Jerusalem, why would He not have hated it in

Egypt? If this great queen had done nothing for them in Jerusalem, why should they think her strong in Egypt? What strange insanity made them persist against all the logic of God and of His many prophets who had risen early to plead with them over the years? The perversion was so complete that they were determined to hate what God loved and to love what God hated. They would rather die than change.

Their reply was filled with insolence. Men, who knew full well that their wives burned incense to other gods, chose to flaunt that knowledge in Jeremiah's face. *"Then all the men . . . with all the women who stood by, a great multitude, and all the people who dwelt in the land of Egypt, in Pathros, answered Jeremiah. . . . We will not listen to you! But we will certainly do whatever has gone out of our own mouth, to burn incense to the queen of heaven and pour out drink offerings to her, as we have done . . . in the cities of Judah and in the streets of Jerusalem. For then we had plenty of food, were well-off, and saw no trouble"* (vv. 15–17).

During their early years of idolatry it was the mercy and the patience of God that continued to keep them in plenty. It was the righteous leadership of Josiah and the faithful presence of Jeremiah that God honored on their behalf. They were all that time subjects of the mercy of God. Yet the defection in their thinking was so complete that they attributed that time of plenty to the queen of heaven. Not only had they forsaken the fountain of living waters, but they had also "hewn themselves cisterns . . . that can hold no water" (2:13). The mission given Jeremiah had come full circle. They fulfilled completely those early words spoken of them by God; they left the prophet almost catatonic with the horror of human defection from God. No wonder he could write so eloquently, "The heart is deceitful above all things, And desperately wicked" (17:9). Instead, it is a heart that does not deceive God but only itself. That which is false, it chooses to worship. That which is profoundly merciful, it chooses to hate.

The painful truth was that God would allow them their choices. He would not violate the human will. Jeremiah's final words to them ring out over the land of their defection. The people once delivered from Egypt had forgotten that deliverance. They had forgotten the youthful love of their betrothal to God when they went after Him in the wilderness in a land not sown (2:2). Both by word and deed they had confirmed their choice, they had retracted their vows to God.

"You and your wives have spoken with your mouths and fulfilled with your hands, saying, 'We will surely keep our vows that we have made, to burn incense to the queen of heaven and pour out drink offerings to her'" (v. 25). Jeremiah understood who the people would serve. If it wasn't God, then it would be something else. Out of his painful understanding of this reality he finally said to them, *"You will surely keep your vows and perform your vows!"* (v. 25). By word and deed, against His many mercies, His many pleadings, they had asked for a divorce from God. The prophet gave them His answer: *"My name shall no more be named in the mouth of any man of Judah in all the land of Egypt, saying, 'The Lord GOD lives'"* (v. 26). What a divorce—even to retracting His name from their identity. What will not be retracted from them, however, is His scrutiny.

"Behold, I will watch over them for adversity and not for good. And all the men of Judah who are in the land of Egypt shall be consumed by the sword and by famine, until there is an end to them" (v. 27). God has the last word. If we refuse the word of grace, then we will hear the word of justice. Against the solemn backdrop of this great divorce, with all its heartbreak and devastation, comes a single note of hope: *"Yet a small number who escape the sword shall return from the land of Egypt to the land of Judah; and all the remnant of Judah, who have gone to the land of Egypt to dwell there, shall know whose words will stand, Mine or theirs"* (v. 28). The Jewish nation would not be utterly extinguished. God would always maintain her identity. This little Semitic people from the small country of Palestine, nomads from God, pursuers of emptiness, nonetheless, is a chosen race. They have made a greater impact on humanity, on its ideas, ethics, and beliefs than mighty Babylon, Egypt, Assyria, and all the great cultures of the world. Because God has the last word, He speaks it now concerning Pharaoh Hophra.

Along with the queen of heaven, the fleeing people had put their trust in this monarch, the fourth king of the twenty-sixth dynasty.[3] He had come to their aid during the Babylonian siege and had been responsible for the temporary lifting of the siege. Too much pressure from Nebuchadnezzar forced him to withdraw his forces, and Jerusalem fell. Yet here they continue to hope in him. *"I will give Pharaoh Hophra king of Egypt into the hand of his enemies and into the hand of those who seek his life, as I gave Zedekiah king of Judah into the hand of Nebuchadnezzar"* (v. 30). The alliance between Zedekiah and Hophra had been a futile one. It could not stem the tide of Babylonian advances nor of the God who orchestrated those advances.

Indeed, Jeremiah had been a prophet to the nations. He had just spoken his last words. It had been a faithful journey, even though it had ended in a strange and foreign land. A more blessed homeland waited for Jeremiah.

BARUCH'S BLESSED ASSURANCE

> 45:1 The word that Jeremiah the prophet spoke to Baruch the son of Neriah, when he had written these words in a book at the instruction of Jeremiah, in the fourth year of Jehoiakim the son of Josiah, king of Judah, saying,
> 2 "Thus says the LORD, the God of Israel, to you, O Baruch:
> 3 'You said, "Woe is me now! For the LORD has added grief to my sorrow. I fainted in my sighing, and I find no rest."'
> 4 "Thus you shall say to him, 'Thus says the LORD: "Behold, what I have built I will break down, and what I have planted I will pluck up, that is, this whole land.
> 5 "And do you seek great things for yourself? Do not seek *them;* for behold, I will bring adversity on all flesh," says the LORD. "But I will give your life to you as a prize in all places, wherever you go."'"
>
> *Jer. 45:1–5*

Being a prophet to the nations had exposed Jeremiah to duties and dangers quite beyond the normal sphere of one human life. Being a secretary to that prophet exposed Baruch as well. This brief chapter records an encounter between the two men. Even though it took place during the fourth year of Jehoiakim, it was placed at the end of their public ministry together, a tender conclusion, a high note of consolation.

There must have been a great bonding between them. For all the exile and rejection that Jeremiah suffered, for the life of loneliness, deprived of the comforts of marriage, Baruch's loyalty must have been to him as a stream in the desert. To have someone to talk to as he stood alone against the world must have kept Jeremiah going on more than one occasion. Baruch must have become familiar in the process of taking dictation, with the flow and cadence of Jeremiah's words, the very rhythm of his thought. In some strange way, the prophet too had come to know the inner world of his loyal secretary which now he enters in order to give assurance.

"You said, 'Woe is me now! For the LORD has added grief to my sorrow. I fainted in my sighing, and I find no rest" (v. 3). The words are similar to Jeremiah's own confessions. He remembered well the day his own cries lifted up to God; "Woe is me, my mother, That you have borne me" (15:10). He remembered wanting to run away from his awesome mission, but the words were as a consuming fire shut up in his bones. He felt that he could not live with it, yet at the same time he could not live without it.

The heart of Baruch's short plea is found in the five personal pronouns woven through it—me, my, I, my, I—they capture the self-involvement of all humanity. No one else's woe is as bad as my woe. No one else's sorrow is as bad as my sorrow. When asked to give a definition of minor surgery, the perceptive humorist answered, "someone else's operation." I am not meaning to make light of Baruch's distress but rather to capture the intrinsic self-centeredness of all humanity, particularly under stress, in order to capture the great liberty God offers us from it.

"Thus says the LORD: 'Behold, what I have built I will break down, and what I have planted I will pluck up, that is, this whole land'" (v. 4). Baruch had labored for the prophet for so many years. Together they had watched everything they had tried to build get broken down. They had tried to bring repentance and reformation to Jerusalem, yet that hope had been defeated. Now they stood on the foreign soil of Egypt with a company of lawless renegades. They were forced to watch the ruin of everything for which they had cared. Baruch felt robbed: *"I find no rest."* The world had let him down. His life had been invested in an enterprise of failure. There was no vocational satisfaction to be found.

What if God had looked at His own mission in those terms? Baruch had served but one human lifetime. God had been about His enterprise for hundreds of human lifetimes. He had planted a people of His choosing in a land of His choosing and then had meticulously cultivated them, invested heavily in them, allowed them to bear His name. When God plucked up Jerusalem, He was destroying not a lifetime of work, but ages and eons of work. What was the dashing of one man's hopes up against that? We humans measure things by too small a compass, as small as time is up against eternity.

Baruch had forgotten how enormous was the business of God. Jeremiah challenged him with the words of God: *"And do you seek great things for yourself? Do not seek them"* (v. 5). Breaking in upon Baruch was the wonderful news that simply because he had not achieved greatness in the sphere of his lifetime did not mean that he was a failure. There was a much larger compass by which to measure success. The borders of his mind were being stretched. How was he to know that the document he had so carefully taken in dictation, that had seemed to fail the people for whom it was directly written, would one day be providing spiritual richness to Western civilization hundreds and hundreds of years later in God's great army of the church? In the light of this reality, what was one man's adversity? *"'I will bring adversity on all flesh,' says the LORD"* (v. 5).

Now Jeremiah introduced to Baruch the colossal proportions of God's economy. He has a different economic index than we do. It was from this same perspective that the Apostle Paul wrote, "For I consider that the sufferings of this present time are not worthy *to be compared* with the glory which shall be revealed in us" (Rom. 8:18). In the context of God's economy, Baruch's woe, his failure, his seemingly unfulfilled life would absolutely shrivel when the final glory is revealed. That which was causing Baruch to "faint," "sigh," and "find no rest" would not even be worthy of a moment's attention. From the standpoint of final glory, Baruch would say "what woe?" "what suffering?"

God sealed this grand consolation with a present and very practical promise to Baruch through Jeremiah: *"But I will give your life to you as a prize in all places, wherever you go"* (v. 5). While the sphere of God's enterprise is the eternal, He does take care of His own in the temporal. This same assurance was delivered to Ebed-Melech, the Ethiopian who pulled Jeremiah out of the miry pit. To that little-known hero, to Baruch, and to Jeremiah, God promised survival and something more. When the curtain falls on this drama of human history, many of the kings and princes and power brokers of the world will lie fallen. These three men would be the last ones standing, unsung heroes for a time, but in the age to come they would receive the applause of a universe.

NOTES

1. R. K. Harrison, *Jeremiah and Lamentations,* The Tyndale Old Testament Commentary (Downers Grove, Ill.: Inter-Varsity Press, 1973), 165.
2. Ibid., 168.
3. Ibid., 168–69.

SECTION THREE

Prophecies to Foreign Nations

Jeremiah 46:1–51:64

CHAPTER TWENTY-ONE

Who Is in Charge of the World?

Jeremiah 46:1–51:64

These six chapters proclaim divine judgment on pagan nations. Each oracle leaves us with the inexorable question, "Who is in charge of the world?" Characteristic of all Hebrew prophecy was the recognition that the God they served was more than a provincial deity. Not only did Yahweh exercise supreme control over them as individuals and over their nation, He was also the God of all nations. As a nation, the Jews were charged with the responsibility and the dignity of taking God's revelation to the other nations of the world. Yet they had abdicated this calling. So the prophetic voices, including that of Jeremiah, have a unique message to the world. The content of these messages is similar to that found in Isaiah 13–33, Ezekiel 25–32, and Amos 1–2. Most of the nations included in this collection are also referred to in Jer. 25:19–26, when the prophet was told to pass the cup of God's fury from Jerusalem to the nations surrounding her.

ORACLES TO EGYPT AND OTHER NATIONS

46:1 The word of the LORD which came to Jeremiah the prophet against the nations.
2 Against Egypt.
Concerning the army of Pharaoh Necho, king of Egypt, which was by the River Euphrates in Carchemish, and which Nebuchadnezzar king of Babylon defeated in the fourth year of Jehoiakim the son of Josiah, king of Judah:
3 "Order the buckler and shield,
And draw near to battle!

4 Harness the horses,
And mount up, you horsemen!
Stand forth with *your* helmets,
Polish the spears,
Put on the armor!

5 Why have I seen them dismayed *and* turned
   back?
Their mighty ones are beaten down;
They have speedily fled,
And did not look back,
For fear *was* all around," says the LORD.

6 "Do not let the swift flee away,
Nor the mighty man escape;
They will stumble and fall
Toward the north, by the River Euphrates.

7 "Who *is* this coming up like a flood,
Whose waters move like the rivers?

8 Egypt rises up like a flood,
And *its* waters move like the rivers;
And he says, 'I will go up *and* cover the earth,
I will destroy the city and its inhabitants.'

9 Come up, O horses, and rage, O chariots!
And let the mighty men come forth:
The Ethiopians and the Libyans who handle the
   shield,
And the Lydians who handle *and* bend the bow.

10 For this *is* the day of the Lord GOD of hosts,
A day of vengeance,
That He may avenge Himself on His
   adversaries.
The sword shall devour;
It shall be satiated and made drunk with their
   blood;
For the Lord GOD of hosts has a sacrifice
In the north country by the River Euphrates.

11 "Go up to Gilead and take balm,
O virgin, the daughter of Egypt;
In vain you will use many medicines;
You shall not be cured.

12 The nations have heard of your shame,
And your cry has filled the land;

316

> For the mighty man has stumbled against the
>   mighty;
> They both have fallen together."

13 The word that the LORD spoke to Jeremiah
the prophet, how Nebuchadnezzar king of Babylon
would come *and* strike the land of Egypt.

14 "Declare in Egypt, and proclaim in Migdol;
    Proclaim in Noph and in Tahpanhes;
    Say, 'Stand fast and prepare yourselves,
    For the sword devours all around you.'

15 Why are your valiant *men* swept away?
    They did not stand
    Because the LORD drove them away.

16 He made many fall;
    Yes, one fell upon another.
    And they said, 'Arise!
    Let us go back to our own people
    And to the land of our nativity
    From the oppressing sword.'

17 They cried there,
    'Pharaoh, king of Egypt, *is but* a noise.
    He has passed by the appointed time!'

18 "*As* I live," says the King,
    Whose name *is* the LORD of hosts,
    "Surely as Tabor *is* among the mountains
    And as Carmel by the sea, *so* he shall come.

19 O you daughter dwelling in Egypt,
    Prepare yourself to go into captivity!
    For Noph shall be waste and desolate, without
      inhabitant.

20 "Egypt *is* a very pretty heifer,
    But destruction comes, it comes from the north.

21 Also her mercenaries are in her midst like fat
      bulls,
    For they also are turned back,
    They have fled away together.
    They did not stand,
    For the day of their calamity had come upon
      them,
    The time of their punishment.

22 Her noise shall go like a serpent,

317

For they shall march with an army
And come against her with axes,
Like those who chop wood.

23 "They shall cut down her forest," says the LORD,
"Though it cannot be searched,
Because they *are* innumerable,
And more numerous than grasshoppers.

24 The daughter of Egypt shall be ashamed;
She shall be delivered into the hand
Of the people of the north."

25 The LORD of hosts, the God of Israel, says: "Behold, I will bring punishment on Amon of No, and Pharaoh and Egypt, with their gods and their kings—Pharaoh and those who trust in him.

26 "And I will deliver them into the hand of those who seek their lives, into the hand of Nebuchadnezzar king of Babylon and the hand of his servants. Afterward it shall be inhabited as in the days of old," says the LORD.

27 "But do not fear, O My servant Jacob,
And do not be dismayed, O Israel!
For behold, I will save you from afar,
And your offspring from the land of their
captivity;
Jacob shall return, have rest and be at ease;
No one shall make *him* afraid.

28 Do not fear, O Jacob My servant," says the
LORD,
"For I *am* with you;
For I will make a complete end of all the
nations
To which I have driven you,
But I will not make a complete end of you.
I will rightly correct you,
For I will not leave you wholly unpunished."

47:1 The word of the LORD that came to Jeremiah the prophet against the Philistines, before Pharaoh attacked Gaza.

2 Thus says the LORD:
"Behold, waters rise out of the north,
And shall be an overflowing flood;
They shall overflow the land and all that is in it,

318

The city and those who dwell within;
Then the men shall cry,
And all the inhabitants of the land shall wail.

3 At the noise of the stamping hooves of his
    strong horses,
At the rushing of his chariots,
At the rumbling of his wheels,
The fathers will not look back for *their* children,
Lacking courage,

4 Because of the day that comes to plunder all the
    Philistines,
To cut off from Tyre and Sidon every helper
    who remains;
For the LORD shall plunder the Philistines,
The remnant of the country of Caphtor.

5 Baldness has come upon Gaza,
Ashkelon is cut off
With the remnant of their valley.
How long will you cut yourself?

6 "O you sword of the LORD,
How long until you are quiet?
Put yourself up into your scabbard,
Rest and be still!

7 How can it be quiet,
Seeing the LORD has given it a charge
Against Ashkelon and against the seashore?
There He has appointed it."

48:1 Against Moab.
Thus says the LORD of hosts, the God of Israel:
"Woe to Nebo!
For it is plundered,
Kirjathaim is shamed *and* taken;
The high stronghold is shamed and
    dismayed—

2 No more praise of Moab.
In Heshbon they have devised evil against
    her:
'Come, and let us cut her off as a nation.'
You also shall be cut down, O Madmen!
The sword shall pursue you;

3 A voice of crying *shall be* from Horonaim:
'Plundering and great destruction!'

4 "Moab is destroyed;
   Her little ones have caused a cry to be heard;
5 For in the Ascent of Luhith they ascend with
        continual weeping;
   For in the descent of Horonaim the enemies
        have heard a cry of destruction.
6 "Flee, save your lives!
   And be like the juniper in the wilderness.
7 For because you have trusted in your works
        and your treasures,
   You also shall be taken.
   And Chemosh shall go forth into captivity,
   His priests and his princes together.
8 And the plunderer shall come against every
        city;
   No one shall escape.
   The valley also shall perish,
   And the plain shall be destroyed,
   As the LORD has spoken.
9 "Give wings to Moab,
   That she may flee and get away;
   For her cities shall be desolate,
   Without any to dwell in them.
10 Cursed is he who does the work of the LORD
        deceitfully,
   And cursed is he who keeps back his sword
        from blood.
11 "Moab has been at ease from his youth;
   He has settled on his dregs,
   And has not been emptied from vessel to vessel,
   Nor has he gone into captivity.
   Therefore his taste remained in him,
   And his scent has not changed.
12 "Therefore behold, the days are coming," says
        the LORD,
   "That I shall send him wine-workers
   Who will tip him over
   And empty his vessels
   And break the bottles.
13 Moab shall be ashamed of Chemosh,
   As the house of Israel was ashamed of Bethel,
        their confidence.

14 "How can you say, 'We *are* mighty
    And strong men for the war'?
15 Moab is plundered and gone up *from* her cities;
    Her chosen young men have gone down to the
        slaughter," says the King,
    Whose name *is* the LORD of hosts.
16 "The calamity of Moab *is* near at hand,
    And his affliction comes quickly.
17 Bemoan him, all you who are around him;
    And all you who know his name,
    Say, 'How the strong staff is broken,
    The beautiful rod!'
18 "O daughter inhabiting Dibon,
    Come down from *your* glory,
    And sit in thirst;
    For the plunderer of Moab has come against
        you,
    He has destroyed your strongholds.
19 O inhabitant of Aroer,
    Stand by the way and watch;
    Ask him who flees
    And her who escapes;
    Say, 'What has happened?'
20 Moab is shamed, for he is broken down.
    Wail and cry!
    Tell it in Arnon, that Moab is plundered.
21 "And judgment has come on the plain country:
    On Holon and Jahzah and Mephaath,
22 On Dibon and Nebo and Beth Diblathaim,
23 On Kirjathaim and Beth Gamul and Beth
        Meon,
24 On Kerioth and Bozrah,
    On all the cities of the land of Moab,
    Far or near.
25 The horn of Moab is cut off,
    And his arm is broken," says the LORD.
26 "Make him drunk,
    Because he exalted *himself* against the LORD.
    Moab shall wallow in his vomit,
    And he shall also be in derision.
27 For was not Israel a derision to you?
    Was he found among thieves?

321

For whenever you speak of him,
You shake *your head in scorn*.
28 You who dwell in Moab,
Leave the cities and dwell in the rock,
And be like the dove *which* makes her nest
In the sides of the cave's mouth.
29 "We have heard the pride of Moab
(He *is* exceedingly proud),
Of his loftiness and arrogance and pride,
And of the haughtiness of his heart."
30 "I know his wrath," says the LORD,
"But it *is* not right;
His lies have made nothing right.
31 Therefore I will wail for Moab,
And I will cry out for all Moab;
I will mourn for the men of Kir Heres.
32 O vine of Sibmah! I will weep for you with the
weeping of Jazer.
Your plants have gone over the sea,
They reach to the sea of Jazer.
The plunderer has fallen on your summer fruit
and your vintage.
33 Joy and gladness are taken
From the plentiful field
And from the land of Moab;
I have caused wine to fail from the
winepresses;
No one will tread with joyous shouting—
Not joyous shouting!
34 "From the cry of Heshbon to Elealeh and to
Jahaz
They have uttered their voice,
From Zoar to Horonaim,
Like a three-year-old heifer;
For the waters of Nimrim also shall be
desolate.
35 "Moreover," says the LORD,
"I will cause to cease in Moab
The one who offers *sacrifices* in the high
places
And burns incense to his gods.
36 Therefore My heart shall wail like flutes for Moab,

And like flutes My heart shall wail
For the men of Kir Heres.
. Therefore the riches they have acquired have
perished.

37 "For every head *shall be* bald, and every beard
clipped;
On all the hands *shall be* cuts, and on the loins
sackcloth—

38 A general lamentation
On all the housetops of Moab,
And in its streets;
For I have broken Moab like a vessel in which
is no pleasure," says the LORD.

39 "They shall wail:
'How she is broken down!
How Moab has turned her back with shame!'
So Moab shall be a derision
And a dismay to all those about her."

40 For thus says the LORD:
"Behold, one shall fly like an eagle,
And spread his wings over Moab.

41 Kerioth is taken,
And the strongholds are surprised;
The mighty men's hearts in Moab on that day
shall be
Like the heart of a woman in birth pangs.

42 And Moab shall be destroyed as a people,
Because he exalted *himself* against the LORD.

43 Fear and the pit and the snare *shall be* upon
you,
O inhabitant of Moab," says the LORD.

44 "He who flees from the fear shall fall into the
pit,
And he who gets out of the pit shall be caught
in the snare.
For upon Moab, upon it I will bring
The year of their punishment," says the LORD.

45 "Those who fled stood under the shadow of
Heshbon
Because of exhaustion.
But a fire shall come out of Heshbon,
A flame from the midst of Sihon,

323

And shall devour the brow of Moab,
The crown of the head of the sons of tumult.
46 Woe to you, O Moab!
The people of Chemosh perish;
For your sons have been taken captive,
And your daughters captive.
47 "Yet I will bring back the captives of Moab
In the latter days," says the LORD.
Thus far *is* the judgment of Moab.
49:1 Against the Ammonites.
Thus says the LORD:
"Has Israel no sons?
Has he no heir?
Why *then* does Milcom inherit Gad,
And his people dwell in its cities?
2 Therefore behold, the days are coming," says
the LORD,
"That I will cause to be heard an alarm of war
In Rabbah of the Ammonites;
It shall be a desolate mound,
And her villages shall be burned with fire.
Then Israel shall take possession of his
inheritance," says the LORD.
3 "Wail, O Heshbon, for Ai is plundered!
Cry, you daughters of Rabbah,
Gird yourselves with sackcloth!
Lament and run to and fro by the walls;
For Milcom shall go into captivity
With his priests and his princes together.
4 Why do you boast in the valleys,
Your flowing valley, O backsliding daughter?
Who trusted in her treasures, *saying*,
'Who will come against me?'
5 Behold, I will bring fear upon you,"
Says the Lord GOD of hosts,
"From all those who are around you;
You shall be driven out, everyone headlong,
And no one will gather those who wander off.
6 But afterward I will bring back
The captives of the people of Ammon," says
the LORD.
7 Against Edom.

Thus says the LORD of hosts:
"*Is* wisdom no more in Teman?
Has counsel perished from the prudent?
Has their wisdom vanished?
8 Flee, turn back, dwell in the depths, O
    inhabitants of Dedan!
For I will bring the calamity of Esau upon him,
The time *that* I will punish him.
9 If grape-gatherers came to you,
    Would they not leave *some* gleaning grapes?
    If thieves by night,
    Would they not destroy until they have
        enough?
10 But I have made Esau bare;
    I have uncovered his secret places,
    And he shall not be able to hide himself.
    His descendants are plundered,
    His brethren and his neighbors,
    And he *is* no more.
11 Leave your fatherless children,
    I will preserve *them* alive;
    And let your widows trust in Me."

12 For thus says the LORD: "Behold, those whose
judgment *was* not to drink of the cup have assuredly
drunk. And *are* you the one who will altogether go
unpunished? You shall not go unpunished, but you
shall surely drink *of it.*

13 "For I have sworn by Myself," says the LORD,
"that Bozrah shall become a desolation, a reproach,
a waste, and a curse. And all its cities shall be perpetual wastes."

14 I have heard a message from the LORD,
    And an ambassador has been sent to the
        nations:
    "Gather together, come against her,
    And rise up to battle!
15 "For indeed, I will make you small among
        nations,
    Despised among men.
16 Your fierceness has deceived you,
    The pride of your heart,
    O you who dwell in the clefts of the rock,

Who hold the height of the hill!
Though you make your nest as high as the
     eagle,
I will bring you down from there," says the
     LORD.
17 "Edom also shall be an astonishment;
Everyone who goes by it will be astonished
And will hiss at all its plagues.
18 As in the overthrow of Sodom and Gomorrah
And their neighbors," says the LORD,
"No one shall remain there,
Nor shall a son of man dwell in it.
19 "Behold, he shall come up like a lion from the
     flood plain of the Jordan
Against the dwelling place of the strong;
But I will suddenly make him run away from
     her.
And who *is* a chosen *man that* I may appoint
     over her?
For who *is* like Me?
Who will arraign Me?
And who *is* that shepherd
Who will withstand Me?"
20 Therefore hear the counsel of the LORD that He
     has taken against Edom,
And His purposes that He has proposed
     against the inhabitants of Teman:
Surely the least of the flock shall draw them
     out;
Surely He shall make their dwelling places
     desolate with them.
21 The earth shakes at the noise of their fall;
 At the cry its noise is heard at the Red Sea.
22 Behold, He shall come up and fly like the
     eagle,
And spread His wings over Bozrah;
The heart of the mighty men of Edom in that
     day shall be
Like the heart of a woman in birth pangs.
23 Against Damascus.
"Hamath and Arpad are shamed,
For they have heard bad news.

326

They are fainthearted;
There is trouble on the sea;
It cannot be quiet.
24 Damascus has grown feeble;
She turns to flee,
And fear has seized *her.*
Anguish and sorrows have taken her like a
woman in labor.
25 Why is the city of praise not deserted, the city
of My joy?
26 Therefore her young men shall fall in her
streets,
And all the men of war shall be cut off in that
day," says the LORD of hosts.
27 "I will kindle a fire in the wall of Damascus,
And it shall consume the palaces of Ben-
Hadad."

28 Against Kedar and against the kingdoms of
Hazor, which Nebuchadnezzar king of Babylon shall
strike.

Thus says the LORD:
"Arise, go up to Kedar,
And devastate the men of the East!
29 Their tents and their flocks they shall take
away.
They shall take for themselves their curtains,
All their vessels and their camels;
And they shall cry out to them,
'Fear *is* on every side!'
30 "Flee, get far away! Dwell in the depths,
O inhabitants of Hazor!" says the LORD.
"For Nebuchadnezzar king of Babylon has
taken counsel against you,
And has conceived a plan against you.
31 "Arise, go up to the wealthy nation that dwells
securely," says the LORD,
"Which has neither gates nor bars,
Dwelling alone.
32 Their camels shall be for booty,
And the multitude of their cattle for plunder.
I will scatter to all winds those in the farthest
corners,

> And I will bring their calamity from all its
> sides," says the LORD.
> 33 "Hazor shall be a dwelling for jackals, a
> desolation forever;
> No one shall reside there,
> Nor son of man dwell in it."
> 34 The word of the LORD that came to Jeremiah the
> prophet against Elam, in the beginning of the reign
> of Zedekiah king of Judah, saying,
> 35 "Thus says the LORD of hosts:
> 'Behold, I will break the bow of Elam,
> The foremost of their might.
> 36 Against Elam I will bring the four winds
> From the four quarters of heaven,
> And scatter them toward all those winds;
> There shall be no nations where the outcasts
> of Elam will not go.
> 37 For I will cause Elam to be dismayed before
> their enemies
> And before those who seek their life.
> I will bring disaster upon them,
> My fierce anger,' says the LORD;
> 'And I will send the sword after them
> Until I have consumed them.
> 38 I will set My throne in Elam,
> And will destroy from there the king and the
> princes,' says the LORD.
> 39 'But it shall come to pass in the latter days:
> I will bring back the captives of Elam,' says
> the LORD."
>
> *Jer. 46:1–49:39*

The battle of Carchemish in 605 B.C. changed everything for Egypt
and the nations that she controlled. Two nations faced each other one
fateful day by the Euphrates River. Pharaoh Necho, confident ruler of
Egypt, had ordered the harnessing of his horses, the polishing of his
spears, and the donning of helmets and armor (vv. 3–4). He never
dreamed they would be *"beaten down,"* that they would be *"turned
back"* to *"stumble and fall"* (vv. 5–6). Young Nebuchadnezzar of Babylon defeated Necho in the fourth year of Jehoiakim's sickly reign over
Judah. The battle of Carchemish stripped Egypt of her designs for

power and signaled five other nations that a similar fate awaited them; a fate that Jeremiah predicted with characteristic passion.

1. *The message to Egypt* (46:1–28). Two poems comprise this message. The first, in verses 2–12, concerned the rout at Carchemish. It presents a vivid picture of the march into battle and the miserable defeat, one that Jeremiah saw as the turning point in the fate of his own nation. There was to be no stopping the foe from the north, mighty Babylon. The second poem continues the imagery of Egypt's defeated gods. Jeremiah was impassioned with the realization that every lesser god would ultimately be defeated by the God he served. *"Egypt is a very pretty heifer"* (v. 20) refers to the bull deity this nation served. *"But destruction comes, it comes from the north"* (v. 20). Carchemish was not merely a human struggle, it was one that was purposed in the mind of God long before it entered the minds of Necho and Nebuchadnezzar. Jeremiah's world-view and that of all God-fearing people are to be shaped by this ultimate reality.

2. *The message to Philistia* (47:1–7). The Philistines were a powerful sea people, settled along the coast of the Mediterranean. They had been longtime rivals of Israel. By virtue of their position on the great highway between Egypt and the Euphrates, they too sustained an attack. Using imagery from their own geography, Jeremiah described *"waters ris[ing] out of the north"* overflowing their land (47:2). Although they were known for their weapons technology, here the Philistines were pictured as fleeing for lack of courage, wailing against the sound of stamping hooves, rushing chariots, and rumbling wheels.

Babylon was relentless, but the real relentless victor was God. *"O you sword of the LORD, How long until you are quiet"*? (47:6). The Philistine cities of Gaza and Ashkelon were just as much under His scrutiny and judgment as were the cities of Israel and Judah. All rebellious men and nations will meet their maker and find Him to be an indomitable warrior. The nations have fallen into obscurity, but the message to the nations is as fresh as today's newsprint.

3. *The message to Moab* (48:1–47). This message is lengthy by comparison to the size of this country. We are not concerned with whether or not the work of other writers has been compiled into this block of prophecy. We know that Jeremiah borrowed heavily from the work of his predecessor, Isaiah, who wrote of the burden of Moab 140 years earlier (Isaiah 15–16).[1] This small nation to the east

of the Dead Sea was one of those that attended the summit conference referred to in Jeremiah 27. Various small states attempted to
form a confederacy against Babylon in 594 B.C., a conspiracy that
came to naught.

These poetic passages are woven with the proper names of cities,
making the imagery realistic. Like vintners who tip over vats of wine,
so would God empty Moab (48:12). Her haughtiness of heart (48:29)
would not have the last word. The summer fruit and the vintage,
the joy and gladness of the plentiful field would be plundered (48:32,
33). There would be no more treading of the grapes with joyous
shouting (48:33). God would break Moab like a vessel. Her national
deity, Chemosh, is referred to three times (48:7, 13, 46), and the
prophetic message is hurled against it: Yahweh is the one warrior that
Chemosh has no strength against. All lesser gods would meet Him on
one battlefield or another and be defeated. This was the message of
the faithful prophet to the nations.

4. *The message to Ammon* (49:1–6). Again the prophetic message
involves a national deity, Milcom, "the king." Ammon, by serving
him, was guilty of trusting *"in her treasures"* (49:4). She had developed an arrogant who-will-come-against-me mentality. Baalis, king
of Ammon, had chosen to conspire with Ishmael in the assassination of Jeremiah's friend, Gedaliah, and the subversion of his good
government over the people left in Jerusalem after its destruction.
For all of her policies, there would be an ultimate penalty. Milcom,
the Ammonite deity who was honored by the ritual of child sacrifice, *"shall go into captivity With his priests and his princes together"*
(49:3).

I well remember the day in 1953 that Elizabeth II was crowned
in Westminster Abbey. She was presented with a Bible by the arch-
bishop of Canterbury with this inscription: "Our most gracious
sovereign, in order that you may know the law that governs the rule
of princes, we present you with this book, the greatest treasure
this world holds." Is not the spirit of Hebrew prophecy echoed
in this inscription?

5. *The message to Edom* (49:7–22). This oracle has particularly strident imagery. This tiny nation lay south of Judah. She too had been
part of the abortive plans to rebel against Babylon. When Nebuchadnezzar finally came against Jerusalem, Edom had joined his side and
actually took part in the plunder of the city and the slaughter of the

Jews. Perhaps it was this treachery for which Jeremiah likened Edom to Esau and then to Sodom and Gomorrah.

Edom was a nation descended from Jacob's twin brother, Esau, the earthy brother who scorned the things of heaven so that he sold his birthright for a mess of pottage. He traded the permanent for the passing, the eternal for the temporal. Like the two infamous cities to which she was likened, Edom was destined to become *"a desolation, a reproach, a waste, and a curse"* (49:13).

Triumphant language from Moses' Song of the Sea is echoed in this oracle. *"Who is like Me? Who will arraign Me? And who is that shepherd Who will withstand Me?"* (49:19; cf. Exod. 15:11). At the Red Sea, God stretched out His hand, and the earth swallowed all lesser gods. So also Jeremiah proclaimed that no earthly leader would ever withstand the sovereign God of the universe.

6. *The message to Damascus* (49:23–27). This prophecy carries the same pictures of defeat. This city, along with Hamath and Arpad,[2] were the capital powers of the Syrian states. Their glory had faded somewhat by Jeremiah's lifetime. Nonetheless they were cited for having *"grown feeble"* when once they had been grand, for becoming *"fainthearted"* and for turning *"to flee."*

7. *The message to Kedar and Hazor* (49:28–33). Jeremiah's message centers around one of his most famous figures of speech. He refers to these Arab tribes as having *"Fear . . . on every side"* (49:29). He may well have been remembering the time when Pashhur put him in the stocks as though he were a common criminal. After suffering that outrageous indignity, Jeremiah publicly gave Pashhur the name of "terror on every side," predicting for him a peculiar alienation and fate.

8. *The message to Elam* (49:34–39). This is the last of those delivered to the nations who were to share the fate of Egypt. Elamites were famous archers. The bow was a symbol of their claim to fame, their power. *"I will break the bow of Elam,"* said the God of the universe (49:35). He went on with a final shout of triumph, *"I will set My throne in Elam, And will destroy from there the king and the princes"* (49:38).

R. K. Harrison noted that Elamites were in Jerusalem when the Spirit was given to the early church (Acts 2:1ff).[3] Perhaps that relates to Jeremiah's final words to this nation. *"'But it shall come to pass in the latter days: I will bring back the captives of Elam,' says the* LORD" (49:39).

331

Concerning Babylon

50:1 The word that the LORD spoke against Babylon
and against the land of the Chaldeans by Jeremiah
the prophet.

2 "Declare among the nations,
Proclaim, and set up a standard;
Proclaim—do not conceal *it*—
Say, 'Babylon is taken, Bel is shamed.
Merodach is broken in pieces;
Her idols are humiliated,
Her images are broken in pieces.'

3 For out of the north a nation comes up against
her,
Which shall make her land desolate,
And no one shall dwell therein.
They shall move, they shall depart,
Both man and beast.

4 "In those days and in that time," says the LORD,
"The children of Israel shall come,
They and the children of Judah together;
With continual weeping they shall come,
And seek the LORD their God.

5 They shall ask the way to Zion,
With their faces toward it, *saying,*
'Come and let us join ourselves to the LORD
In a perpetual covenant
That will not be forgotten.'

6 "My people have been lost sheep.
Their shepherds have led them astray;
They have turned them away *on* the mountains.
They have gone from mountain to hill;
They have forgotten their resting place.

7 All who found them have devoured them;
And their adversaries said, 'We have not
offended,
Because they have sinned against the LORD,
the habitation of justice,
The LORD, the hope of their fathers.'

8 "Move from the midst of Babylon,
Go out of the land of the Chaldeans;
And be like the rams before the flocks.

9 For behold, I will raise and cause to come up
   against Babylon
An assembly of great nations from the north
   country,
And they shall array themselves against her;
From there she shall be captured.
Their arrows *shall be* like *those* of an expert
   warrior;
None shall return in vain.

10 And Chaldea shall become plunder;
All who plunder her shall be satisfied," says
   the LORD.

11 "Because you were glad, because you rejoiced,
You destroyers of My heritage,
Because you have grown fat like a heifer
   threshing grain,
And you bellow like bulls,

12 Your mother shall be deeply ashamed;
She who bore you shall be ashamed.
Behold, the least of the nations *shall be* a
   wilderness,
A dry land and a desert.

13 Because of the wrath of the LORD
She shall not be inhabited,
But she shall be wholly desolate.
Everyone who goes by Babylon shall be
   horrified
And hiss at all her plagues.

14 "Put yourselves in array against Babylon all
   around,
All you who bend the bow;
Shoot at her, spare no arrows,
For she has sinned against the LORD.

15 Shout against her all around;
She has given her hand,
Her foundations have fallen,
Her walls are thrown down;
For it *is* the vengeance of the LORD.
Take vengeance on her.
As she has done, so do to her.

16 Cut off the sower from Babylon,
And him who handles the sickle at harvest time.

> For fear of the oppressing sword
> Everyone shall turn to his own people;
> And everyone shall flee to his own land.
>
> 17 "Israel *is* like scattered sheep;
> The lions have driven *him* away.
> First the king of Assyria devoured him;
> Now at last this Nebuchadnezzar king of
> Babylon has broken his bones."

18 Therefore thus says the LORD of hosts, the God of Israel:

> "Behold, I will punish the king of Babylon and
> his land,
> As I have punished the king of Assyria.
>
> 19 But I will bring back Israel to his home,
> And he shall feed on Carmel and Bashan;
> His soul shall be satisfied on Mount Ephraim
> and Gilead.
>
> 20 In those days and in that time," says the LORD,
> "The iniquity of Israel shall be sought, but
> *there shall be* none;
> And the sins of Judah, but they shall not be
> found;
> For I will pardon those whom I preserve.
>
> 21 "Go up against the land of Merathaim, against
> it,
> And against the inhabitants of Pekod.
> Waste and utterly destroy them," says the
> LORD,
> "And do according to all that I have
> commanded you.
>
> 22 A sound of battle *is* in the land,
> And of great destruction.
>
> 23 How the hammer of the whole earth has been
> cut apart and broken!
> How Babylon has become a desolation among
> the nations!
> I have laid a snare for you;
>
> 24 You have indeed been trapped, O Babylon,
> And you were not aware;
> You have been found and also caught,
> Because you have contended against the Lord.
>
> 25 The LORD has opened His armory,

And has brought out the weapons of His
indignation;
For this *is* the work of the Lord GOD of hosts
In the land of the Chaldeans.

26 Come against her from the farthest border;
Open her storehouses;
Cast her up as heaps of ruins,
And destroy her utterly;
Let nothing of her be left.

27 Slay all her bulls,
Let them go down to the slaughter.
Woe to them!
For their day has come, the time of their
punishment.

28 The voice of those who flee and escape from
the land of Babylon
Declares in Zion the vengeance of the LORD
our God,
The vengeance of His temple.

29 "Call together the archers against Babylon.
All you who bend the bow, encamp against it
all around;
Let none of them escape.
Repay her according to her work;
According to all she has done, do to her;
For she has been proud against the LORD,
Against the Holy One of Israel.

30 Therefore her young men shall fall in the
streets,
And all her men of war shall be cut off in that
day," says the LORD.

31 "Behold, I *am* against you,
O most haughty one!" says the Lord GOD of
hosts;
"For your day has come,
The time *that* I will punish you.

32 The most proud shall stumble and fall,
And no one will raise him up;
I will kindle a fire in his cities,
And it will devour all around him.'

33 Thus says the LORD of hosts:
"The children of Israel *were* oppressed,

Along with the children of Judah;
All who took them captive have held them
     fast;
They have refused to let them go.

34 Their Redeemer *is* strong;
The LORD of hosts *is* His name.
He will thoroughly plead their case,
That He may give rest to the land,
And disquiet the inhabitants of Babylon.

35 "A sword *is* against the Chaldeans," says the
     LORD,
"Against the inhabitants of Babylon,
And against her princes and her wise men.

36 A sword *is* against the soothsayers, and they
     will be fools.
A sword *is* against her mighty men, and they
     will be dismayed.

37 A sword *is* against their horses,
Against their chariots,
And against all the mixed peoples who *are* in
     her midst;
And they will become like women.
A sword *is* against her treasures, and they will
     be robbed.

38 A drought *is* against her waters, and they will
     be dried up.
For it *is* the land of carved images,
And they are insane with *their* idols.

39 "Therefore the wild desert beasts shall dwell
     there with the jackals,
And the ostriches shall dwell in it.
It shall be inhabited no more forever,
Nor shall it be dwelt in from generation to
     generation.

40 As God overthrew Sodom and Gomorrah
And their neighbors," says the LORD,
"*So* no one shall reside there,
Nor son of man dwell in it.

41 "Behold, a people shall come from the north,
And a great nation and many kings
Shall be raised up from the ends of the earth.

42 They shall hold the bow and the lance;

They *are* cruel and shall not show mercy.
Their voice shall roar like the sea;
They shall ride on horses,
Set in array, like a man for the battle,
Against you, O daughter of Babylon.

43 "The king of Babylon has heard the report
about them,
And his hands grow feeble;
Anguish has taken hold of him,
Pangs as of a woman in childbirth.

44 "Behold, he shall come up like a lion from the
flood plain of the Jordan
Against the dwelling place of the strong;
But I will make them suddenly run away from
her.
And who *is* a chosen *man that* I may appoint
over her?
For who *is* like Me?
Who will arraign Me?
And who *is* that shepherd
Who will withstand Me?"

45 Therefore hear the counsel of the LORD that He
has taken against Babylon,
And His purposes that He has proposed
against the land of the Chaldeans:
Surely the least of the flock shall draw them
out;
Surely He will make their dwelling place
desolate with them.

46 At the noise of the taking of Babylon
The earth trembles,
And the cry is heard among the nations.

51:1 Thus says the LORD:
"Behold, I will raise up against Babylon,
Against those who dwell in Leb Kamai,
A destroying wind.

2 And I will send winnowers to Babylon,
Who shall winnow her and empty her land.
For in the day of doom
They shall be against her all around.

3 Against *her* let the archer bend his bow,
And lift himself up against *her* in his armor.

337

Do not spare her young men;
Utterly destroy all her army.

4 Thus the slain shall fall in the land of the
    Chaldeans,
And *those* thrust through in her streets.

5 For Israel is not forsaken, nor Judah,
By his God, the LORD of hosts,
Though their land was filled with sin against
    the Holy One of Israel."

6 Flee from the midst of Babylon,
And every one save his life!
Do not be cut off in her iniquity,
For this *is* the time of the LORD's vengeance;
He shall recompense her.

7 Babylon *was* a golden cup in the LORD's hand,
That made all the earth drunk.
The nations drank her wine;
Therefore the nations are deranged.

8 Babylon has suddenly fallen and been
    destroyed.
Wail for her!
Take balm for her pain;
Perhaps she may be healed.

9 We would have healed Babylon,
But she is not healed.
Forsake her, and let us go everyone to his own
    country;
For her judgment reaches to heaven and is
    lifted up to the skies.

10 The LORD has revealed our righteousness.
Come and let us declare in Zion the work of
    the LORD our God.

11 Make the arrows bright!
Gather the shields!
The LORD has raised up the spirit of the kings
    of the Medes.
For His plan *is* against Babylon to destroy it,
Because it *is* the vengeance of the LORD,
The vengeance for His temple.

12 Set up the standard on the walls of Babylon;
Make the guard strong,
Set up the watchmen,

Prepare the ambushes.
For the LORD has both devised and done
What He spoke against the inhabitants of
Babylon.

13 O you who dwell by many waters,
Abundant in treasures,
Your end has come,
The measure of your covetousness.

14 The LORD of hosts has sworn by Himself:
"Surely I will fill you with men, as with locusts,
And they shall lift up a shout against you."

15 He has made the earth by His power;
He has established the world by His wisdom,
And stretched out the heaven by His
understanding.

16 When He utters *His* voice—
There is a multitude of waters in the heavens:
"He causes the vapors to ascend from the ends
of the earth;
He makes lightnings for the rain;
He brings the wind out of His treasuries."

17 Everyone is dull-hearted, without knowledge;
Every metalsmith is put to shame by the
carved image;
For his molded image *is* falsehood,
And *there is* no breath in them.

18 They *are* futile, a work of errors;
In the time of their punishment they shall
perish.

19 The Portion of Jacob *is* not like them,
For He *is* the Maker of all things;
And *Israel is* the tribe of His inheritance.
The LORD of hosts *is* His name.

20 "You *are* My battle-ax *and* weapons of war:
For with you I will break the nation in pieces;
With you I will destroy kingdoms;

21 With you I will break in pieces the horse and
its rider;
With you I will break in pieces the chariot and
its rider;

22 With you also I will break in pieces man and
woman;

With you I will break in pieces old and young;
With you I will break in pieces the young man
    and the maiden;
23 With you also I will break in pieces the
    shepherd and his flock;
With you I will break in pieces the farmer and
    his yoke of oxen;
And with you I will break in pieces governors
    and rulers.
24 "And I will repay Babylon
And all the inhabitants of Chaldea
For all the evil they have done
In Zion in your sight," says the LORD.
25 "Behold, I *am* against you, O destroying
    mountain,
Who destroys all the earth," says the LORD.
"And I will stretch out My hand against you,
Roll you down from the rocks,
And make you a burnt mountain.
26 They shall not take from you a stone for a corner
Nor a stone for a foundation,
But you shall be desolate forever," says the LORD.
27 Set up a banner in the land,
Blow the trumpet among the nations!
Prepare the nations against her,
Call the kingdoms together against her:
Ararat, Minni, and Ashkenaz.
Appoint a general against her;
Cause the horses to come up like the bristling
    locusts.
28 Prepare against her the nations,
With the kings of the Medes,
Its governors and all its rulers,
All the land of his dominion.
29 And the land will tremble and sorrow;
For every purpose of the LORD shall be
    performed against Babylon,
To make the land of Babylon a desolation
    without inhabitant.
30 The mighty men of Babylon have ceased
    fighting,
They have remained in their strongholds;

Their might has failed,
They became *like* women;
They have burned her dwelling places,
The bars of her *gate* are broken.

31 One runner will run to meet another,
And one messenger to meet another,
To show the king of Babylon that his city is
taken on *all* sides;

32 The passages are blocked,
The reeds they have burned with fire,
And the men of war are terrified.

33 For thus says the LORD of hosts, the God of
Israel:
"The daughter of Babylon *is* like a threshing
floor
When it is time to thresh her;
Yet a little while
And the time of her harvest will come."

34 "Nebuchadnezzar the king of Babylon
Has devoured me, he has crushed me;
He has made me an empty vessel,
He has swallowed me up like a monster;
He has filled his stomach with my delicacies,
He has spit me out.

35 Let the violence *done* to me and my flesh *be*
upon Babylon,"
The inhabitant of Zion will say;
"And my blood be upon the inhabitants of
Chaldea!"
Jerusalem will say.

36 Therefore thus says the LORD:
"Behold, I will plead your case and take
vengeance for you.
I will dry up her sea and make her springs dry.

37 Babylon shall become a heap,
A dwelling place for jackals,
An astonishment and a hissing,
Without an inhabitant.

38 They shall roar together like lions,
They shall growl like lions' whelps.

39 In their excitement I will prepare their feasts;
I will make them drunk,

That they may rejoice,
And sleep a perpetual sleep
And not awake," says the LORD.

40 "I will bring them down
Like lambs to the slaughter,
Like rams with male goats.

41 "Oh, how Sheshach is taken!
Oh, how the praise of the whole earth is seized!
How Babylon has become desolate among the
nations!

42 The sea has come up over Babylon;
She is covered with the multitude of its waves.

43 Her cities are a desolation,
A dry land and a wilderness,
A land where no one dwells,
Through which no son of man passes.

44 I will punish Bel in Babylon,
And I will bring out of his mouth what he has
swallowed;
And the nations shall not stream to him anymore.
Yes, the wall of Babylon shall fall.

45 "My people, go out of the midst of her!
And let everyone deliver himself from the
fierce anger of the LORD.

46 And lest your heart faint,
And you fear for the rumor that *will be* heard
in the land
(A rumor will come *one* year,
And after that, in *another* year
A rumor *will come,*
And violence in the land,
Ruler against ruler),

47 Therefore behold, the days are coming
That I will bring judgment on the carved
images of Babylon;
Her whole land shall be ashamed,
And all her slain shall fall in her midst.

48 Then the heavens and the earth and all that *is*
in them
Shall sing joyously over Babylon;
For the plunderers shall come to her from the
north," says the LORD.

49 As Babylon *has caused* the slain of Israel to fall,
So at Babylon the slain of all the earth shall
fall.
50 You who have escaped the sword,
Get away! Do not stand still!
Remember the LORD afar off,
And let Jerusalem come to your mind.
51 We are ashamed because we have heard
reproach.
Shame has covered our faces,
For strangers have come into the sanctuaries of
the LORD's house.
52 "Therefore behold, the days are coming," says
the LORD,
"That I will bring judgment on her carved
images,
And throughout all her land the wounded
shall groan.
53 Though Babylon were to mount up to heaven,
And though she were to fortify the height of
her strength,
Yet from Me plunderers would come to her,"
says the LORD.
54 The sound of a cry *comes* from Babylon,
And great destruction from the land of the
Chaldeans,
55 Because the LORD is plundering Babylon
And silencing her loud voice,
Though her waves roar like great waters,
And the noise of their voice is uttered,
56 Because the plunderer comes against her,
against Babylon,
And her mighty men are taken.
Every one of their bows is broken;
For the LORD *is* the God of recompense,
He will surely repay.
57 "And I will make drunk
Her princes and wise men,
Her governors, her deputies, and her mighty men.
And they shall sleep a perpetual sleep
And not awake," says the King,
Whose name *is* the LORD of hosts.

343

58 Thus says the LORD of hosts:
"The broad walls of Babylon shall be utterly
broken,
And her high gates shall be burned with fire;
The people will labor in vain,
And the nations, because of the fire;
And they shall be weary."

59 The word which Jeremiah the prophet commanded Seraiah the son of Neriah, the son of Mahseiah, when he went with Zedekiah the king of Judah
to Babylon in the fourth year of his reign. And Seraiah
was the quartermaster.

60 So Jeremiah wrote in a book all the evil that
would come upon Babylon, all these words that are
written against Babylon.

61 And Jeremiah said to Seraiah, "When you ar-
rive in Babylon and see it, and read all these words,

62 "then you shall say, 'O LORD, You have spoken
against this place to cut it off, so that none shall remain in it, neither man nor beast, but it shall be desolate forever.'

63 "Now it shall be, when you have finished reading this book, *that* you shall tie a stone to it and throw
it out into the Euphrates.

64 "Then you shall say, 'Thus Babylon shall sink
and not rise from the catastrophe that I will bring
upon her. And they shall be weary.'" Thus far *are* the
words of Jeremiah.

Jer. 50:1–51:64

Almost as much space is given to the oracle concerning Babylon as
to all the other nations combined. This national power was by far the
greatest tragedy Jerusalem had ever faced. All the skirmishes with
the previously named nations pale in comparison to the grand clash
with Nebuchadnezzar. Yet here we have the words, *"Babylon is taken,
Bel is shamed. Merodach is broken in pieces"* (50:2). Their god, who
claimed to be creator and king, was found to be but one more impotent and useless deity in the face of the great finality of Yahweh.

Jeremiah was accused by his countrymen of loving Babylon more
than Judah because he had urged them to surrender. Here we see
how preposterous were those allegations. The prophet hurled fire at

344

Babylon, to whom he said, *"You were glad, because you rejoiced, You destroyers of My heritage . . . you have grown fat . . . you bellow like bulls"* (50:11). He who laughs best, however, laughs last. Without trying to sound irreverent, I want to affirm that it is God who has the last word. It will be the laughter of redeemed men and women that will finally ring out over the universe. All lesser rejoicing will be silenced. There will be a final triumph of the church over the world.

In essence, Babylon is any and every nation that chooses to act as if it has existence independent from God. In these oracles is the wonderful assurance that there is something more than just the here and now. There is a moral absolute that rules over everything and everyone, quite beyond the temporal gods of this world. Other ideologies will one day respect and affirm this world-view. "Who is in charge of the world?" Was it Egypt's pretty heifer, Moab's Chemosh, Ammon's Milcom, or Babylon's Merodach? Jeremiah, in all his prophetic ministry, was ever tracking on the truth in order that the real course of the nations might be proclaimed.

These oracles call out to modern man. Our deities have different names now, but we nonetheless bow to them and to their petty visibility when we could be bowing to sheer majesty. These words of Jeremiah offer us a vision of sovereignty that could change forever the way we view the universe. We are not meant to be "conformed to this world" but to be "transformed by the renewing of our minds" (Rom. 12:2). We are meant to be modern-day Jeremiahs, with a passion for ultimate reality and with a fire for serving it in a world that is racing after empty humanism. We are meant to be like bronze walls for what we believe, bastions for the sovereignty of God, that His will may be done on earth as it is in heaven.

NOTES

1. E. W. Nicholson, *The Book of the Prophet Jeremiah,* 2 vols., The Cambridge Bible Commentary (New York: Cambridge University Press, 1975), 2:177.

2. Ibid., 2:196.

3. R. K. Harrison, *Jeremiah and Lamentations,* The Tyndale Old Testament Commentary (Downers Grove, Ill.: Inter-Varsity Press, 1973), 183.

Lamentations of the Prophet

Lamentations 1:1–5:22

Introduction to Lamentations

Authorship of Lamentations

Much has been said both for and against Jeremiah's authorship of Lamentations. Obviously it was the work of a person who was an eyewitness to the fall of Jerusalem, who was gifted in poetic expression, and who was emotionally and spiritually involved with the calamity. The consensus of Jewish tradition ascribes it to Jeremiah. This reasoning springs from the text of 2 Chronicles: "Jeremiah also lamented for Josiah. And to this day all the singing men and the singing women speak of Josiah in their lamentations. They made it a custom in Israel; and indeed they *are* written in the Laments" (2 Chron. 35:25). Skeptics temper that logic by introducing the possibility that the Chronicler may have been referring to another collection of dirge material that has since perished. They go on to draw attention to the anonymity of the work itself, and then to point out what they see as radical ideological differences between the books of Lamentations and Jeremiah. Many feel that there are greater affinities in language and attitude between Lamentations, parts of Ezekiel, and some of the latter psalms.[1] Others say that certain of the dirges lack the literary excellence of Jeremiah.

In line with Jewish tradition, the Septuagint and Vulgate have cast their weight in favor of Jeremianic authorship by prefacing their translations with the statement, "And it came to pass, after Israel was led into captivity and Jerusalem laid waste, that Jeremiah sat weeping and lamented with this lamentation over Jerusalem and said. . . ." We could stand forever in the courtroom of this debate and never move on to relish the content of the text nor to its application to daily living. Rather than referring to the author as only "the poet," I will refer to him as Jeremiah and treat the collection of five dirges as coming from his hand.

Place in Canon

Lamentations is one of the five rolls (or megilloth) of the Hebrew Old Testament. The megilloth are read liturgically once a year: Song of Songs at Passover, Ruth at Pentecost, Lamentations on the anniversary of the destruction of the temple, Ecclesiastes at Tabernacles, and Esther at Purim. In the Hebrew Bible the megilloth is in the third division called "the Writings"—the other two divisions being the Law and the Prophets. In the Septuagint, however, Lamentations came to be placed in the division of the Prophets in order that it might follow Jeremiah and preserve a chronological order.[2] Regardless of the difference in the positioning of the book between the Hebrew and the Greek versions, the canonicity of Lamentations has never been questioned.

The Title and Content

The first word of the book speaks in the universal language of all humanity: a great sigh—"how!" or "alas!" The Hebrew custom of naming a book by its first word is carried out here. The Jewish mind learned to identify the five books of the law by their beginning words. Genesis (*Bereshith*, "in beginning of"), Exodus (*We'eleh shemoth*, "and these are the names of"), Leviticus (*Wayyiqra*, "and he called"), Numbers (*Bemidhbar*, "in the wilderness of"), and Deuteronomy (*Eleh had-debharim*, "these are the words").[3] Another Hebrew tradition was to name a book with a title descriptive of its contents. In the Talmud and Rabbinic writings, the title is *Qinoth* (Lamentations). This was adopted by the Greek translators, who believed it to be more readily intelligible to the non-Hebrew reader.

The two traditions for titling the book are closely related. The first word, "how," launches the lament over Jerusalem with a moan that collects the sufferings of all people bereaved of God and battered by their own sinfulness. Every year, in mid July, the event is commemorated liturgically as the mournful song of universal suffering is heard again by faithful Jews. Dramatic images are cast upon all minds, sharper perhaps than we are ready for. "How lonely lies the city!" launches the first dirge. She is a widow weeping in the night. The tears that glisten on her cheeks are seen by no one, for she is alone, like the city of Jerusalem. In the first half of the dirge, we see her. In the second half, she turns and speaks to us, refusing to let us be merely casual passersby. What she says is sung for the Western world in Handel's *Messiah:* "Behold and see if there is any sorrow like my sorrow. How the Lord has covered the daughter of Zion with the cloud of His anger!"

The second dirge begins with a siege upon the mind, shocking it out of complacency. God is the dread warrior, not fighting for Jerusalem this time, but against her. The air is filled with smoke because He has blazed against the city wall. It is no longer a great rampart. It burns; houses burn, palaces burn, even the sanctuary burns. Starving infants choke in the street. A mighty arm has swept across Jerusalem, tumbling her walls like a house of cards. The poetry rises to a peak of literary excellence.

"I am the man who has seen affliction," introduces the third poem which is not a dirge but a personal lament, as its opening words suggest. The pages of a private journal are laid bare. Its poetry is highly subjective, a stream of consciousness at times, which explains why it is less cohesive than the other poems and three times as long. The journey recorded here begins in despair and ends with rediscovered hope, much like that of C. S. Lewis in the journal that was later published as *A Grief Observed.*

"How the gold has become dim! How changed the fine gold!" The fourth dirge rises to the same poetic heights as did the second. The temple no longer glistens in the sunlight. Her golden age has passed into blackened streets where temple stones have been tumbled and all the brilliant things of God have become cheap and common. The sons of Zion are no longer precious, no longer mortised together as living stones of the spiritual house. The daughters too have lost their glory, have become less than human. They eat their dying infants in order to survive. Like the second dirge, it has all the marks of vivid, eyewitness experience.

"Remember, O Lord" begins the fifth poem. How fitting to end with a national prayer, one that they had been unwilling to offer in their pleasant times under Jeremiah's prophetic urgings. The last verse of this last poem leaves the reader with an uncomfortable and haunting feeling of solemn suspense, of waiting for the action of a sovereign God, but of not being able to take it for granted.

Metrical and Literary Structure

The first four poems are in the *qinah* rhythm, one used particularly for funeral dirges. A peculiar halting effect is achieved by the 3-2 rhythm. A similar tone was achieved by Samuel Taylor Coleridge in the more tragic parts of his "Rime of the Ancient Mariner."[4]

Four of the five poems are twenty-two stanzas long, matching the twenty-two consonants of the Hebrew alphabet. In this way the poems can take the literary form of acrostics, each stanza beginning with a successive letter of the alphabet. This was a highly elaborate poetic discipline that at its best functioned as an aid to memory and at its worst became contrived and awkward. The third poem is not twenty-two verses long but is an acrostic; the fifth poem is twenty-two verses long but is not an acrostic. Such irregularities force us to remain elastic in our thinking as was the thinking of the ancient writer, particularly since our purpose is not to dissect the poems in a technical way but to meet the more impelling challenge of Scripture for its application to our personal lives.

NOTES

1. R. K. Harrison, *Jeremiah and Lamentations,* The Tyndale Old Testament Commentary (Downers Grove, Ill.: Inter-Varsity Press, 1973), 197, 198.
2. James Hastings, *The Speaker's Bible* (Aberdeen, Scotland: Speaker's Bible Office, 1944), 133–34.
3. Ibid., 133.
4. Ibid., 135.

An Outline of Lamentations

CHAPTER ONE

How Lonely Sits the City

Lamentations 1:1–22

1:1 How lonely sits the city
That was full of people!
How like a widow is she,
Who *was* great among the nations!
The princess among the provinces
Has become a slave!
2 She weeps bitterly in the night,
Her tears *are* on her cheeks;
Among all her lovers
She has none to comfort *her*.
All her friends have dealt treacherously with
her;
They have become her enemies.
3 Judah has gone into captivity,
Under affliction and hard servitude;
She dwells among the nations,
She finds no rest;
All her persecutors overtake her in dire straits.
4 The roads to Zion mourn
Because no one comes to the set feasts.
All her gates are desolate;
Her priests sigh,
Her virgins are afflicted,
And she *is* in bitterness.
5 Her adversaries have become the master,
Her enemies prosper;
For the LORD has afflicted her
Because of the multitude of her transgressions.
Her children have gone into captivity before
the enemy.

6 And from the daughter of Zion
All her splendor has departed.
Her princes have become like deer
That find no pasture,
That flee without strength
Before the pursuer.
7 In the days of her affliction and roaming,
Jerusalem remembers all her pleasant things
That she had in the days of old.
When her people fell into the hand of the
    enemy,
With no one to help her,
The adversaries saw her
And mocked at her downfall.
8 Jerusalem has sinned gravely,
Therefore she has become vile.
All who honored her despise her
Because they have seen her nakedness;
Yes, she sighs and turns away.
9 Her uncleanness *is* in her skirts;
She did not consider her destiny;
Therefore her collapse was awesome;
She had no comforter.
"O LORD, behold my affliction,
For *the* enemy is exalted!"
10 The adversary has spread his hand
Over all her pleasant things;
For she has seen the nations enter her
    sanctuary,
Those whom You commanded
Not to enter Your assembly.
11 All her people sigh,
They seek bread;
They have given their valuables for food to
    restore life.
"See, O LORD, and consider,
For I am scorned."
12 "*Is it* nothing to you, all you who pass by?
Behold and see
If there is any sorrow like my sorrow,
Which has been brought on me,

Which the LORD has inflicted
In the day of His fierce anger.

13 "From above He has sent fire into my bones,
And it overpowered them;
He has spread a net for my feet
And turned me back;
He has made me desolate
And faint all the day.

14 "The yoke of my transgressions was bound;
They were woven together by His hands,
And thrust upon my neck.
He made my strength fail;
The Lord delivered me into the hands of *those*
whom I am not able to withstand.

15 "The Lord has trampled underfoot all my
mighty *men* in my midst;
He has called an assembly against me
To crush my young men;
The Lord trampled *as* in a winepress
The virgin daughter of Judah.

16 "For these *things* I weep;
My eye, my eye overflows with water;
Because the comforter, who should restore my
life,
Is far from me.
My children are desolate
Because the enemy prevailed."

17 Zion spreads out her hands,
But no one comforts her;
The LORD has commanded concerning Jacob
That those around him *become* his adversaries;
Jerusalem has become an unclean thing among
them.

18 "The LORD is righteous,
For I rebelled against His commandment.
Hear now, all peoples,
And behold my sorrow;
My virgins and my young men
Have gone into captivity.

19 "I called for my lovers,
But they deceived me;

My priests and my elders
Breathed their last in the city,
While they sought food
To restore their life.

20 "See, O LORD, that I *am* in distress;
My soul is troubled;
My heart is overturned within me,
For I have been very rebellious.
Outside the sword bereaves,
At home *it is* like death.

21 "They have heard that I sigh,
But no one comforts me.
All my enemies have heard of my trouble;
They are glad that You have done *it.*
Bring on the day You have announced,
That they may become like me.

22 "Let all their wickedness come before You,
And do to them as You have done to me
For all my transgressions;
For my sighs *are* many,
And my heart *is* faint."

Lam. 1:1–22

We are participating in a funeral service for a nation. A grieving sigh is heaved by the poet who mourns the fall of his beloved Jerusalem. "Lamentation" is a word that has fallen on hard times. It is virtually dead to our contemporary ears. B. B. Warfield, referring to a different word has said, "It is sad to witness the death of any worthy thing—even a worthy word. And worthy words do die, like any other worthy thing—if we do not take good care of them. Sadder still is the dying out of the hearts of men of the things for which the word stands."[1] The moan issued here by the grieving prophet knows no counterpart in today's culture.

"How lonely sits the city That was full of people" (v. 1). This opening verse sets the tone for the whole collection. Judging from his passion and the richness of his detail, we can assume that the writer was an eyewitness to the fall of Jerusalem and was most likely recording his impressions within a reasonable time frame of the actual event. He watches the city from the perspective of the third person for the first half of the dirge and then performs a literary stroke of genius by

switching the perspective to the first person in the last half of the work. The shift carries with it a powerful intimacy that invites a personal response from the reader or the listener. I say "listener" because Lamentations is one of the five books that make up the megilloth that were read aloud once a year for liturgical purposes in their appropriate season. Every year in mid July, the Hebrew ear is fed again with these mournful strains as they assemble in their synagogues to commemorate the destruction of the temple.[2]

The Hebrews were renowned throughout the Middle East as singers and musicians. Their poetry had rather striking features that loses something in its translation. One of the most striking features was the use of parallelism. "How like a widow is she, Who was great among the nations!" (v. 1). This second part is synonymous with the first. Each part is a total unit of thought and syntax, yet the second is laid alongside of the first, in this case, repeating the same idea but clothing it in a different image.

In order to keep loneliness from being an abstraction, we are invited to picture a widow, recently bereaved. Not only is force created by this parallel repetition, but it is also created by a strong accentual quality. Major words carry one stress and minor words are unstressed or often linked together. The groupings then result in a strong rhythmic pattern that lends dramatic resonance.

When the Roman emperor Titus conquered Jerusalem in A.D. 70, he stamped a coin to commemorate her loss and his gain. The image on that coin was none other than the image of a widow, bowed and shrouded in grief. *"The princess among the provinces Has become a slave!"* (v. 1). Once *"full of people,"* she is now all alone. The husband she has lost is none other than the Lord Himself, the generous provider, the gentle protector, and the lover whose love she had never returned. No wonder there are sleepless nights filled with tears (v. 2). They are not simply tears of remembrance; they are tears of bitterness over lost opportunities for reconciliation. No one comforts her; *"She finds no rest"* (v. 3). This strain will be caught again in the final prayer of chapter 5.

If only she could forget *"the days of her affliction and roaming"* (v. 7), it might not then be so painful. In a great rush of remorse, *"Jerusalem remembers all her pleasant things That she had in the days of old"* (v. 7). Instead of the sweetness of these memories being a comfort to her, they haunt her because they are now irretrievable. The *"roaming"* she had so desired is now all that she has. Like all sin, it had masqueraded as a desirable thing but now is nothing but an affliction.

When she had the chance, *"she did not consider her destiny"* (v. 9). If only we could hear these words today and think seriously about our destiny and about the consequences of our roamings. In this culture we insure ourselves against all kinds of losses. We take out policies that cover disability, health, fire, theft, casualty, and so on. We insure ourselves against so many calamities, most of which will never happen, but we don't take care enough about our souls, to insure them against the one thing that most certainly will happen.[3] We make so little provision for our eternal destiny.

"The adversary has spread his hand over all her pleasant things" (v. 10). The whole collection of dirges and poetry never departs from the theme of old Jerusalem's loneliness and calamity. Brighter images, however, are found in the whole sweep of Scripture. Centuries later, John described the New Jerusalem, showing this time the bride and not the widow. "Then I, John, saw the holy city, New Jerusalem, coming down out of heaven from God, prepared as a bride adorned for her husband" (Rev. 21:2). Here is another writer using the same metaphor hundreds of years later, seeing the city as a woman. This time she is in her splendor, adorned for her husband in the full dignity of her redemption, under a new marriage covenant.

The last half of the dirge is told from the first person. *"Is it nothing to you, all you who pass by?"* (v. 12). The widow clutches at each passerby, not allowing them an escape. *"Behold and see If there is any sorrow like my sorrow"* (v. 12). Grief over lost opportunity for repentance is meant to be observed and not ignored.

"From above He has sent fire into my bones" (v. 13). The physical feelings of grief are handled with candor in verses 13–15. The feeling of being tangled in a net, of being faint, of being weighed down with a yoke of guilt, of being trampled underfoot and crushed, all become stark realities by virtue of being made personal in the metaphor of one grieving widow. Yet, at the same time, they describe aspects of the siege. Fiery darts, catapulted over the wall, would light up the night sky with their terror and then burn in the bones of the city.

"My eye, my eye overflows with water; Because the comforter, who should restore my life, Is far from me" (v. 16). The husband who had so yearned to comfort was gone. How like the words of Jesus as He

looked over the same city, soon to undergo its siege from the Romans, soon to be widowed again: "O Jerusalem, Jerusalem. . . . How often I wanted to gather your children together, as a hen gathers her chicks under *her* wings, but you were not willing!" (Matt. 23:37). Now the widow is inconsolable. All pleas for comfort seem unprofitable. *"Zion spreads out her hands, But no one comforts her"* (v. 17). Those who should be friends have become adversaries. So it was with the nations around Jerusalem. They did not come to her aid. Moab even joined forces with the Babylonians during the final siege. *"I called for my lovers, But they deceived me; . . . They have heard that I sigh, But no one comforts me. All my enemies have heard my trouble; They are glad that You have done it"* (vv. 19–21).

In the final verses of this dirge, the widow continues to appeal to the passersby to learn from her example. *"Hear now, all peoples, And behold my sorrow"* (v. 18). The senses of sight and sound are being appealed to, not merely for pity but for the lesson of righteousness. *"The LORD is righteous, For I rebelled against His commandment"* (v. 18). Finally the cause of the tragedy is identified. It rises in a moan that echoes through the dirges to follow. *"My heart is overturned within me, For I have been very rebellious"* (v. 20).

Jerusalem was not the only city, Israel was not the only nation who would suffer for their rebellion. She is the great example, the conscience of the nations. Addressing the God who holds the whole world in His hands and inviting His inexorable justice, the widow cries, *"Let all their wickedness come before You, And do to them as You have done to me"* (v. 22). This funeral is the business of every nation and of every individual.

NOTES

1. B. B. Warfield, *Person and Work*, 345, 347, as quoted by John R. W. Stott, *Cross of Christ* (Downers Grove, Ill.: Inter-Varsity Press, 1986), 176.

2. R. K. Harrison, *Jeremiah and Lamentations*, The Tyndale Old Testament Commentary (Downers Grove, Ill.: Inter-Varsity Press, 1973), 195.

3. James Montgomery Boice, *The Parables of Jesus* (Chicago: Moody Press, 1983), 116.

CHAPTER TWO

How the Lord Has Covered

Lamentations 2:1–22

2:1 How the Lord has covered the daughter of Zion
With a cloud in His anger!
He cast down from heaven to the earth
The beauty of Israel,
And did not remember His footstool
In the day of His anger.
2 The Lord has swallowed up and has not pitied
All the dwelling places of Jacob.
He has thrown down in His wrath
The strongholds of the daughter of Judah;
He has brought *them* down to the ground;
He has profaned the kingdom and its princes.
3 He has cut off in fierce anger
Every horn of Israel;
He has drawn back His right hand
From before the enemy.
He has blazed against Jacob like a flaming fire
Devouring all around.
4 Standing like an enemy, He has bent His bow;
With His right hand, like an adversary,
He has slain all *who were* pleasing to His eye;
On the tent of the daughter of Zion,
He has poured out His fury like fire.
5 The Lord was like an enemy.
He has swallowed up Israel,
He has swallowed up all her palaces;
He has destroyed her strongholds,
And has increased mourning and lamentation
In the daughter of Judah.
6 He has done violence to His tabernacle,

As if it were a garden;
He has destroyed His place of assembly;
The LORD has caused
The appointed feasts and Sabbaths to be
    forgotten in Zion.
In His burning indignation He has spurned the
    king and the priest.

7 The Lord has spurned His altar,
He has abandoned His sanctuary;
He has given up the walls of her palaces
Into the hand of the enemy.
They have made a noise in the house of the
    LORD
As on the day of a set feast.

8 The LORD has purposed to destroy
The wall of the daughter of Zion.
He has stretched out a line;
He has not withdrawn His hand from
    destroying;
Therefore He has caused the rampart and wall
    to lament;
They languished together.

9 Her gates have sunk into the ground;
He has destroyed and broken her bars.
Her king and her princes *are* among the
    nations;
The Law *is* no *more,*
And her prophets find no vision from the
    LORD.

10 The elders of the daughter of Zion
Sit on the ground *and* keep silence;
They throw dust on their heads
And gird themselves with sackcloth.
The virgins of Jerusalem
Bow their heads to the ground.

11 My eyes fail with tears,
My heart is troubled;
My bile is poured on the ground
Because of the destruction of the daughter of
    my people,
Because the children and the infants
Faint in the streets of the city.

12 They say to their mothers,
   "Where *is* grain and wine?"
   As they swoon like the wounded
   In the streets of the city,
   As their life is poured out
   In their mothers' bosom.

13 How shall I console you?
   To what shall I liken you,
   O daughter of Jerusalem?
   What shall I compare with you, that I may
      comfort you,
   O virgin daughter of Zion?
   For your ruin *is* spread wide as the sea;
   Who can heal you?

14 Your prophets have seen for you
   False and deceptive visions;
   They have not uncovered your iniquity,
   To bring back your captives,
   But have envisioned for you false prophecies
      and delusions.

15 All who pass by clap *their* hands at you;
   They hiss and shake their heads
   At the daughter of Jerusalem:
   "*Is* this the city that is called
   'The perfection of beauty,
   The joy of the whole earth'?"

16 All your enemies have opened their mouth
      against you;
   They hiss and gnash *their* teeth.
   They say, "We have swallowed *her* up!
   Surely this *is* the day we have waited for;
   We have found *it*, we have seen *it!*"

17 The LORD has done what He purposed;
   He has fulfilled His word
   Which He commanded in days of old.
   He has thrown down and has not pitied,
   And He has caused an enemy to rejoice over
      you;
   He has exalted the horn of your adversaries.

18 Their heart cried out to the Lord,
   "O wall of the daughter of Zion,
   Let tears run down like a river day and night;

Give yourself no relief;
Give your eyes no rest.
19 "Arise, cry out in the night,
At the beginning of the watches;
Pour out your heart like water before the face
    of the Lord.
Lift your hands toward Him
For the life of your young children,
Who faint from hunger at the head of every
    street."
20 "See, O LORD, and consider!
To whom have You done this?
Should the women eat their offspring,
The children they have cuddled?
Should the priest and prophet be slain
In the sanctuary of the Lord?
21 "Young and old lie
On the ground in the streets;
My virgins and my young men
Have fallen by the sword;
You have slain *them* in the day of Your anger,
You have slaughtered *and* not pitied.
22 "You have invited as to a feast day
The terrors that surround me.
In the day of the LORD's anger
There was no refugee or survivor.
Those whom I have borne and brought up
My enemies have destroyed."

Lam. 2:1–22

"How the Lord has covered the daughter of Zion With a cloud in His anger!" (v. 1). This covering is not a comfortable one. Jeremiah's prophetic voice had offered his people the love of God, His provision, and His protection if they would only abandon their idolatry and turn again to Him. In this second dirge, the prophet describes a punitive God. How different this God appears. In order to dramatize this difference, Jeremiah makes God the subject of almost half the sentences.[1] His awesome presence is painted with bold strokes as the poet uses explicit verbs with military connotations, not only to describe the war but to identify the attacker as God Himself. The poetry rises to a height of literary excellence that matches that of chapter 4.

In 1741 Jonathan Edwards delivered what has become one of the most famous sermons in the history of this nation. It was meant to destroy the religious complacency of his congregation in Enfield, Connecticut.[2] Not only did it succeed in doing just that, but it also succeeded in fanning the fires of the Great Awakening, causing them to rage across this country with an unprecedented spirit of repentance and life-changing power. "Sinners in the Hands of an Angry God" seemed such an offensive title then, let alone now. Today it is preserved in textbooks of American literature for its genius of expression rather than for its biblical integrity. This sermon is commendable for both and bears striking similarity to this second dirge of Lamentations. Both dare to speak of the anger of God with courage and passion, letting the chips fall where they may. With the very first line, the poet is launched into the incredible world of his memories, or perhaps we should say his nightmares. The interplay between heaven and earth preoccupies verses 1 and 2. The cloud descends, not as the benevolent presence of glory that wrapped around Solomon and the whole assembly when he brought the ark of the covenant into the temple. Then "the glory of the LORD filled the house of the LORD" (1 Kings 8:11). The cloud here does not come in a gentle descent, but it is *cast down from heaven to the earth*" (v. 1). It comes filled with God's anger, to destroy *the beauty of Israel*" (v. 1).

The poet was haunted by the memory of a cloud of smoke enveloping Jerusalem, filling his lungs with the stench of burning walls and of burning flesh. *"The Lord has swallowed up and has not pitied All the dwelling places of Jacob"* (v. 2). The weight of His presence consumes her in one gulp. The parallel line reinforces the picture of physical anger with its strong verb: *"He has thrown down in His wrath The strongholds of the daughter of Judah; He has brought them down to the ground; He has profaned the kingdom and its princes"* (v. 2).

When Nebuchadnezzar's battering rams hit the gates of Jerusalem, their heavy beams drove wedges into what complacent Judah had presumed impenetrable. The poet saw beyond the hand of a Babylonian king. He saw the hand of an angry God operating the engines of war. Now that mighty hand wielded a flashing sword. *"He has cut off in fierce anger Every horn of Israel"* (v. 3). Once this same hand had protected her; now *"He has drawn back His right hand From before the enemy"* (v. 3). He has moved from being a protective God to being a punitive God, proving that dual dimension of His love and His wrath.

There is nothing wimpy about God or about the poet charged with describing Him. *"He has blazed against Jacob like a flaming fire devouring all around"* (v. 3). The enemy had rained missiles and firebrands over her walls; she tried to douse them with water but to no avail. Just as Jerusalem was bombarded, so the poet bombards the listener in order that no mistake be made as to the nature of God's anger, in order that we not spiritualize it too much and try to explain it away. *"Standing like an enemy, He has bent His bow; With His right hand, like an adversary, He has slain all who were pleasing to His eye"* (v. 4).

Edwards preached that day in 1741 without voice inflection, simply allowing the words to strike their mark. "The bow of God's wrath is bent, the arrow made ready on the string and justice bends the arrow at your heart and strains the bow."[3] Enemy archers, lancers, and slingers were a fearsome sight to the citizens of Jerusalem. More fearsome than any human enemy, however, is the anger of a holy God, pictured here in the same anthropomorphic detail meant to arouse the senses and the soul. He takes a determined stand and bends the bow with the muscular power of His right arm that had hitherto been the symbol of His help. Now He takes careful aim at everything in His path, regardless of how pleasant. This is no God who is soft on sin. This is the God who later did not spare His own Son. He releases the bow *"On the tent of the daughter of Zion, He has poured out His fury like fire"* (v. 4).

Early in his ministry Jeremiah preached a famous sermon long remembered for its eloquent repetition, "the temple of the LORD, the temple of the LORD, the temple of the LORD" (Jer. 7:4). They had trusted that its architecture would somehow magically protect them, would cover the multitude of their sins, regardless of the state of their hearts. They even said, "We are delivered to do all these abominations" (Jer. 7:10). What cheap grace they believed in! As though a little repetitive chanting would prove the temple inviolate. Look now at what God thinks of their cheap grace.

"He has done violence to His tabernacle, As if it were a garden; He has destroyed His place of assembly; The LORD has caused The appointed feasts and Sabbaths to be forgotten in Zion" (v. 6). They did not believe that God would really destroy His place and the institutions of His appointment. Perhaps they thought that at the last minute He would lose courage and find them all quite irresistible. Instead, *"In His*

burning indignation He has spurned the king and the priest. The Lord has spurned His altar, He has abandoned His sanctuary; He has given up the walls of her palaces Into the hand of the enemy" (vv. 6–7). The Arch of Titus in Rome commemorates a similar event. A Roman general conquered the Jews in A.D. 70, destroyed the temple, and carried away the sacred vessels. They are pictured in the frieze on this arch being handled irreverently and savagely by the enemy. Jerusalem's scandal was forever cast in stone, arching over the passersby, like a giant trophy to all her enemies, as a solemn reminder that a sovereign God will judge.

Not only the wall, not only the temple, but also the gates of the city were desecrated. Those proud avenues of commerce where many times Jeremiah had stood and preached *"have sunk into the ground; He has destroyed and broken her bars"* (v. 9). This image is found again in the final prayer. Not only the king and the priest are spurned, but *"the elders of the daughter of Zion Sit on the ground and keep silence; They throw dust on their heads And gird themselves with sackcloth"* (v. 10). Leadership carries with it a solemn responsibility and ultimately a solemn accountability. All of this devastation was the result of apostate leadership.

"Is this the city that is called The . . . joy of the whole earth?" (v. 15). In this second half of the dirge the imagery shifts away from God as the dread warrior and onto the city and her sufferings. What was meant to shock the listener was not just the calamity but the shocking contrast between what Jerusalem became and what she was meant to be. This parallels how we have felt the difference between the protective God and the punitive God in the first half of the dirge. How like Jeremiah are these next candid words. *"My eyes fail with tears, My heart is troubled; My bile is poured on the ground"* (v. 11). He had no stomach for this part of the prophetic ministry. It sickened him to have seen it coming and then to have lived through it and now to tell of it. In the year he stepped into prophetic office, Jerusalem was a disaster waiting to happen, and now the disaster had happened. How easily Jeremiah could have said, "See, I told you so." Instead, he offers the most tender sympathy. *"The children and infants Faint in the streets of the city"* (v. 11). All the while he was forced to deal with human suffering, to steady himself in the face of it, and to keep on going. To see a child suffer was more than he could take. Now he understood, perhaps even thanked God for forbidding

him to marry and to procreate. What if it was his child, dying in the
arms of his wife? *"They say to their mothers 'Where is grain and wine?'*
As they swoon like the wounded In the streets of the city, As their life is
poured out In their mothers' bosom" (v. 12). What if it was his wife
raising the anguished question, *"Should the women eat their offspring,*
The children they have cuddled?" (v. 20).

Like a journalist obligated to report the carnage and like a pastor
obligated to bring comfort, he strained himself professionally,
searching for imagery. *"How shall I console you? To what shall I liken*
you, O daughter of Jerusalem? What shall I compare with you, that I may
comfort you?" (v. 13). Like a doctor working in a trauma unit during a
disaster, he must keep going even though the *"ruin is spread wide as*
the sea" (v. 13).

Perhaps it was his own adrenalin that energized him and forced
him to speak of the false prophets. They had always worked against
his warnings with their "peace, peace" euphoria. *"Your prophets have*
seen for you False and deceptive visions; They have not uncovered your
iniquity, To bring back your captives, But have envisioned for you false
prophecies and delusions" (v. 14). They have played right into the
hands of the world system that wants to see the work of God dis-
graced on this earth. *"All who pass by clap their hands at you; They*
hiss and shake their heads At the daughter of Jerusalem: 'Is this the city
that is called The . . . joy of the whole earth'?" (v. 15). The enemies of
God revel in the demise of His city; *"They hiss and gnash their teeth.*
They say, 'We have swallowed her up! Surely this is the day we have
waited for; We have found it, we have seen it!" (v. 16). For a moment,
one can almost see Satan dancing in the street. The next line, however, blasts him away! *"The LORD has done what He purposed; He has*
fulfilled His word Which He commanded in days of old. He has . . .
exalted the horn of your adversaries" (v. 17). The world had wanted to
destroy the city of God, but God beat them to it. His sovereign judgment of apostasy was executed, and He used the world system to do
it. He was not the victim. He was the victor.

The only option left is prayer. *"Arise, cry out in the night. . . . Lift*
your hands toward Him For the life of your young children, Who faint
from hunger at the head of every street" (v. 19). How like so many of
us! We wait until we are desperate before we pray. They passed by
Jeremiah's countless appeals to them, his countless warnings of how
they could have averted the disaster now upon them. Not only do

we suffer the consequences of our own stubborn hearts, but so do our children, so does the whole generation to which we give birth. *"Young and old lie On the ground in the streets; My virgins and my young men Have fallen by the sword"* (v. 21). The future strength of our society lies in our youth; they are our greatest natural resource. Jerusalem slaughtered hers. There would be no next generation. "Zion has now learned the bitter lesson that the sowing of the wind inevitably reaps the whirlwind, and that this cause-effect nexus is based strictly upon the immutability and consistency of the divine nature."[4]

What does this lesson say to us? Are we giving our next generation a real chance to live according to God's order of things? Or will we say as Jerusalem does here, "Those whom I have borne and brought up My enemies have destroyed" (v. 22).

NOTES

1. Theophile J. Meek, "The Book of Lamentations: Introduction and Exegesis," in *The Interpreter's Bible*, vol. 6, ed. George A. Buttrick et al. (Nashville: Abingdon Press, 1956), 16.

2. George McMichael, ed., *Anthology of American Literature* (New York: Macmillan Publishing Co., 1985), 251.

3. Ibid., 256.

4. R. K. Harrison, *Jeremiah and Lamentations*, The Tyndale Old Testament Commentary (Downers Grove, Ill.: Inter-Varsity Press, 1973), 222.

CHAPTER THREE

I Am the Man

Lamentations 3:1–66

3:1 I *am* the man *who* has seen affliction by the rod
of His wrath.
  2 He has led me and made *me* walk
In darkness and not *in* light.
  3 Surely He has turned His hand against me
Time and time again throughout the day.
  4 He has aged my flesh and my skin,
And broken my bones.
  5 He has besieged me
And surrounded *me* with bitterness and woe.
  6 He has set me in dark places
Like the dead of long ago.
  7 He has hedged me in so that I cannot get out;
He has made my chain heavy.
  8 Even when I cry and shout,
He shuts out my prayer.
  9 He has blocked my ways with hewn stone;
He has made my paths crooked.
10 He *has been* to me a bear lying in wait,
Like a lion in ambush.
11 He has turned aside my ways and torn me in
pieces;
He has made me desolate.
12 He has bent His bow
And set me up as a target for the arrow.
13 He has caused the arrows of His quiver
To pierce my loins.

14 I have become the ridicule of all my people—
   Their taunting song all the day.

15 He has filled me with bitterness,
   He has made me drink wormwood.

16 He has also broken my teeth with gravel,
   And covered me with ashes.

17 You have moved my soul far from peace;
   I have forgotten prosperity.

18 And I said, "My strength and my hope
   Have perished from the LORD."

19 Remember my affliction and roaming,
   The wormwood and the gall.

20 My soul still remembers
   And sinks within me.

21 This I recall to my mind,
   Therefore I have hope.

22 *Through* the LORD's mercies we are not
      consumed,
   Because His compassions fail not.

23 *They are* new every morning;
   Great *is* Your faithfulness.

24 "The LORD *is* my portion," says my soul,
   "Therefore I hope in Him!"

25 The LORD *is* good to those who wait for Him,
   To the soul *who* seeks Him.

26 *It is* good that *one* should hope and wait
      quietly
   For the salvation of the LORD.

27 *It is* good for a man to bear
   The yoke in his youth.

28 Let him sit alone and keep silent,
   Because *God* has laid *it* on him;

29 Let him put his mouth in the dust—
   There may yet be hope.

30 Let him give *his* cheek to the one who strikes him,
   And be full of reproach.

31 For the Lord will not cast off forever.

32 Though He causes grief,
   Yet He will show compassion
   According to the multitude of His mercies.

33 For He does not afflict willingly,
   Nor grieve the children of men.

34 To crush under one's feet
   All the prisoners of the earth,
35 To turn aside the justice *due* a man
   Before the face of the Most High,
36 Or subvert a man in his cause—
   The Lord does not approve.
37 Who *is* he *who* speaks and it comes to pass,
   When the Lord has not commanded *it?*
38 *Is it* not from the mouth of the Most High
   That woe and well-being proceed?
39 Why should a living man complain,
   A man for the punishment of his sins?
40 Let us search out and examine our ways,
   And turn back to the LORD;
41 Let us lift our hearts and hands
   To God in heaven.
42 We have transgressed and rebelled;
   You have not pardoned.
43 You have covered *Yourself* with anger
   And pursued us;
   You have slain *and* not pitied.
44 You have covered Yourself with a cloud,
   That prayer should not pass through.
45 You have made us an offscouring and refuse
   In the midst of the peoples.
46 All our enemies
   Have opened their mouths against us.
47 Fear and a snare have come upon us,
   Desolation and destruction.
48 My eyes overflow with rivers of water
   For the destruction of the daughter of my
        people.
49 My eyes flow and do not cease,
   Without interruption,
50 Till the LORD from heaven
   Looks down and sees.
51 My eyes bring suffering to my soul
   Because of all the daughters of my city.
52 My enemies without cause
   Hunted me down like a bird.
53 They silenced my life in the pit
   And threw stones at me.

54 The waters flowed over my head;
   I said, "I am cut off!"
55 I called on Your name, O LORD,
   From the lowest pit.
56 You have heard my voice:
   "Do not hide Your ear
   From my sighing, from my cry for help."
57 You drew near on the day I called on You,
   And said, "Do not fear!"
58 O Lord, You have pleaded the case for my
      soul;
   You have redeemed my life.
59 O LORD, You have seen *how* I am wronged;
   Judge my case.
60 You have seen all their vengeance,
   All their schemes against me.
61 You have heard their reproach, O LORD,
   All their schemes against me,
62 The lips of my enemies
   And their whispering against me all the day.
63 Look at their sitting down and their rising up;
   I *am* their taunting song.
64 Repay them, O LORD,
   According to the work of their hands.
65 Give them a veiled heart;
   Your curse *be* upon them!
66 In Your anger,
   Pursue and destroy them
   From under the heavens of the LORD.
                                        Lam. 3:1–66

Again the first line hints at the content of the whole poem. The first two poems have been dirges beginning with "how" or "alas." This poem, however, is a personal lament; its style is more stream of consciousness, as though it were written for a private journal. As a result, it is three times as long and decidedly less cohesive. The acrostics are at times contrived, but the journey here described involves a road we all must travel sometime in our lives.

After the death of his wife, C. S. Lewis found that writing in his journal was his only consolation, his only touch with sanity. This private world of personal lament began with desolation but slowly led to a rediscovery of faith that was ultimately offered to the reading public as *A Grief Observed*. Like Lewis's work, this third chapter moves from intense introspective suffering to acceptance and hope and finally to prayer. "The order of thought is affliction, resignation, repentance, and prayer."[1] The first two chapters were dirges for the funeral of Jerusalem, and as such they take the standard form of twenty-two lines written in acrostics. This lament maintains the acrostic form; each letter of the Hebrew alphabet appears three times, most likely for the same reason as in the dirges—to aid memorization.

The highly subjective nature of this section becomes immediately apparent. This is no clinical report on the grieving process. It is instead flowing with the tears of the griever himself. During this early stage, the sufferer is totally preoccupied with his own pain, almost as though the whole world turns on it. Lewis described it as "the monotonous treadmill march of the mind around one subject."[2] Note the profusion of first-person pronouns: *"I am the man who has seen affliction by the rod of His wrath. He has led me and made me walk In darkness and not in light"* (vv. 1–2). Jeremiah has become so identified with his people and their pain that he himself becomes a metaphor of the city, a phenomenon of which we have already noted. Therefore, these words can be read as though spoken by either the poet or the city. They can be taken both personally and corporately.

The grieving process involves the whole person physically, mentally, psychologically, and spiritually. *"He has aged my flesh and my skin, And broken my bones"* (v. 4). By now Jeremiah was an old man, perhaps not conscious of his age until now in the midst of his grief when that bone-tired feeling seemed overwhelming. Similarly, Lewis says, "No one ever told me about the laziness of grief. Except at my job—where the machine seems to run on much as usual—I loath the slightest effort."[3]

Not only is there the physical nature of grief; there is also a spiritual dimension as well. *"He has besieged me And surrounded me with bitterness and woe. He has set me in dark places Like the dead of long ago. He has hedged me in so that I cannot get out; He has made my chain heavy"* (vv. 5–7). Typical of the grief process is the feeling that there is no future, that things will never get better, that God simply cannot be reached. I am ever amazed at the honesty of Scripture.

There is no glossing over the realities of our humanity. It walks right up to them and looks them in the face. Here Jeremiah describes something of a Catch-22 situation. He needs God to comfort him in his grief, but he can't reach God because he is too overwhelmed with grief.

Lewis noticed that when we are happy we have no real sense of needing God. "But go to Him when your need is desperate, when all other help is vain, and what do you find? A door slammed in your face, and a sound of bolting and double bolting on the inside. After that, silence."[4] Lewis wrote in the privacy of his own grief with the same shocking candor that Jeremiah expressed in Lamentations. *"Even when I cry and shout, He shuts out my prayer"* (v. 8). It is as though these realities must be expressed before the griever can move on to higher ground.

There are also psychological matters with which we must deal. For more than forty years, Jeremiah had prepared himself and his people first for the possibility and then for the inevitability of Jerusalem's fall. One would expect then that he would have been psychologically prepared. The harsh reality of death and tragedy, however, is that we are never prepared. It still comes as a surprise. *"He has been to me a bear lying in wait, Like a lion in ambush"* (v. 10). Lewis writes, "I had been warned—I had warned myself not to reckon on worldly happiness. We were even promised sufferings. They were part of the program. We were even told, 'Blessed are they that mourn' and I accepted it. I've got nothing that I hadn't bargained for." Jeremiah must have felt something like that over the course of his prophetic ministry. Then Lewis writes such telling words that they ring true to our humanity: "Of course it is different when the thing happens to oneself, not to others, and in reality, not in imagination."[5]

"I have become the ridicule of all my people —Their taunting song all the day" (v. 14). Jeremiah was giving expression to an isolation that characterized his whole prophetic ministry. He lived as a one-man resistance movement. Now, as a metaphor of the people, he expressed what all Jerusalem felt in her scandal, the jeers she now endured. *"Remember my affliction and roaming, The wormwood and the gall"* (v. 19).

In the next unit of Jeremiah's personal lament we find a note of hope emerging—he had begun to pray. The anguish hitherto described was never meant to become an end in itself. He did not allow himself to get stuck in its mire. Just as he was pulled out of the miry cistern, so also was he gradually pulled out of this sense of total despair. The man who at one time said that God had shut out his prayer was once again praying to be remembered. God indeed calls His people to be rememberers. The Book of Lamentations is read once a year, liturgically, and all because we are to recall and rehearse the events of His dealings with us. The acrostic literary form confirms that fact. It provides us with the abc's of repentance and remembrance. Just before Jesus was to suffer death on the cross, He celebrated the Lord's Supper with his disciples and with the express command, "Do this in remembrance of Me" (Luke 22:19). He did not say, "Now when this is over I want you to forget all about it."

Remembrance brings comfort. *"This I recall to my mind, Therefore I have hope"* (v. 21). Suddenly the mind that was hedged in and chained is now able to think in terms of God's compassion and to say, *"They are new every morning"* (v. 23). The grieving mind was learning to live one day at a time. It is an art we all must learn, but it is a difficult one. We would much rather see the burden removed once and for all. Yet as we see Jeremiah submit to this process, we feel a fresh breeze blowing across the pages of his personal journal, bringing with it a threefold reference to goodness. *"The LORD is good to those who wait for Him. . . . It is good that one should hope and wait quietly. . . . It is good for a man to bear The yoke in his youth"* (vv. 25–27). The language is like streams in a desert and so is the hope that God does not cause suffering just for the sake of suffering. It always has a purpose. *"Though He causes grief, Yet He will show compassion"* (v. 32). Lewis writes of a similar breakthrough: "You can't see anything properly while your eyes are blurred with tears. . . . Is it the very intensity of the longing that draws the iron curtain, that makes us feel we are staring into a vacuum when we think about our dead? I have gradually been coming to feel that the door is no longer shut and bolted. Was it my own frantic need that slammed it in my face?"[6]

When Jeremiah describes the posture of hope in verses 22–30, we feel a lifting of that frantic intensity so characteristic of the earlier verses. He instructs us to *"wait quietly"* (v. 26), *"bear the yoke"* (v. 27), *"sit alone and keep silent"* (v. 28), *"put [our mouths] in the dust"* (v. 29), and *"give [our] cheek to one who strikes [us]"* (v. 30). The language moves from resistance to resignation. In this same process, Lewis speaks of "the senseless writhings of a man who won't accept the fact that there is nothing we can do with suffering except to suffer it."[7] Once that fact is accepted, then a healing process begins.

Jeremiah continued to climb out of his total subjectivity. *"For the Lord will not cast off forever"* (v. 31). Suddenly he sees God not as the afflicter but as a great champion of human justice. *"For He does not . . . subvert a man in his cause"* (vv. 33, 36). He was focusing on the positive side of God's justice. *"Is it not from the mouth of the Most High That woe and well-being proceed?"* (v. 38). In the move from resistance to resignation, there is also a move from woe to well-being. He who had so pitied himself now says, *"Why should a living man complain, A man for the punishment of his sins?"* (v. 39).

Nothing could hold him back now. Jeremiah almost shouted to his people: *"Let us search out and examine our ways, And turn back to the LORD; Let us lift our hearts and hands To God in heaven"* (vv. 40–41). I can almost see him putting down his pen, lifting his hands, trembling and old, and turning from his people, looking up to his God, and saying, *"We have transgressed and rebelled; You have not pardoned"* (v. 42). The great and holy law of sowing and reaping has been enforced. It was as though Jeremiah was proud of God for staying true to His laws. His justice is inexorable. There is something triumphant yet frightening about this discovery. *"You have covered Yourself with a cloud, That prayer should not pass through"* (v. 44) Herein begins an address to this frightening God. In chapter 2 he described the cloud of anger that held the city in its grip. Now that same cloud obscured God. Again Jeremiah referred to the inscrutableness of God. *"You have covered Yourself with anger And pursued us"* (v. 43). The very suffering of which Jeremiah bemoaned had now brought a more expansive sense of God's holiness.

God does not want us to hold images of Himself that are less than He really is. Perhaps through suffering, more than through happiness, we have hammered out before us more and more of what He is really like. Lewis admits to his own imperfect ideas about God when he says, "My idea of God is not a divine idea. It has to be shattered time after time. He shatters it Himself. He is the great iconoclast. Could we not almost say that this shattering was one of the marks of His presence?"[8] In the long run, don't we really want God to triumph over our narrow vision of Him—regardless of the cost? Surely Jeremiah did.

Through tears came a more perfect vision. The threefold reference sets up a memorable rhythm. *"My eyes overflow with rivers of water. . . . My eyes flow and do not cease. . . . My eyes bring suffering to my soul"* (vv. 48–49, 51). The weeping prophet wept not in vain. *"I called on Your name, O LORD, . . . You drew near on the day I called on You, And said, 'Do not fear!'"* (vv. 55, 57). Is this the same man who felt the Lord to be so far away, so unresponsive? Now he was absolutely rhapsodic over the instancy of God, who answered on the day He was called! This same God who covered Himself with a cloud was now covering Jeremiah with redemption and with vindication. *"O Lord, You have pleaded the case for my soul; You have redeemed my life. O LORD, You have seen how I am wronged; Judge my case"* (vv. 58–59). The aged prophet rested his case under the covering of the Almighty. All the reproach, all the whispering, all the taunting song ever to come from the lips of his enemies would not go unpunished. When we have taken the blows of God for our own sins, when we have made fresh discoveries about His perfect justice, when He has shattered in us all false images of Himself, then we can draw greater and greater comfort from His holiness, but His holiness must first be afflicting before it can be comforting. On this solemn principle, Jeremiah ended his personal lament.

"Give them a veiled heart; Your curse be upon them! In Your anger, Pursue and destroy them From under the heavens of the LORD" (vv. 65–66).

NOTES

1. Theophile J. Meek, "The Book of Lamentations: Introduction and Exegesis," in *The Interpreter's Bible*, vol. 6, ed. George A. Buttrick et al. (Nashville: Abingdon Press, 1956), 23.
2. C. S. Lewis, *A Grief Observed* (Toronto: Bantam Books, 1963), 10.
3. Ibid., 3.
4. Ibid., 4.
5. Ibid., 41–42.
6. Ibid., 53.
7. Ibid., 38.
8. Ibid., 76.

CHAPTER FOUR

How the Gold Has Become Dim

Lamentations 4:1–22

4:1 How the gold has become dim!
How changed the fine gold!
The stones of the sanctuary are scattered
At the head of every street.

2 The precious sons of Zion,
Valuable as fine gold,
How they are regarded as clay pots,
The work of the hands of the potter!

3 Even the jackals present their breasts
To nurse their young;
But the daughter of my people *is* cruel,
Like ostriches in the wilderness.

4 The tongue of the infant clings
To the roof of its mouth for thirst;
The young children ask for bread,
But no one breaks *it* for them.

5 Those who ate delicacies
Are desolate in the streets;
Those who were brought up in scarlet
Embrace ash heaps.

6 The punishment of the iniquity of the daughter
of my people
Is greater than the punishment of the sin of
Sodom,
Which was overthrown in a moment,
With no hand to help her!

7 Her Nazirites were brighter than snow
And whiter than milk;
They were more ruddy in body than rubies,
Like sapphire in their appearance.

8 *Now* their appearance is blacker than soot;
They go unrecognized in the streets;
Their skin clings to their bones,
It has become as dry as wood.
9 *Those* slain by the sword are better off
Than *those* who die of hunger;
For these pine away,
Stricken *for lack* of the fruits of the field.
10 The hands of the compassionate women
Have cooked their own children;
They became food for them
In the destruction of the daughter of my
  people.
11 The LORD has fulfilled His fury,
He has poured out His fierce anger.
He kindled a fire in Zion,
And it has devoured its foundations.
12 The kings of the earth,
And all inhabitants of the world,
Would not have believed
That the adversary and the enemy
Could enter the gates of Jerusalem—
13 Because of the sins of her prophets
And the iniquities of her priests,
Who shed in her midst
The blood of the just.
14 They wandered blind in the streets;
They have defiled themselves with blood,
So that no one would touch their garments.
15 They cried out to them,
"Go away, unclean!
Go away, go away,
Do not touch us!"
When they fled and wandered,
Those among the nations said,
"They shall no longer dwell *here.*"
16 The face of the LORD scattered them;
He no longer regards them.
The people do not respect the priests
Nor show favor to the elders.
17 Still our eyes failed us,
Watching vainly for our help;

In our watching we watched
For a nation *that* could not save *us*.
18 They tracked our steps
So that we could not walk in our streets.
Our end was near;
Our days were over,
For our end had come.
19 Our pursuers were swifter
Than the eagles of the heavens.
They pursued us on the mountains
And lay in wait for us in the wilderness.
20 The breath of our nostrils, the anointed of
the LORD,
Was caught in their pits,
Of whom we said, "Under his shadow
We shall live among the nations."
21 Rejoice and be glad, O daughter of Edom,
You who dwell in the land of Uz!
The cup shall also pass over to you
And you shall become drunk and make
yourself naked.
22 *The punishment of* your iniquity is
accomplished,
O daughter of Zion;
He will no longer send you into captivity.
He will punish your iniquity,
O daughter of Edom;
He will uncover your sins!

Lam. 4:1–22

The temple no longer glistened in the sunlight because the gold was tarnished. *"How the gold has become dim! How changed the fine gold! The stones of the sanctuary are scattered At the head of every street"* (v. 1).

How far Jerusalem had come from her past glories. David passed the kingdom to Solomon with these words, "I go the way of all the earth; be strong, therefore, and prove yourself a man. And keep the charge of the LORD your God; to walk in His ways, to keep His statutes, His commandments, His judgments, and His testimonies" (1 Kings 2:2–3). In proving himself a man, Solomon requested wisdom from the Lord. It was a request that pleased the Lord and led to the building of the temple to exacting specifications. "And the temple, when it was being built, was built with stone finished at the quarry, so that no hammer or chisel *or* any iron tool was heard in the temple while it was being built" (1 Kings 6:7). It was to be the temple of the God of peace, built without noise, without clamoring. Yet it was thrown down with barbaric axes and battering rams. The trauma that Jeremiah described was beyond imagining.

He looks at each stone, having been so carefully hewn, so brilliantly fitted together, now wrenched from its position and tumbled carelessly into the streets of Jerusalem as though they were random chunks of nothing. He was pained to see them out of place, no longer joined together for the glory of God. The Apostle Peter in speaking to the body of believers under the persecution of Nero said, "You also, as living stones, are being built up a spiritual house, a holy priesthood, to offer up spiritual sacrifices acceptable to God through Jesus Christ" (1 Pet. 2:5). Peter was catching the vision that the temple was not merely a piece of architecture but was a corporate body of living stones, people fitted together, their rough edges hewn silently by the work of God, that they might form a spiritual house for His work on earth.

"The precious sons of Zion, Valuable as fine gold, How they are regarded as clay pots, The work of the hands of the potter!" (v. 2). Jeremiah saw the scattered stones as the scattered sons who had allowed themselves to be tossed from their dignity in the Lord, to lose their value as gold and become nothing but clay. They had lost their sacred usefulness and had become vessels of dishonor. The memories of his visions in the potter's house were still fresh in his mind, as fresh as the clay he smelled that day spinning on the wheel. "And the vessel that he made of clay was marred in the hand of the potter" (Jer. 18:4).

Jerusalem's most precious treasure, her sons, had fallen in value from gold to clay. Nevertheless the hand of the potter was still upon them; "So he made it again into another vessel, as it seemed good to the potter to make" (Jer. 18:4). Out beyond lamenting the shame and scandal of Jerusalem's destruction, the note of hope rings, another characteristic of Jeremiah. Not only have her sons fallen from their intended glory, but so have the daughters of Jerusalem. *"Even the jackals present their breasts To nurse their young; But the daughter of my people is cruel, Like ostriches in the wilderness"* (v. 3). Another reference to the effects of the famine creeps into the poet's imagery; he cannot escape the dreadful sight of starving infants and of mothers becoming far less than human, less even than jackals who at least nurture their young. Jerusalem's daughters were more like ostriches who were known for their indifference to their young. Not only were they becoming like animals, but they were becoming like the very worst representatives of the animal kingdom—the lowest of the low. *"The hands of the compassionate women Have cooked their own children; They became food for them In the destruction of the daughter of my people"* (v. 10). The desperation of survival instincts knows no bounds. We shock ourselves with what we are capable of becoming in a crisis.

Perhaps Jeremiah chose such degrading language out of his anger and frustration over the sight of suffering. *"The tongue of the infant clings To the roof of its mouth for thirst; The young children ask for bread, But no one breaks it for them"* (v. 4). To think that all of this could have been prevented if Zedekiah had been willing to surrender to Nebuchadnezzar! How costly is prideful leadership. The innocent suffer.

The streets were meant to be proud avenues of commerce and communion, busy sidewalks leading into the city of God. Instead they were empty, like a ghost town but for the scattered rubble of temple stones and dying children. Now the poet's eye falls on the derelict, lying on an ash heap like so many homeless in today's cities. In looking closely into their smudged faces, the prophet was shocked to realize who they once were. *"Those who ate delicacies Are desolate in the streets; Those who were brought up in scarlet Embrace ash heaps"* (v. 5). He was not looking at the dregs of society but at her elite, at the filthy robes that once were scarlet and aristocratic.

Prophets and priests wandered blind in the streets (vv. 13–14). They who once were untouchable for the purity they represented, now are untouchable for the leprosy of their sin. Like the nobles, many of them might be unrecognizable, so deformed and disfigured by the effects of famine and destruction. To anyone who approached them they cried out, *"Go away, unclean! Go away, go away, Do not touch us!"* (v. 15). They who had caused Jeremiah so much anguish were now exposed for what they were, contaminators of the revelation of God. In writing these verses, Jeremiah may well have remembered pouring out his heart to the Lord over the opposition he was receiving from the prophets and priests. "The prophet who has a dream, let him tell the dream," God answered. "And he who has

382

My word, let him speak My word faithfully" (Jer. 23:28). God had now separated the chaff from the wheat. The false prophets were now wearing their emptiness and their scandal while Jeremiah continued in the aftermath of his prophetic mission.

Jeremiah concludes that Jerusalem's fate was worse than that of Sodom and Gomorrah—at least theirs came in an instant. *"The punishment of the iniquity of the daughter of my people Is greater than the punishment of the sin of Sodom, Which was overthrown in a moment, With no hand to help her!"* (v. 6). Theirs came swiftly and directly from the hand of God, not by the agency of human violence nor the agency of famine. Jeremiah concluded that of the two, famine was worse than violence. *"Those slain by the sword are better off Than those who die of hunger; For these pine away, Stricken for lack of the fruits of the field"* (v. 9).

No one would have imagined it would come to this. *"The kings of the earth, And all inhabitants of the world, Would not have believed That the adversary and the enemy Could enter the gates of Jerusalem"* (v. 12). We do not want to believe that God will punish sin, that any righteousness we have built for ourselves is only a house of cards. We think that we can save ourselves, that our own walls are impregnable. All of this tragedy exposes the feebleness of our own efforts to save ourselves. *"Still our eyes failed us, Watching vainly for our help; In our watching we watched For the nation that could not save us"* (v. 17). Jerusalem had preferred to look to Egypt rather than repent, even when the enemy peered down upon them from Babylonian siege walls. *"They tracked our steps So that we could not walk in our streets. . . . Our pursuers were swifter Than the eagles of the heavens"* (vv. 18–19).

Nebuchadnezzar's armies swooped down upon Jerusalem as an eagle does its prey. While this event was painfully etched into the history of the Jewish nation, and this is a lament over that event, we would do it a great injustice to deny its value to the conscience of other nations. *"Rejoice and be glad, O daughter of Edom. . . . The cup shall also pass over to you"* (v. 21). While Edom was delighting over the fate of her rival Israel, gloating over her demise, she sat precariously under the judgment of God herself. Jeremiah takes a certain satisfaction in the great principle of sovereignty that weaves its way through all of his writing. God is not just the God of Israel. He has the whole world in His hands. These elegies were solemn warnings not merely of a private nature but to the world community.

CHAPTER FIVE

Remember, O Lord

Lamentations 5:1–22

5:1 Remember, O LORD, what has come upon us;
Look, and behold our reproach!
2 Our inheritance has been turned over to
aliens,
And our houses to foreigners.
3 We have become orphans and waifs,
Our mothers *are* like widows.
4 We pay for the water we drink,
And our wood comes at a price.
5 *They* pursue at our heels;
We labor *and* have no rest.
6 We have given our hand *to* the Egyptians
And the Assyrians, to be satisfied with bread.
7 Our fathers sinned *and are* no more,
But we bear their iniquities.
8 Servants rule over us;
There is none to deliver *us* from their hand.
9 We get our bread *at the risk* of our lives,
Because of the sword in the wilderness.
10 Our skin is hot as an oven,
Because of the fever of famine.
11 They ravished the women in Zion,
The maidens in the cities of Judah.
12 Princes were hung up by their hands,
And elders were not respected.
13 Young men ground at the millstones;
Boys staggered under *loads of* wood.
14 The elders have ceased *gathering at* the gate,
And the young men from their music.

15 The joy of our heart has ceased;
   Our dance has turned into mourning.
16 The crown has fallen *from* our head.
   Woe to us, for we have sinned!
17 Because of this our heart is faint;
   Because of these *things* our eyes grow dim;
18 Because of Mount Zion which is desolate,
   With foxes walking about on it.
19 You, O LORD, remain forever;
   Your throne from generation to generation.
20 Why do You forget us forever,
   And forsake us for so long a time?
21 Turn us back to You, O LORD, and we will be
      restored;
   Renew our days as of old,
22 Unless You have utterly rejected us,
   And are very angry with us!

Lam. 5:1–22

The first lines of this last elegy indicate that it is a prayer. Plural pronouns "we," "us," and "our" thread their way through the text, casting the image of a nation on its knees. What a perfect way to seal forty years of prophetic ministry! What a final triumph to a ministry so characterized by failure! The flavor of the corporate complements the extremely personal content of chapter three. Many of the details suggest the plight of the remnant left in Palestine after the Babylonian defeat. *"Our inheritance has been turned over to aliens"* (v. 2). Jerusalem no longer belonged to herself. Nebuchadnezzar had appointed Gedeliah to exercise good government, but nonetheless he represented the alien occupation.

"We have become orphans and waifs, Our mothers are like widows" (v. 3). The inhabitants of Jerusalem were called her sons and her daughters, but now that the city was dead they were orphans without proper care, without even the basic commodities of life. *"We pay for the water we drink, And our wood comes at a price"* (v. 4). The price for such basic necessities was obviously so inflated that they had to work constantly just to survive. *"We labor and have no rest"* (v. 5). There is a note of irony here. God had made abundant provision for rest in His sabbath day. He had never intended that work would become oppressive and burdensome, but rather He meant that it be

385

balanced by regular Sabbath intervals of refreshment and reverence. He even sent Jeremiah to stand in the gates of Jerusalem on the Sabbath, to be a one-man resistance movement to the practice of bringing burdens through these gates on that day. One day in seven the gates were to rest and so were the people. As long as that ordinance, that tempo for life, was observed, "then shall enter . . . kings and princes sitting on the throne of David" (Jer. 17:25). Against the appeal of Jeremiah, the people insisted on making the Sabbath one more day of getting and spending. Now they paid the inexorable price. They got what they wanted and found it to be a horror. They have no rest. They have no king on the throne. The sabbath ordinance had been for their own good, but after all, what did God know?

"We have given our hand to the Egyptians And the Assyrians, to be satisfied with bread" (v. 6). These countries were used here to indicate two parts of the world, the west and the east.[1] The land of promise was anything but that. This prayer now begins to penetrate the reason why this was so.

"Our fathers sinned and are no more, But we bear their iniquities" (v. 7). Up to this point the prayer has been preoccupied with the problems facing the remnant in Palestine. Now the first note of penitence was sounded, but only the first note. The subtle implication was that the fathers have caused the whole trouble by their sins, and that now the destitute are left to pay the price. They saw themselves more as victims of sin than as sinners themselves, when in real truth they are both. The prayer does not rise to this awareness until verse 16.

This once-proud people was now being subjected to every form of humiliation. The economic humiliation of having to beg for bread from foreigners, to pay for their water, to force their children into heavy labor, to "stagger under loads of wood" (v. 13)—and yet the social humiliation was even worse. When the soldiers entered the city, they took from it a brutal pleasure. "They ravished the women in Zion, The maidens in the cities of Judah" (v. 11). The women, another element of society, suffered tragic humiliation. "Princes were hung up by their hands, And elders were not respected" (v. 12). It does not appear that hanging by the hand was ever used as a mode of judicial punishment by the ancients. It must have been practiced on these princes as a matter of sheer cruelty.[2] A similar image might flash across the modern memory. Benito Mussolini, the dictator of Italy for more than twenty years, was captured by Italian partisans in 1945, along with his mistress. Both of them were executed, taken to Milan, and hung there by their heels in a public place. The text does not suggest that the princes of Judah were slain, but their defeat was made a public spectacle as they lived. Their shame was deserved. Jeremiah's was not. He too had suffered public humiliation when Pashhur had put him in the stocks and caused him public shame when the prophet should have received public fame.

"The elders have ceased gathering at the gate" (v. 14). One of the enduring images in the mind of the poet was the assembly of elders at the city gates for the administration of justice. They were one of the city's most valuable natural resources, known for their wisdom, their memories, and their willingness to use them for the welfare of the community. He could remember the day that Ahikam saved his life in a dispute with the priests and prophets. He was old enough to remember the words of Micah and wise enough to know how to apply them to the case at hand (Jer. 26:24).

Now Judah was no longer politically self-determining. She was an occupied land. Her elders did not even bother coming to the gates. *"The gates have sunk into the ground"* (2:9). There was no more wisdom in the elders. There were no more gates. When there is no justice, there is also no joy. *"The joy of our heart has ceased; our dance has turned into mourning"* (v. 15).

Now at last comes the great moment of accountability in the prayer. *"The crown has fallen from our head. Woe to us, for we have sinned"* (v. 16). The poet becomes the voice of the nation that speaks now as one man. A crown had been placed upon the head of this corporate entity called the people of God. They were to reflect His majesty in the conduct of their affairs, to bear the weight of that crown with such noble bearing that other nations would come to know a better government, that orphans, widows, and strangers would find refuge in her gates and know that the kingdom of God had come on earth, that His will was being done on earth. Instead of cresting the mountain of Jerusalem, the royal diadem had fallen— not for any fault of God's and not only for the faults of their fathers, but because "we have sinned."

With surgical precision, the poet has found the cancer. The healthy lives they could have had now languished. Mount Zion could have been a city populated by men and women whose splendor was a beacon to the world, whose streets and gates streamed with tired and poor humanity hungry for a better way. Instead the mountain was desolate, *"With foxes walking about on it"* (v. 18). *"Woe to us, for we have sinned"* (v. 16).

The only hope for us is that our sin is not the last word. *"You, O LORD, remain forever; Your throne from generation to generation"* (v. 19). Jeremiah no longer rehearsed their woes as in the early section of the prayer. Every attention was riveted on God. *"Turn us back to You, O LORD, and we will be restored; Renew our days as of old"* (v. 21). Every trembling and penitent heart pauses here, having reached the overwhelming conclusion that unless God renews there will be no renewal, unless God turns, there will be no turning. The days of old were irretrievable to the humanity that had destroyed them. Hopeful faces now turned toward heaven in this verse, clinging to its note of hope.

In their synagogues across the world, Jews even to this day read these words as though they wished that verse 22 was simply not there. Yes they read it, but before the words have had time to land they quickly read again verse 21. These last words, solemn though they be, crucify the human ego which can never presume upon the goodness of God. *"Unless You have utterly rejected us, And are very angry with us!"* (v. 22). Forty years of prophetic ministry are rolled into these words. They rest the final case into the courts of heaven. A final tribute to God's sovereignty is a nation on its knees, a final echo to the weeping prophet, "well done good and faithful servant."

NOTES

1. Theophile J. Meek, "The Book of Lamentations: Introduction and Exegesis," in *The Interpreter's Bible*, vol. 6, ed. George A. Buttrick et al. (Nashville: Abingdon Press, 1956), 36.

2. E. Henderson, *Jeremiah and Lamentations* (Philadelphia: Smith, English and Co., 1868), 314.

Bibliography

Albrektson, Bertil. *Studies in the Text and Theology of the Book of Lamentations.* Lund: C. W. K. Gleerup, 1963.

Boice, James Montgomery. *The Parables of Jesus.* Chicago: Moody Press, 1983.

Edersheim, Alfred. *Old Testament Bible History.* Grand Rapids, Mich.: Eerdman's Publishing Co., 1977.

Harrison, R. K. *Jeremiah and Lamentations.* Tyndale Old Testament Commentaries. Downers Grove, Ill.: Inter-Varsity Press, 1973.

Hastings, James. *The Speaker's Bible.* Aberdeen, Scotland: Speaker's Bible Office, 1944.

Henderson, E. *The Book of the Prophet Jeremiah.* Philadelphia: Smith, English, and Co., 1868.

Henry, Matthew. *Commentary on the Whole Bible.* Edited by Leslie F. Church. Grand Rapids, Mich.: Zondervan Publishing House, 1960.

Hopper, Stanley. "The Book of Jeremiah: Exposition." In *The Interpreter's Bible,* vol. 5. Edited by George A. Buttrick et al. Nashville: Abingdon Press, 1956.

Hyatt, James P. "The Book of Jeremiah: Introduction and Exegesis." In *The Interpreter's Bible,* vol. 5. Edited by George A. Buttrick et al. Nashville: Abingdon Press, 1956.

Josephus, Flavius. *Antiquities of the Jews.* 3 vols. Grand Rapids, Mich.: Baker Book House, 1984.

Lewis, C. S. *A Grief Observed.* Toronto: Bantam Books, 1963.

Lloyd-Jones, D. Martyn. *Studies in the Sermon on the Mount.* Leichester, England: Inter-Varsity Press; Grand Rapids, Mich.: Eerdman's Publishing Co., 1985

McMichael, George, ed. *Anthology of American Literature.* New York: Macmillan Publishing Co., 1985.

Meek, Theophile J. "The Book of Lamentations: Introduction and Exegesis." In *The Interpreter's Bible,* vol. 6. Edited by George A. Buttrick et al. Nashville: Abingdon Press, 1956.

Meyer, F. B. *Jeremiah.* Fort Washington, Pa.: Christian Literature Crusade, 1980.

Morgan, G. Campbell. *Studies in the Prophecy of Jeremiah.* Old Tappan, N.J.: Fleming H. Revell, 1969.

Nicholson, E. W. *The Book of the Prophet Jeremiah.* The Cambridge Bible Commentary. 2 vols. New York: Cambridge University Press, 1975.

Petersen, William J. *Jeremiah: The Prophet Who Wouldn't Quit.* Wheaton, Ill.: Victor Books, 1984.

Stott, John R. W. *Cross of Christ.* Downers Grove, Ill.: Inter-Varsity Press, 1986.

Unger, Merrill F. *Unger's Bible Dictionary.* Chicago: Moody Press, 1966.